A History of the Scottish Labour Party

A History of the Scottish Labour Party

David Torrance

EDINBURGH
University Press

Edinburgh University Press is one of the leading university presses in the UK. Publishing new research in the arts and humanities, EUP connects people and ideas to inspire creative thinking, open new perspectives and shape the world we live in. For more information, visit www.edinburghuniversitypress.com.

© David Torrance, 2026

Edinburgh University Press Ltd
13 Infirmary Street, Edinburgh EH1 1LT

Typeset in 10.5/13pt Sabon by
Cheshire Typesetting Ltd, Cuddington, Cheshire

A CIP record for this book is available from the British Library

ISBN 978 1 3995 4479 5 (hardback)
ISBN 978 1 3995 4480 1 (paperback)
ISBN 978 1 3995 4481 8 (webready PDF)
ISBN 978 1 3995 4482 5 (epub)

The right of David Torrance to be identified as the author of this work has been asserted in accordance with the Copyright, Designs and Patents Act 1988, and the Copyright and Related Rights Regulations 2003 (SI No. 2498).

EU Authorised Representative:
Easy Access System Europe
Mustamäe tee 50, 10621 Tallinn, Estonia
gpsr.requests@easproject.com

Contents

Introduction: Labour and Scotland   1
1 'The Cause of Labour and of Scottish Nationality': 1888–1915   8
2 Scottish Council of the Labour Party: 1915–1940   23
3 'Socialist Planning on a United Kingdom Scale': 1940–1958   56
4 'Signposts for Scotland': 1958–1979   78
5 The Party of Scotland: 1979–1994   131
6 The Scottish Labour Party: 1994–2011   181
7 The Strange Death of Labour Scotland? 2011–2026   238
Conclusion: Whither Scottish Labour?   264

Appendix 1 – Party Leaders   279
Appendix 2 – Election Results   281
Bibliography   283
Index   303

Introduction
Labour and Scotland

For several decades, and indeed within living memory, it was possible to speak of 'Labour Scotland' without any fear of contradiction. If the story of Scottish politics is successive periods of single-party hegemony followed by a relatively sudden shift to whomever was seen to 'stand up for Scotland', then Labour's period of dominance could be said to have lasted between the UK general elections of 1959 and 2010.

In keeping with the approach of the first two volumes in this series,[1] however, an account is also provided of the Labour Party's 'rise' in Scotland (beginning with Keir Hardie's first Scottish Labour Party in 1888) and its later 'fall' (between the Scottish Parliament elections of 2007 and 2011). The aim is to explore Scottish politics since the late nineteenth century from the vantage point of what was initially most accurately called the Labour Party in Scotland and only since 1994 the Scottish Labour Party.

Indeed, a major theme is Labour's organisation in Scotland, its nomenclature, internal constitution and relationship with the 'British' Labour Party,[2] as well as other elements of the wider Labour movement, most notably in a Scottish context the trades councils, Independent Labour Party, Scottish Trades Union Congress, the party in local government and, to a lesser extent, the Scottish Co-operative movement and Communist Party of Great Britain. More broadly, also examined are Scottish Labour's relations with 'the Union', the media, and political parties of the centre and centre-right.

Methodologically, the author makes no apology for remaining 'fixated' on a chronological approach,[3] this being the most efficient (and indeed coherent) means of bringing together a large amount of primary and secondary material. And as with the author's previous studies of the Scottish Liberals/Liberal Democrats and Scottish Conservatives/Unionists, the goal is partly one of consolidation. Although it would be incorrect in this case to complain of a lack of competing secondary sources, the last single-volume history of Labour in Scotland (an edited collection) was published in 1989.[4]

Reviewing Hassan's 2004 edited publication *The Scottish Labour Party: History, Institutions and Ideas*, Knox criticised writers 'obsessed with committees, institutions and personalities', but with 'no understanding of forces that shape them or change them, far less any concern for their impact on the people of Scotland'.[5] Although doing full justice to such an approach would require a much longer book (or indeed books), the present volume adopts the approach of Bealey in analysing three factors which have impacted the Labour Party in Scotland since 1888: (1) its 'situation within the polity', in other words the party's relative strength, either in government or in opposition, (2) the state of the national (or sub-national) economy, and (3) 'externality', the impact of 'experiences and ideas' of those outside the Labour movement.[6]

Also deployed are the three themes identified by Kellas and Fotheringham, 'nationalism, religion and separate interest', which ensured working-class politics in Scotland never became 'entirely British in character or aims'. They made the important point that Scottish politics must be understood in terms of 'attitudes, interests and decision-making as well as party affiliation'.[7] At around the same time, Drucker identified Labour's 'apparently unshakeable support' in Scotland as resting on municipally owned housing, trade unions and the Roman Catholic Church,[8] and although these 'three pillars' later weakened, they remain a useful frame through which to view the Labour Party in Scotland, particularly its activity between the First World War and the early part of the twenty-first century.[9]

Marwick was among the first systematically to chart and analyse the history of the Labour movement in Scotland. *Labour in Scotland: A Short History of the Scottish Working Class Movement* appeared as early as 1948,[10] and was expanded two decades later to become, ironically, *A Short History of Labour in Scotland*.[11] MacDougall's edited *Essays in Scottish*

Labour History paid tribute to Marwick in 1978,[12] while the same author's *A Catalogue of Some Labour Records in Scotland and Some Scots Records Outside Scotland* remains an impressive attempt to capture the then available source material, not just for the Labour and Independent Labour parties but also the broader Labour movement in Scotland.[13]

Keating and Bleiman's *Labour and Scottish Nationalism* (1979)[14] and to a lesser degree Drucker and Brown's *The Politics of Nationalism and Devolution* (1980)[15] reflected a growing interest in analysing more specific aspects of Labour in Scotland, which continued with activist Iain McLean's two-part *Labour and Scottish Home Rule* (1991), which he called 'a positive assertion of Labour's nationalist traditions',[16] and Mitchell's *Strategies for Self-government: The Campaigns for a Scottish Parliament* (1996).[17] There was also a continuing fascination with 'Red Clydeside', mythological or real, which began with Keith Middlemas's *The Clydesiders: A Left Wing Struggle For Parliamentary Power* (1965),[18] and continued in more scholarly (though subsequently contested) form with McLean's *The Legend of Red Clydeside* (1983).[19]

As already noted, it took until the late 1980s for a single-volume history of Labour in Scotland to emerge, the still stimulating *Forward! Labour Politics in Scotland, 1888–1988*, edited by Donnachie, Harvie and Wood. The early 1990s saw an important account by E. Gordon of *Women and the Labour Movement in Scotland, 1850–1914*,[20] while in the 2000s Hassan established himself as the main chronicler, either solo or in partnership with Shaw, of the contemporary Scottish Labour Party, first in *The Scottish Labour Party: History, Institutions and Ideas* (2004)[21] and later *The Strange Death of Labour Scotland* (2012). The latter was the first 'declinist' study of the party and argued that 'Labour Scotland' had 'passed into history, leaving the Labour Party with a shortage of ideas and resources and little sense of what to do'.[22]

Accounts of the British Labour Party and movement have been rather better at incorporating Scotland than equivalent studies of the Conservatives and Liberal Democrats, particularly McKibbin's *The Evolution of the Labour Party, 1910–1924* (1974)[23] and Kenneth D. Brown's *The First Labour Party, 1906–1914* (1985).[24] Biographically, however, the party in Scotland has been poorly served. Studies of Keir Hardie,[25]

James Maxton[26] and Tom Johnston[27] have tended towards hagiography, while later figures have been curiously neglected. Beyond this author's necessarily brief treatment of William Ross,[28] Scottish Labour's most significant figure of the 1960s and 1970s still lacks a major biography, and while Wendy Alexander edited an occasionally useful volume in 2005, the same is true of Donald Dewar. Of the post-1999 trio of Labour First Ministers, only Henry McLeish has produced a memoir; Lorraine Davidson's *Lucky Jack: Scotland's First Minister*, an approving and journalistic account which appeared in 2005, does not add much.

As Bennie et al. and Hassan have noted, Drucker's notion of 'doctrine and ethos' as the two facets of Labour ideology provides a useful device for analysing Scottish Labour thought. While doctrine is 'a more or less elaborate set of ideas about the character of ... social, economic and political reality which lead to a programme of action', ethoses are 'sets of values which spring from the experience of the British working class and a shared past, a series of folk memories of shared exploitation, common struggle and gradually increased power'.[29]

Scottish Labour doctrine as captured in manifestos and other statements of party policy is another major preoccupation of this book, as is the party's ethos, which connects neatly with the importance of mythology. As Bennie et al. have observed, Labour's apparent 'Scottish radicalism is an inbuilt part of its ethos but whether that translates well into its doctrine is another matter'.[30] If doctrine has necessarily shifted – as Herbert Morrison famously put it, socialism is whatever the Labour Party says it is – discourse since the late nineteenth century suggests the party's ethos has been rather more consistent.

As per Mitchell, a myth is 'an idea or set of ideas whose importance lies in being believed or accepted by a significant body of people sufficient to affect behaviour or attitudes whether grounded in fact or fiction'.[31] Red Clydeside is an early example of such a myth in a Scottish Labour context, promoted by the media and party actors as early as 1918 and ever since to varying degrees. A related but broader myth took hold in the 1980s and had three 'interconnected assumptions': (1) that Labour in Scotland was 'a radical party', something grounded in its nationalist-unionism and willingness to co-operate with other parties, (2) that it was a 'popular' party, a belief which arose from Scottish Labour's long-standing electoral hegemony vis-à-vis the party in England (if not Wales), and (3) the perceived but erroneous 'historical linkage' of support for 'Home Rule' or devolution as extending uninterrupted from Keir Hardie in 1888 through to Donald Dewar and John Smith a century later. This, to quote Hassan, constituted a view of itself 'as the party of Scotland able to speak without equivocation for all Scotland'.[32] This, too, frames much of the account that follows.

As ever, researching this book has been a largely but not exclusively solo undertaking. First, I must express thanks for the research bursary granted by the Society for the Study of Labour History which facilitated two trips to my native Scotland to explore the extensive archival holdings at, among others, the National Library of Scotland in Edinburgh and the superb Scottish Political Archive at Stirling University. Curiously, while the Scottish Labour Party's own papers were transferred to Glasgow's Mitchell Library in 1998 there is no publicly available catalogue and even its existence is not obvious from any online archival database. Perhaps as a result, it has not been widely utilised by historians and political scientists. Hopefully, this book will stimulate further investigation of what is undeniably a rich and important resource.

Thanks also to Baroness Ramsay of Cartvale, Lord Foulkes of Cumnock and Lord Robertson of Port Ellen, all of whom generously contributed financially to make this book possible. As an independent researcher, private donations take the place of funding streams available to academics, but the outcome is the same: an absence of any influence over my judgements, for which responsibility – including any errors or omissions – is mine alone. Finally, colleagues at the House of Commons Library, particularly Paul Little and Greg Howard, helped probably more than either realised, cheerfully tracking down often obscure pamphlets, books and journal articles. I owe you both several pints.

Dr David Torrance
Peckham, South London
April 2025

NOTES

1. *A History of the Scottish Liberals and Liberal Democrats* (2022) and *A History of the Scottish Conservative and Unionist Parties* (2024), both Edinburgh University Press.
2. The Labour Party is not a registered political party in Northern Ireland and does not contest elections there. Those resident in Northern Ireland have only been eligible to apply for membership of the British party since 2003.
3. The term 'fixated' was used by Nathan Sands in his otherwise positive review of *A History of the Scottish Conservative and Unionist Parties in Party Politics* (2025, online).
4. I. Donnachie, C. Harvie & I. S. Wood (eds) (1989), *Forward! Labour Politics in Scotland, 1888–1988*, Edinburgh: Polygon.
5. W. W. Knox (2006), 'The Scottish Labour Party: History, institutions and ideas (review)', *Scottish Historical Review* 85:1, 172–4.
6. F. Bealey (1970), *The Social and Political Thought of the British Labour Party*, London: Weidenfeld and Nicolson, 2.
7. J. G. Kellas & P. Fotheringham (1976), 'The political behaviour of the working class', in A. A. MacLaren (ed.), *Social Class in Scotland: Past and Present*, Edinburgh: John Donald, 143, 161.
8. H. Drucker (1978), *Breakaway: The Scottish Labour Party*, Edinburgh: EUSPB, 8.
9. G. Hassan & E. Shaw (2012), *The Strange Death of Labour Scotland*, Edinburgh: Edinburgh University Press, 1.
10. Penicuik: Scottish Secretariat.
11. Edinburgh and London: Chambers, 1967.
12. Edinburgh: John Donald, 1978.
13. Edinburgh: Scottish Labour History Society, 1978. This flowed from I. MacDougall (ed.) (1965), *An Interim Bibliography of the Scottish Working-Class Movement, and of Other Labour Records held in Scotland*, Edinburgh: Scottish Committee, Society for the Study of Labour History.
14. London: Macmillan. See also M. Keating (1983), 'Labour and Scottish Nationalism: An update', *Cencrastus* 12, 29–31.
15. London: Longman.
16. Whitburn: Scottish Labour Action.
17. J. Mitchell (1996), *Strategies for Self-government: The Campaigns for a Scottish Parliament*, Edinburgh: Polygon. Most recently, see D. Torrance (2020), *'Standing Up for Scotland': Nationalist Unionism and Scottish Party Politics, 1884–2014*, Edinburgh: Edinburgh University Press, 121–47.
18. K. Middlemas (1965), *The Clydesiders: A Left Wing Struggle For Parliamentary Power*, London: Hutchinson.

Introduction 7

19. I. McLean (1983), *The Legend of Red Clydeside*, Edinburgh: John Donald. The same publisher issued a new paperback edition in 1999.
20. E. Gordon (1991), Oxford: Clarendon Press.
21. Edinburgh University Press. Hassan appears to have planned a volume entitled 'A History of Scottish Labour and Home Rule' to be published by Lawrence and Wishart in 1999, but this was not published.
22. Hassan & Shaw, 1.
23. Oxford: Clarendon Press.
24. London: Croom Helm.
25. W. Stewart (1925), *J. Keir Hardie*, London: Cassell; E. Hughes (1956), *Keir Hardie*, London: George Allen and Unwin.
26. G. Brown (1986), *Maxton*, Edinburgh: Mainstream.
27. R. Galbraith (1995), *Without Quarter: A Life of Tom Johnston*, Edinburgh: Mainstream. The author's 2018 reworking (with the different subtitle '*A Biography of Tom Johnston*' and published by Birlinn) represented a considerable improvement upon the original.
28. D. Torrance (2006), *The Scottish Secretaries*, Edinburgh: Birlinn, 248–69.
29. H. Drucker (1979), *Doctrine and Ethos in the Labour Party*, London: HarperCollins, 8–9.
30. L. Bennie, J. Brand & J. Mitchell (1997), *How Scotland Votes: Scottish Parties and Elections*, Manchester: Manchester University Press, 55.
31. J. Mitchell (1990), *The Myth of Dependency*, Glasgow: Scottish Centre for Economic and Social Research, 4.
32. G. Hassan (1996) 'New Labour and the politics of a new Scotland', in M. Perryman (ed.), *The Blair Agenda*, London: Lawrence and Wishart, 172–3.

1

'The Cause of Labour and of Scottish Nationality': 1888–1915

Harvie has argued that Labour in Scotland made a 'significant contribution' to the nature of the early British Labour movement, 'its leadership, its language and its ideology'. He cited trades councils in Glasgow (1858) and Edinburgh (1859), which intervened to help elect Liberals favourable to trade union legislation. But although the first 'Lib-Lab' MP was a Scot, the miners' leader Alexander Macdonald (he won Stafford in 1874), no Lib-Labs were returned for a Scottish seat.[1] The birth of the Labour Party in Scotland has, therefore, most often been traced to the events of 1888.

James Keir Hardie was born in Lanarkshire in 1856 and began work in coal mines aged ten. Preaching gave way to public speaking and a leadership role in miners' unions. Keir, as he was generally known, was also a Liberal, and continued to identify as such even after establishing what might be called the first Scottish Labour Party. This was the product of two working-class movements in Scotland, one concerned with miners' trade unionism and the other Highland land reform. Frustrated at Liberal inaction on a statutory eight-hour day, Hardie became convinced that miners needed their own party to represent them in Parliament. And when Stephen Mason, the Liberal MP for Mid-Lanarkshire, resigned in 1888, he hoped to secure the Liberal nomination.[2]

When it became obvious the local Liberal association did not share Hardie's desire, Hardie resolved to fight Mid-Lanarkshire under his own steam. Several organisations supported his candidacy, including the Highland Land League, the Glasgow Trades Council, the Scottish Miners' Federation and the Scottish Home

Rule Association, whose London secretary was James Ramsay MacDonald. MacDonald implored Hardie not to withdraw:

> The cause of Labour and of Scottish Nationality will suffer much thereby. Your defeat will awaken Scotland, and your victory will reconstruct Scottish Liberalism. All success be yours, and the National cause you champion. There is no miner – and no other one for that matter – who is a Scotsman and not ashamed of it, who will vote against you.[3]

As McLean and McMillan have pointed out, MacDonald's letter mentioned Liberalism, Labour and Scottish nationality 'as if they were the same, or at least overlapping'.[4]

Hardie polled a disappointing 617 votes at the by-election on 27 April 1888, and MacDonald's premonition of restructured Liberalism did not transpire. Instead, and following a preliminary meeting in Glasgow, the Scottish Labour Party (SLP) was born on 25 August. Hardie's actions had convinced a few prominent Liberals to excommunicate themselves from their old political faith and join the new party, but while the SLP's programme was 'more socialist' than Hardie's in the recent by-election, it was 'not a definitely Socialist body'.[5]

Rather the SLP's object was to 'educate the people politically, and to secure the return to Parliament and all local bodies of members pledged to its programme'. Given the SLP's broad range of support, that programme was the result of obvious compromises, encompassing adult suffrage, triennial parliaments, payment of MPs, 'Home Rule for each separate nationality or country in the British Empire', abolition of the House of Lords, land nationalisation, labour legislation (including an eight hours' bill), prohibition of liquor, Commons consent for acts of war, free education, disestablishment and state acquisition of railways, waterways and tramways. 'After reading this plain recital of origins and aims', noted David Lowe, who was present, 'no man can convict the wage-worker of unseemly haste in the pursuit of his own business'.[6]

There was press criticism that the party's office-bearers, particularly the aristocratic R. B. Cunninghame-Graham (president), were not what Emrys Hughes called 'bona fide horny-handed sons of toil'. In response, Hardie declared that:

> The Labour Party in Scotland is now fairly on its feet and ready for action. It will embrace within its ranks not only those working men

who have grown tired of playing at politics as a game for the amusement of the rich, and who want to see social legislation pushed to the front, but also such men as have shown by years of devotion to the cause that they are worthy of trust.[7]

Nevertheless, the Scottish Labour and Scottish Liberal parties remained hard to differentiate, grounded in what Kellas characterised as a political idealism rooted in the 'myth of Scottish history, philosophy and religion ... a compound of presbyterianism, Robert Burns and Robert Owen'.[8] As David Lowe put it:

> The Scottish Labour movement was not founded on materialism. The instinct for freedom and justice which animated the Covenanters and Chartists also inspired the Nineteenth Century pioneers. Their teachers and prophets were Jesus, Shelley, Mazzim, Whitman, Ruskin, Carlyle and Morris. The economists took a secondary place. The crusade was to dethrone Mammon and to restore spirit, and to insist that the welfare of the community should take precedence of the enrichment of a handful.[9]

Class-consciousness was yet to emerge as a key cleavage in Scottish electoral politics, and the Scottish Labour Party had 'no strong, native ideological strength which the Liberal Party did not already possess'.[10] Fred Reid described the SLP as 'labour activists with Christian socialist leanings', and indeed this found expression in the formation of Socialist Sunday Schools during the 1890s. Future inter-war Labour leaders such as Patrick and Agnes Dollan and other members of the Hardie family were their driving forces.[11]

The SLP, meanwhile, was not ready to sponsor its own candidates in by-elections, instead supporting Liberal candidates. An attempt to run a Labour candidate in West Fife in July 1889 failed, while John Burns withdrew in Dundee when Edward Marjoribanks, the Scottish Liberal Whip, offered him a safe seat at Battersea. The fledgling party was further hobbled by internal divisions. In Aberdeen, H. H. Champion formed his own Labour Party based on trades councils rather than trade unions (the Scottish United Trades Councils' Independent Labour Party, or SUTCILP), while at a Trades Union Congress meeting in Dundee in September 1889 a spat between Hardie and the Stirlingshire miners' leader, R. Chisholm Robertson (who had been chosen as secretary of the SUTCILP), saw the latter remove much of the SLP's trade union support.

There were renewed negotiations between the SLP and Scottish Liberals during 1890. At a private meeting, Marjoribanks offered Cunninghame-Graham, James Shaw Maxwell (SLP chairman) and Hardie a clear run in three constituencies (including Greenock) if they agreed not to oppose the Liberals in a forthcoming by-election,[12] but the compact was attacked by the Liberal-supporting *Daily Mail* on the basis that Liberals would lose support by consorting with 'extremist' socialists. Local Liberal associations then repudiated the arrangement, including by rejecting Cunningham-Graham as a candidate in Greenock. At the 1892 general election, therefore, five SLP candidates faced Liberal opposition and accordingly none were elected. Dr G. B. Clark was returned as a Gladstonian despite leading the Crofters' Party and serving as a member of the SLP executive. At its fourth annual conference in January 1893, the Scottish Labour Party therefore resolved to prohibit office holders belonging to outside political organisations and Clark – one of its founding members – was compelled to resign.[13]

At that gathering Hardie attempted to spin the election result as 'a good beginning'. The fledgling party was at least solvent, with twenty-three branches extending from Dumfries to Dundee (one of which was for women; the first, claimed Lowe, 'of its kind in Great Britain').[14] Also speaking to the SLP's lack of progress was the fact Hardie had finally managed to get himself elected to Parliament, just not for a seat in Scotland. So, it was as the Labour Member for South-West Ham that he attended a conference in Bradford, a city chosen as the most convenient centre for Scotland and the industrial north.[15]

SLP delegates unanimously backed Hardie as president and Shaw Maxwell as secretary of the new 'Independent Labour Party' (ILP), to which the SLP was to be affiliated. The ILP's goal was 'collective ownership of all the means of production, distribution and exchange' and 'the independent representation of Labour on all legislative, governing and administrative bodies'. Three Scots joined the ILP's Administrative Council, all from Glasgow or the west coast, including Shaw Maxwell as secretary. Hardie dominated the Bradford conference, stating from the chair that its purpose was:

> to direct the attention of the workers away from reforms of political machinery, no matter how important they may be, and concentrate

their whole energies on this one problem of how to restore to the working classes of the community the capital and the land.[16]

But as Bealey has observed, the ILP had no 'very well defined set of ideas'; Hardie described socialism as 'the kingdom of God upon earth', while Ramsay MacDonald saw it in terms of harmony and co-operation.[17] The new party's essentially ethical vision of socialism, much like the Scottish Labour Party it subsumed, had much in common with Liberal radicalism: land reform, temperance, free trade and the right to national self-determination. Scottish delegates had unsuccessfully moved that 'Socialist Labour Party' be adopted as its name, George Carson (a tinplate worker and later secretary of the Scottish Trades Union Congress) remarking that in Scotland 'the Labour Party had come to the conclusion that it was best to call a spade a spade'. This was opposed as too narrow, English opponents arguing that the ILP 'had to appeal to the vast mass of the workers outside, and not only to the Socialists'.[18]

Back in Scotland, Scottish Labour Party branches in Glasgow agreed to fight municipal elections in 1893 on distribution, temperance, artisan dwellings, trade union rates and a maximum eight-hour day for all municipal employees. When a letter from H. H. Champion to R. Chisholm Robertson (the Stirlingshire miners' leader) was inadvertently opened at the Labour Literature Society office in Glasgow, an apparent attempt to present Hardie and his associates as 'catspaws of Liberalism' provoked uproar, although this had the useful side effect of withering support for Champion's alternative labour party and bolstering the ILP's Bradford programme. Champion left for Australia soon after.[19]

And while those active in the SLP 'formed the nucleus of an army which in the process of time took many citadels in Parliament, Corporation, School Board, County Council, and Parish Council', in 1894 it was unanimously agreed (on Hardie's motion) that the Scottish Labour Party be wound up. An alternative proposal to form a 'Scottish Council' of the Independent Labour Party was rejected by twenty-eight votes to twenty-two. Nevertheless, Robert McLean later viewed the SLP as 'a key intermediary in passing the mantle of Scottish Home Rule from the Liberal Party to an infant labour movement'.[20]

At the 1895 general election Labour and the Liberals again competed for the same Scottish votes. While the ILP fielded seven candidates, two more than the SLP in 1892, their number of votes fell from 5,267 to 4,878. Fraser considered this 'disastrous for the ILP, with a heavy drain on limited finances and plummeting morale at the results, and nearly threatened its demise'.[21] Kellas concluded that the SLP had been simply too radical to advance on the basis of class representation alone:

> This aim was alien to the traditions of Scottish society, and received practically no support from the working-class electorate, which preferred either the old sentiments of the Liberals, or the bread-and-butter appeal of the Unionists. The leaders of the Scottish Labour Party were socialists, but there was still a strong individualism in most of Scotland.[22]

Yet for the remainder of the nineteenth century, it was the ILP which 'provided the thread of continuity' in Labour's electoral campaigns until its eventual disaffiliation in the early 1930s. In 1896, the ILP sent delegates to a new Workers' Municipal Election Committee established by the Glasgow Trades Council. This backed eight Labour and radical candidates returned at that year's Glasgow Town Council election.[23] By 1900, the ILP had thirteen town councillors in Scotland, including five in Glasgow and three in Paisley.[24]

As the Scottish Council of the Labour Party (SCLP) later put it, the nascent Labour movement attracted:

> Radicals impatient with the orthodox Liberals; trade unionists inspired by Keir Hardie and Bob Smillie; non-conformists whose democratic instincts gave proper importance to every member of society; Christian Socialists who believed that dogmas meant deeds as well as words; Fabians who knew that society was capable of reorganisation that would fairly benefit all; Marxists who sought to end the exploitation of the mass of the people by an elite with economic power; Women's Labour League who fought for the franchise and better social conditions; the Cooperatives who offered an experiment in corporate effort as a means of democratic expression.[25]

In 1897, meanwhile, a Scottish Trades Union Congress (STUC) was formed to take a more active part in politics, trades councils in Scotland having been barred from the Trades Union Congress by the Lib-Labs.[26]

The SCLP later lauded Scotland for bringing together its two 'streams' of activity – industrial and political – to form a Scottish

Workers' Representation Committee (SWRC) in Edinburgh on 6 January 1900. This anticipated 'a British conference for the same purpose' held at London's Memorial Hall a few weeks later.[27] Marwick considered the SWRC more 'broadly based' than what was now known as the Labour Representation Committee (LRC), comprising representatives from trade unions (particularly the miners), trades councils (predominantly in Glasgow), Co-operative Societies, the ILP and the SLP. Robert Smillie, the Belfast-born son of a Scottish crofter, became the SWRC's first chairman.[28] But despite high hopes at its inauguration, the SWRC won no seats at the general election in September–October 1900. As one union leader told Ramsay MacDonald, 'it certainly does not accomplish the good results that its founders anticipated'.[29] The SWRC seems to have assumed some kind of equality with the LRC, which MacDonald, despite being a Scot and a Home Ruler, was never going to accept.[30]

According to Hutchison, the SWRC failed to publicise its presence, and even when it did, the benefits were not apparent; George Carson, its secretary and a founder member of the SLP, had a drink problem, and only in 1906 did it begin centrally to encourage the formation of local committees. The SWRC could not even compile a list of prospective candidates, and its finances were so bad it could not afford to send any delegates to the 1905 STUC conference. At the LRC, Ramsay MacDonald called for 'some rearrangement so that the movement for Labour consolidation may go ahead in Scotland as it has done in the South', and in 1904 the LRC's assistant secretary was instructed to explain to the SWRC's chairman '1) the deadness of the Scottish Committee, 2) [and] the imminent necessity of our taking over the whole country'.[31] At the 1906 general election, nine Labour candidates (four LRC and five SWRC) stood, but only two (both LRC) won in Dundee and in Glasgow Blackfriars, Alexander Wilkie and George Barnes respectively.

The result nationally was a Liberal landslide, which compounded that party's view of Labour as driven by the 'perverse personal ambition of a clique of upstart politicians'.[32] The MacDonald–Gladstone arrangement of 1903 – under which Labour and Liberal candidates left the field clear for each other in certain constituencies – had yielded results in England and Wales but specifically excluded Scotland. Although the Scottish Liberal Association had formed a Conciliation Committee, it had still to meet six months before polling day.³³ At their first meeting after the election, LRC MPs decided to call themselves 'the Labour Party' and Keir Hardie was elected the first chairman of the Parliamentary Labour Party. Under a new agreement between Ramsay MacDonald and the Irish-Scots Arthur Henderson, the party in Scotland became the 'Labour Party (Scottish Section)'.

As Harvie has observed, turn of the century Scottish socialism was a paradox in that figures such as Keir Hardie, MacDonald, Henderson and Smillie 'gave the Labour "establishment" a marked Scottish air', while organisation in Scotland remained 'relatively weak'.³⁴ To Hutchison, Labour in Scotland lagged behind the party in England because of organisational defects, ideological conflict between constituent sections, divisions within the working class and limitations imposed by the electoral franchise.³⁵ There were, however, pockets of progress. Agnes Hardie, who in 1909 married George, half-brother of Keir and later the Labour MP for Glasgow Springburn, proved a gifted platform speaker and won election to the Glasgow School Board, later becoming the first female member of Glasgow Trades Council.³⁶

LRC policy was not to contest both seats in two-member constituencies, an electoral understanding with the Liberals which had yielded considerable success in England and Wales. When the Scottish Section indicated its intention to defy this at by-elections in Dundee and Montrose during 1908, MacDonald – fearing retaliatory moves from the Liberals in the rest of Great Britain – telegrammed that 'his committee' had decided to 'affiliate Scottish societies and place their own candidates in the constituencies there'. Two unions – the Scottish Ironmoulders and the Blacksmiths – swiftly transferred their allegiance from the SWRC to the LRC and, anticipating a stampede, the Scottish Section voted to dissolve itself in February 1909.³⁷ Instead, Scottish activists agreed to 'approach the Labour Party with a proposal to establish a Scottish Committee to be directly financed and controlled by the Labour Party'.³⁸

At around the same time, the Scots-Irish publisher John Wheatley (who joined the ILP in 1907) tried to build support for a Catholic Socialist Society, although this encountered hostility from those who feared any weakening of support for Irish Home Rule together with suspicions that Labour stood for an 'atheist materialism'. But while small, Cameron believes the Society 'did vital work in engaging with a section of the population which otherwise retained a strong commitment to Liberalism'.[39] For Kellas, this marked the point at which a Protestant–Catholic split entered the industrial wing of the labour movement, 'for the trade unions could not be effective when cheap labour in the form of Irish Catholic immigrants was readily available'. This tension was strongest in Glasgow and the west, although in the east – Aberdeen, Dundee and the Fifeshire coalfield – there was 'a more united Labour movement and better industrial relations'.[40]

At the January 1910 general election, Labour's twelve candidates received nearly 38,000 votes, a share of more than 5 per cent, enough to secure – as in 1906 – Glasgow Blackfriars and Dundee. Only five candidates contested a second election in December 1910, and despite a fall to 25,000 votes and 3.1 per cent of the vote, the Fife miners' leader William Adamson joined Alexander Wilkie and George Barnes in the House of Commons. They represented a minority of Labour's forty MPs, hardly, as Kellas noted, 'an indication that the Scots were in any sense "red"'.[41] At five Scottish by-elections between 1911 and 1914, there was little evidence Labour's position was improving. On the contrary, Scottish workers remained happy to vote Liberal or Unionist.[42]

By August 1911 there were persistent complaints from the party in Scotland to the Labour Party's National Executive Committee (NEC) about remote and insensitive treatment from London, not least the absence of specifically Scottish propaganda material. The result was a conference of Scottish delegates in Edinburgh at which the NEC was represented by Ramsay MacDonald and Ben Turner of the National Union of Textile Workers. They concluded that:

> the political organisation of Scotland is not quite as good as it might be ... The steady and persistent work of local Labour parties is not so marked as in England. For this, to some extent there is an inclination to blame the Central Executive, but we do not think our Scottish friends quite appreciate how much this form of excellence depends upon local workers.

MacDonald and Turner concluded that the creation of a Scottish advisory committee 'might prevent a good deal of the resentment which some of the older workers of the Movement in Scotland undoubtedly feel'. This proposal, however, was not immediately acted upon.[43]

More generally, George Barnes, who had briefly acted as PLP chairman, lamented the situation in Scotland going 'from bad to worse', with what he called 'that raw declamatory sort of thing' getting 'more general', something encouraged by the *Forward* newspaper.[44] Tom Johnston, its editor, was indeed inclined to pungent rhetoric. In 1909 he published *Our Scots Noble Families* with an approving introduction by Ramsay MacDonald, which accused the Scottish nobility of benefitting from generations of 'pillage, butchery and theft'.[45] Very few Scottish trade union candidates were bona fide socialists and they flinched at such blatant class warfare. At the 1908 Scottish Section conference, its chairman had remarked that the 'bogey' most often raised 'was that they were a Socialist party'.[46]

Instead, the Labour movement in Scotland continued to be animated by what MacDougall called 'a powerful moralism' which rejected the established Church of Scotland despite the Kirk's adoption of a 'social gospel' and related social programmes. The Church of Scotland, meanwhile, feared that 'socialism would also mean atheism, as was believed to be the case on the continent'. Flowing from this was temperance – Keir Hardie and George Barnes were both appalled by drunkenness – and 'a considerable element of romanticism of the William Morris sort', a 'brotherly utopianism' which rested upon the dignity of craftmanship. As described by Harry McShane in his reminiscences of Glasgow: 'The skilled workers who dominated Clydeside unionism were respectable Protestants, running their unions on principles as democratic as their Calvinist Churches, attending meetings in their blue Sunday suits, bowler hats and often rolled umbrellas.'[47]

The Independent Labour Party, meanwhile, remained the lifeblood of the movement in Scotland: in 1910 it had about 5,000 members (one sixth of the ILP's British total) and some 130 branches. A Scottish Division had been established in 1906. Its essential strength, judged Hutchison, was as an 'educational and evangelising movement' rather than as an organised election machine. The party was famous for its public campaigning, street-corner meetings, addresses in cinemas on Sunday nights and summer sessions at holiday resorts. James Maxton likened this approach to 'sowing the seeds which would come to fruition in some distant harvest-time'.[48]

ILP/Labour representation on Glasgow's town council also began to increase from 1910, when it made three gains, with another four the following year and extended city boundaries in 1912 adding another quartet, including John Wheatley. A Glasgow City Labour Party was finally formed in 1913 while Edinburgh elected its first labour councillors in 1909 which, on the eve of the First World War, had risen to six. In Scotland as a whole, Labour could boast sixty-nine town and thirteen county councillors by 1915.[49]

In 1912 Arthur Henderson arranged conferences in Glasgow, Aberdeen, Dundee and Edinburgh to discuss Scottish organisation. By January 1913 his scheme for a Scottish Advisory Council (SAC) was ready to be presented to that year's Scottish conference. It was opposed, however, by trade unions on the basis that they were under-represented. Other unions could see no need; textile worker Tom Shaw could not see 'any earthly reason for setting up an organisation in an organisation':

> If a separate organisation of this character was to be set up for Scotland, should one be set up for Ireland, one for Wales, one for the individual districts of England, and one for the agricultural districts? ... If there were any problems ... there were sufficient Scotsmen on the Executive to deal with them ... Scotland was no worse situated than any other part of the country.

Henderson's plan was defeated by 225 votes to 105. A revised scheme more favourable to Scottish unions was presented to the 1914 conference. The SAC was now to have its own secretary, although his salary was to be paid by the NEC. Scottish conference provided their consent, and an inaugural conference was planned. This, however, was delayed by a dispute between Glasgow's Labour party and trades council over representation. This inflamed similar tensions in Edinburgh and the NEC then used the outbreak of war as a pretext for postponing the conference indefinitely.[50] The only progress made during 1914 was the appointment of Huddersfield-born Ben Shaw as the new SAC's first secretary.

Housing, meanwhile, began to emerge as a core part of Labour's Scottish programme. John Wheatley had a degree of success with his 1914 pamphlet, *Eight Pound Cottages for*

Glasgow Citizens, which at a propaganda level 'benefited from being straightforward, self-contained (the finance was to come from the tramway surplus), and offered a qualitatively better form of public housing than tenement flats'.[51] The proposal, however, met with obstruction and a ruling from Glasgow's town clerk that the policy would be illegal.[52]

When housebuilding ceased at the outbreak of the 'Great War', landlords used the opportunity provided by an influx of workers to raise rents in parts of Glasgow. This sparked industrial action at shipyards and munitions factories, while bringing to the fore female Labour activists such as Helen Crawfurd (a Communist), Mary Barbour (a housewife), Mary Laird and Agnes Dollan, many of whom remained active for decades.[53] Barbour organised women's committees who met in kitchens and closes to gather information on impending evictions. They then used bells and 'ricketies' (rattles) to get women out on the streets to drive off sheriff officers. On 17 November 1915, this culminated with a huge demonstration at Glasgow Sheriff Court. The result was the Rent Restrictions Act 1915 – which froze rents at their August 1914 levels for the duration of the war – and Mary Barbour 'became a Govan legend'.[54]

When it became clear the war was not coming to a swift conclusion, the Scottish Advisory Council's inaugural conference finally took place on 21 August 1915 at Glasgow's YMCA Hall. An executive committee was elected from delegates representing trade unions, trades councils, Labour Representation Committees, the Independent Labour Party, the Women's Labour League and Fabian societies, a composition which would remain unchanged for several decades. The first chairman was Robert Smillie of the Scottish Mineworkers' Association, while Ramsay MacDonald was the tactful choice as the NEC's representative. Scotland, he told delegates, 'needs a lot of stirring up', while the Aberdeenshire-born NEC chairman William Anderson cautioned that:

> conference had been called not to discuss passing affairs, but with a view to building up a better organisation of the Labour Party in Scotland. There was no doubt that Scotland had its own industrial and political problems and the work of solving them would be better left in their own hands. [But] Better organisation was wanted before they could expect to win more seats and send more Labour representatives to Parliament.[55]

As McKibbin observed, the tortuous establishment of the SAC illustrated both particular and general problems of 'regional devolution' within the Labour Party:

> In the particular, Scotland differed perceptibly in degree from most of England in the balance of its working-class organizations: the unions relatively were weaker and the socialist societies relatively more influential. On the other hand, the unions were strong enough to ensure that the socialists could not be predominant. The result was that Party organization in Scotland was both more ineffective than in England, and more politically divided.[56]

Nevertheless, in the SAC's first year it acquired permanent premises on Glasgow's West Regent Street, held a joint meeting with the parliamentary committee of the STUC, forged links with Co-operative organisations and established Parliamentary Divisional Labour Parties to select Labour candidates, particularly in industrial areas. The new party executive set itself the modest goal of raising £50 to fund the production of 'special Scottish literature' and assist 'in other ways local developments throughout Scotland'. In fact, it raised £59 13s.[57]

NOTES

1. C. Harvie, 'Before the breakthrough, 1886–1922' (1989), in I. Donachie, C. Harvie & I. S. Wood (eds), *Forward! Labour Politics in Scotland, 1888–1988*, Edinburgh: Polygon, 8.
2. This account relies heavily on J. G. Kellas's 1964 article, 'The Mid-Lanark by-election (1888) and the Scottish Labour Party (1888–1894)', *Parliamentary Affairs* XVIII:3, 321–4.
3. E. Hughes (1956), *Keir Hardie*, London: George Allen and Unwin, 42.
4. I. McLean & A. McMillan (2005), *State of the Union: Unionism and the Alternatives in the United Kingdom since 1707*, Oxford: Oxford University Press, 120.
5. Kellas, 324.
6. D. Lowe (1919), *Souvenirs of Scottish Labour*, Glasgow: W. and R. Holmes, 2–5.
7. Hughes, 47.
8. Kellas, 318. Ramsay MacDonald said of Hardie that he 'got more Socialism from Burns than from Marx' (Introduction to W. Stewart, 1925, *J. Keir Hardie*, London: Cassell, xviii–xix).
9. Lowe, 125.
10. Kellas, 320.

11. W. W. Knox (1988), 'Religion and the Scottish Labour movement, c.1900–39', *Journal of Contemporary History* 23:4, 613.
12. *The Times*, 1 March 1890.
13. Kellas, 325–7.
14. This section relies heavily on D. Lowe's narrative of the SLP's early life in *Souvenirs of Scottish Labour*.
15. Hughes, 65.
16. J. R. MacDonald (1921), *The History of the ILP: Notes for Lecturers and Class Leaders*, London: ILP Information Committee.
17. F. Bealey (1970), *The Social and Political Thought of the British Labour Party*, London: Weidenfeld and Nicolson, 5.
18. Independent Labour Party (1893), *Report of the First General Conference*, Glasgow: Labour Literature Society.
19. W. H. Fraser (2000), *Scottish Popular Politics From Radicalism to Labour*, Edinburgh: Polygon, 131.
20. R. McLean (1991), *Labour and Scottish Home Rule: Mid Lanark to Majority Government, Part 1: 1888–1945*, Whitburn: Scottish Labour Action, 12–13.
21. Fraser, 132.
22. Kellas, 328–9.
23. J. J. Smyth (2000), *Labour in Glasgow, 1896–1936: Socialism, Suffrage, Sectarianism*, Edinburgh: John Donald, 7.
24. Harvie, 13.
25. Scottish Council of the Labour Party (1965), *Golden Jubilee, 1915–1965: Labour Party Scottish Council*, Glasgow: SCLP, 12.
26. I. MacDougall (1985), *Labour in Scotland: A Pictorial History from the Eighteenth Century to the Present*, Edinburgh: Mainstream, 151.
27. SCLP (1965), 12.
28. W. H. Marwick (1967), *A Short History of Labour in Scotland*, Edinburgh: Chambers, 71.
29. I. G. C. Hutchison (1986), *A Political History of Scotland, 1832–1924: Parties, Elections and Issues*, Edinburgh: John Donald, 250.
30. W. H. Fraser (1985), 'The Labour Party in Scotland', in K. D. Brown (ed.), *The First Labour Party, 1906–1914*, London: Croom Helm, 44.
31. Hutchison (1986), 251–3.
32. Kellas, 321.
33. Hutchison (1986), 260.
34. Harvie, 12.
35. I. G. C. Hutchison (2000), *Scottish Politics in the Twentieth Century*, Basingstoke: Palgrave, 20.

36. E. Ewan, S. Innes & S. Reynolds (2007), *The Biographical Dictionary of Scottish Women: From the Earliest Times to 2004*, Edinburgh: Edinburgh University Press, 159.
37. Hutchison (1986), 251–3.
38. Fraser (1985), 51.
39. E. A. Cameron (2010), *Impaled Upon a Thistle: Scotland since 1880*, Edinburgh: Edinburgh University Press, 89. For a detailed study of Wheatley's religion and politics, see G. C. Gunnin (1987), *John Wheatley, Catholic Socialism, and Irish Labour in the West of Scotland, 1906–1924*, USA: Routledge. The Catholic Socialist Society existed until 1924.
40. J. G. Kellas (1968), *Modern Scotland: The Nation since 1870*, London: Pall Mall Press, 194–5.
41. Kellas (1968), 195.
42. C. M. M. Macdonald (2017), 'Following the procession: Scottish Labour, 1918–45', in M. Worley (ed.), *Labour's Grass Roots: Essays on the Activities of Local Labour Parties and Members, 1918–45*, London: Routledge, 36.
43. R. McKibbin (1974), *The Evolution of the Labour Party, 1910–1924*, Oxford: Clarendon Press, 39–40.
44. Hutchison (1986), 254–5.
45. S. Checkland & O. Checkland (1989), *Industry and Ethos: Scotland, 1832–1914*, Edinburgh: Edinburgh University Press, 191. Johnston later regretted his youthful vitriol.
46. *The Times*, 3 February 1908.
47. I. MacDougall (ed.) (1978), *Essays in Scottish Labour History: A Tribute to W. H. Marwick*, Edinburgh: John Donald, 189–90.
48. Hutchison (2000), 21–2.
49. Fraser (1985), 57.
50. McKibbin, 41–2.
51. Smyth, 8.
52. D. Howell (1986), *A Lost Left: Three Studies in Socialism and Nationalism*, Manchester: Manchester University Press, 238.
53. Cameron, 118–19.
54. Ewan et al., 29.
55. SCLP (1965), 15–16.
56. McKibbin, 42–3.
57. SCLP (1965), 16.

2

Scottish Council of the Labour Party: 1915–1940

The Scottish Advisory Council of the Labour Party was born a year into what was then considered the 'Great' War, that which would end, or so it was hoped, all wars. The First World War also had a profound impact on Scotland's economy, society and politics. This – although accounts of precisely how are contested – influenced the nascent Labour Party in Scotland. As Bealey has recounted, war meant a considerable expansion of the state, with the Liberal–Conservative coalition government taking over mines and railways, while trade unions suspended their protective practices.[1]

Initially, much of the Labour movement supported the Great War, including the three Scottish Labour MPs. Particularly enthusiastic were the miners, whose Scottish representative William Adamson (West Fife) became chairman of the Parliamentary Labour Party in 1917 but proved 'as weak and ineffective as any man who ever held the post'.[2] From 1915 Labour MPs were also included in the coalition government, largely to placate the unions which were so important to expanded munitions production. The most significant group of dissenters, meanwhile, joined Ramsay MacDonald and the campaigning journalist E. D. Morel (later a Labour MP for Dundee) in the Union of Democratic Control, which was critical of 'secret diplomacy' and the lack of parliamentary control over foreign policy.[3] Dissidents were disdained by the majority. At one trade union conference, David Graham, a Lanarkshire miners' leader and later a Scottish Labour MP, read an anti-war declaration by MacDonald before tearing it up to the acclaim of delegates.[4]

As Kenefick has noted, the Labour anti-war movement received little or no press coverage beyond the columns of *Forward* or the *Labour Leader*. Although more than 5,000 turned out for a Glasgow Peace Demonstration, they were nevertheless a 'dedicated minority'.[5] Deeply affected by the European conflict, the pacifist Keir Hardie died in September 1915, although some of his own statements in the year before his death had been, in the eyes of some socialists, equivocal.[6] By December 1916 Labour's Scottish Advisory Council supported peace by negotiation.[7] And when Arthur Henderson was dismissed from the coalition in August 1917 for advocating the same policy, he was succeeded by Gorbals MP George Barnes.

Another aspect of the Great War was industrial. As a centre of munitions, the Clyde was subject to constant pressure to increase production. And as the war progressed, skilled labour was 'diluted' by unskilled male and female workers. The result was a militant protest movement calling itself the Clyde Workers Committee (CWC). Its aim was to: 'organise the workers upon a class basis and to maintain the class struggle until the overthrow of the wages system, the freedom of the workers, and the establishment of industrial democracy have been obtained'. For Kellas, this was 'something new in Scottish politics, and quite alien to its previous history'.[8] In response to the unrest, Liberal MP David Lloyd George, then Minister of Munitions, travelled to Glasgow (accompanied by Arthur Henderson) to charm the CWC into submission. According to David Kirkwood, both Lloyd George and 'Uncle Arthur' handled proceedings badly at a Christmas Day mass meeting,[9] a version of events which influenced a report in the 31 December edition of *Forward*. When the Welsh Wizard failed to work his magic on editor Tom Johnston, the government seized unsold copies, arrested leading members of the CWC and imprisoned them for between six and twelve months.[10] While disputes soon returned to pre-war levels, the unrest radicalised many of those on the Labour left, particularly as Liberals were increasingly perceived as an establishment party of the 'bosses'.

In December 1917 the Scottish Advisory Council submitted a new draft constitution to the NEC. This proposed a return to the 'Scottish Labour Party' nomenclature last used by Keir Hardie and demanded a 'special position' within the national party, with automatic representation on its NEC and at its annual conference. At the last minute, Scottish secretary Ben Shaw persuaded the SAC executive to reinsert the word 'Council', so when the constitution was despatched on 8 December it was headed 'The Scottish Council of the Labour Party'. An irritated Arthur Henderson travelled north ('notwithstanding very great pressure at the office') and stated bluntly that:

> The presentation of the Scottish draft to the [British] Conference would raise wide territorial issues and it would be impossible to reconcile the territorial and other elements at this Conference, as the main structure was, and must remain, largely one of Trades Union and Socialist Organisations, most of which were national bodies stretched throughout Great Britain. Were Scotland granted separate representation, London, Lancashire, Yorkshire, Wales and perhaps other sections of the country differing in type, would each present a similar claim, with a great show of reason.

The SAC executive agreed to withdraw its proposals and reconvene once the 'great work' of the national conference was out of the way. On 9 May 1918 James Maxton, a middle-class schoolteacher, presented further amendments to the NEC where they received what McKibbin called 'a pretty rough reception', not least because they were largely unaltered from those first submitted in 1917 and rejected by Henderson shortly afterwards. On 27 August, the NEC's organisation committee:

> rejected entirely the proposed clause 4, which provided for separate union and local party affiliation to the Scottish Advisory Council (as distinct from affiliation to the national Party), struck out the clause which would have permitted separate Scottish representation at the national conference and similarly rejected separate Scottish representation on the national executive.

The Scottish executive finally admitted defeat. At a further meeting in January 1919, final revisions gave the party an 'autonomy more nominal than real': an increased budget, certain rights regarding a distinctly Scottish policy programme and a new name: 'Scottish Council of the Labour Party'. This at least dovetailed with the regional (almost federal) reorganisation of the national Labour Party which followed in 1920 and, together with electoral advances in the west of Scotland, helped 'still dissatisfaction'.[11]

The ILP had, however, survived with its own separate organisation, membership and leadership, and of course a major power base in Scotland. In 1917 it had 3,000 members in Scotland, and by 1919 three times that figure,[12] In 1918 Maxton issued a May Day manifesto calling for 'A living wage for all', the abolition of food profiteers, as well as justice for soldiers and their families.[13] That same year the ILP activist Roland Muirhead revived the Scottish Home Rule Association (SHRA), this time with Labour and socialist organisations (rather than Liberal) providing its dominant components.[14]

By the end of 1918 'a distinctively nationalist tone' had crept into Scottish party discourse.[15] At that year's 'khaki' election, the first in eight years, Labour's Scottish programme promised both 'The Self-Determination of the Scottish People' and the 'Complete Restoration of the Land of Scotland to the Scottish People'. A joint appeal issued with the Highland Land League (which had been reconstituted by Tom Johnston in 1909) asserted that:

> The English people show a marked disposition to conservatism, while the Scottish people on the other hand, are undoubtedly progressive in political thought and action. The result of the Union has been that Celtic culture and Scottish ideals are discouraged, while the tendency is for the ideals and culture of England to be thrust on our country. Large areas of Scottish land have been denuded of people, in order to provide sporting grounds for the idle rich.[16]

This framing owed much to the Labour movement's Liberal ancestry and would resurface at various points during the twentieth century. With the Representation of the People Act 1918 having extended the vote to all males aged over twenty-one and women over thirty who met a property qualification, the Scottish electorate had almost doubled, including a greater number of working-class voters in industrial areas. Labour's capacity to mount constituency election campaigns in Scotland, however, remained heavily dependent upon its federated components, the ILP, the Co-operative Party (which had increasingly allied itself with Labour during the war), trades councils and even lodges of the miners' union.[17] The party was virtually absent in rural areas, with most of its forty-three candidates standing in Glasgow constituencies as well as five in Edinburgh.[18]

Three hitherto Labour MPs stood as coalition 'coupon' candidates, which meant that in the Gorbals, George Barnes, who had served as Minister without Portfolio, faced an 'official'

Labour candidate, the sometime Soviet consul in Glasgow John Maclean. His British Socialist Party affiliation meant Maclean's candidacy came before the NEC, which reluctantly endorsed him under pressure from local activists. Although Maclean's health prevented active campaigning and Barnes held the seat, he was greeted with a mass procession and the waving of the Red Flag, all 'dramatic statements of his distinctive position', on returning to Glasgow.[19] John Wheatley also lost Shettleston by just seventy-four votes. Seven Scottish members subsequently took the Labour whip; three had been strong supporters of the war (F. H. Rose in Aberdeen North, James Brown in Ayrshire South and Duncan Graham in Hamilton) and two were associated with the ILP (former town councillor William Graham in Edinburgh Central and Neil Maclean in Govan). In England and Wales, Labour had secured a further fifty-two MPs.

Although women remained disadvantaged by the expanded franchise, Labour had begun engaging with that section of the electorate as early as 1916. It took until a year after the 1918 election, however, for Agnes Hardie, a former Glasgow shop girl and sister-in-law of Keir, to be appointed the first Scottish Women's Organiser.[20] That same year the Scottish Council's executive (on which women's organisations had one representative, later increased to four) subsidised a Scottish Labour Women's Conference, which was confirmed as an annual event in 1926.[21] Also in 1919, Clarice McNab Shaw, the first Labour woman member of a Scottish town council, also became the first woman to chair the Scottish conference. Her address argued that as women were the 'chief victims' of Scotland's 'wretched social conditions' it was:

> of extreme importance ... to arouse women to a sense of the political weapon which they now wield by means of the vote. In many districts the requirement of the Constitution for the development of the women's sections had not been complied with, and in very few instances are facilities given to the women to proceed with the necessary educational work.[22]

By 1923, however, Agnes Hardie was reporting forty-two Scottish women's sections comprising between thirty and 200 members, many of whom had been politicised by the Glasgow rent strikes of 1915–16. Breitenbach and Gordon calculated this to equal a Scottish female membership of between 1,266 and 8,400, although in this period that was still considerably less than the Scottish Unionists.²³ There followed more firsts. In November 1919 Agnes Dollan became the first woman Labour candidate selected to contest a municipal election in Glasgow while Mary Barbour was the first to be elected in 1920. The latter went on to establish municipal baths, laundries and crèches, as well as free school milk for children.²⁴

Reinforcing the image of Clydeside as politically militant was a general strike in the west of Scotland which culminated with extraordinary scenes in George Square during January 1919 (though not tanks, as later mythology had it). Inspired by 'Bolshevism', according to the *Daily Record and Mail*, or 'the first step towards that squalid terrorism', according to the *Glasgow Herald*,²⁵ Labour's Scottish Council, the Scottish Division of the ILP, the STUC and the Glasgow Trades Council all officially supported the strike's demand for a forty-hour week.²⁶

Even at the time, Patrick Dollan, a former miner and journalist who had been active in the Clyde Workers Committee, told the ILP's 1920 conference that 'all the talk of Glasgow being the Petrograd of Britain was a great deal of moonshine'.²⁷ Rather the events of 1919 gave rise to what Levitt called 'Labour Unionism', a political culture which sought to 'fuse the needs of the radical Scottish voter to the well-oiled wheels of the British administrative system ... satisfying the basic wants of a job, a house and social security'.²⁸

There were also significant shifts within Scotland's Irish Catholic community. Historically reluctant to abandon support for the Liberals on account of Home Rule, following the 1916 Easter Rising and 1921 Anglo-Irish Treaty of 1921, this began to fade. In 1920 the *Dundee Catholic Herald* had already urged Irish and Catholic citizens to be 'Labour men, pure and simple', doubtless motivated by Labour's support for the Education (Scotland) Act 1918 and its segregated state-funded denominational schooling. Opponents called it 'Rome on the Rates'.²⁹

In this context, the way was open for the Irish Catholic community to 'accept its class identity'. The Church of Scotland Act 1921, meanwhile, drew a line under almost a century of presbyterian strife by recognising the Kirk's spiritual independence and paving the way for reunion with the Free Church in 1929.³⁰ Rosie used the term 'secular canopy' to describe how Labour offered a space in which religious identity could be placed behind class without threatening it.[31] The inter-war Labour Party, however, could point to only three Catholic MPs (vis-à-vis two Unionists) and no more than six Catholic Labour councillors in Glasgow. In Hutchison's view: 'The close relations between Catholicity and Labour in the inter-war years reinforced the essential moderation of Labour. The church hierarchy was much exercised by tears of Communism and turned to Labour to best resist the menace of Bolshevism.'[32] As Knox put it, Labour was seen by the Catholic Church as the lesser of two evils, while the 'rapprochement' between the two tended to 'obscure the class message of the labour movement and obstruct the growth of progressive social reform', not least the reciprocal silence from Labour on abortion, birth control and the desegregation of education.[33] The British Labour leader Ramsay MacDonald, a Scottish Presbyterian, was also perceived by the Catholic press to be 'bitterly anti-Catholic', and possibly with some justification.[34]

By the 1922 general election – prompted by the Unionists' withdrawal from the Conservative–Liberal coalition – the total size of the Scottish electorate had grown from 779,000 in 1910 to 2,205,000. 'We had little money in the bank and only a skeleton organisation in each division', recalled Patrick Dollan in his unpublished memoirs, 'we borrowed most of the money for deposits and raised the election expenses by collections at meetings'. Nevertheless, the ILP managed to sponsor twenty-one Labour candidates and there was a definite sense of momentum. As Philippou concluded, the 'heart and soul of Labour in Scotland in 1922 was the ILP'. In January 1922, Scottish party secretary, Ben Shaw, had predicted winning between twenty-three and twenty-five seats in Scotland.[35]

Labour's electoral breakthrough on 15 November 1922 was sudden and emphatic,[36] commanding, for the first time, more votes than any of its Scottish rivals and capturing the disproportionately large tally of twenty-nine MPs (compared with 113 in England and Wales). Labour also achieved a larger share of Scottish vote than in England, a pattern repeated at every election until 1935. There were heady scenes as a contingent of apparently 'red' Clydesiders headed to Parliament from Glasgow's St Enoch Station.[37] The ILP's Scottish organiser John Paton, however, was under no illusions as regards the enthusiastic crowd:

> The great majority of them had little real understanding of the purposes of these men they were cheering. Socialism probably conveyed as little meaning to them as did the higher mathematics ... What they did understand was that they'd witnessed a portent: a working class party of formidable power had emerged; whether or not they'd voted for it, they could identify themselves with it in its moment of victory.[38]

If anything, posited McLean, the Clydesiders were not class or nationalist 'heroes' but religious. At St Enoch they sang the 124th psalm ('Scotland's psalm of deliverance'), while in David Kirkwood's account: 'We were all Puritans. We were all abstainers. Most of us did not smoke. We were the stuff of which reform is made.'[39]

A few months before the election, James Maxton and Patrick Dollan had finally rejected Communism in a statement of ILP goals, making it clear they did not advocate the use of force as a means of achieving socialism. In 1921 the Scottish Division of the ILP had repudiated its endorsement of the Third International and Tom Johnston prayed that before long the 'current spasm of excitement about how many Soviet angels will sit comfortably on a Parliamentary needle' would be 'spent'.[40]

But Communism existed beyond the ILP. At the election the Lancashire-born academic J. T. Walton Newbold was returned as the Communist MP for Motherwell, endorsed by the local trades and Labour council despite the opposition of Labour's NEC, which retained responsibility for candidates across Great Britain. Indeed, Communists had been able to run as locally sanctioned Labour candidates in several constituencies, including Alec Geddes of the Communist Party of Great Britain (founded in 1920) in Greenock and Aitken Ferguson in Glasgow Kelvingrove.[41]

As more than a dozen ILP MPs headed south, meanwhile, they discussed the British Labour leadership, then in the hands of Manchester MP J. R. Clynes. Opinion strongly favoured Ramsay MacDonald, who had resigned at the outbreak of the First World War, and at an informal meeting the following morning – which included sixteen Scots – a majority endorsed the illegitimate son of a Morayshire farm hand. A full meeting of the Parliamentary Labour Party then took place and MacDonald was elected by a margin of four votes.[42]

What, then, explained Labour's result in 1922? Seismic elections often give rise to the quixotic pursuit of a single overarching explanation, but there was a myriad of factors at play. The most famous (but now contested) thesis is that of McLean, who identified two elements: (1) high levels of unemployment, deteriorating industrial relations and a bleak economic outlook, all of which diminished trust in the coalition government, and (2) the politically potent issue of rents.[43]

Tenants' and housing associations had recently scored a notable triumph in the case of *Kerr v. Bryde*, in which a sheriff ruled that a formal 'notice to quit' was necessary from property owners before rents could legally be increased. Upheld in the Court of Session, an owner appealed to the House of Lords, which by a majority agreed with the Scottish courts. The Law Lords' judgment on 3 November 1922 caused a 'great stir', with *Forward* claiming 'every tenant of a working-class house in Scotland is entitled to have returned to him a sum equal to about 12 months' rent and rates combined'. But Labour, as McLean observed, 'stood to gain votes not simply through gratitude for services rendered, but from the threat of an immediate reversal of the [judgment] by the other parties'.[44]

Philippou also emphasised 'long years of propaganda and unremitting effort' – particularly from the ILP – not least in the areas of unemployment and housing.[45] Hutchison's clear-sighted view was that the 'hectic episodes' of 1915–19 suggested that Red Clydeside was, at worst, 'a figment of the imagination, and, at best, only a partial explanation of the rise of Labour after 1918', which owed more to a 'broader' set of forces relating to a range of socio-economic rather than ideological trends, including the widened franchise system, the homogenisation of the working class, greater solidarity created by the growth of working-class institutions, a diminution in the sectarian divide and dramatically increased trade union membership.[46] As McLean has shown, municipal election results between 1919 and 1922 also indicated that the Labour vote had spread from 'labour-aristocratic' to 'unskilled' districts and went 'some way towards explaining the differences between the 1918 and 1922 General Elections'.[47]

What of the new Scottish MPs? A disproportionate number were ILP members, mainly from Glasgow. In John Paton's sober analysis, they:

> were an exceedingly diverse selection, they had nothing whatever of the homogeneity of outlook and action expressed by such

picturesque titles as 'the Clydesiders' or 'the Scottish Rebels'. The men from Clydeside, as from all the other districts, were men of the Right, the Centre and the Left, as their temperaments, experiences and habits of thought dictated.[48]

But while most of the Clydeside ILP members had supported MacDonald as party leader, the relationship between the two quickly became uneasy. James Maxton had told the crowds in Glasgow that they would soon see the atmosphere of the Clyde get the better of the House of Commons, and for a while he and his colleagues remained ostentatiously aloof from what others considered the best club in London. Paton believed:

> The popular illusion of the superior 'revolutionary' fervour of these Scots members had its origin, probably, in their effective team-work in the first days of the new Parliament, when they astonished the House by their capacity for effective speech and by the vigour of their language. For perhaps a week, in the roving discussion of the King's Speech, they displayed a unity never again to be achieved.[49]

This peaked on 27 June 1923 when, during a debate on cuts to subsidised milk for children, Maxton called 'the persons who sent that order murderers, and the hon. gentlemen opposite who went into the division lobby in favour of that policy are murderers, cold callous murderers, with the blood of infants on their hands'.

MacDonald apparently groaned, 'noble head' in hands, that this was 'the end of the Labour Party', while Maxton (now supported by John Wheatley) refused to retract, which led to their suspension from the House. 'A recent speech by Maxton in Glasgow is really terrible', MacDonald subsequently told ILP chairman Clifford Allen. 'It is fearful nonsense. And Maxton is such a good fellow. [Arthur] Henderson writes me complaining of the pronouncements being made by the ILP without consultation committing us to this, that and the other thing.'[50] To Smout, rather than changing Westminster, the Clydesiders 'allowed themselves to be overwhelmed by it'.[51] But, as Paton has argued, the 'revolt' was 'immensely popular with the masses of the common folk throughout the country', the ILP rebels ended up in huge demand at public meetings and, ultimately, inflicted no obvious electoral damage on Labour's advance.[52]

1924 ELECTION AND GOVERNMENT

Ramsay MacDonald at least appeared at one with the ILP when it came to Home Rule. From its inception in 1915, the Scottish Council of the Labour Party had passed an annual resolution supporting a Scottish Parliament, as had the STUC from 1914.[53] To Howell, this was symptomatic of an increasing emphasis on specifically Scottish issues by the Labour movement.[54] Importantly, the objective was 'Home Rule', which meant the sort of autonomy granted to Northern Ireland in 1921, although some in the ILP came to prefer the Dominion status of the Irish Free State.

This emphasis also manifested itself in organisational terms. At its March 1924 conference, a majority of Scottish Council delegates again demanded separate Scottish representation on British Labour's NEC.[55] The eighteen-member executive committee of the Scottish Council met monthly and was 'stuck somewhere between Unionist integration and Liberal autonomy', comprising six trade union representatives, four from constituency parties and trades councils, four from women's sections, two from the ILP and one apiece from the moribund Social Democratic Federation and the Fabians.[56] The 1923 conference had also backed one or two annual meetings between the Scottish executive and Scottish Labour MP group 'to talk over Scottish business, past or future, and make plans'.[57]

Finlay has posited that Labour embraced self-government because:

> it appealed to popular nationalist sentiment and, in the absence of properly defined policies, could be used as a panacea for a whole range of social, political and economic problems. Also, it acted as a unifying force, bringing together disparate elements, such as the Rev. James Barr and James Maxton, together in common cause. The use of nationalist rhetoric was a speciality with Labour politicians when addressing large audiences who, probably because of the simplicity of the Home Rule idea, responded enthusiastically to the demands for a redress of Scottish grievances.[58]

This rhetoric naturally embraced and celebrated national 'heroes'. In June 1923, the ILP organised a Bannockburn Rally with David Kirkwood as the main speaker, while in Elderslie a few months later, Tom Johnston (author of *The History of the Working Classes in Scotland*, published in 1920) and James Maxton addressed a (William) Wallace rally, the sort of events which would later become the preserve of the Scottish National Party. One contemporary account found it 'curious' that a 'simple' speech by Kirkwood was 'far more concerned with Bannockburn, Stirling Bridge, Bruce and Wallace', than it was with 'the dictatorship of the proletariat and Karl Marx'.[59] John Paton recalled making himself unpopular when he 'openly blasphemed' against the ILP's new nationalist 'gods'. Although he had:

> no difficulty in giving assent to the general idea of a Scottish Parliament to deal with exclusively Scottish affairs ... it was not long before much of the argument for this eminently reasonable proposal began, probably naturally enough, to have a flavour against which I was in instant revolt ... There were traces of a separatist argument and a steady drift into a fervent Scottish Nationalism.[60]

The Clydesiders, meanwhile, viewed themselves 'as advance agents of a hitherto unrepresented public, carrying with them some special authority of a new and final order',[61] and their experience as MPs after 1922 made them burn with even greater zeal for Scottish autonomy. This rested at least in part on the perception of a radical Scottish majority, as Maxton put it, 'steadily voted down by the votes of the English members pledged to a policy of social stagnation'.[62] In October 1923 Ramsay MacDonald told the Educational Institute for Scotland that if 'anything established the claim to Self-government and Self-determination', it was watching Scotland's distinctive 'advantages' preserved in 1707 being 'taken away from them by hostile majorities from another nation that owed no allegiance to the Scottish people'.[63]

But within weeks of that fiery peroration, MacDonald began to cool. Although Labour did not win the unexpected general election of December 1923,[64] the refusal of a depleted Unionist Party to coalesce with the hated Liberals meant that within days it looked certain that the Labour Leader of the Opposition was headed for Downing Street as the head of a minority government – Labour's first. Unlike Maxton, who believed taking office would be a mistake, Patrick Dollan, Labour's leader on Glasgow Town Council, argued that the party in government would 'be able to do more for the workers and the nation than Labour in opposition'.[65]

MacDonald did not enjoy assembling his first government. Apart from himself as premier and Foreign Secretary, other prominent Scots included John Wheatley, who was considered essential on account of the need for an ILP representative. Fittingly, his great success came in housing policy, finally convincing trade unions and construction industry leaders to work together, underpinned by a Treasury grant. Even so, Paton recalled that Wheatley 'was little understood, and it is no exaggeration to say that he was disliked and even distrusted by large numbers who were repelled by his enigmatic personality'.[66] There was bitter disappointment among Scottish Labour women when Wheatley (in his capacity as Minister for Health) refused to revoke regulations banning doctors and health visitors from giving advice on contraception, a clear example of his Catholicism trumping progressive policy.[67]

Why had MacDonald cooled on Home Rule for Scotland? In his survey of Labour's constitutional policy, Dorey identified three factors, ideological, economic and electoral. Ideologically, developments on the Continent had gradually convinced the party that nationalism was a destructive rather than a progressive force, while many Labour politicians had come to see it as potentially damaging to the unity and solidarity of the British working class, encouraging the idea that Scottish workers had different interests from those in England and Wales.[68] Economically, meanwhile, recession had pointed the movement towards closer involvement with a unified 'British' economy.[69] As British Labour's assistant secretary James Middleton put it, he did 'not think [that] all the large measures in which the Scottish, English and Welsh peoples are interested necessarily depend upon self-government for their success'.[70] Finally, as Labour became more electorally successful, it feared that devolution – and a commensurate reduction in Scottish representation at Westminster – might deprive it of a parliamentary majority.[71]

Frustrated at the Prime Minister's evident loss of interest, some Clydesiders decided to take the initiative. At a well-attended meeting organised by the Scottish Home Rule Association on 27 April 1924, the Gorbals MP George Buchanan gave details of a forthcoming private member's bill,[72] while Maxton spoke of having 'no greater job in life than to make English-ridden, capitalist-ridden, landowner-ridden Scotland into the Scottish Socialist Commonwealth'.[73] A remarkable crowd of 30,000 attended a march in August 1924 in which ten Scottish MPs took part.[74] Other ILP MPs such as Tom Johnston eschewed 'a narrow, sterile, wha's-like-us pride' and prayed for something more constructive.[75] Johnston's nationalism complimented his support for Union and Empire and he helped found the Commonwealth Labour Group.[76] In 1925, by contrast, the STUC declared its 'complete opposition to Imperialism'.[77]

The second reading of the Government of Scotland Bill proved memorable. Buchanan claimed support from fifty-six out of Scotland's seventy-four MPs, but while William Adamson, now the Secretary for Scotland, said the government endorsed the 'general principle' of the bill, he proposed the fudge of 'a Committee to examine this whole question and report to the House'.[78] When the Speaker appeared to facilitate Unionist attempts to 'talk out' the bill without the question being put to a vote, there was so much uproar from Liberal as well as Labour members that the chair took the procedurally nuclear option of adjourning the sitting due to 'grave disorder'.[79]

The Cabinet subsequently made desultory efforts to follow through with Adamson's promised committee but in the Commons on 18 June 1924 MacDonald said the government had been unable to secure cross-party support.[80] Tom Johnston, Neil Maclean and Duncan Graham visited Downing Street the following month but to no avail.[81] While Home Rule ostensibly remained Labour policy, it was, judged Keating and Bleiman, simply 'too far down the list of national priorities for it to be worth putting the Government's survival at risk'.[82] Having incurred the ILP's wrath for nominating two Unionist MPs as Lord Advocate and Solicitor-General, MacDonald's only sop to Scottish sentiment was the recommendation of mining MP James Brown as Lord High Commissioner to the General Assembly of the Church of Scotland, an office hitherto occupied by Tory aristocrats.[83]

MacDonald also had other concerns. His foreign policy triumphs in the summer of 1924 were soon engulfed by personal scandal (the whiff of cash-for-honours over shares gifted by the newly knighted Alexander Grant, a childhood friend), opposition intransigence (ostensibly over a City loan to the newly recognised Soviet Union) and the 'Campbell Case', a botched prosecution of a Scottish Communist. The culmination was the third general election in as many years, and while Labour entered the campaign confident of its record, the fabricated Zinoviev Letter aided a Conservative landslide on 29 October.[84]

With the 1922 election having spooked Conservatives and Liberals into a series of 'anti-socialist' electoral pacts, Labour faced single opponents in many seats in the west of Scotland and their representation was reduced from thirty-four to twenty-six, despite an increased poll – almost a million votes across Great Britain. MacDonald licked his wounds as Stanley Baldwin returned to Downing Street, although both leaders welcomed the disastrous performance of the Liberals. In Paisley, Rosslyn Mitchell, a Glasgow magistrate radicalised by the Clydeside rent strikes, had defeated the Liberal leader and former premier H. H. Asquith.[85] In a post-mortem on the first Labour government, Patrick Dollan challenged ILP critics to put up or shut up; either accepting MacDonald had increased the party's vote or moving to replace him as leader.[86]

The Scottish Labour MPs elected in 1924 were predominantly working class (Dyer judged only nine to be 'unequivocally' middle). The most distinct group were territorially concentrated miners, 'the working-class equivalent of the landowners' (such as William Adamson), while the second major group remained the Clydeside-based ILP, a mix of middle-class intellectuals such as Maxton, skilled workmen like David Kirkwood and small businessmen, of which John Wheatley had been the undisputed star of the first Labour government.[87] In 1925, the ILP's Scottish Division peaked with 307 branches out of the British total of 1,028, while Neil Maclean told the 1926 Scottish Council conference that he and his colleagues were in Parliament 'to do their best, and it was the duty of the Labour supporters in the country to tell them when they were not doing right'.[88]

A recent Liberal convert was the Revd James Barr, whose Motherwell election address had boasted of being 'closely connected with all that is best in Scottish life – with Scottish Religion, with Scottish Education, with Scottish Temperance, and with Scottish Political Idealism'.[89] Once active in the Liberal-aligned Young Scots Society, Barr relished the opportunity to pursue Home Rule via another bill, this time drafted by the Scottish Home Rule Association.[90] Rejecting charges of 'narrow nationalism', Barr believed 'true and free Scottish nationalism would make its distinctive contribution to a true internationalism, the welfare of humanity'.[91]

Barr's Government of Scotland Bill reflected both its sponsor's political priorities ('matters of temperance, matters of religious equality and the great principles of moral and social advance') as well as a hardening of Home Rule demands, which now included Dominion status for Scotland and the withdrawal of its MPs from Westminster. Although supported by Tom Johnston, John Wheatley and the Revd Campbell Stephen (like Barr a presbyterian dissenter), the bill was once again talked out. McLean noted the irony that within a matter of months Home Rule was far from Barr's mind when he led the rejection of a revised Anglican Prayer Book in the Commons. Although Scottish Labour frontbenchers had not intended to vote, they were swayed by Rosslyn Mitchell's warning that the move would legitimise the Catholic doctrine of transubstantiation. Crucial to the draft prayer book's rejection were the votes of thirty-five Scottish MPs, nine of them Labour.[92] Support for temperance also lingered despite only forty-one Scottish burghs voting to be alcohol free (508 backed 'no change') at 'local option' ballots in 1920. Only in 1965 did the Labour Party in Glasgow abandon its policy of maintaining 'dry' council estates.[93]

Another decisive event in the mid-1920s was the General Strike, which not only offended Ramsay MacDonald's centrist strategy but convinced the Labour leadership that any involvement with the Communist Party of Great Britain (CPGB) – blamed by Baldwin and the *Daily Mail* for the 'unconstitutional' attempt to overthrow parliamentary government – was electorally toxic. The Labour movement had long held the CPGB at arm's length and rejected affiliation by large majorities, while Constituency Labour Parties in Scotland which declined to expel Communists were suspended or dissolved.[94] Addressing the Scottish Council's 1928 conference, Arthur Henderson said delegates should not be 'ashamed to tell the people we are a constitutional party'.[95] James Maxton's rejoinder was the vigorously Marxist Cook-Maxton manifesto, which criticised Labour's apparent abandonment of the class struggle.[96] At the 1928 British Labour conference, John Wheatley attacked *Labour and the Nation* (the official programme endorsed at that conference) as an 'undertaking' to do nothing more than 'run capitalism successfully'.[97]

Despite their earlier friendship, this confirmed Patrick Dollan's conviction that Maxton now advocated revolutionary policies and Communist alliances which had limited popular and electoral appeal.⁹⁸ While Maxton and his followers seized control of the British ILP during 1925–6, Dollan persuaded the Scottish Division of the ILP to reject the Cook-Maxton manifesto. As Hutchison has observed, the Scottish Labour vote at the 1924 and 1929 elections rather undermined the charge that MacDonald's moderate approach had alienated working-class voters in Scotland.⁹⁹ Marxist analysis was thus replaced by empiricism, something epitomised by Arthur Woodburn's *An Outline of Finance* in 1928.

When in February 1928 Roland Muirhead emerged as a Home Rule candidate in West Renfrewshire despite being an ILP member in that constituency, George Mathers (a Labour candidate in Edinburgh) complained to Arthur Henderson that:

> In the Annual Conferences of the Scottish Council of the Labour Party we have repeatedly passed resolutions in favour of Home Rule but there is no appearance of result … more attention must be paid to Scottish opinion (regarding Scotland) by our National Party … there should be room for Scotland as a separate country with a different outlook and sufficient national pride to sometimes resent being tacked on at the tail of England in respect of legislation and even in the pronouncements of our own Party.¹⁰⁰

Scottish Labour MPs including William Adamson, Tom Johnston, George Hardie and the Revd James Barr also lobbied MacDonald and Henderson a few weeks later, and in response both expressed support for 'a great scheme of devolution in Scottish affairs'.¹⁰¹ Although MacDonald backed Mathers's candidacy in West Edinburgh on this basis (praising his 'sound views' on the 'future Government of Scotland'),¹⁰² *Labour and the Nation* had done little more than reaffirm a 1918 commitment to create 'separate legislative assemblies in Scotland, Wales and England with autonomous powers in matters of local concern'. Roland Muirhead ultimately contested West Renfrewshire in May 1929 on behalf of the newly formed National Party of Scotland (NPS) but received only 1,667 votes. Labour responded by ruling NPS members ineligible for Labour membership or affiliation, the SHRA dissolved itself, and thereafter nationalism became the property of the CPGB and Scottish National Party formed in 1934.¹⁰³

Once again Prime Minister, Ramsay MacDonald offered another committee, primarily into local administration but also, he hoped, 'the larger question of Scottish self-government'.[104] No inquiry took place. Gordon Brown concluded that 'lying behind Labour's inability to meet its policy on home rule was the fact that the sense of Scottish separateness was never sufficiently strong to force Labour into a more decisive stand'.[105] Labour had emerged from the 1929 general election with a plurality of seats. Neither the General Strike of 1926 nor the defeat of Home Rule legislation in 1927 had dented the party's advance in Scotland, indeed the former event (together with the longer-lasting miners' lockout) helped push Labour representation on Glasgow Town Council to new heights.[106]

A Leith by-election back in May 1927 had revealed a certain degree of dysfunctionality. The incumbent was Liberal MP William Wedgwood Benn (father of Anthony/Tony), although he was keen to stand on a Labour ticket, something supported by the British Labour NEC. When the Leith CLP instead selected the ineffective R. F. Wilson, an English Liberal called Ernest Brown entered the race and won the seat by 111 votes.[107] An NEC post-mortem noted that the contest had been 'typically Scottish in character', with 'extremely successful meetings' but only a partial canvass, not least because 'Scottish traditions in the matter of canvassing are very hard to break down'.[108]

Of the sixty-eight candidates Labour fielded at the 1929 general election, however, thirty-six were elected, ten more than in October 1924. Re-elected in North Lanarkshire was Jennie Lee, a twenty-four-year-old miner's daughter who had won the seat at a by-election despite being unable to vote for herself given remaining franchise restrictions.[109] She was the first female Scottish Labour MP and in 1934 would begin a long partnership with Nye Bevan. Between 1918 and 1945, just eleven women were selected as Labour or ILP candidates and only five returned as Scottish MPs.

The second Labour government was not a happy one. Despite the party's strengthened position across Great Britain, within months it had fallen victim to external events in the form of a global financial crash. Tom Johnston, now a junior minister at the Scottish Office, visited the Soviet Union during 1930, which sparked an enthusiasm for economic and social planning and dampened his commitment to Home Rule. Increasing support for a strongly centralised (British) state was hardly compatible with radical autonomy for Scotland, not least when the global economy appeared to be in meltdown. Thus a new orthodoxy had it that:

> Scottish interests were best promoted by a strong UK government, with a strong Scottish Labour presence at Westminster and a large degree of administrative devolution to ensure Scotland's voice was heard, that Scotland received a fair share of the UK cake and that special conditions were recognised in the administration of policy.[110]

Knox and Mackinlay called this a 'dualist perception' of the British state: on the one hand an 'agent of oppression' during periods of industrial unrest, but on the other one capable of redressing 'social injustices'. Such pragmatism also allowed Labour to reach an understanding with moderate Scottish businessmen via corporatist initiatives such as the Scottish National Development Council established in 1931.[111] Figures like John Wheatley were in complete agreement with this modified position, although by the late 1920s he was so estranged from the party mainstream that MacDonald did not include the star of the first Labour government in his second. Wheatley died just shy of his sixty-first birthday in May 1930 and was succeeded in Shettleston by John McGovern.[112] By 1932, meanwhile, even James Maxton believed the struggle 'for mere political liberty' to be 'out of date' with economic reality, be it in Ireland, India or Scotland.[113]

Johnston had increasingly become the public face of the Scottish Office, not least because William Adamson was such a weak Secretary of State for Scotland, the office having been upgraded in 1926. In March 1930 Johnston was forced publicly to defend his chief when Ellen Wilkinson attacked Adamson as unfit for office in the official journal of the ILP.[114] That year a new system of local government had been inaugurated under the Local Government (Scotland) Act 1929. Apart from Fife and in the Clyde valley, Labour managed only meagre representation on the new county councils and also fared badly in PR elections to short-lived Local Education Authorities.[115]

Adamson was among those uneasy at the direction of government policy in the summer of 1931. 'I've never voted against the poor yet', the Scottish Secretary told colleagues when confronted with cuts to unemployment benefit, 'and I can't now'.

Subsequent events have been well charted, although it is notable that James Maxton was surprisingly generous regarding Ramsay MacDonald's decision to head a National Government which included Conservatives and Liberals: 'he did what he believed right. Accusations from the Labour party about treachery seem to me quite out of place.'[116] The general election in October 1931 proved what Arthur Woodburn remembered as 'a terrible blow to our people', the defection of MacDonald and Philip Snowden to the 'other side' having broken 'the hearts of many of the older socialists who ... on this account dropped out of the movement'.[117] Labour won just seven seats in Scotland, one fewer than both the Liberals and National Liberals. Robert Forgan, the only Scottish Labour MP to have joined Oswald Mosley's New Party, polled negligibly in West Renfrewshire. The 'National' Labour Party, subsequently formed by supporters of MacDonald, also had little support in Scotland. Only the Lord Advocate Craigie Aitchison retained both his office and constituency, although he soon departed for the Scottish Bench.[118]

As Donnachie has argued, the electoral omens for Labour in Scotland had not been good even before the 'Great Betrayal', certainly judging by swings against the party in the St Rollox and Rutherglen by-elections. Labour had not been defeated by its own failure or that of its policies, 'but by the unity of the opposition'.[119] An internal post-mortem identified this as one of three areas of concern, the others being poor organisation and inadequate canvassing.[120] Indeed, the second Labour government – much like the first – added up to rather more than might have been expected given its circumstances. Not only was the Wheatley subsidy restored via the Housing Act 1930, but coal mining was partially reorganised and there were notable advances in alleviating unemployment, developing agriculture and extending social welfare, including the provision of free milk for children in Lanarkshire.[121]

DISAFFILIATION AND REBUILDING

The relationship between Labour and the Independent Labour Party had deteriorated sharply since 1929, and although formal disaffiliation had long been rumoured it finally came a year after Labour's electoral collapse and, ironically, a resulting pitch to the left. While the ILP's Scottish Division and conference backed a Patrick Dollan–Manny Shinwell axis which opposed disaffiliation, the more populous Glasgow ILP supported the secessionist James Maxton, a testament to his personal following.[122]

Nineteen ILP branches in Scotland left the Labour Party, proportionately a more painful breach than in England and Wales. Both parties suffered, the ILP losing members and Labour in Scotland much of its campaigning vitality. The latter was left with just three MPs and a stark decline from one of Labour's strongest British 'regions' to one of its weakest.[123] Those ILP members (including Tom Johnston, now an ex-MP) who chose to remain within the Labour Party organised themselves under the banner of the 'Scottish Socialist Party' (SSP), which led to a lengthy legal battle over 'halls and property all over Scotland which had been accumulated by the sacrifice and work of hundreds of people'.[124] This dragged on until 1939 when the Court of Session found in the continuing ILP's favour.[125]

Arthur Woodburn had recently been appointed secretary to the Scottish Council of the Labour Party in succession to Ben Shaw. His only condition was that he remain secretary of the Scottish Labour College, whose treasurer William Elger also doubled up as secretary of the Scottish Trades Union Congress.[126] Elger had helped lend trade unionism a clearer and more powerful voice since the war, a 1922 reorganisation having formed an STUC General Council and permanent secretariat.[127] Between them, Woodburn detected the possibility of 'keeping the movement in Scotland going harmoniously' and, in time, rebuilding it. But there was, as he noted in his unpublished memoirs:

> practically no Labour Party in Scotland. The Labour Party was still largely a federated body and the real drive was in the ILP. But the ILP had just broken away from the Labour Party and my job was practically to build from scratch.

The Scottish Council was merely 'a piece of internal machinery providing the movement with advice on Scottish affairs'.[128]

The existence of the Scottish Socialist Party was an additional complication in that party workers were duplicated in several towns and villages. As of September 1932, the SSP had 100 branches and more than 1,000 members.[129] Its driving force, Patrick Dollan, was also Scottish editor of the Labour-supporting *Daily Herald*. He and Tom Johnston at *Forward* publicised the activities of the SSP at the expense of Labour, although Woodburn skilfully exploited the latter's correspondence columns to carry on 'polemic discussions on the theories that were dividing us'.[130] Neither the SSP nor Labour, however, could afford what Knox and Mackinlay called 'another round of blood-letting', and they were at least united in their opposition to Communism.[131]

Keating believed the Labour Party that emerged was 'more pragmatic, cautious, and unimaginative' than that which had existed prior to the ILP's exit, not to mention 'smaller in membership and activism'.[132] At the 1933 East Fife by-election, Joseph Westwood gave Labour its first increased vote since 1932, while the party advanced in local government. The dominant figure in Glasgow was Dollan, whom Smout depicted as 'unemotional organizer, Catholic, party-machine man par excellence', and the Labour leader who 'really understood the Scottish working-class voter of the years after 1920'. Under Dollan's guidance, municipal Labour became synonymous with council housing, heavy industry and denominational education, although this had little to do 'with participatory democracy, enthusiasm for socialism or hope for the future'.[133]

The Dollan era peaked in 1933 when Labour moved from almost permanent opposition on Glasgow Town Council to form its first (minority) administration, ironically aided by divisions on the Conservative right caused by the emergence of Alexander Ratcliffe's Scottish Protestant League (SPL).[134] While the SPL soon petered out, Labour retained control, with the Scottish Socialist Party accounting for around twenty-five of its councillors. Between 1933 and 1938, Dollan served as finance spokesman, city treasurer and ultimately council leader, committing Labour to:

> build new hospitals, houses, and schools; to develop road schemes; to ensure the 'humanisation of Public Assistance'; to introduce a direct labour department which would not only build houses but venture into other areas of activity such as the building of coach bodies; the introduction of a system for the bulk purchase of departmental supplies; and to establish a municipal bank.

While the hostile *Glasgow Herald* predicted 'an orgy of extravagance', much of this ambitious agenda was realised and in 1935 Labour gained a majority in Glasgow for the first time. Dollan accepted a knighthood on becoming Lord Provost in 1938, and Smyth has argued convincingly that although Sir Patrick was subsequently assessed more harshly than Maxton, Wheatley et al., he was in fact a 'highly nuanced figure: a socialist campaigner as well as an effective administrator ... a powerful working class advocate, as well as a political reformist'.[135]

THE LATER 1930S

By the general election of November 1935, the National Government was four years old, and an exhausted Ramsay MacDonald had recently resigned as Prime Minister. Labour selected candidates to fight five incumbent ILP MPs, something Arthur Woodburn deemed necessary to prevent them spreading 'over the whole of Scotland [and] losing us, perhaps, many seats'. Oliver Baldwin, Labour's candidate in Paisley and the estranged (and homosexual) son of Stanley, once again Prime Minister, offered to negotiate an electoral truce, but in the event Maxton 'preferred the privileged position in Parliament of being the leader of a small party without responsibility'.[136]

The ILP retained four of its five MPs and Oliver Baldwin was narrowly defeated in Paisley. Labour won twenty seats, although none of the four candidates sponsored by the SSP (which included Jean Mann and Hector McNeil, a future Scottish Secretary) were successful. Another high-profile victim was MacDonald, who was defeated in Seaham by the Anglo-Scottish (and Jewish) Manny Shinwell, who had served as Secretary for Mines in the first Labour government. Despite failing health, MacDonald was re-elected to Parliament at a by-election for the Combined Scottish Universities constituency in January 1936. William Adamson, a MacDonald loyalist who had fought a gruelling battle to maintain control of his miners' union, failed to regain his seat, which was taken by William Gallacher of the Communist Party of Great Britain. Adamson's wife Jennie, on the other hand, thrived as the 1935–6 chair of British Labour's NEC, of which she was a member for two decades. She was later elected the MP for Dartford at a 1938 by-election.[137] An energetic rural campaign, meanwhile, had yielded the Western Isles, Liberal decline having persuaded Labour that rural seats were worth targeting.[138] By this point, 'complete harmony' existed between Labour and the Scottish Co-operative Party, which since 1931 had engaged in political activity. The Co-op Society in Dumfriesshire had provided seventy cars for Labour on polling day.[139]

In 1936 the British Labour conference took place at Edinburgh's Usher Hall. There, what Woodburn called 'a vital change of policy' was made, with delegates resolving that 'the armed strength of the countries loyal to the League of Nations must be conditioned by the armed strength of the potential aggressors'. The party in Scotland, however, remained strongly pacifist. In 1935 Patrick Dollan had declared the SSP an 'anti-war party', predicting '1,000 conscientious objectors in Scotland for every score in 1914' should there be another war, although he was also vehemently anti-Communist, castigating the CPGB for supporting the Nazi-Soviet pact.[140] *Forward* adopted a pacifist stance under the editorship of Emrys Hughes, a Welsh journalist who had married Keir Hardie's daughter Nan in 1924. This soured relations with the Scottish Council.[141]

Foreign policy, over which the Scottish Council possessed no authority, increasingly dominated domestic politics. As Mussolini geared up to invade Abyssinia in September 1935, Labour stuck to its then support for League of Nations sanctions during the Dumfriesshire by-election, while shortly after the same dictator's invasion of Albania in April 1939, another by-election took place in South Ayrshire. A National Liberal defeated a Labour Co-operative candidate in the former, while miner Alexander Sloan easily held James Brown's seat in the latter.[142] George Lansbury, who opposed sanctions against Italy, was compelled to resign as British Labour leader in October 1935 and was succeeded by Clement Attlee.

As British Labour secretary James Middleton had told the 1935 Scottish Council conference, some were 'making comparisons between our own nation and the nations who were suffering abroad and were thanking God for a constitutional monarchy'. This was an expression of the almost romantic monarchism imbibed by the party during 1924, when King George V was seen to have dealt fairly with his first Labour ministers. The left rationale a decade later was that a popular monarch would act as a bulwark against a right-wing coup. Dollan was pacifist but not republican, claiming in early 1936 (following the death of George V) that workers had 'made more progress in Great Britain in the past 25 years than in any other country', something which proved that 'constitutional monarchy doesn't interfere with the progress of Democracy'. The following year the Labour-controlled Glasgow Town Council marked the coronation of King George VI despite criticism from within the labour movement.[143]

At the Glasgow Springburn by-election of September 1937 (a rare Tuesday poll), Agnes Hardie easily retained her late husband George's seat in a straight fight with a Unionist, becoming Scotland's second female Scottish MP and retaining the seat until 1945. Individual membership doubled between 1929 and 1932 from 11,099 to 22,292, peaked at 29,510 in 1935, and then dropped slightly to 29,159 by 1939.[144] By the close of that decade the Scottish Socialist Party had all but collapsed through a steep 'diminution in membership' and finally merged with Labour.[145] In local government, however, Labour's municipal gains of 1932–5 – a period in which it took control of most of Scotland's larger towns and cities – were checked. In November 1936 the party even lost Dundee and was yet to take control of a single county authority.[146]

Organisationally, meanwhile, the 1938 Scottish Council conference adopted what Marwick considered an 'over-elaborate' federal constitution.[147] This separated trades and labour councils from local Constituency Labour Parties (CLPs), which meant candidate selection became the exclusive preserve of CLPs, and trade unionists could only exert influence as individual affiliated members. CLPs, however, were what Knox and Mackinlay called 'a new institution and alien to Scottish labour tradition', which was more accustomed to the vibrant ILP model.[148] Only twenty-three of sixty-nine Scottish CLPs sent delegates to the British Labour conference in 1939.

Although the 1937 *Plan for Scotland* noted that Scotland had 'been ruthlessly exploited and bled white, not by England, but by her own industrialists', a preface by Clement Attlee recognised a tendency among socialists to 'underrate the force of National Sentiment':

> To-day we ought all to recognise that nationalism has an immense attractive force for good or evil. Suppressed, it may poison the political life of a nation. Given its proper place it can enrich it ... Nothing is easier than to make windy speeches on the right of Self-Government, in which little attention is given to construction, but much to the fomenting of ill between nations.

The *Plan for Scotland*, added Attlee, situated self-government in its 'right place' as part of a 'plan for giving a better and fuller life to all the people of these islands', particularly its 'careful consideration of the economic questions which many so-called nationalists ignore'.[149] A Labour enquiry the same year also recommended that Central Scotland (including Glasgow) be 'considered as an economic unit and its future systematically planned'.[150]

The *Plan* was sponsored by the London Scots Self-Government Committee (LSSGC), which had been formed in 1936 to recalibrate 'Home Rule' along federalist lines. It believed that only through 'Labour and progressive politics' could self-government be achieved, stressing the 'clear-cut choice' between the 'grasping, anti-social individualism of the Big Business interests which have almost ruined Scotland and the collective, community ownership of the Labour Party'.[151] Another LSSGC publication, *The Real Rulers of Scotland*, depicted Home Rule as a crucial weapon in breaking the hold of monopoly capitalism in Scotland.[152]

On 1 September 1939 Germany invaded Poland and when a Franco-British ultimatum to cease military operations was ignored, the UK and France declared war on Germany. Arthur Woodburn, secretary to the Scottish Council for the past seven years, became one of the first beneficiaries of a wartime electoral truce, although he was warned that in 'all probability the House will meet infrequently ... and you may find yourself an MP without scope or responsibility'.[153] At the October Clackmannanshire and East Stirlingshire by-election arising from the death of Labour MP Lauchlin MacNeill Weir, Woodburn easily defeated a pacifist by the name of Andrew Stewart, whose candidacy had been supported by the continuing ILP, some Labour MPs and Emrys Hughes of *Forward*. The Second World War, much like the First, was to transform Labour's fortunes, not only in Scotland but across Great Britain during its finest – and indeed darkest – hour.

NOTES

1. F. Bealey (1970), *The Social and Political Thought of the British Labour Party*, London: Weidenfeld and Nicolson, 13.
2. 'He was not a heaven-born leader', concluded another account. 'The faculty of rapid decision is not his nor is his the most flexible of minds' (Anonymous, *The Scottish Socialists:*

A Gallery of Contemporary Portraits, London: Faber and Faber, 106).
3. Bealey, 18.
4. I. G. C. Hutchison (2000), *Scottish Politics in the Twentieth Century*, Basingstoke: Palgrave, 57.
5. W. Kenefick (2007), *Red Scotland! The Rise and Fall of the Radical Left, c. 1872 to 1932*, Edinburgh: Edinburgh University Press, 136.
6. I. MacDougall (1985), *Labour in Scotland: A Pictorial History from the Eighteenth Century to the Present*, Edinburgh: Mainstream, 183.
7. I. McLean ([1983] 1999), *The Legend of Red Clydeside*, Edinburgh: John Donald, 95.
8. J. G. Kellas (1968), *Modern Scotland: The Nation since 1870*, London: Pall Mall Press, 196.
9. D. Kirkwood (1935), *My Life of Revolt*, London: George G. Harrap and Co, 107–8. Christmas Day was not yet a public holiday in Scotland.
10. J. Grigg (1985), *Lloyd George: From Peace to War, 1912–1916*, London: Methuen, 299–301.
11. R. McKibbin (1974), *The Evolution of the Labour Party, 1910–1924*, Oxford: Clarendon Press, 163–7.
12. R. Finlay & C. Wood (2013), 'A House Divided? The Impact of the First World War on the Scottish Liberals and Labour', *History Scotland* May/June 2013.
13. B. Winter (2023), *The ILP: Past and Present, Part 1*, Leeds: Independent Labour Publications Trust, 22.
14. W. W. Knox (ed.) (1984), *Scottish Labour Leaders, 1918–39: A Biographical Dictionary*, Edinburgh: Mainstream, 42.
15. M. Keating & D. Bleiman (1979), *Labour and Scottish Nationalism*, London: Macmillan, 56, 60.
16. D. Howell (1986), *A Lost Left: Three Studies in Socialism and Nationalism*, Manchester: Manchester University Press, 208.
17. The Scottish Co-operative Union had approved in April 1917 the formation of a Joint Advisory Committee with Labour and trade union organisations and thereafter the Co-operative Party sponsored candidates (W. H. Marwick, *A Short History of Labour in Scotland*, Edinburgh: Chambers, 107).
18. M. Dyer (1996), *Capable Citizens and Improvident Democrats: The Scottish Electoral System, 1884–1929*, Aberdeen: Scottish Cultural Press, 135. For more on Labour in Edinburgh during this period, see J. Holford (1988), *Reshaping Labour: Organisation, Work and Politics – Edinburgh in the Great War and After*, London: Croom Helm.

19. Howell, 191–2.
20. Agnes Hardie held this post until moving to London with her husband in 1923.
21. The conference was abolished in the late 1990s as part of a reorganisation of women's structures.
22. F. Mackay (2004), 'Women and the Labour Party in Scotland', in G. Hassan (ed.), *The Scottish Labour Party: History, Institutions and Ideas*, Edinburgh: Edinburgh University Press, 106. See also A. Hughes (2013), '"A clear understanding of our duty": Labour women in rural Scotland, 1919–1939', *Scottish Labour History* 48, 136–57. Clarice McNab Shaw had married Scottish party organiser Ben Shaw in 1918.
23. E. Breitenbach and E. Gordon (eds) (1992), *Out of Bounds: Women in Scottish Society, 1800–1945*, Edinburgh: Edinburgh University Press, 156–8.
24. E. Ewan, S. Innes & S. Reynolds (2007), *The Biographical Dictionary of Scottish Women: From the Earliest Times to 2004*, Edinburgh: Edinburgh University Press, 29, 98.
25. G. Brown (1981), 'The Labour Party and Political Change in Scotland, 1918–1929: The Politics of Five Elections', Edinburgh: University of Edinburgh, PhD thesis.
26. McLean, 182.
27. I. G. C. Hutchison (1986), *A Political History of Scotland, 1832–1924: Parties, Elections and Issues*, Edinburgh: John Donald, 278.
28. I. Levitt (1993), 'Scottish sentiment, administrative devolution and Westminster, 1885–1964', in M. Lynch (ed.), *Scotland, 1850–1979: Society, Politics and the Union*, London: Historical Association, 36.
29. W. W. Knox (1988), 'Religion and the Scottish Labour movement, c.1900–39', *Journal of Contemporary History* 23:4, 618.
30. The Reverend James Barr, a Scottish Labour MP, defied reunion to become the first moderator of the United Free Church of Scotland minority.
31. P. S. Philippou (2018), '"The fruits of long years of propaganda and unremitting effort": Labour's "breakthrough" in Scotland in 1922', *Scottish Labour History*, 53, 149.
32. Hutchison (2000), 58.
33. Knox (1984), 32–3.
34. N. Riddell (1997), 'The Catholic Church and the Labour Party, 1918–1931', *Twentieth Century British History* 8:2, 176.
35. Philippou, 145, 172.
36. Although there had been healthy by-election performances in Bothwell (1919), in Paisley (1920) and in Kirkcaldy (1921).

37. T. C. Smout (1986), *A Century of the Scottish People, 1830–1950*, London: Collins, 271.
38. J. Paton (1936), *Left Turn! The Autobiography of John Paton*, London: Martin Secker & Warburg, 144.
39. McLean, 98; Kirkwood, 192.
40. McLean, 139–41.
41. M. Petrie (2019), *Popular Politics and Political Culture in Urban Scotland, 1918–1939*, Edinburgh: Edinburgh University Press, 20.
42. A. Marwick (1964), 'James Maxton: His place in Scottish Labour history', *Scottish Historical Review* XLIII:135, 30–1.
43. McLean, 5–27.
44. McLean, 172.
45. Philippou, 176.
46. Hutchison (2000), 53–6.
47. McLean, 161–2, 177–8. At the 1920 local elections Labour won forty-four councillors in Glasgow.
48. Paton, 145. Two leading 'Clydesiders' actually sat for West Stirlingshire (Tom Johnston) and West Lothian (Manny Shinwell).
49. Paton, 146.
50. Marwick, 32–3.
51. Smout, 272.
52. Paton, 163–4.
53. According to a 1924 STUC survey around 'a third, or 536,432 Scots ... were members of a trade union, of which 14.6 per cent were female' (Kenefick, 186).
54. Howell, 209.
55. I. S. Wood (1989), 'Hope deferred: Labour in Scotland in the 1920s', in I. Donnachie, C. Harvie & I. S. Wood (eds), *Forward! Labour Politics in Scotland, 1888–1988*, Edinburgh: Polygon, 35–6.
56. C. Harvie (2016), *No Gods and Precious Few Heroes: Scotland, 1900–2015* (Fourth Edition), Edinburgh: Edinburgh University Press, 97.
57. Labour Party Scottish Council (1923), *Report of the Eighth Annual Conference*, Glasgow: SCLP.
58. R. J. Finlay (1994), *Independent and Free: Scottish Politics and the Origins of the Scottish National Party, 1918–1945*, Edinburgh: John Donald, 9.
59. Anonymous, *The Scottish Socialists*, 22.
60. Paton, 181–2.
61. R. W. Lyman (1957), *The First Labour Government*, London: Chapman & Hall, 232.
62. G. Brown (1986), *Maxton*, Edinburgh: Mainstream, 160.

63. *Glasgow Herald*, 15 September 1923.
64. The funeral of John Maclean, who had died aged only forty-four, took place the same month. He had refused to join the Communist Party of Great Britain and instead established the Scottish Workers' Republican Party (R. J. Morris, 1991, 'The ILP, 1893–1932: introduction', in A. McKinlay & R J. Morris (eds), *The ILP on Clydeside, 1893–1932: From Foundation to Disintegration*, Manchester: Manchester University Press, 208).
65. D. Carrigan (2016), 'Patrick Dollan and the Glasgow labour movement: A reappraisal', *Scottish Labour History* 51, 145.
66. Paton, 146.
67. Mackay, 107.
68. P. Dorey (2008), *The Labour Party and Constitutional Reform: A History of Constitutional Conservatism*, London: Palgrave Macmillan, 206–7.
69. Keating & Bleiman, 83.
70. M. Taylor (2000), 'Labour and the constitution', in D. Tanner, P. Thane & N. Tiratsoo (eds), *Labour's First Century*, Cambridge: Cambridge University Press, 159.
71. A *Punch* cartoon portrayed Ramsay MacDonald as a London railway booking clerk selling 'single' tickets to Wheatley, Maxton and other Clydesiders.
72. *The Times*, 28 April 1924.
73. Brown, 161. For more on Maxton's nationalism, see W. Ferguson (1978), *Scotland: 1689 to the Present*, Edinburgh: Oliver and Boyd, 375.
74. Wood, 36–7.
75. G. Walker (1988), *Thomas Johnston*, Manchester: Manchester University Press, 70. For more on Johnston and the Scottish Home Rule Association, see R. Galbraith (2018), *Without Quarter: A Biography of Tom Johnston*, Edinburgh: Birlinn, 180–94.
76. See, for example, HC Debs 26 May 1922 Vol 154 c1645.
77. E. Breitenbach (2016), 'For workers' rights and self-determination? The Scottish labour movement and the British empire from the 1920s to the 1960s', *Scottish Labour History*, 51, 113.
78. HC Deb 09 May 1924 Vol 173 cc789–874.
79. HC Deb 9 May 1924 Vol 173 cc872–74.
80. HC Deb 18 June 1924 Vol 174 c2119.
81. 'Material for Reply to Deputation on Scottish Home Rule', 21 July 1924, PRO 30/69/59, Ramsay MacDonald Papers, London: The National Archives.
82. Keating and Bleiman, 82.

83. Anonymous, *The Scottish Socialists*, 168.
84. For more on the first Labour government, see D. Torrance (2024), *The Wild Men: The Remarkable Story of Britain's First Labour Government*, London: Bloomsbury Continuum.
85. See C. M. M. Macdonald (2001), *The Radical Thread: Political Change in Scotland, Paisley Politics, 1885–1924*, East Linton: Tuckwell Press, and (2011), 'The Radical Thread – Liberalism and the rise of Labour in Scotland, 1886–1924', *Mémoire(s), identité(s), marginalité(s) dans le monde occidental contemporain* 7 (online).
86. Wood, 40.
87. Dyer, 165.
88. Labour Party Scottish Council (1926), *Report of the Eleventh Annual Conference*, Glasgow: SCLP.
89. G. Walker & J. Greer (2019), 'Religion, Labour, and national questions: The general election of 1924 in Belfast and Lanarkshire', *Labour History Review* 84:3, 234.
90. See J. Barr (1948), *Lang Syne: Memoirs of the Rev. James Barr*, Glasgow: William Maclellan.
91. W. H. Marwick (1973), 'James Barr: Modern Covenanter', *Scottish Journal of Science* 1:3, 187.
92. McLean, 99; HC Deb 15 December 1927 Vol 211 cc2531–655 [Prayer Book Measure].
93. Knox, 25–6. Remarkably, it took until 1982 for that decision to be fully implemented.
94. Hutchison (2000), 61.
95. Petrie, 21, 41.
96. A. Marwick, 35.
97. Howell, 279.
98. Carrigan, 135.
99. Hutchison (2000), 60.
100. C. M. M. Macdonald (2017), 'Following the procession: Scottish Labour, 1918–45', in M. Worley (ed.), *Labour's Grass Roots: Essays on the Activities of Local Labour Parties and Members, 1918–45*, London: Routledge, 47.
101. *Daily Herald*, 29 March 1928.
102. Ramsay MacDonald to George Mathers, 1 May 1929, Mathers Papers Acc 4826/1, Edinburgh: National Library of Scotland.
103. Knox (1984), 44–5.
104. HC Deb 10 Jul 1929 Vol 229 cc933–34.
105. Brown (1981), 527.
106. J. J. Smyth (2003), 'Resisting Labour: Unionists, Liberals, and moderates in Glasgow between the wars', *Historical Journal* 46:2, 375–401.

107. G. Pentland (2017), *The Autobiography of Arthur Woodburn (1890–1978): Living with History*, Woodbridge: Boydell and Brewer, 70–1.
108. Hutchison (2000), 66.
109. Lee won despite claims the Catholic Church had advised parishioners to vote against her because of her support for birth control (Mackay, 108).
110. Keating & Bleiman, 115–16.
111. W. W. Knox & A. Mackinlay (1995), 'The re-making of Scottish Labour in the 1930s', *Twentieth Century British History* 6:2, 184–6.
112. For an account of the by-election, see J. McGovern (1960), *Neither Fear Nor Favour*, London: Blandford Press, 67–70. McGovern claimed the 'clergy and the die-hard section of the Catholic voters' had operated against him. He was subsequently expelled from Labour following allegations that he had fixed his selection as candidate.
113. Knox (1984), 45.
114. D. Torrance (2006), *The Scottish Secretaries*, Edinburgh: Birlinn, 107.
115. W. H. Marwick, 107.
116. A. Marwick, 38.
117. Pentland, 77.
118. W. H. Marwick, 106.
119. W. H. Marwick, 106.
120. Hutchison (2000), 64.
121. I. Donnachie (1989), 'Scottish Labour in the Depression: the 1930s', in I. Donnachie, C. Harvie & I. S. Wood (eds), *Forward! Labour Politics in Scotland, 1888–1988*, Edinburgh: Polygon, 51–5.
122. I. S. Wood (1981), 'Labour Politics in Glasgow', Edinburgh: Napier College, 69. Unpublished thesis.
123. Knox & Mackinlay, 176.
124. Pentland, 73.
125. C. Harvie (1999), *Travelling Scot*, Glendaruel: Argyll Publishing, 62.
126. Founded in Glasgow in March 1917, the Scottish Labour College had become part of the National Council of Labour Colleges which, for a time, was run from Edinburgh. It transferred to London in 1927 but returned to Scotland (Tillicoultry) as a war precaution in 1940 (W. H. Marwick, 104).
127. Hutchison (2000), 82.
128. Knox & Mackinlay, 179.
129. Knox & Mackinlay, 179.

130. Pentland, 73–7.
131. Knox & Mackinlay, 181.
132. G. Hassan & E. Shaw (2020), 'The Scottish Labour Party', in M. Keating (ed.), *The Oxford Handbook of Scottish Politics*, Oxford: Oxford University Press, 257.
133. Smout, 274.
134. E. A. Cameron (2010), *Impaled Upon a Thistle: Scotland since 1880*, Edinburgh: Edinburgh University Press, 158.
135. J. J. Smyth (2000), *Labour in Glasgow, 1896–1936: Socialism, Suffrage, Sectarianism*, Edinburgh: John Donald, 135–47. See also T. Gallagher (2010), 'Scottish Catholics and the British Left, 1918–1939', *Innes Review* 34:1, 17–42.
136. Pentland, 82.
137. Ewan et al., 6.
138. Hutchison (2000), 68.
139. Hutchison (2000), 67.
140. Carrigan, 143.
141. Knox & Mackinlay, 190.
142. Pentland, 87.
143. Knox & Mackinlay, 191.
144. C. Harvie (1983), 'Labour in Scotland during the Second World War', *Historical Journal* 26:4, 922.
145. Knox & Mackinlay, 190.
146. Harvie (1983), 922.
147. W. H. Marwick, 106.
148. Knox & Mackinlay, 178.
149. T. Burns (1937), *Plan for Scotland*, London: London Scots Self-Government Committee, 1.
150. Labour Party (1937), *Central Scotland: Report of the Labour Party's Commission of Enquiry into the Distressed Areas*, London: Labour Party, 22.
151. Burns (1937), 1.
152. T. Burns (1939), *The Real Rulers of Scotland*, London: London Scots Self-Government Committee.
153. Harvie (1983), 927.

3

'Socialist Planning on a United Kingdom Scale': 1940–1958

At its 1940 conference, the executive of the Scottish Council of the Labour Party expressed its support for the government, which it believed would:

> increasingly trust the common people [and] at long last throw off disastrous reliance on class and privilege; get rid of the idea that blue blood and ability are synonymous and will demand real equality of sacrifice and service – then this nation will be invincible.

The Scottish executive also decided to co-opt a representative of the Scottish Labour MP group to 'establish a closer relationship between the Council and the Members of Parliament representing Scottish constituencies' for the duration of the war.[1]

While the Scottish Unionists essentially disbanded their party organisation at the outbreak of war, Labour in Scotland maintained its party structures, although some thirty Constituency Labour Parties (CLPs) reconstituted themselves as local information bureaus. The Scottish Council's loudspeaker van was also handed over to the Ministry of Information. Marginalised were several Scottish MPs who identified with the Scottish Peace Congress, which was banned by the Labour's National Executive Committee in October 1940.[2]

But despite Arthur Woodburn's efforts, Labour organisation in Scotland was still recovering from the after-effects of the Independent Labour Party's disaffiliation. There were particular problems in Dundee and Glasgow. In the former, Communist pressure via the Linen Workers' Union had selected an Indian left-winger called Krishna Menon in June 1939, although he was soon disqualified by the NEC for sharing platforms with proscribed speakers. Owing to his 'natural allegiance to India', it argued, the NEC did not believe he could 'give full support to Labour Party policy'.[3] Pollok CLP was disaffiliated for defying the electoral truce and (unsuccessfully) opposing the Unionists at an April 1940 by-election, while in 1943 the NEC forcibly reformed the Glasgow Labour Party and appointed a new secretary.[4]

John Taylor, Woodburn's successor as secretary to the Scottish Council, despaired that:

> There is an absence of Party spirit and team work in most of the C.L.P.s and the general attitude of querulous criticism of every party action is encouraged by the lead given by the Burgh party which invariably plays to its gallery of disgruntled individuals with a grudge against life. People of balanced mind and outlook have thus been frozen out or have left in disgust.

Forward had also morphed into what Woodburn called 'a definitely anti-Labour paper', while the monthly *Edinburgh Clarion*, founded in November 1939, was similarly pacifist.

In 1942, meanwhile, the Scottish Council's privilege of having its minutes tabled at NEC meetings came to an end as additional 'regional' councils were established within the British party. Transport House, Labour's London headquarters, wielded enormous influence given it provided funding for 90 per cent of Scottish party operations, including by-elections and salaries for the Scottish secretary, organiser and women's organiser.[5] Individual membership stood at 15,993 in 1942. Taylor's aim was simply to keep the party's general organisation in existence.

There were no servicemen among Scottish Labour MPs given their average age was fifty-eight. Initially, only one of their number, Aberdeen North's George Garro-Jones (a Welsh lawyer) served as a minister in the wartime coalition, although Edinburgh East's Frederick Pethick-Laurence (an Old Etonian lawyer) was also de facto Leader of the Opposition for a few months between late 1941 and early 1942. The party's apparent saviour amidst all this gloom was Tom Johnston, 'shadow' Scottish Secretary since his return to the Commons in 1935 and Scotland's regional commissioner for civil defence. Winston Churchill, who became premier in May 1940 and had a soft spot for the Clydesiders, quickly earmarked Johnston, whom he considered 'one of the best of the Labour Party', for the Cabinet.[6]

The Prime Minister mooted health, but Johnston himself suggested replacing Ernest Brown (who had humiliated Labour at the 1927 Leith by-election) as Secretary of State for Scotland.[7]

The timing was fortuitous, for not only had Johnston completed his remarkable political journey from left-wing firebrand to pragmatic centrist, but the Scottish Office had recently been reorganised in a way that allowed the Scottish Secretary virtually to take full control of wartime government in Scotland as well as guide thinking on post-war reconstruction. The Unionist Lord Provost of Edinburgh, Sir William Darling (great uncle of Alistair, a future Labour Scottish Secretary), assessed Johnston within months of his arrival at Fielden House, the temporary London base of the Scottish Office:

> Gone, apparently, is the ardent propagandist of a political theory. He has no theories now – he asks if this is desirable, practical, worthwhile, and if so – on with it. Don't inquire – don't stop – don't write about it – don't harangue – don't ask if it is Christian or Marxian – on with it. This turbulent intensity commends itself to me. He knows he has his chance, his opportunity, his hour, and he wants to give it all to Scotland.[8]

Johnston's achievements over the next four years have been widely charted,[9] particularly the grandly titled 'Council of State', which comprised every surviving Scottish Secretary. Remaining ILP members in the Commons warned their old comrade he would become a 'prisoner' of his Liberal and Unionist predecessors (William Adamson having died in 1936),[10] but this did Johnston a disservice. Not only did the Council chime with the ecumenical spirit of the times, but many of its members, like the Liberal Sir Archibald Sinclair and Unionist Walter Elliott, were not far removed from Johnston's thinking on most major issues. Crucially, Churchill indicated that he would endorse anything agreed by the Council.

Johnston had argued since the mid-1920s that issues such as unemployment and manufacturing 'ought not to be ... the shuttlecock of party politics', and through the Scottish Council on Industry (established in February 1942), largely Tory industrialists worked with the Convention of Royal Burghs and the Scottish Trades Union Congress to drive down unemployment and increase wartime production. By the end of 1942, meanwhile, 3,210 patients had been referred from voluntary waiting lists to emergency hospitals, but the *pièce de résistance* was agreement on a comprehensive scheme of hydro-electric power in the Highlands, something which had first captured Johnston's fertile imagination in the late 1920s. Six previous legislative schemes had come and gone but the Scottish Secretary seized the opportunity to make the seventh a reality. All this not only represented 'a great vindication' of administrative devolution,[11] but added enormously to Johnston's personal and political prestige. Harvie, however, judged that this owed more to 'publicity' than genuine policy innovation (the Johnston myth, he observed, had endured 'almost as tenaciously as the Red Clyde'),[12] while Hutchison believed that by pursuing such a non-partisan approach, Johnston may have 'diluted the credit for any progressive plans given to Labour'.[13]

It was an irony of Johnston's four energetic years as Scottish Secretary that although he was a life-long Home Ruler, the cumulative effect of his achievements (perceived or real) was to erode many well-rehearsed arguments in favour of a separate Scottish Parliament. In Cabinet, Johnston was neither the first nor the last Scottish Secretary to wield the threat apparently posed by 'extreme' nationalism to bolster a 'nationalist-unionist' alternative.[14] In 1943, Lord Reith was warned there was 'a great danger of Scottish Nationalism coming up ... a sort of Sinn Féin movement as he called it'.[15] This was exaggerated, although during the war the Scottish National Party, which ignored the electoral truce, grew steadily in by-elections.

Johnston, however, took care to treat Home Rule delegations with respect. Following one such meeting on 10 November 1944, Naomi Mitchison, a contemporary of Johnston on the London Scots Self-Government Committee, recorded that he:

> won't do anything political during the coalition. [He] Emphasised all the economic things he had done, and the machinery for progress which he had produced, the Grand Council etc. The difficulty is it may all be swept away by his successor and he doesn't seem to want to stand again which is an awful pity.[16]

Johnston assumed office a little too late to influence a Scottish Labour initiative dating from 1939 in which A. B. MacKay, secretary of the Scottish Banker's Association, had been instructed to prepare a 'Scottish economic survey'. In May 1941, and acknowledging a pro-devolution motion at the 1940 Scottish

Council conference, the Scottish executive transformed McKay's inquiry into a committee on Post-War Policy in Scotland, but without consulting the NEC. Published in August 1941, this recognised: 'the first broad principle that, although Scotland is a nation with its own traditions, customs, culture and law, and with problems not encountered or understood outside its borders, it is also part of the island of Britain'.[17] The policy went on to propose a 'parliament' of Scottish MPs meeting in Edinburgh with responsibility for housing and education while nationalised heavy industries would remain controlled by Westminster. Although Scottish party secretary John Taylor had written to the *Scots Independent* in September 1940 with a similar proposal,[18] the NEC was unimpressed and moved quickly to censure this attempt at independent policy making. In February 1942, Manny Shinwell kept even a watered-down version away from British Labour's formal policy agenda and the Scottish Council admitted defeat.[19]

Scottish party organisation, such as it was, remained sub-optimal. In 1943 J. T. Anson was appointed acting Scottish secretary on account of Taylor's illness. At a by-election in Midlothian and Peebles Northern that February, Labour stuck to the electoral truce in a Unionist-held seat but was spooked by a near win from the Common Wealth Party, an alliance of two socialistic groups formed in 1942. Taylor returned to his duties in October 1944, at which point Labour in Scotland began preparations for the first general election in almost a decade.[20]

There were two further electoral jolts early in 1945. On 12 April Dr Robert McIntyre became the SNP's first MP in Motherwell, while the following day Sir John Boyd Orr won a Combined Scottish Universities by-election as a nationalist-inclined independent. The South Ayrshire MP Alexander Sloan,[21] whom the SNP leader Douglas Young considered the 'most fully nationalist' of the Scottish Labour MPs, and the Revd James Barr eventually sponsored McIntyre's rather fraught introduction to the Commons.[22] Commentators began to note what the *New Statesman* called 'pent-up Scots irritations' such as the government's failure to construct road bridges across the Forth and Tay and the threat to Prestwick Airport on the Ayrshire coast. Belatedly realising it had to, as per Attlee's observation in 1937, take national sentiment seriously, the NEC instructed Harold Laski to examine the phenomenon.[23]

While *Let Us Face the Future*, Labour's 1945 manifesto, avoided Home Rule, republished Scottish Council speakers' notes from 1941 did not, a compromise recommended by Laski. These made it clear the party did not support 'Dominion status or complete autonomy', and Douglas Young claimed most Scottish Labour candidates placed 'a Scottish Parliament for Scottish affairs' as their top priority after the defeat of Japan.[24] Nat Jackson in Cathcart stated that:

> Labour stands for a Scottish Parliament for Scottish affairs and a British Parliament for British affairs. We believe that thus Scotland's special problems will receive increased and more effective attention. We therefore advocate the establishment of an Executive Authority in Scotland to deal with all matters which have solely Scottish Interest. But, although Scotland is a nation with its own traditions, customs, culture, and law, we reject the idea of complete separation.[25]

Harvie calculated that twenty-three of those subsequently elected had thus declared themselves, although during the campaign itself MacCallum and Readman found the issue marginal compared with 'bread and butter' issues such as housing, jobs, social security and welfare.[26]

Tom Johnston was the public face of the 'first' election on 5 July 1945, in which sixty Scottish constituencies polled, while at the 'second', a week later, the remaining fourteen seats selected their MPs as Transport House dispatched Herbert Morrison, Arthur Greenwood, Ernest Bevin and Ellen Wilkinson to speak north of the border. The count took several weeks on account of transporting servicemen's ballots from overseas.[27] The results were not declared until 26 July, and despite MacCallum and Readman's rather dim view of Labour candidates – 'One is left to speculate whether something of the old vigour of Scottish radicalism has passed out of the Scottish Labour Party or, as some might think, has never sufficiently entered it'[28] – thirty-seven were returned to Westminster. These included Clarice McNab Shaw in Kilmarnock, although illness would prevent her making a maiden speech.[29] Across Great Britain, Labour had 393 seats and an overall majority of 147.

'A new and proud chapter in the history of our land was written by Britain's first majority Labour Government', gushed a later Scottish Council publication. 'The great edifice of the

Welfare State began to rise.'[30] To Knox, 1945 also marked the moment the Labour movement in Scotland became 'thoroughly incorporated into the modern state':

> In the process it became more prone to middle-class ideologies and to rely on the bureaucrat and the planner rather than the people. Scottish labour lost its former idealistic drive, its sense of historical mission, and its distinctiveness, and has found no substitute since.[31]

When Clement Attlee addressed the Scottish Council's Musselburgh conference in 1945, he made clear his disappointment. The turnout and swing to Labour in Scotland had been two to three points lower than the British average, which if matched would have yielded a further nine seats. In his speech, the Prime Minister alluded to:

> the election of December 1923, which resulted in the first Labour Government, Scotland contributed 34 members, London and Middlesex only 28. In 1945, when Labour for the first time gained a majority, Scotland has contributed 37, London and Middlesex 62. It is surely up to you to find out the reason.

What explained the disparity? MacCallum and Readman believed Glaswegians had already experienced twelve years of Labour government (at local level) and did not think much of it, while Harvie concluded that most of Labour's problems, 'moribund parties, unpopular councils, bitter press hostility' were 'authentically Scottish and, untended by the Scottish leadership, might have been beyond such remedy'. In that context, and although Tom Johnston had given a Labour 'focus' to the 'collectivist and quasi-nationalist initiatives generated by depression and war', the result was 'a kind of stasis' electorally.[32] The King's Speech of August 1945, meanwhile, weakly promised 'the special problems of Scotland and Wales' would receive the attention of His Majesty's Government.[33]

Sixty per cent of Scotland's Labour MPs were new, although proportionately fewer were younger, middle-class professionals and ex-officers as was the case in England. The average Scottish MP still tended to be middle-aged (average age of fifty-two, compared to forty-six in Great Britain as a whole). When James Maxton died in July 1946, the ILP's James Carmichael, long groomed to succeed Maxton, held the seat against Labour's John

Wheatley, the middle-class nephew of the eponymous star of the first Labour government.[34] With Campbell Stephen's passing in October 1947, the ILP crumpled. By 1950 Carmichael had rejoined Labour (and trounced his ILP opponent in that year's election), as had John McGovern, 'part of a bizarre political and intellectual odyssey' which ended in 1959 with him supporting the Conservatives.[35] A proposal for Tom Johnston to continue as Scottish Secretary from the House of Lords had been rejected by Labour MPs,[36] and instead Joseph Westwood became Attlee's first Secretary of State for Scotland. Dubbed 'Little Joe' or 'Wee Joe' on account of his stature (little more than five feet), the former industrial and political organiser for the Fife miners knew the Scottish Office well from his time as PPS to William Adamson and as under-secretary between 1940 and 1945. It fell to Westwood to adapt ground-breaking health and education legislation for Scottish purposes, although even Labour admitted the Education (Scotland) Act 1945 had not quite the same 'revolutionary character' as its English counterpart (Education Act 1944).[37]

In May 1946, the Scottish Secretary also explained how the UK New Towns Bill would help Scotland 'deal with the whole problem of rehousing and industrial rehabilitation'.[38] East Kilbride and Glenrothes were subsequently designated under the New Towns Act 1946 in May 1947 and June 1948 respectively. On leaving Glasgow Corporation in 1947, Sir Patrick Dollan became the first chairman of the East Kilbride Development Corporation.[39] Labour had made 'great advances' in the Scottish burgh and county council elections of November–December 1945, while a *Scottish Local Government Handbook* issued by the Scottish and British parties in 1946 spoke of 'completing' Labour's 1945 general election victory by electing 'many more' councillors across Scotland.[40]

Before long, however, the Scottish Labour MP group was writing to Herbert Morrison, the Lord President of the Council, to complain about the lack of parliamentary time for specifically Scottish business. In response, Westwood initially proposed an additional Minister of State at the Scottish Office but then changed tack to suggest:

> An independent committee to enquire into the administrative set up in Scotland and to make recommendation as to whether and to

what extent further legislative devolution ... is necessary, practical and advisable, whilst retaining the integrity of the United Kingdom.

By this point (June 1947) both London and Scottish-based Unionists had embraced a quasi-nationalist agenda centred around the reduction of 'Whitehall control' over Scotland's governance and industry. Despite Westwood's increasing agitation and a degree of support from the Prime Minister (while 'our Scots friends are apt to be unduly alarmed at Scottish Nationalism', scribbled Attlee, 'I think it might be wise to have some kind of inquiry'), Herbert Morrison instead suggested a PR offensive. Before this could take effect Westwood was sacked on 7 October 1947 and replaced with the more substantial Arthur Woodburn.[41] Attlee's brutal response to Westwood's pathetic 'why?' was, in some accounts: 'Cos you don't measure up to the job. That's why. Thanks for coming. Secretary will show you out.'[42]

With John MacCormick's devolutionary Scottish Covenant Association (SCA) on the rise, Scottish Labour MPs (who were cautioned against attending its National Assemblies) again urged an inquiry into Scottish administration, only for it to be rejected by Morrison. In a Cabinet paper circulated in December 1947, Woodburn concluded that the 'agitation for a greater measure of devolution of legislative and executive responsibility' did not 'follow party lines' but had crystalised around the 'organisation of socialised industries on a Great Britain basis'. In a striking passage, the new Scottish Secretary observed that:

> The danger of this widespread feeling in Scotland is that it is hidden to some extent by the fact that elections are fought between the main parties. But it betrays itself in the general uneasiness that Scotland is held to be of no account by British Governments. There is, therefore, a kind of smouldering pile that might suddenly break through the party loyalties and become a formidable national movement. This is the more possible as the Labour Party programme comes to fulfilment and the great dividing issues are settled, leaving the cleavages between the parties less deep and intense.[43]

Woodburn's proposed solution had three limbs: at Westminster, a reorganisation of specifically Scottish business; in Edinburgh, a new Scottish Production Council to direct industry; and overarching both, a government inquiry into Scottish administration. Again, Herbert Morrison emerged as the main opponent of what he regarded as hasty concessions to nationalism, and by early the following year Woodburn's White Paper advocated only an all-party Scottish Grand Committee in the Commons and a Scottish Economic Council without executive authority.

Presentationally, what the Scottish Secretary hyperbolically called 'almost a constitutional revolution' proved a disaster. Publication coincided with Labour's defeat at the Glasgow Camlachie by-election, its vote split by the intervention of the ILP's Annie Maxton, younger sister of James. The NEC was so disturbed it despatched Manny Shinwell and National Agent R. T. Wardle to investigate party organisation in Glasgow. They found things 'far from satisfactory' and recommended the appointment of a full-time organiser. Yet there was little subsequent improvement, membership remaining a fifth of what it ought to have been and Glasgow party finances giving 'great cause for alarm'. By contrast, the Scottish Unionists had a substantial membership and plentiful resources in Scotland's largest city.[44]

While the largely Unionist media contrasted Labour's proposals unfavourably with the quasi-nationalist agenda now being promoted by the Scottish Unionists, the Scottish Covenant Association went from strength to strength. Already convinced it was a Tory front given John MacCormick's Unionist-backed Liberal candidacy at the February 1948 Paisley by-election (comfortably won by Labour's Douglas Johnston), a blistering speech from Margaret (Peggy) Herbison at the 1949 Scottish Council conference led delegates to reject a Scottish Parliament by a large majority. By contrast, the SCA's Scottish National Assembly endorsed the sort of legislative autonomy Labour in Scotland had once supported. Only the economic historian and former ILP candidate William Marwick urged the formation of a 'Scottish legislative assembly' with 'devolved powers ... on Scottish domestic matters'.[45]

Woodburn inadvertently poured oil on these flames by suggesting during a Unionist-sponsored adjournment debate on Scottish nationalism that John MacCormick had indulged in 'dangerous talk', including speeches in which he had used the word 'bomb'.[46] Shettleston's John McGovern condemned the Scottish Secretary's remarks as 'unworthy', while the *Bulletin* newspaper asked: 'Haven't we in Scotland had just about enough of Arthur Woodburn?'[47] He summoned a press conference to provide evidence of the violent nationalist threat, but only *Forward* and the *Catholic Herald* took it seriously.

Unionist strategy reached its apex with Winston Churchill's speech at Ibrox stadium in May 1949 in which the Leader of the Opposition depicted Labour's nationalisation programme as:

> detrimental and offensive to Scotland. It affects not only its prosperity but the independence which Scotland has exercised in so many fields, no sharper challenge could be given to Scottish national sentiment than is now launched by the Socialism of Whitehall.[48]

Although Unionists did not actually promise to reverse nationalisation (except in the case of the iron and steel), the party cleverly promoted a 'Home Rule' light programme encapsulated in *Scottish Control of Scottish Affairs*, published in 1949. Its 'offer' to voters included Westwood's old idea of an additional Minister of State as well as a Royal Commission on Scottish Affairs. Even senior Labour figures such as Sir Patrick Dollan believed it was:

> high time our people in London, whether connected with the Government, newspapers, trade unions and other organisations, consulted local officials in Scotland in matters affecting our side of the border. There is far too much done in London on the assumption that we will be glad to fall into line with anything they may want done. They can strain one's loyalty almost to the breaking point.[49]

There had also been complaints at the 1947 Scottish Council conference of the government's 'fine record' being 'underestimated, belittled, jeered at or ignored by Labour's opponents in Scotland'. Individual membership was at 43,125 (17,817 of whom were women), a slight decrease on the previous year. The average membership per Scottish constituency was 616 as compared with just over 1,000 in Britain generally, although the Scottish party executive was confident this gap 'could be eliminated if the membership in Glasgow and Edinburgh could be organised on the same scale as in the majority of the other Scottish constituencies'.[50] John Taylor, however, informed an NEC sub-committee that only:

> About a third of our Scottish M.P.s do what they can to assist us. Of the other two-thirds about half are heavily involved with government duties, and the remainder are mainly poor propagandists who are unlikely to do us much credit at public meetings.[51]

In May 1949 Labour lost control of Dundee Corporation amid 'sweeping defeats' in town halls all over Scotland.[52]

At least at the February 1950 general election Labour no longer had to contend with the ILP, although as a study of that contest noted, a 'sombre photograph of Jimmy Maxton' at the ILP's committee rooms in Bridgeton urged passers-by to 'Be Faithful to Old Faithful'. Labour's fifteen candidates in Glasgow were supported by the Revd Dr George MacLeod of the Iona Community, who emphasised the party's 'ethical and spiritual ... attempt to remove social evil'. Although voters generally regarded politicians as 'all the same', Glasgow University recorded both a working-class housewife from Clydebank and a middle-class woman leaving a Unionist meeting as acknowledging Labour's achievements over the past five years.[53]

After polling day – at which Labour held its thirty-seven Scottish seats but only just beat the Unionists in terms of vote share – Attlee decided to despatch Woodburn as he had Westwood a few years earlier. His failure to consult Scottish ministerial colleagues irritated John Wheatley, now Lord Advocate, who felt the Prime Minister paid greater 'heed to Arthur's critics both in the party and in the media'. In Wheatley's view, Woodburn's 'true worth' as Secretary of State was never properly recognised, although he acknowledged a tendency acquired at the National Council of Labour Colleges 'to lecture rather than address his audience'.[54]

What of Knox's charge that post-war Scottish Labour had lost its 'former idealistic drive'? In 1949, Naomi Mitchison had spoken of being 'deeply disturbed' by the fact the Labour government had 'made certain promises about Scotland before it came into power, has not so far kept them and does not appear to be going to do so'.[55]

If that was a nationalist rather than a socialist critique, Emrys Hughes, the former *Forward* editor and now the maverick MP for South Ayrshire, also attacked the Linlithgowshire MP George Mathers's decision to serve as the King's Lord High Commissioner to the General Assembly of the Church of Scotland in 1946, 1947, 1948 and 1951, echoing similar disapproval which had greeted the appointment of miners' MP James Brown in 1924.[56] Mathers joined the House of Lords in 1952 (as had David Kirkwood in 1951) and was created a Knight of the Thistle in 1956. His heraldic crest incorporated the badge of the Railway Clerks' Association, of which Lord Mathers had been chairman.[57]

Of the Scottish Labour Members new to Parliament in 1945, only Margaret Herbison achieved ministerial rank as joint under-secretary at the Scottish Office between 1950 and 1951, the first female Labour MP from a Scottish constituency to do so. She worked alongside Hector McNeil, who was reluctantly prised away from foreign affairs to become Attlee's third – and easily the most able – Secretary of State. In his first Commons outing, he said:

> There always will be a concern and a zeal among Scots people to protect these Scottish characteristics, and they should be assisted. It must not be lightly concluded that we will assist Scotland or Britain by pressing hurriedly towards any measure of self-government. There has been a gradual transfer, and it is unlikely that that transfer will be stopped at any one stage.[58]

McNeil initiated a 'return' on Anglo-Scottish finance and trade to be compiled by Lord Catto, a former Governor of the Bank of England. This reported in 1952, by which point Labour was out of office, but it revealed the Scottish economy's growing reliance on state subsidies. McNeil also launched a new handbook on Scottish Administration in July 1950, something contrived to emphasise that Scotland already possessed 'a substantial measure of devolution in the present structure of government'. McNeil's American contacts proved useful in luring International Business Machines (IBM) to Greenock, where it remained a major employer for several decades.[59]

By May 1950, the Scottish Covenant Association's demand for a Scottish Parliament claimed more than a million signatures and on Christmas Day the ancient Stone of Scone was taken from Westminster Abbey, an incident McNeil handled with considerable tact. Although Morgan considered the party's 'unresponsive attitude' towards the aspirations of some Scots 'very much unfinished business in October 1951',[60] as Hutchison has noted Labour's Scottish share of the vote in 1950 had been 10 per cent higher than in 1945, and 15 per cent higher in 1951, suggesting that voters were 'pretty pleased with Labour, at least in the party's traditional areas'.[61]

Out of office, Labour entered what Robert McLean called its 'unionist interregnum', from which it 'only slowly and reluctantly' emerged in the late 1960s.⁶² But as the party turned decisively away from its nationalist past, it had also succeeded in refashioning unionism in its own image. As Moran has observed, a 'new sense of civic identity' emerged after the Second World War, one based upon 'the notion of universalism – a new way of thinking of ourselves as British, involving common social entitlements and common social obligations'.⁶³ The 'greatest emblem' of this new 'welfare unionism' was the National Health Service,⁶⁴ separately administered in Scotland and now embraced by Scottish Unionists as a central part of a 'reimagined state'.⁶⁵

Labour regained control of Glasgow Corporation in 1952, to which it later added four more councils including Aberdeen and Dundee, making it the major party of local government across urban Scotland.⁶⁶ Around 15 per cent of Labour councillors were trade union or party officials.⁶⁷ Turnout in elections, however, was often low; although Labour gained four seats at municipal elections in Glasgow in May 1954, only 17 per cent bothered to vote in the Dalmarnock ward and fewer than 20 per cent in the Gorbals, leading *The Times* to conclude that it was 'hard to find any signs of an upsurge of working class feeling'.⁶⁸ In 1953, meanwhile, the Scottish Council produced a dedicated 'programme' for the Highlands and Islands, the centrepiece of which was a development corporation with 'powers of ownership and control of the use of all land'.⁶⁹ There had been a dedicated Labour organiser there since 1946 and a Highland conference met annually until 1957, yet the party had made no gains in 1950 or 1951. If anything, the party appeared to lose ground in an historically Liberal region which Unionists were increasingly accused of neglecting.⁷⁰

At the 1955 general election the Unionists famously peaked in Scotland, winning a majority of seats and of the popular vote, an electoral feat unmatched before or since by any Scottish party. They made much (as did the press) of Labour's 'uninspiring' manifesto pledge, which merely promised to give the 'fullest consideration' to any recommendations arising from the recent Royal Commission on Scottish Affairs⁷¹ (commissioners had included Agnes, Lady Dollan, wife of Sir Patrick). Reducing Lady Tweedsmuir's majority in Aberdeen South was the Lancashire-born Judith Hart, who bucked Labour's post-war tendency to select more authentically 'Scottish' candidates.⁷²

Compared with their English counterparts, Scottish Labour MPs remained 'older, more working class, more likely to have been local councillors and less likely to lose their seats'.[73] Between 1945 and 1970, 83 per cent of Glasgow Labour MPs were former councillors.[74] Despite this durability, only one Scottish MP, Tom Fraser, was elected to Labour's Shadow Cabinet between 1951 and 1964, serving as Shadow Secretary of State for Scotland. Had he not died suddenly in 1955, Hector McNeil might have offered Labour in Scotland 'more dynamic leadership'.[75] A brilliant orator with policy ideas and managerial abilities, his departure 'left Scottish Labour looking somewhat lacklustre for a generation'.[76] The party was at least aided by the Mirror Group's acquisition of the *Daily Record* (and its sister title the *Sunday Mail*) in 1956, which transformed it into the 'staple reading diet for the working-class, particularly in the industrial Lowlands'.[77] *Forward*, which had thrived as recently as 1951, was practically dead by 1959.[78] The local media scene, which since August 1957 also included commercial broadcasting in the form of Scottish Television, was beginning to shift in Labour's favour.

Labour performed poorly, however, when it came to giving women a visible role within party structures. A 1951 NEC survey revealed that proportionately five times as many Scottish constituencies lacked a women's section as in England or Wales, while in 1956 the Scottish executive complained that 'all too often Women's Sections are only recognised and thought useful when money is needed', leading them to resent 'the impression that raising money and canvassing is their only function'.[79] There had been seven women candidates at the 1955 general election, of which three – Alice Cullen (Gorbals), Margaret Herbison (North Lanark) and Jean Mann (Coatbridge) – had been returned with healthy majorities. In 1955, the Labour League of Youth was also disbanded by the Scottish Council 'in the face of Trotskyite permeation and discord'. Although it had been slow to take off in Scotland, as recently as 1951 the League had boasted eighty-six out of 777 branches in Great Britain.[80]

The key party figure of the mid-1950s was William Marshall, who had succeeded John Taylor as the party's Scottish secretary in 1951. Marshall made a point of cultivating a lively group of students at the Glasgow University Labour Club, which included the future UK party leader John Smith and future

Secretary of State for Scotland Donald Dewar, although this was resented by young female activists such as Maria Fyfe, a future Scottish Labour MP.[81] Significantly, Smith and Dewar were ardent devolutionists as well as Gaitskellites, Hugh Gaitskell having succeeded Attlee as party leader towards the end of 1955. When Sir Anthony Eden, Churchill's initially popular successor as premier, covertly authorised military action in supposed 'defence' of the Suez Canal, the anti-imperialist STUC instructed trades councils across Scotland 'to act in conjunction with the local Labour Parties to engender the greatest possible public opinion against the Government's action and to join in the demand for a cease-fire and the withdrawal of British troops from the area of conflict'.[82]

The Suez Crisis served to paper over cracks in the British Labour Party, particularly when it came to foreign policy. Yet while a Bevanite split gripped the London media and Tony Crosland's *The Future of Socialism* urged the party to shed its class image and focus instead on social equality and economic growth, the party in Scotland played little part in these debates. Few individualistic MPs were returned in the post-war decade other than Dundee West's John Strachey. As Hutchison has observed, hardly any Scottish MPs were identified with the various internal left-wing revolts of the era (Victory for Socialism, the Bevanites and the Tribune Group); only Emrys Hughes and John McGovern stood out as left-wing mavericks. Even the former ILP firebrand Jean Mann was by the late 1950s a loyal Gaitskellite.[83] Keating concurred that there was 'probably less that is distinctive about Scottish Labour in this period than at any other in its history', the 1930s and 1940s having 'seen an almost complete integration of the party in Scotland into the British party, in terms of policies and priorities as in terms of organisation.'[84]

In January 1957, Labour's Scottish executive expressed its opposition to legislative devolution 'on compelling economic grounds', with which the NEC concurred. An executive report mused that it was:

> not clear what the Scottish people themselves desire. Greater control over purely Scottish affairs by Scottish representatives and the preservation of the Scottish national life are the broadly accepted and stated aims ... [but] It is difficult to obtain a detailed statement

of intentions which are at the same time an accurate reflection of widely held views in the Labour Party. What does appear clear is the almost unanimous desire to play our full part in the United Kingdom Parliament.

Rather the party's 'aim should remain the maximum possible self-government for Scotland' but in the 'administrative field' rather than via legislative or economic 'separation'.[85] Although 'no enthusiast' for devolution, even Labour's Edinburgh North candidate Gordon Stott (a future Lord Advocate) had 'no difficulty' in voting for the executive's report to be remitted back, something which was carried by a large majority.[86]

Later that year, Hugh Gaitskell visited Scotland for a meeting of the STUC but did not bother to take in the Scottish Council conference in session at the same time.[87] At the latter gathering, the Scottish executive announced that while it had halted a decade-long membership decline (with an increase of almost 4,000 to 58,653), A. L. Williams, the party's national agent, bluntly informed delegates that Scotland still had the worst membership record in Great Britain and needed 'a changed attitude to party affairs'. The Scottish Council's discussions on policy, added William Marshall equally bluntly, 'cut no ice unless Labour had power – and power meant organization'.[88] Several 'organising assistants' had recently been appointed by the NEC, including Bunty Urquhart in Glasgow,[89] who would go on to serve as Scottish women's organiser and assistant Scottish organiser.

Already unhappy at the unequivocal rejection of the party's historic commitment to Home Rule, some delegates proceeded to debate a resolution critical of Transport House's neglect of the party in Scotland – another long-standing complaint. John P. Mackintosh, a politics lecturer active in the Edinburgh Pentlands CLP, also pressed the 'need for a Labour Scottish policy' in letters to Gaitskell, who replied that there existed a 'good deal of sympathy for your point of view in the National Executive and I think you may take it that we will do what we can on the lines you suggest'.[90]

A Scottish Working Party subsequently comprised representatives from the NEC (Peggy Herbison and Jean Mann), the Scottish Labour MP group (Tom Fraser, Arthur Woodburn, William Ross and George Thomson) and the Scottish Council (E. G. Willis and E. J. Milne from USDAW). The Working

Party's report, which formed part of a wider restatement of British Labour's programme, was endorsed at a special Scottish Council conference held in Glasgow during September 1958. The opening passages of what was later published as *Let Scotland Prosper: Labour Plans for Scotland's Progress*, attempted to distil, and indeed reconcile, decades of Labour contortions regarding the 'Scottish Question':

> The Labour Party is proud of its Scottish traditions. Its roots lie deep in the history of Scottish radicalism. Keir Hardie's Scottish Labour Party was the parent of the political party we know today ... the Labour Party in Scotland today realises that Scotland's problems can best be solved by Socialist planning on a United Kingdom scale ... The unemployed Greenock worker is suffering from exactly the same scourge as the worker in Wales or Durham. He is the victim of living within a declining part of the British capitalist system.[91]

This, the party's first separately published policy statement on Scotland, went on to stress its preparation by 'Scottish Socialists' who were nevertheless members of the 'British Labour Party' because they believed it was 'only through Socialist planning on a United Kingdom scale ... that Scotland's many special problems can be tackled'.[92] This set the tone for two decades in which Labour would consolidate its position as Scotland's dominant political party.

NOTES

1. Scottish Council of the Labour Party (1940), *Report of the Executive Committee presented to the Annual 25th Conference*, Glasgow: SCLP. The first representative was Neil Maclean.
2. C. Harvie (1983), 'Labour in Scotland during the Second World War', *Historical Journal* 26:4, 928.
3. M. Sherwood (2007), 'Krishna Menon, Parliamentary Labour Party candidate for Dundee, 1939–1940', *Scottish Labour History* 42, 29–48.
4. C. Harvie (1989), 'The recovery of Scottish Labour, 1939–51', in I. Donnachie, C. Harvie & I. S. Wood (eds), *Forward! Labour Politics in Scotland, 1888–1988*, Edinburgh: Polygon, 71.
5. Harvie (1983), 925–7.
6. J. Colville (1986), *The Fringes of Power: Downing Street Diaries, Volume One: 1939–October 1941*, London: Sceptre, 419.
7. T. Johnston (1952), *Memories*, London: Collins, 147–8.

8. W. Y. Darling (1945), *King's Cross to Waverley*, London: William Hodge, 42.
9. See G. Walker (1988), *Thomas Johnston*, Manchester: Manchester University Press, and R. Galbraith (2018), *Without Quarter: A Biography of Tom Johnston*, Edinburgh: Birlinn.
10. Specifically, James Maxton and John McGovern (see HC Deb 11 September 1941 Vol 379 cc304–06).
11. M. Keating & D. Bleiman (1979), *Labour and Scottish Nationalism*, London: Macmillan, 129.
12. C. Harvie (1981), 'Labour and Scottish government: The age of Tom Johnston', *Bulletin of Scottish Politics* 2, 11, 17.
13. I. G. C. Hutchison (2000), *Scottish Politics in the Twentieth Century*, Basingstoke: Palgrave, 92.
14. See D. Torrance (2020), *'Standing Up for Scotland': Nationalist Unionism and Scottish Party Politics, 1884–2014*, Edinburgh: Edinburgh University Press.
15. C. Stuart (ed.) (1975), *The Reith Diaries*, London: HarperCollins, 300–1.
16. D. Sheridan (ed.) (1986), *Among You Taking Notes: The Wartime Diary of Naomi Mitchison, 1939–1945*, Oxford: Oxford University Press, 300.
17. C. M. M. Macdonald (2009), *Whaur Extremes Meet: Scotland's Twentieth Century*, Edinburgh: John Donald, 230.
18. D. Young (1949), *Labour Record on Scotland, 1945–1949*, Glasgow: Scottish Secretariat, 9.
19. Harvie (1983), 'Labour in Scotland', 933–4.
20. Harvie (1983), 935.
21. Sloan's great-great-granddaughter, Katy Clark, became the Labour MP for North Ayrshire and Arran between 2005 and 2015.
22. Young (1949), 8.
23. Harold Laski had published *Studies in the Problems of Sovereignty* in 1917 (New Haven: Yale University Press).
24. Young, 8–9.
25. Nat Jackson election address, TD 1617/1/6, Records of James Carmichael and Neil Carmichael, Glasgow: Mitchell Library. Jackson was defeated by a Unionist.
26. R. B. MacCallum & A. Readman (1947), *The British General Election of 1945*, Oxford: Oxford University Press, 104.
27. Harvie (1983), 939–40.
28. MacCallum & Readman, 105.
29. McNab Shaw resigned in October 1946 and was succeeded by William Ross, who had been one of her Sunday school pupils.

30. Scottish Council of the Labour Party (1965), *Golden Jubilee, 1915–1965: Labour Party Scottish Council*, Glasgow: SCLP, 17.
31. W. Knox (ed.) (1984), *Scottish Labour Leaders, 1918–39: A Biographical Dictionary*, Edinburgh: Mainstream, 52.
32. Harvie (1983), 941–5.
33. HL Deb 15 August 1945 Vol 137 c10 [The King's Speech].
34. J. Wheatley (1987), *One Man's Judgment: An Autobiography*, London: Butterworths, 105–7.
35. I. G. C. Hutchison, *Scottish Politics in the Twentieth Century*, 97.
36. Harvie (1989), 78.
37. Labour Party (1946), *Scottish Local Government Handbook*, London: Labour Party and Glasgow: Scottish Co-operative Wholesale Society, 57.
38. HC Deb 8 May 1946 Vol 422 c1127 [New Towns Bill].
39. Another Glasgow Labour councillor, William Taylor, later chaired the Livingston Development Corporation. It was designated a New Town under a Conservative government in 1962.
40. Labour Party (1946), 1.
41. I. Levitt (1998), 'Britain, the Scottish Covenant movement and devolution, 1946–50', *Scottish Affairs* 22, 37–47.
42. Harvie (1989), 67–8.
43. 'Scottish Demands for Home Rule or Devolution', Cabinet paper dated 6 December 1947, HH36/92, Edinburgh: National Records of Scotland.
44. Hutchison (2000), 89.
45. W. H. Marwick (1950), *Scottish Devolution: A Study to Further Discussion*, London: Fabian Society, 26.
46. HC Deb 16 November 1949 Vol 469 c2097.
47. *Bulletin*, 17 November 1949.
48. Torrance, 63.
49. E. A. Cameron (2024), 'The Bulletin, "Londonisation" and Scottish Politics in the 1940s and 1950s', *Scottish Historical Review* 1:261, 156–77.
50. Labour Party Scottish Council (1948), *Report of the Executive Committee to the Annual Conference*, Glasgow: SCLP.
51. Harvie (1983), 944.
52. *The Times*, 6 May 1954.
53. S. B. Chrimes (ed.) (1950), *The General Election in Glasgow February, 1950: Essays by Members of the Staff of the University of Glasgow*, Glasgow: Jackson, Son and Company, 28, 44–8.
54. Wheatley, 112–14.
55. Young, 2.
56. See 'Miscellaneous Press Cuttings' in Acc 4826/14, Mathers Papers, Edinburgh: National Library of Scotland.

57. *Edinburgh Evening News*, 29 October 1956.
58. HC Deb 10 March 1950 Vol 472 c635.
59. D. Torrance (2006), *The Scottish Secretaries*, Edinburgh: Birlinn, 210.
60. K. O. Morgan (1985), *Labour in Power, 1945–1951*, Oxford: Oxford University Press, 308.
61. Hutchison (2000), 93.
62. R. McLean (1991), *Labour and Scottish Home Rule, Part 1*, Whitburn: Scottish Labour Action, 3.
63. M. Moran (2017), *The End of British Politics?*, London: Palgrave Macmillan, 23–4.
64. I. McLean and A. McMillan (2005), *State of the Union: Unionism and the Alternatives in the United Kingdom since 1707*, Oxford: Oxford University Press, 157.
65. Moran, 29.
66. Cameron, 269.
67. I. McLean (1978), 'Labour Elites and Electorates in Glasgow', ESRC Study 1007, University of Essex.
68. *The Times*, 6 May 1954.
69. Labour Party Scottish Council (1953), *Programme for the Highlands and Islands*, Glasgow: SCLP. Tom Johnston was critical of this programme (*Scotsman*, 20 November 1954).
70. Hutchison (2000), 91. See also A. MacNeill Weir (1945), *Highland Plan: An Outline of Labour Policy for the Highlands*, Glasgow: SCLP.
71. Conservative and Unionist Central Office (1955), *The Campaign Guide 1955: The New Political Encyclopædia*, London: CUCO.
72. In the immediate post-war era, John Strachey, Emrys Hughes and William Hamilton (all non-Scots) had been elected Labour MPs in Scotland.
73. M. Keating (1989), 'The Labour Party in Scotland, 1951–1964', in I. Donnachie, C. Harvie & I. S. Wood (eds), *Forward! Labour Politics in Scotland, 1888–1988*, Edinburgh: Polygon, 90.
74. M. Keating (1975), 'The Role of the Scottish MP', Glasgow: Glasgow College of Technology, PhD thesis.
75. Harvie (1989), 82.
76. Hutchison (2000), 93.
77. Hutchison (2000), 100–1.
78. Harvie (1989), 82.
79. Labour Party Scottish Council (1956), *Report of the Executive Committee to the 41st Annual Conference*, Glasgow: SCLP.
80. Hutchison (2000), 90.
81. See M. Fyfe (2020), *Singing in the Streets: A Glasgow Memoir*, Edinburgh: Luath.

82. E. Breitenbach (2016), 'For workers' rights and self-determination? The Scottish Labour movement and the British empire from the 1920s to the 1960s', *Scottish Labour History* 51, 125.
83. Hutchison (2000), 95.
84. Keating (1989), 87.
85. Labour Party Scottish Council (1957), *Report of the Executive Committee to the 42nd Annual Conference*, Glasgow: SCLP.
86. 'The Scottish Executive had with unusual temerity submitted a report concluding baldly, and without anything substantial in the way of argument or evidence, that a separate Parliament for Scotland was impracticable' (G. Stott, 1998, *Q.C.'s Diary, 1954–1960*, Edinburgh: Mercat Press, 127).
87. A. Midwinter, M. Keating & J. Mitchell (1991), *Politics and Public Policy in Scotland*, Edinburgh: Edinburgh University Press, 27.
88. *The Times*, 13 April 1957.
89. Labour Party Scottish Council (1958), *Report of the Executive Committee to the 43rd Annual Conference*, Glasgow: SCLP.
90. Hugh Gaitskell to John P. Mackintosh, 5 September and 14 October 1957, Acc 13476/55, John P Mackintosh MP papers, Edinburgh: National Library of Scotland.
91. Labour Party (1958), *Let Scotland Prosper: Labour Plans for Scotland's Progress*, London: Labour Party, 1.
92. Labour Party (1958), 81.

4

'Signposts for Scotland': 1958–1979

The general election of October 1959 found Scotland in transition between a long period of Unionist hegemony and a new political era in which Labour would dominate almost every level of Scottish governance. Labour gained thirty-eight seats, an increase of four on 1955, and although the Unionists lost five seats Harold Macmillan's government maintained a slight plurality of the popular vote in Scotland. Scotland's swing to Labour, meanwhile, was a preference shared only by Lancashire.[1]

Campaigning had not exactly been energetic. At the launch of the Scottish Council's 'Into Action' initiative, only half the 1,800 activists expected at a Glasgow rally turned up and Jim Griffiths (deputy British Labour leader), Tom Fraser (shadow Scottish Secretary) and Jennie Lee made what *The Times* called 'somewhat heavy weather of rousing enthusiasm for the cause'. Lee even resorted to 'nostalgically' recalling more exciting political times on Clydeside, an early example of the party's revolutionary mythology being weaponised at election time.[2]

In other respects, however, the Scottish party was deeply conservative. Coatbridge MP Jean Mann viewed the Wolfenden Report as part of an 'evil thread' that ran 'through the theatre, through the music hall, through the Press, and through the BBC'. She could not:

> imagine the miners' lodges welcoming a Report which will mean that it will no longer be an offence to procure an adult male and set up a house in a mining village for a male friend. I cannot see the Co-operative women's guilds welcoming this, or the townswomen's guilds.

Of the thirty Scottish MPs who voted in a 1960 Commons motion supportive of Wolfenden, twenty were opposed, of whom six were Labour members.[3]

Party organisation remained curiously sluggish. While Jimmy Allison, a future Scottish party organiser, resolved to join Labour in June 1959, it took until January 1961 for him to receive a membership card. Attending his first ward meeting in early 1961, Allison found:

> only eight people in the room including three Labour councillors. I had gone along expecting a political debate on issues such as nuclear disarmament but instead we spent our time talking about trivial matters such as street lighting or the state of the pavements.[4]

The debate on nuclear weapons was taking place elsewhere. The General Council of the Scottish Trades Union Congress (STUC) had called on Labour to join its opposition to the presence of both British and American Polaris (later Trident) submarines on the Clyde.[5] A critical 1961 Scottish Council motion, however, was ruled out of order as it was not a Scottish issue.[6] The Campaign for Nuclear Disarmament (CND) nevertheless found willing supporters from among pacifists on the Scottish left,[7] while the Scottish National Party – whose new logo evoked that of the CND – also came to benefit.

These tensions came to a head at the 1962 May Day march and rally in Glasgow. Scottish party secretary William Marshall had arranged for Donald Dewar and other Glasgow University Gaitskellites to form a protective shield around the leader, but when he came to address a 5,000-strong crowd, Hugh Gaitskell was heckled by Young Socialists (YS) and CND activists, prompting indelicate remarks about East Germany and the Kremlin. 'You're nothing', was YS Maria Fyfe's recollection of one tirade from the Leader of the Opposition. 'You're just peanuts!'[8] Dewar called it a 'yelling mass of hysterical men and women ... which will leave a memory and a scar'. The Glasgow Federation of Young Socialists was subsequently disbanded, and Woodside CLP subjected to a party inquiry on account of its members' involvement.[9] Maria Fyfe resented Marshall's obvious preference for middle-class students over working-class Young Socialists.[10]

Jim Sillars viewed the 'clan' who ran the Scottish Labour MP group in the early 1960s – Peggy Herbison, Willie Ross and

Tom Fraser – as similarly 'snobbish', particularly their sidelining of John Robertson, who had beaten off a strong Liberal challenge at a by-election in Paisley. His offence was a July 1961 speech in which he stated that:

> If we believe, as I do, that Scotland as a cultural unity is worth preserving, then we must provide the economic base from which it can go on. I have never thought of myself as a Scottish nationalist, but in the few months that I have been in this House I have been rapidly coming to the conclusion that the only solution is a Scottish government.[11]

'Those sentiments', recalled Sillars, 'damned him at the start of his parliamentary life.'[12]

Since the Scottish party executive's move against Home Rule in 1957, any hint of nationalism had become anathema to Labour in Scotland, attacks on the party by the Covenant movement and the Scottish National Party having 'left a bitter aftertaste'.[13] As Bealey has observed, demands for decentralisation and devolution were increasingly directed 'against the state as a political entity rather than the state as a centre of capitalist dominance', while remedies 'lay in reform of political institutions rather than in social and economic innovation'.[14]

In September 1958 the Scottish executive reported to a special Scottish Council conference in Glasgow, the 'Scottish Parliament' section of its 1957 report having been remitted back the previous year. This, however, restated its 'belief in the principle of the maximum possible self-government for Scotland, consistent with the right to remain in United Kingdom Parliament and continue full Scottish representation there ... The Scottish problem is part of the general problem.' The only compromise was the suggestion of a 'Special Committee or Speaker's Conference to examine and consider the question of Scottish Government',[15] but while this was endorsed by the special conference, it was ignored by the British party.[16] Aberdeen North MP Hector Hughes criticised the report as 'airy-fairy stuff' which offered 'no solutions'.[17]

According to Keating and Bleiman:

> Labour's attitude to the Scottish question was based upon the assumptions that the basis of any discontent was economic, and that the electorate were more concerned about the economic goods which they received than with the constitutional mechanism by which they were delivered.[18]

When unemployment reached the symbolically significant level of 100,000 in 1961, Scottish MPs from all parties – including thirty-seven from Labour – conferred with trade union representatives at Glasgow City Chambers, something the *Sunday Post* described as the biggest gathering of MPs in Scotland since the Act of Union.[19] Among them was Willie Ross, whom Gaitskell had appointed shadow Scottish Secretary in place of the less strident Tom Fraser. A dour ex-schoolmaster, Ross fitted well into the image of the Scots dominie:

> stern, old-fashioned and a Kirk elder given to quoting the Bible in his orations. Firmly on the right of the Labour Party, Ross was also a conservative member of the Church of Scotland, reflecting its traditionalist wing's views on 'such matters as liquor licensing, Sunday observance, homosexuality, family planning and divorce'.[20]

Ross combined strident attacks on the SNP with accusations that Unionists were neglecting Scotland, cleverly deploying the same arguments levelled against Labour in the late 1940s. With the collapse of the Scottish Covenant movement and nascent Unionist decline, such actions allowed Labour to 'command the centre of the Scottish political stage as never before and to turn the Scottish question to its own advantage'.[21]

The party grew steadily in local government. In elections to a new authority for East Kilbride (a New Town) in May 1963, Labour gained control of its fortieth authority.[22] The West Lothian by-election of 1962 also marked both the beginning of a long Commons career for Tam Dalyell (who was married to Kathleen Wheatley, a niece of John) as well as a foretaste of the SNP's advance, its candidate Billy Wolfe winning almost a quarter of the vote. At this point, however, it made more of an impression on the Old Etonian than it did his party.

In 1962 the Scottish Council had an independent income of just £760 pounds a year and employed only five full-time agents (the Scottish Unionists had fifty-five).[23] Journalist Magnus Magnusson observed that Labour in Scotland was 'just a branch office' of the British Labour Party.[24] At its 1961 conference the Scottish Council's executive said the time had come for an improvement in the 'status and an extension' of its power. There was obvious frustration at the SCLP's 'advisory' role on policy, which it could only determine within the 'framework' of British Labour policy as laid down by its national conference. All policy initiatives from the Scottish executive or Scottish Council were passed on to the Scottish Labour MP group at Westminster, while there was a constitutional obligation to consult the STUC on anything relating to employment and industry. The NEC, of course, had the final say. The Scottish executive asserted that:

> members of the Labour Party in Scotland and Scottish Labour M.P.s are concerned not only with Scottish affairs ... We therefore have a national party, not a federation of autonomous Regional Councils; the Regional Councils are functional parts of the National Party and must therefore be subsidiary to the whole.[25]

Signposts for Scotland, Labour's 1963 policy statement, acknowledged Scotland's 'rich national culture', which it said would be 'preserved' by British planning:

> Scotland will stand to gain more from this fairer sharing of both benefits and burdens just because of our present relatively greater needs. This is the answer to those who claim that Scotland should cut herself off from the rest of Britain and make herself economically and politically independent. Such a separation would give Scotland the worst of both worlds.[26]

'A PROVING GROUND FOR PROGRESSIVE LEGISLATION'

At the October 1964 general election, Labour in Scotland decisively entered its hegemonic phase, gaining five more MPs (a total of forty-three) and 1,283,667 votes, which put it comfortably ahead of the increasingly moribund Unionists. Labour's Scottish executive considered it a measure of the 'calibre and importance' of the Scottish Labour MP group that it provided the new government with eleven ministers, including two of Cabinet rank.[27] Gordon Stott, a son of the manse, editor of the *Edinburgh Clarion* (a wartime Labour journal) and failed parliamentary candidate, was appointed Lord Advocate, relieved at not having 'done the slightest thing' to advance his 'claims'.[28] Harold Wilson, meanwhile, largely left Ross to his Scottish fiefdom.

The Secretary of State was not inactive during the short 1964–6 Parliament. In 1965 the Scottish Education Department issued Circular 600 which, as in England and Wales, abolished selective transfer in favour of fixed-catchment area comprehensive schools for twelve to eighteen-year-olds.[29]

The Education (Scotland) Act 1969 later removed the power of local authorities to charge fees, although this was largely symbolic given not many did. In the Highlands and Islands, meanwhile, Ross addressed what he had called the 'man on Scotland's back' and legislated to create a Development Board (HIDB) equipped with a huge budget and wide-ranging powers to acquire land and grant financial assistance, a considerable improvement upon the advisory Highland Panel established by the last Labour government. Michael Noble, Ross's shadow, called it 'undiluted Marxism'.[30]

The HIDB also tied in with the new political orthodoxy of regional and national economic planning. The result was an ambitious Command Paper, *The Scottish Economy 1965–1970*, which designated the whole of Scotland, except for Edinburgh and Leith, a development area. It also committed to limiting emigration and cutting unemployment by rapidly developing Central Scotland and the Borders. A New Town at Irvine would be designated in November 1966. Labour's reward was three more Scottish MPs and very nearly 50 per cent of the popular vote at the March 1966 general election. An unexpected gain was Donald Dewar in Aberdeen South, where he defeated Conservative Lady Tweedsmuir (daughter-in-law of John Buchan) by 1,799 votes. The Scottish executive hailed Dewar as representing a 'new element of youth, ability and experience' in the Scottish Labour MP group, which also included Robert Maclennan (Caithness and Sutherland) and John P. Mackintosh (Berwick and East Lothian).[31]

Dewar's election address had emphasised 'thirteen wasted years' of Conservative rule, its 'neglect of Scotland' and lack of concern regarding the 'social consequences in the towns and villages affected by the loss of tens of thousands of jobs'.[32] Kellas and Fotheringham explained Labour's superior strength in Scottish constituencies (vis-à-vis English) on the basis of class structure and the much greater provision of council housing in Scotland, and indeed Budge and Urwin found a 'strong link' between an elector's tenancy and party support, owner-occupiers voting Unionist and corporation tenants Labour.[33] A later study by Rose also showed that a third of Scottish Labour support came from Roman Catholics,[34] while McLean found 'class and Catholicism' to be reliable predictors of a Labour vote,[35] a tendency which did not exist in England. Drucker noted that

Scottish Labour was an 'anomaly' in Western European terms: 'In no other Western country can the party of the Left count on support from Catholic voters: more important, in no other country of the West are all of the trade unions united behind one Socialist Party.'[36]

Increasingly dominant, Willie Ross lobbied relentlessly within the Cabinet for more jobs, securing a new prototype fast breeder (nuclear) reactor for Dounreay and an aluminium smelter at Invergordon, but failing when it came to the Royal Mint and the DVLA, both of which went to Wales (which had recently gained its own Secretary of State). Unemployment had fallen by 10,000 during Labour's first year in office, but from 1966 the National Plan began to fail and by 1969 the Scottish Council conference was debating resolutions highly critical of the government.[37] The Scottish Labour MP group remarked defensively that 'too many supporters of the Labour Party think that because we have not done everything, we have done nothing. The record shows differently.'[38]

Ross also believed Scotland could be made 'a proving ground for progressive legislation', of which the Social Work (Scotland) Act 1968 became the most enduring example. This drew together disparate services provided by different local authority departments – education, welfare and the probation service – to form a single social work department for each Scottish council under its own director, as well as a Children's Hearings System. This was a distinctly Scottish agenda later followed by England in less comprehensive form.

Although Richard Crossman, then Leader of the House of Commons, admired the policy, he was infuriated when Ross ordered him to be kept out of the Chamber during its parliamentary consideration. 'You and Willie Ross', Crossman thundered to Tam Dalyell, his parliamentary private secretary: 'You're just as bad as he is ... [you] go around shouting about the Scottish Nationalists wanting separation, but what both of you and your friends actually want is to keep your Scottish business absolutely privy from English business.'[39] As Keating observed, the Scottish Secretary's strategy was 'assimilationist on the one hand, [Scotland's] problems British problems', yet at the same time territorial institutions like the Scottish Office 'were to be used to extract and maintain an advantage over other parts of the UK'.[40]

On homosexual law reform, however, Ross was markedly less progressive. With 'Calvinist Scots', notably the Scottish miners, having helped defeat Leo Abse's motion to introduce a bill amending the law in 1965, Ross went on to ensure the exclusion of Scotland from Abse's subsequent ten-minute rule bill, which the government supported. While Ross's stance was arguably consistent with Scottish public opinion,[41] his opposition did not extend to David Steel's private member's bill to decriminalise abortion, which applied across Great Britain.

Kellas characterised the Scottish Labour of the late 1960s as 'a staid, socially-conservative and rather dull body':

> While they are no longer a left-wing ginger group like the old ILP, the Scottish Labour MPs are to the left in their party on foreign or economic matters, but more conservative on 'moral issues' such as abortion, homosexuality and Sunday Observance. Many have inherited the puritanism which was so noticeable in the make-up of the early Scottish Labour leaders and which is part of Scottish life generally. Unfortunately, they cannot be said to have maintained the pioneers' disdain for the status quo, since they are so much a part of it themselves.[42]

In 1968, Jimmy Allison caused controversy by attending the Scottish Labour women's conference, where he got heckled for his opposition to separate women's organisations.[43] Scottish Labour women were, however, prominent in the Wilson governments of the era: Peggy Herbison as Minister of Social Security (1964–7), Jennie Lee as Minister for the Arts (1964–70) and Judith Hart as Minister for Overseas Development (1969–70).

Dundee MP George Thomson (a former *Forward* journalist) also impressed as Secretary of State for Commonwealth Affairs (1967–8), typifying one breed of Scottish Labour MP who avoided purely Scottish affairs. In 1967 William Hamilton, the English and strongly republican MP for West Fife, complained to Harold Wilson about being overlooked for ministerial office, suspecting 'the Palace' had been 'at work', a thought which in the 'context of a Labour Govt & a Labour P.M.' he found 'inexplicable'. When the Prime Minister eventually offered to make Hamilton Chairman of Ways and Means (a deputy Commons Speaker), he declined on the basis he was not yet prepared to 'go into the political purdah ... and in such ridiculous garb'.[44] But beyond Hamilton, William Baxter in West Stirling and Emrys

Hughes, James McMillan judged Labour's 'Scottish contingent' a 'docile one'.[45]

In another contemporary survey by the nationalist Douglas Young, the Scottish Labour organisation was described as 'run on a shoe-string budget' from Glasgow's Royal Crescent by its secretary William Marshall, 'a frank straightforward Scot' of 'great integrity and diligence, with all the dour loyalty of the mining communities'. In 1968 only four local Labour parties could afford full-time agents (Dundee, North Lanark, Central Ayrshire and South Ayrshire) and beyond the historic mining and industrial constituencies, party organisation was indeed 'often very sketchy'.[46] There were recurrent crises, including the disbandment of the Glasgow City Labour Party. A 1969 NEC enquiry found that total individual membership in the fifteen Glasgow constituencies was just 1,786 with 'only the devoted work of two or three people' preventing 'a complete collapse of organisation'.[47]

Writing in 1967, Marwick found that local parties sprang to life only at election time and were otherwise characterised by apathy or inertia.[48] Across Scotland, individual membership stood at 74,446 in 1968, trade affiliated membership at 578,500, the allied Co-operative Party at 10,000 and the affiliated Socialist Societies at 3,000. This, to Young, meant 665,946 persons in Scotland 'more or less committed to backing Labour candidates', about a sixth of the qualified electorate before eighteen-year-olds were permitted to vote at the 1970 general election.[49] An NEC rule implemented in 1963, however, required CLPs to affiliate 1,000 members regardless of actual membership (something known as 'the minimum'), so the individual membership figure must be treated with caution.[50] Even so, the party in Scotland appeared to fare better than that in Great Britain, with individual membership falling by only 9 as opposed to 20 per cent between 1964 and 1969.[51]

As Kellas had detected, 'disaffected radicals' who wished for 'a more emotional or revolutionary approach' were increasingly turning to the Liberals, who had increased their vote at the 1966 election, or to the SNP, then rapidly professionalising. 'Their attack is now aimed at a new Establishment', observed Kellas, 'the vested interest of Labour in trade union and town hall, which has replaced some of the privilege of the past.'[52] The first indication of such a protest vote came at the Pollok by-election of March 1967, at which a significant SNP showing split the anti-Tory vote and handed the rebranded Scottish Conservative and Unionist Party an unexpected victory. Next were municipal elections and then, in the biggest shock, the November Hamilton by-election, which resembled the great 'smouldering pile' of nationalist sentiment Arthur Woodburn had anticipated back in 1947. It did not help that the victorious SNP MP Winnie Ewing had grown up reading *Forward* in an ILP family. She was introduced to the Commons by South Ayrshire MP Emrys Hughes and another Nationalist by-election victor, Plaid Cymru's Gwynfor Evans.

Tam Dalyell called it an 'electoral atom bomb' which left party leaders in Scotland 'shell-shocked for weeks'. For Hamilton was 'not just any old Labour seat' but 'a Scottish Ebbw Vale, with close links to Keir Hardie, Bob Smillie and other pioneers and folk-heroes of the movement, it embodied the socialist heartland'. Dalyell attributed the result to a combination of the abrupt manner in which the incumbent MP Tom Fraser had quit Parliament for a 'well-paid appointment' at the Hydro-Electric Board, ill feeling among local teachers, troubles at the Ravenscraig steelworks, a spate of local traffic accidents and even a row involving a 'friendly' international football match.[53] The Scottish Labour MP group spoke of the 'menace that is Nationalism' having reared its head. 'We as a Group have taken note of these happenings and shaped our course accordingly. We hope the Party is doing likewise.'[54] In May 1968 the SNP polled 30 per cent in local elections, including a strong showing in Glasgow, which had been controlled by Labour since 1933. Now the Conservatives formed an administration with SNP support. Aiding the SNP had been cases of corruption, nepotism and favouritism among Labour councillors.[55] This crumbling of Labour support, however, at least meant a 'swathe of elderly and rather ineffectual councillors' was eventually replaced by younger and more able Labour representatives.[56]

Initially the Labour response was to 'ride out the Nationalist storm' and go on the attack.[57] Willie Ross stepped up his anti-SNP vitriol and resisted any concessions beyond a new Select Committee on Scottish Affairs (formed in 1968 with Donald Dewar as a member). As McLean and McMillan have observed, Labour divided between 'hedgers and ditchers'. Harold Wilson and Crossman led the hedgers, believing that 'some gestures to devolution would head off the Scottish Nationalist threat', while the ditchers, led by Ross, 'believed that any concession to the SNP was dangerous. For them, devolution was a dangerous precedent, a slippery slope, the start of the breakup of Britain'.[58] As Miller put it, Labour's attitude to devolution in the late 1960s 'owed as much to an hysterical reaction to party defeats as to consideration of the issue itself'.[59]

Long disdainful of the party's devolutionists, Ross was also suspicious of the STUC ('the Scottish Trades Union Congrouse'), which he refused to accept was truly representative of the workers' movement, instead being full of Communists and nationalists. That body had been moving towards support for legislative devolution since 1967, and in 1969 Mick McGahey, president of the National Union of Mineworkers Scotland Area (NUMSA), said he 'did not believe in total separation' and instead 'approached the National question in class terms'.[60] Adding to the pressure on Ross was Labour in Wales, which had long agitated (unsuccessfully) for greater devolution, as well as the Scottish Conservatives, whose 'Declaration of Perth' in May 1968 made it the first British party to commit to a form of legislative devolution. Labour had 'become accustomed to thinking of itself as the political voice of Scotland', judged Drucker and Brown, 'and did not take kindly to being displaced from that role'.[61]

At the March 1968 Scottish Council conference Ross had stamped all over a pro-devolution motion from John P. Mackintosh and other 'young turks'. It was rejected by a large majority, a victory for the Scottish Secretary, as *The Economist* reported, and 'the elderly phalanx of machine-run Scottish Labour MPs who have graduated from union branch to town council to safe seat in plodding progression, and who thought no cataclysm could ever touch them'.[62] Devolution on the Northern Ireland model was rejected out of hand and the Scottish Labour MP group even dismissed a modest proposal for the Scottish Grand Committee to meet in Edinburgh. Instead, the usual formula was intoned: 'the greatest possible devolution consistent with our absolute determination to retain the maximum possible influence on the economic and political policies of the United Kingdom'. As Donald Dewar later remarked, that was little different from the position adopted in 1958. 'It is an acceptable sentiment which could offend no one', he wrote.

'The difficulty is that ten years later the party is not one bit the nearer knowing what it means'.[63]

Ross's conference move, meanwhile, convinced Dick Crossman that the time had come for the Scottish Secretary to move on, a view he believed the Prime Minister had come to share.[64] At a parliamentary committee meeting in June 1968, Crossman recalled ministers considering:

> a strange, sad, melancholy paper by Willie Ross, saying how awful life is in Scotland and how Scotland is penalized in comparison with other regions. He is mainly complaining about the loss of the Edinburgh-Carlisle railway and the closing down of a brand-new pit at Dumfries. But the whole of the country is suffering and the North of England has a higher rate of unemployment. The fact is that the Scots' peculiar problem is one of nationalism and Willie Ross is in these difficulties only because he is determined to treat nationalism as a mere emotional attitude which can be cured by economic policies alone.[65]

Jim Sillars, an Ayrshire councillor, STUC official and Ross protégé, was becoming known in the party as 'the Hammer of the Nats'.[66] With the Midlothian MP Alex Eadie he wrote the pungent pamphlet *Don't Butcher Scotland's Future*. This rejected the 'separatist case' not because it was 'emotional' but on the utilitarian grounds that the Scottish economy had become so 'fully integrated' with the rest of the UK that 'to separate them now would be as difficult as extracting the original acorn from the giant oak'. Instead, the authors promoted a two-tier system of local government as well as a 'Scottish Ombudsman' committed to 'righting grievances at all levels of government both national, regional and local'.[67]

In another pamphlet Dick Douglas, also a Labour councillor and the defeated candidate at the 1967 Pollok by-election, hinted at a federalist system of ten 'area assemblies' which might be 'involved in fundamental decisions affecting the allocation of resources from the central government'.[68] John P. Mackintosh, whose 1968 book *The Devolution of Power* had proved influential,[69] spoke of 'dual' identities, telling the Commons towards the end of 1969 that nationalism was 'not altogether bad':

> My constituency contains the site of the last battlefield on which the Scots defeated the English, at Prestonpans, and I have a certain mild form of national pride of my own. But this does not mean

that I dislike other tribes, such as the Welsh, that I have any hostile feelings towards foreigners or that I lack pride in being British. It does not mean that I am not eager to join the European Economic Community or that I am not enthusiastic for the development of the United Nations.[70]

From outside the movement, meanwhile, came a memorable broadside from the theorist Tom Nairn, who called on Labour to build up its own 'socialist nationalism' to compete with that of the SNP.[71]

On 19 December 1968, the government announced the chairman (Lord Kilbrandon) of a Royal Commission on the Constitution. Only the Edinburgh City Labour Party and Central Edinburgh CLP submitted pro-devolution evidence, while the party's Scottish secretary, William Marshall, denied there was such thing as a 'separate political culture in Scotland'. The Scottish Council's chairman John Pollock, meanwhile, bluntly argued that 'substantial legislative devolution' would be the 'slippery slope towards total separation'. He added:

> We believe that would be disastrous for Scotland, because it would lead to Scotland becoming a separate small nation economy instead of remaining part of a major economic unit. That would be so disastrous in the long run that even the hypothetical situation of another Conservative Government ruling in Great Britain would be preferable.[72]

Donald Dewar begged to differ. In his contribution to a book published shortly before the 1970 general election, *The Scottish Debate: Essays on Scottish Nationalism* (ed. MacCormick), he said the:

> matter should not be reduced to a narrow exercise in political tactics when what is required is anxious debate about the case for change ... The present Government had been committed as no other to balanced industrial growth and the even spread of economic power. It would be in no way dishonourable or inconsistent for the Labour Party to think in terms of parallel political developments.

Dewar, like Mackintosh, believed the existence of a devolved parliament at Stormont had destroyed 'the common view that separate control of internal finance would leave Scotland struggling on with the same handicaps as would arise from complete independence', not least because Northern Ireland was getting social services 'at a bargain basement price'.[73] And if that meant Scots – like Ulster Unionists – being excluded from the UK Cabinet, then so be it.

Norman Buchan, the MP for West Renfrewshire since 1964, on the other hand, feared a Stormont approach would weaken Scotland's voice at Westminster, the calibre of its elected representatives and share of resources. Delving into the party's historical position, Buchan asked why Labour had proved incapable of implementing Keir Hardie's vision 'of a kind of Commonwealth status':

> It is not just that the implications at that time were in any case never thought through, but because since then there has been increasing intermeshing of the capitalist economy and its interlinking with Government agencies ... It has been curious to notice how the exponents of the constitutional panacea have been invoking the names of Keir Hardie and John Maclean in that one context – while ignoring in both of them their real radical content. Their priorities, too, were socialism first and devolution second.[74]

Meanwhile the political tide – as measured in by-elections, local elections and opinion polls – appeared to have turned in Labour's favour. Frank McElhone comfortably held the Gorbals in October 1969 and Jim Sillars South Ayrshire in March 1970,[75] while at local elections in May 1969 the SNP fell back to 22 per cent of the vote, in part due to inexperienced SNP councillors, and Scotland returned 'to the dependable, if stolid, charms of Labour councillors'. Lord Wheatley's proposed reforms to local government, published in September 1969, were welcomed by Labour, although Willie Ross initially argued against the huge Strathclyde region, advocating four smaller authorities instead.[76]

The general election of June 1970 consolidated this electoral recovery. On one level, it appeared the SNP threat had dissipated, with the party losing Winnie Ewing in Hamilton and gaining Donald Stewart in the Western Isles, although its share of the vote more than doubled to 11.4 per cent. Ewing's claim at the South Ayrshire by-election that she was witnessing 'the beginning of the end of a great movement, the Labour Party in Scotland' now looked hubristic.[77] Retirees included Arthur Woodburn and Peggy Herbison, who had recently served as the first female Lord High Commissioner to the General Assembly of the Church of Scotland. Described as 'austere, religious and right-wing',[78] Herbison (a long-serving member of Labour's NEC) refused the offer of a life peerage and was succeeded in North Lanark by John Smith.[79]

Labour's Scottish vote dipped by almost as much as the SNP's increased, losing it two seats, one of which was Donald Dewar. Tony Crosland, whom Dewar had served as PPS in the previous Parliament, wrote to commiserate ('You have the huge advantage of youth'),[80] as did Willie Ross despite their differences over devolution. Reflecting that the party had 'underestimated' Conservative organisation in Aberdeen South, he said he:

> had been hoping in post-election changes to see you in office and would have welcomed you in the Scottish Office. In the present situation where the Scottish Dep[artmen]t. is bereft of my benign presence you would have revelled. I sincerely hope that you are back with us, sooner rather than later. If I may presume to advise you – don't tie yourself too tightly to Aberdeen. By the very nature of things there are bound to be by-elections – and retirals; and as you will know, the older the member, the safer the seat.[81]

'A SCOTTISH PARLIAMENT WOULD BE A WORKERS' PARLIAMENT'

Willie Ross reverted to pre-1964 form in presenting himself and Labour as defenders of Scottish interests against the ill-fated Conservative government of Edward Heath, with its weak 'mandate' in Scotland (although that critique had yet to find resonance on the Labour benches) and industrial woes. Following a resolution passed in 1968, meanwhile, from 1972 the Scottish Council was finally able to discuss wider British and international issues at its annual conference, if not adopt an official position. 'Over the next two decades', observed Hassan, 'the Scottish conference was to be transformed into a forum that debated some of the most intractable problems on the planet'.[82]

Opposition brought certain internal tensions into the open. In late 1971 the Revd Wotherspoon formed a breakaway 'Labour Party of Scotland' in Glasgow, although it disbanded in the spring of 1973. Another party with the same name was also established in Dundee and contested local elections and a by-election, albeit without much success.[83] The Local Government (Scotland) Act 1973 was about to create eight regional authorities, forty-seven district councils and three island authorities. Although Scottish organiser Peter Allison (no relation to Jimmy) admitted it might be difficult to find suitable candidates in some areas, he anticipated 'tremendous competition' for seats in Scotland's industrial central belt. 'If ever there was a chance of making inroads in the peripheral areas this is it', he added, 'and we intend to take advantage of the chance.'[84]

In January 1973 George Thomson was appointed a European Commissioner (the UK having recently joined the European Economic Community) and there was a by-election in Dundee East. Labour selected George Machin, a trade union-sponsored candidate from Sheffield who 'did not have a clue about Scottish politics'.[85] Although Machin held the seat by 1,410 votes and the Labour Party of Scotland polled just 1,409, the SNP's Gordon Wilson had established himself as a major local campaigning force with 30 per cent of the vote.

Parts of the Labour movement had been moving in an obviously nationalist direction since the late 1960s, something Keating attributed to the fact that:

> unease about the threat from the SNP, frustration at Labour's impotence in the face of the Heath government's housing legislation, North Sea oil and the as-yet uncertain implications of EEC membership caused a reawakening of interest. This coincided with a general move on the European left, away from the centralised model of state planning and back to the earlier socialist ideas of local and community-based action.[86]

In February 1972 the STUC had convened a 'Scottish Assembly' on unemployment, during which general secretary James Jack declared there was 'not the slightest doubt' in his mind 'that a Scottish Parliament would be a workers' Parliament'.[87] A similarly nationalistic approach was taken by a group of industrial workers during the 1971–2 Upper Clyde Shipbuilders (UCS) work-in, a response to the Conservative government's proposal to withdraw credit from UCS and risk up to 8,000 jobs. Gordon Brown, then an Edinburgh undergraduate, first met Donald Dewar on the 1972 UCS 'March for Jobs', full of admiration that the former MP had chosen to help 'make Scotland's children's panel system work in one of our poorest communities'.[88] This 'neo-nationalist' element extended to a group of MPs led by Jim Sillars, who had 'been moving in an increasingly nationalist direction' since his by-election victory in 1970.[89] Drucker pointed to a series of meetings attended by MPs and journalists in the wake of the September 1971 Stirling and Falkirk by-election, at which Robert McIntyre – the SNP's first MP in 1945 – had attracted 35 per cent of the vote.[90] In June 1973, Sillars even told Tony Benn he had become a 'convinced Scottish nationalist', and that he would 'become a Scottish nationalist member' if the UK stayed in Europe.[91]

The closing months of 1973 brought a perfect constitutional and political storm. In October the Scottish Council executive restated its opposition to legislative devolution in a pamphlet entitled *Scotland and the UK*, which Andrew Marr called 'a flimsier, less coherent' version of its 1970 evidence to the Royal Commission on the Constitution,[92] albeit one which acknowledged 'new factors' including the EEC and North Sea oil. Its suggestion that 'local democracy as it now exists can be strengthened and extended over greater areas' was hardly inspiring and jarred with the recommendations of the Royal Commission, a directly-elected 'Scottish Assembly' with legislative and executive autonomy.[93] Hutchison, meanwhile, reckoned the SNP's cry of 'It's Scotland's oil' resonated because it appeared a 'more realisable opportunity for economic recovery and social improvement than Labour's approach'.[94]

Finally there was the Govan by-election on 8 November with all its uncomfortable echoes of Hamilton in 1967, including an articulate female candidate with a Labour background. Labour's candidate was the sixty-one-year-old Harry Selby, a local barber and veteran chairman of a 'very small' local party. 'No wonder it was such a small CLP', mused Jimmy Allison, for 'Harry was a devout socialist who did not allow people into the party unless they were familiar with Marx and Engels'.[95] Karl and Frederick could not save Selby, and Margo MacDonald took the seat by 571 votes on a remarkable 31.2 per cent swing. Although she was not in Parliament long, the SNP had again come from nowhere to displace Labour in one of its heartlands.

'AN ASSEMBLY WITH ECONOMIC TEETH'

At the 'snap' general election on 28 February 1974, Labour gained a few more seats than the Conservatives in a hung Parliament. In Scotland, the party lost four seats while the SNP gained six on a remarkable 22 per cent vote share. Labour's Scottish Council had produced no distinctly Scottish campaign literature, too preoccupied with the upcoming (and first reformed) local government elections to focus adequately on the House of Commons.[96]

A week after the election Labour's Scottish executive endorsed a devolution statement drafted by John Pollock, Donald Dewar, Bruce Millan and Willie Ross, who was once again Scottish Secretary. This said there was:

> a real need to ensure that decisions affecting Scotland are taken in Scotland wherever possible ... we believe this might best be done by the setting up of an elected Scottish Assembly ... [but] there can be no question of reducing the number of Scottish MPs or of abolishing the office of Secretary of State.

Two weeks later the Scottish Council's conference at Ayr accepted this statement and rejected all other pro- or anti-devolution resolutions.[97] Dewar said:

> I personally believe that we have made mistakes. I think we have been so keen to man the barricades that we have perhaps swept aside the possibility of constructive reform within the framework of the United Kingdom, and I believe that now is the time to put that right and to look at the possibilities.[98]

Despite this plea the debate that followed was 'bitter, bad-tempered and disfigured by personal attacks'.[99] Causing a stir was the distribution of a pamphlet by Jim Sillars, Harry Ewing, John Robertson and Alex Eadie (now energy minister) entitled *Scottish Labour and Devolution*,[100] which emphasised the need for an Assembly to possess significant economic powers. This, recalled Sillars, 'had a good reception everywhere, except in the Labour Party'.[101]

Meanwhile the Bradford-born scholar Lord Crowther-Hunt had produced a consultative document which recommended legislative devolution, although it seems this progressed partly because Prime Minister Harold Wilson had failed to realise that the proposed Scottish Assembly and Executive would need 'something to do'.[102] When this paper was put to the Scottish Council executive at Keir Hardie House (recently purchased by the Labour Party Properties Company[103]) on 23 June 1974, another chaotic series of events unfolded.

In Tam Dalyell's second-hand account (he did not join the executive until the following month), Willie Ross was 'very properly' in Frankfurt for a football match (Scotland v. Yugoslavia) and as others were keen to watch the game, only eleven of twenty-nine executive members were present. As Dalyell recounted:

> When the vote was taken, all eyes turned to the one member of the Scottish Executive not to have spoken, the petite and comely Mrs Sadie Hutton of Glasgow, who had drifted in after doing her morning's shopping. Loyal to her Chairman, and resentful of the pressure that was being put on him from Transport House, she raised her hand. Thus are momentous decisions actually made! So, by six votes to five, the Scottish Executive of the Labour Party reaffirmed their policy that an Assembly was 'irrelevant to the real needs of the people of Scotland'.[104]

Newspaper reports provided a full break down. Those in favour of devolution were Tom Fulton, Donald Dewar, Hugh Brown, George Robertson and Frank Gormill, while those against were Sadie Hutton, David Davidson, Jean McVey, Geoff Shaw, Allan McLean and Peter Talbot.[105]

Even had there been a fuller attendance, Dalyell judged this to have reflected the majority view of the executive. *The Times* concurred and quoted Thomas Fulton, chairman of the executive's devolution subcommittee, who admitted that as a matter of political expediency it might have been easier to have supported an Assembly but 'one has to be more fundamental and truthful'. Allan McLean, the party's leading anti-devolutionist, said it would have been 'absurd' to interpose another layer of government between the new regional and district authorities and Westminster.[106] 'Six silly men', screamed the Labour-supporting *Daily Record*, forgetting that Sadie Hutton had been among them.

A few days later British Labour's National Executive Committee met at Transport House, where the Scottish executive's decision was lambasted by Alex Kitson of the Transport and General Workers' Union and South Lanark MP Judith Hart. Harold Wilson later called Kitson the man who 'turned the tide of history' by proposing the NEC 'should support Scottish devolution', a motion which was carried.[107] Confronted with a demand for a recall conference, a meeting of the Scottish executive on 6 July could hardly refuse. Although initially Dalyell and McLean and other anti-Assembly members were confident of persuading conference to uphold the executive's original decision, Alex Kitson energetically lobbied major trade unions, which given the drift of STUC thinking since 1967 was not difficult.[108] *The Times* characterised the split as follows:

> there remain fears that an assembly might provoke even greater support for the Scottish National Party, with the added threat that a Scottish assembly would be set up at the expense of Scottish seats in the Commons. In that case the Labour Party in Scotland would be likely to lose more than its opponents, but the pro-devolutionists in the party find that less daunting than the possible result of ignoring clear popular opinion and entering the new shape of Scottish politics with apparent reluctance.[109]

Meanwhile a Cabinet committee on devolution was increasingly 'frightened' at the direction of travel. Willie Ross launched what the adviser Bernard Donoughue called a 'savage attack' on Crowther-Hunt, saying they had no choice but to back legislative devolution as the 'pass has already been sold by the NEC'. Only the Secretary of State for Wales supported the scheme, with Roy Jenkins, Tony Crosland and Denis Healey arguing that the government 'should announce the minimum and deal with it after the general election'.[110] Barbara Castle recalled Ross remarking that 'we ought not to have gone so far ... but having started the whole [Kilbrandon] enquiry, we had aroused expectations we could not resist'.[111]

The recall conference took place at Glasgow's Dalintober Street on 17 August 1974.[112] Allan McLean stressed the potential for 'scapegoat politics', with all Scotland's ills being 'blamed on the lack of power vested in an Edinburgh Assembly and their subservience to Westminster'; Jim Sillars now spoke eloquently in favour of devolution; Brian Wilson, editor of the radical *West Highland Free Press* and Labour's candidate in Ross and Cromarty 'just thought the party should square up to the challenge of the SNP and not run away, instead of sheltering under the umbrella of a Scottish Assembly'. Wilson added that it would lead to the 'destruction of the Labour Movement'. Devolution, as John Burns of the West Lothian CLP 'acidly' remarked to Tam Dalyell, was 'little more than a political life jacket – and a life jacket, what's more, that will not inflate at the right time'.[113]

Eventually, conference resolved by an overwhelming majority that:

> recognising the desire of the Scottish people for a greater say in the running of their own affairs calls for the setting up of a directly elected Assembly with legislative powers within the context of the political and economic unity of the UK.

This, as *The Times* observed, avoided 'an embarrassing clash between the Labour Government and the party in Scotland'.[114] Although a Scottish Assembly was not yet viewed as intrinsically desirable, there were principled devolutionists in the Scottish Labour ranks. John P. Mackintosh suggested the 'one thing' that would 'spike' the SNP's guns was:

> a Scottish Parliament which would really excite the Scottish people, which would unleash their constructive energies and absorb their attention. This is the choice facing the Labour Government when it brings in its Devolution Bill this winter. Will it rise to the occasion and produce a piece of constructive statemanship or will it fail and allow power in Scotland (and in the UK in consequence) slip from its hands because of a mixture of timidity, of failure to realise the seriousness of the situation and of the old imperial belief that any decisions made outside London must be inferior decisions?[115]

Scotsman polling in May and September confirmed that devolution was a popular policy even if it was seldom mentioned as a priority. On this basis, Labour geared up for an aggressive campaign at the second general election of 1974. The party in Scotland produced its own manifesto for the first time,[116] largely the work of Bruce Millan and the party's new research officer Alex Neil, and in which Willie Ross claimed it was from Scotland that 'the men and the ideas came that created the great Labour Party of today'. Meanwhile a publication entitled *Labour News* and a televised broadcast on 7 October went beyond the text of the manifesto. The former promised 'an Assembly with economic teeth' while the broadcast, a discussion between Jim Sillars, Helen Liddell and George Foulkes chaired by John P. Mackintosh, referred several times to a 'Scottish Parliament', which Liddell categorically stated would have control of the planned Scottish Development Agency.[117]

On 10 October the Labour vote held up in Scotland and the party even gained a seat, although the SNP emerged with a total of eleven MPs and 30.4 per cent of the vote. British Labour's vote was 40.1 per cent against Scottish Labour's 36.3 per cent. Holding on with a much-reduced majority in Stirling, Falkirk and Grangemouth was the former postman Harry Ewing, who was appointed to the Scottish Office with responsibility for devolution and home affairs, a position he was to hold until 1979. Willie Ross's authority was diminishing, for Ewing was appointed against his wishes, as was Frank McElhone (a Catholic) the following year, apparently to counter the impression that St Andrew's House was the political wing of the Church of Scotland.[118] McElhone was one of only eight Catholic Labour MPs in Scotland elected between 1945 and 1970, but all voting surveys confirmed the importance of Catholic electors to the Scottish party.[119] The continued existence of segregated Catholic state schools, however, found the party 'torn between an ideological commitment to comprehensive education and a practical need not to shake the very bedrock of its electoral support', i.e. the Roman Catholic Church in Scotland.[120]

Harry Ewing later admitted that for all Willie Ross's undoubted abilities he had made the mistake of outstaying his welcome, his twenty years' 'unquestioned dominance' of the party in Scotland having given rise to an unhealthy 'personality cult'.[121] While Bernard Donoughue admired Ross for being 'totally uninterested in anything except Scotland's interests' ('Nothing phoney about him ... Straight out of the 19th-century manse'), by late 1974 the Scottish Secretary had developed the same characteristics Donoughue had seen in 'so many politicians as they get older: vanity, talking endlessly, never listening to anybody else, in fact never really noticing who they are taking to'.[122]

By March 1975, with a referendum on continuing membership of the Common Market looming, Donoughue believed Ross's opposition (although the Cabinet was free to campaign either way) 'may finish him as Scottish Secretary'. Even Harold Wilson agreed that Ross was 'very vulnerable'.[123] The Scottish Secretary voiced his dissent in television interviews and even tried to disrupt the referendum date by claiming Scottish local authorities would not be ready in time, partly motivated by a desire to outflank the anti-EEC SNP. At the March 1975 Scottish Council conference delegates ignored the Prime Minister's call to enter the referendum campaign in an 'adult, mature, comradely and friendly spirit' and Janey Buchan (ironically a future MEP) launched a bitter attack on the pro-EEC MP John P. Mackintosh.[124] Although Scotland proved less enthusiastically European than England and Wales, most voters ultimately disagreed with conference's rejection of continuing membership.[125]

With the Cabinet having resolved to 'go-slow' on devolution during an all-day meeting at Chequers earlier that year, Ross at least had space to address some pressing industrial and economic concerns. In January 1975 the Scottish Secretary had insisted on more money for what would become the interventionist Scottish Development Agency (SDA). The brainchild of Bruce Millan, now Minister of State at the Scottish Office, by the end of the decade the SDA had kickstarted what would later be known as 'urban regeneration'. Towards the end of 1975, Ross fought just as hard to save the Chrysler factory at Linwood, even threatening resignation. Wilson wanted closure without losing any ministers, although Bernard Donoughue feared another Upper Clyde Shipbuilders, i.e. 'a government rescue of hundreds of millions which staves off inevitable closure for a few years'.[126] Phillips et al. have suggested all this contributed to an uptick in the Scottish Labour vote during the late 1970s, in sharp contrast to the party's decline in England.[127] A subsequent Scottish Council publication on industrial strategy called for 'a strong Scottish voice in the formation of policy' once the Scottish Assembly was up and running.[128]

In other respects, Ross's social conservatism was undimmed. He was 'totally opposed' to a Downing Street Policy Unit paper on council house sales in March 1976, something eventually taken forward by the Conservatives. The Prime Minister thought it a good illustration of why 'old men should retire': 'They made up their minds in 1965 and they have been closed to new ideas ever since.'[129] When it came to Scottish candidate selection, however, the trade union and local government strand declined appreciably, while the typical MPs elected for the first time during the 1970s were more middle class, lawyers, teachers and lecturers rather than those with shop-floor experience.[130]

Although he would not be elected until 1983, emblematic was Gordon Brown, a Labour member since 1969, a son of the manse and high-profile student rector of Edinburgh University. McInnes has argued that Brown acted as 'a bridge' between the pro-devolution trade union movement in Scotland and a Labour Party in Scotland still learning to live with new constitutional realities.[131] According to Henry Drucker, with whom Brown would later write a book, all the 'older people' in the Scottish party 'just couldn't stand him. He was too fast for them, too clever, too popular, too good with the press'.[132] Brown was nevertheless elected to the Scottish party executive in 1976 aged just twenty-six, and Keir Hardie House also modernised: in 1975 a network of sub-committees and research groups was established, with policy seminars, day schools for key organisers and detailed guides for branch officials following in 1977.[133]

The Red Paper on Scotland, edited by Brown in 1975, sought to 'adapt socialist views to the Scottish national framework'.[134] Other contributors (there was not a single woman) included Robin Cook, Tom Nairn, Jim Sillars and 'Vincent' Cable, until recently a Labour councillor, an ecumenical approach which did not necessarily endear Brown to his party colleagues. He later reflected on a 'divisive' debate at the 1976 Scottish Labour conference: 'A large number of Labour leaders whom I respected saw devolution as a diversion from the effort to secure a Labour government in the UK. In response, I argued that a commitment to devolution was rooted in Labour's ideals.'[135]

'DEVOLUTION NOT SEPARATION'

Now that the Labour Party in Scotland and London had resolved its differences as to the principle of devolution, the process of actually legislating for a Scottish Assembly took almost three years – from November 1975 to July 1978 – involving two separate bills and ongoing intra-party debates as to the precise shape of the devolution settlement. In February 1975 Harry Ewing went out on a limb by claiming everything was 'bang on target' for a 142-member Assembly in Edinburgh from which would be drawn a ministerial Scottish executive. He even said the Assembly could be elected as soon as late 1976 or early 1977. This alarmed the Cabinet's go-slow contingent as well as what *The Economist* called the 'political dinosaurs who run Labour's Scottish fiefdom'.[136]

At the Scottish Council conference in Aberdeen the following month, most trade unions backed an Assembly with revenue-raising powers, but delegates instead endorsed an executive motion denying it any economic, trade or industry levers. Willie Ross sat 'granite-faced in the granite city' as Harold Wilson appeared to accept that this would influence the contents of a devolution bill due later that year.[137] Robert Maclennan and other Scottish Labour MPs told Bernard Donoughue they thought Labour in Scotland was 'behaving suicidally and giving the Scot Nats seats on a plate'.[138] Internal party research concluded that the SNP had a 'firm grip' on Scottish voters aged under forty – a growing trend since the late 1960s – and that west coast Labour strongholds constituted that party's 'soft underbelly'.[139] Sure enough, in the first test of public opinion since the October 1974 election, the SNP's Stephen Maxwell took the Slateford Hailes ward on the new Lothian Regional Council with a majority of 759. Labour was pushed into third place.[140]

In an unusually well attended election for chair of the Scottish Labour MP group, the Tribunite Norman Buchan (West Renfrewshire), who had taken a strong line against 'separatism', stood against the more centre-right Dr Dickson Mabon (Greenock and Port Glasgow), who had not been so outspoken. Mabon won by twenty-six votes to fifteen, while James McCrandle, acting Scottish secretary, said in a statement that only one organisation spoke for the Labour Party in Scotland, a remark directed at Buchan's recent call in *The Times* for a referendum on independence.[141]

Labour's long-awaited proposals, *Our Changing Democracy: Devolution to Scotland and Wales*, finally appeared on 27 November 1975. At the press launch, Willie Ross almost sounded enthusiastic:

> I believe Scotland is best placed to lead the way in a new style of Government. It has a strong sense of its own identity; an established administration in Edinburgh; a separate system of education, local government and above all of law. And indeed already in Westminster we have a distinctive way of handling Scottish legislation. The difference devolution will make will depend on the Assembly and on the Executive.

The 'whole point' of devolution, added the Scottish Secretary with all the zeal of a convert, was 'to enable people to be different'.[142] The White Paper committed the government to a Scottish Assembly with 142 members but excluded the Scottish

Development Agency from its remit.[143] This fudge pleased no one, neither going far enough for supporters of devolution nor appeasing English fears regarding a 'slippery slope'.[144] Just days later Labour suffered two more defeats in regional council by-elections: in the coal town of Bo'ness the SNP polled 48.5 per cent, while in the middle-class Glaswegian suburb of Bishopbriggs it managed 42 per cent. Labour again came third in both wards.[145]

The White Paper proved the final straw for Jim Sillars, who believed Labour had reneged on repeated commitments to grant the Assembly economic teeth. When the Scottish Labour MP group backed the White Paper by a 'crushing majority' on 10 December 1975, he quit both the group and the Scottish Council executive.[146] Alex Neil also resigned as research officer at Keir Hardie House, branding *Our Changing Democracy* 'a sell-out and insult to the intelligence of every Scotsman'.[147] Together they established the breakaway 'Scottish Labour Party' (SLP), which consciously evoked Keir Hardie's party of the same name. As Maria Fyfe later reflected, although no one sympathetic to Sillars supported full independence, 'some of us had begun to think that our people would be better served by a sister party operating in Scotland', just as the Social Democratic and Labour Party did in Northern Ireland.[148]

The split, although modest, had a demoralising impact on Labour in Scotland, not least because Sillars and Neil were not 'mad extremists but young moderates', not to mention two of the party's most effective propagandists.[149] Neil later referred to support for Labour 'just melting away',[150] and indeed that is how it must have felt, particularly when the Paisley MP John Robertson and Scottish executive member Danus Skene also defected. The Scottish Labour Party's inaugural meeting at Glasgow's Grosvenor Hotel on 18 January 1976 was attended by around 400 people, including John McAllion, Maria Fyfe and Sheila Gilmore, all future Scottish Labour MPs, as well as writers and journalists such Neal Ascherson (who tipped Sillars as 'a future Prime Minister of Scotland'[151]), George Kerevan, Tom Nairn, Bob Brown of *The Times* (the SLP's first chair) and Ruth Wishart.[152] What it lacked, recalled Maria Fyfe, was 'skilled and unskilled workers'.[153] The 'greatest fear' as *The Times* put it, was that the SLP could 'dangerously split the Labour vote in Scotland, where thirty-five Labour MPs have nationalists immediately behind them'.[154] 'We are', declared Sillars, 'Scottish with a capital S and Socialist with a capital S.'[155]

At around the same time, Labour launched a campaign – 'Devolution not Separation' – which was intended to shore up support for *Our Changing Democracy*.[156] 'If you do not agree with this White Paper', declared the Scottish Secretary dramatically, 'you can say goodbye to the Labour Party in Scotland and probably Willie Ross as well', an allusion to an SNP advance so great that it would include his Kilmarnock constituency.[157] Although Ross was not among them, every other Scottish Office minister subsequently took part in an unprecedented push to prevent the Calderwood–St Leonard's ward on Strathclyde Regional Council falling to the SNP in another by-election. Despite what *The Economist* called 'a first-class candidate and a sound local organisation', the SNP once again 'contemptuously swept Labour aside' in what ought to have been a safe seat. Just days earlier a Nationalist had also come within forty-five votes of winning a district by-election in Cumnock, Keir Hardie's hometown.[158]

To make matters worse, on 3 February 1976 the government's Commons majority disappeared when the Scottish party executive ruled that no members of the Scottish Labour Party were to be permitted dual membership. Sillars and Robertson were therefore expelled along with dozens of other Labour members, although Sillars said he would retain the Labour whip until the Parliamentary Labour Party ruled otherwise.[159] 'Is the Labour Party in Scotland on the point of collapse?', asked *The Times*,[160] while System Three polling suggested the SLP could attract a quarter of Labour's already faltering support.[161]

The Scottish party's propaganda machine, meanwhile, went into overdrive. In January 1976 the Scottish Council published *Labour's Analysis of the Economics of Separation*, which despite the title was intended as 'an economic analysis rather than a political act against the Scottish National Party'.[162] Its main charge was that the economic case advanced by 'the separatists' was 'ill-thought out, lacking in substance and understanding, and based more on the emotional rhetoric that oil revenues alone can bring success'. Also targeted were sins of omission:

> the separatists have said virtually nothing about questions that we as socialists regard as important – namely the effect of independence

upon the distribution of income and wealth; and about the policies, if any, that they have for altering the whole basis of society towards a more just and equitable system ... the Labour Party rather than the SNP has attitudes and policies towards such issues ... which are in keeping with the political and economic realities of modern Scotland.[163]

A second publication, *Can Scotland Go it Alone? The Menace of Separation: A Labour Party Analysis*, attempted to separate economic facts from nationalist myths, mainly as regards North Sea oil,[164] while predicting more division:

> Scotland has voted Labour since the war and there is no doubt that the Scottish people want socialist policies. We can therefore see a major clash between the economic policies of the nationalists and the social priorities of the Scottish people if independence were ever to become a reality ... The Labour Party is proud to defend, an economically integrated, politically devolved United Kingdom in which Scotland's role is one of willing partner.[165]

At the Scottish Council conference in Troon, delegates did their best to appear unified on constitutional policy, endorsing the White Paper but demanding the Secretary of State's 'veto' powers be abolished, tax-raising powers investigated, control of universities and industrial assistance transferred to the Assembly and a Stormont-style 'block grant'. Invited to Troon by pro-devolutionists, the vehemently anti-devolution Liverpool MP Eric Heffer accepted there was no choice but to 'carry it through with the minimum of damage', although he demanded that voters in 'the three countries' of the UK be simultaneously (but separately) consulted in referenda.[166] 'What I got from this conference', Heffer told a packed fringe meeting, 'is that none of you is really happy about devolution. You're going to accept it because you've got to.'[167]

There had been rumours that Willie Ross was about to resign as Secretary of State, but in the event, he demitted office shortly after James Callaghan succeeded Harold Wilson as Labour leader and premier in April 1976. A towering presence since the early 1960s, by the mid-1970s Ross had come to be viewed as increasingly out of kilter with the pro-Common Market, pro-devolution era. 'Held responsible for every disappointment', Donald Dewar had observed in 1970, 'Secretaries of State are remembered only for their failures.'[168] Only Tom Johnston had left office with an enhanced reputation, though of course he had operated during a wartime truce. Ross himself later reflected on a 'tough' job made all the tougher by Scots' 'Archangelic' expectations:

> For the Scot it is the top job; any other job would be dull indeed after the hectic, crisis-ridden life as Scotland's Secretary of State. The post has changed beyond all recognition since 1885. The Secretary of State now has a new St. Andrew's House in Edinburgh. His Cabinet status is assured. But has his office a future? Devolution within the United Kingdom is the next logical step. But Scotland's voice will still be needed in the Cabinet of the U.K. government and further afield in Europe.[169]

Ross's successor was the Govan MP Bruce Millan, his deputy since 1974 and long tipped as a future Scottish Secretary. Having campaigned for Callaghan during the recent leadership election, the 'engaging but politically wayward' Dick Mabon had hoped to join the Cabinet, but Ross had threatened to 'raise the roof'.[170] An accountant by background, Millan brought a calmer, more methodical and collegiate style to a ninety-year-old Scottish Office which at that point looked to be on the wane. For John P. Mackintosh, Millan had been appointed 'with some reluctance' on account of all the other candidates having 'something against them'.[171] Leader of the House Michael Foot, meanwhile, took charge of the devolution legislation, assisted by John Smith, Minister of State at the Privy Council Office.

In August 1976 the new Prime Minister visited the former Royal High School in Edinburgh, which had been earmarked to accommodate the Scottish Assembly. Press speculation had prematurely turned to the likely identity of 'Scotland's first prime minister',[172] with the Glasgow *Evening Times* putting its money on Geoff Shaw, the forty-seven-year-old clergyman and convener of Strathclyde Regional Council, despite the fact he had been among those to reject devolution in the summer of 1974. From a professional Edinburgh middle class background, the 'foundation' of Shaw's social and political views had been the Gorbals Group initiative, the object of which was to 'live among the people with whom it was concerned'.[173] Shaw's name was also among those tipped for the first Scottish Cabinet by the *Glasgow Herald* in February 1978, alongside John

P. Mackintosh, Gordon Brown, Jimmy Reid, George Robertson, Donald Dewar and George Foulkes.[174]

The government, however, had to consider a more immediate political challenge – carrying the Scotland and Wales Bill in both Houses of Parliament. 'Some still have to be won', noted *The Times* of English Labour MPs, 'and they will be more difficult to win if the legislation contains anything which appears to put Scotland at a material advantage over English regions.'[175] At the British Labour conference in September 1976, delegates backed devolution by a majority of six to one, but only after Michael Foot conceded a post-legislative referendum, a device he had hitherto rejected.

Aided by this concession, the now minority Labour government had a majority of forty-five when the Scotland and Wales Bill passed its second reading on 16 December 1976.[176] Ten Labour rebels voted with the Conservatives[177] but only West Lothian's Tam Dalyell, now chairman of the Scottish Labour MP group and the emerging focal point for anti-Assemblyites, represented a Scottish constituency. Another thirty Members, almost all of them English, abstained. The referendum requirement, meanwhile, was inserted via a well-supported amendment in the name of Welsh Labour MP Leo Abse.

After much 'hesitation, arm-twisting, and head-counting', the government finally risked a guillotine motion on 22 February 1977. Humiliatingly for Callaghan, Millan et al., this was defeated by Labour votes. A now retired Willie Ross told the Scottish Council conference he was 'outraged to see how people went back on a manifesto commitment', but as Miller correctly judged, the government had also 'lacked the nerve to make devolution an issue of confidence'.[178] A subsequent opinion poll suggested that in a snap election seventeen Scottish Labour MPs would lose their seats, including Tam Dalyell. A fifth of those who had voted Labour in October 1974 now intended to vote SNP; 64 per cent supported an immediate referendum on devolution while support for independence had risen to 31 per cent.[179]

'LABOUR'S ORGANISATION IS CRUMBLING'

The academic David Heald was not alone in believing that Labour in Scotland did not have the 'professional organisation, research capacity, membership or propaganda machine to fight off the Nationalist challenge'. He said:

> what must also be accepted is that the Party in Scotland ... must put its own house in order. It should look at the quality of its elected representatives, the moribund state of many constituencies and branches and its failure to generate the funds necessary to run a political party outside elections without relying on Transport House for funds it does not have.[180]

In 1975 Transport House had found that in Glasgow, a city with thirteen Labour MPs, most CLPs had fewer than 100 members.[181] To Neil Williamson, local parties in Dundee, Lanarkshire and Glasgow were 'notorious for their inefficient corruption'. In April 1977 the Gorbals councillor Catherine Cantley was forced to resign following allegations of favouritism in housing allocation, 'epitomising a generation of local government complacency by Labour politicians'.[182] Just weeks later, the Glasgow District Labour Party suggested that Keir Hardie House might take over the party, a potential 'burden' rejected through fear of being 'obliged' to do the same for every failing local organisation.[183]

On top of an affiliation fee paid to British Labour, Scottish CLPs and allied trade unions also paid a small affiliation fee to the Scottish Council. In 1977 this amounted to just £4,222.67.[184] All the Scottish Council's full-time political officials, meanwhile, continued to be paid for and therefore chosen by Transport House. By the late 1970s there were just five full-time paid constituency agents, fewer than the Scottish Conservative Party. The Scottish party executive was elected by CLPs and affiliated trade unions at the party's annual conference every March. Conference debated and voted on any subject for which there was a resolution. But given only it could mobilise support from major trade unions, the executive could usually control the debate.[185]

Rumblings about the party's lack of autonomy in Scotland had resurfaced upon publication of the devolution White Paper back in November 1975. As *The Economist* observed, Westminster politicians could not 'convincingly argue that they favour devolution of powers to a Scottish Assembly, while denying a measure of home rule for their own party organisation'.[186] In a 1976 Young Fabians pamphlet, David Heald said the time had come:

for the Scottish and Welsh Councils of the Labour Party to be transformed into autonomous, self governing bodies affiliated to the British Labour Party in parallel to the existing arrangements of the Conservatives and Liberals ... Labour's future in Scotland and Wales depends on it translating its majorities from paper ones which might go with the wind into a vibrant political movement.[187]

Imminent devolution made some reforms along those lines inevitable. Until 1977, the Scottish party secretary had been the pivotal link with Transport House in London, but early that year the role was split in two. Jimmy Allison, a 'small wiry man with a sharp mind and sharper tongue',[188] was appointed Scottish organiser while Helen Liddell, BBC Scotland's former economics correspondent, became secretary. The latter appointment was met with 'a degree of hostility' from several members of the Scottish executive.[189] Not only was Liddell a woman, 'a rare creature among the Labour hierarchy', but she was young (in her mid-twenties), from a working-class background and a university graduate.[190]

Liddell, however, proved an immediate success. Indeed, by May, Bernard Donoughue wished 'she was in Ron Hayward's place running the whole Party'.[191] Conscious of tensions within the Labour movement, Liddell worked hard to forge the 'closest possible relationship' between her and the Scottish Labour MP group at Westminster, while she also wanted to see an 'improved relationship' between MPs and the Scottish executive.[192] Within a few weeks she was reporting 'increased warmth' from the MP group and increasing 'goodwill' from trade unions.[193] Liddell also attempted to thaw what she called a 'cold war' which had existed between Labour in Scotland and the STUC earlier that decade, something exacerbated by the General Council's occasional flirtations with the SNP.[194]

At its 1977 Perth conference, meanwhile, the Scottish Council adopted new rules which changed the nature of the party in Scotland. These:

> were riddled with references to the Assembly, Assemblymen, and the ALP [Assembly Labour Party] which was to be an Assembly version of the PLP. Throughout, Assemblymen generally had the same rights and duties as MPs. The Scottish executive and the ALP were given the right to draw up the Assembly manifesto and validate candidates and the Scottish conference would decide the party programme. The British NEC retained no more than the formal

right to be consulted. Like the proposals for the nation itself these changes conceded devolution within the party – not federalism or independence – on devolved subjects.[195]

Although the failure of the Scotland and Wales Bill had not produced the anticipated backlash, Willie Ross reminded delegates that devolution had been Labour policy since 1945 (this, observed the journalist Hugo Young, 'rewrote autobiography with a passion that would make even a member of the politburo blush'). With the onward march of the SNP everywhere apparent, conference also voted for a referendum at the earliest opportunity to enable the people of Scotland to choose between devolution, 'separation' and the status quo.

The Times took this as the mark of a party both 'baffled and bewildered', not only by its declining support but the new Lib–Lab 'pact' and ongoing cuts to public spending. The newspaper's correspondent ended with a gloomy prediction:

> Labour's organization is crumbling. Its appeal rests upon habit, its strength upon the continued loyalty of the established trade union movement. That may be enough to save it, if not from the humiliation expected at the Scottish district elections in May, at any rate from too severe a fate in the general election. But it could hardly be more vulnerable. The radical tradition in west central Scotland is the politics of people looking for a sign of hope to relieve their dreary living conditions. The Labour Party in Scotland is not much of a symbol.[196]

DISTRICT COUNCIL ELECTIONS

The thirty-four Scottish district council elections certainly represented a daunting challenge. The SNP was gearing up to fight more than 350 wards in Scotland's central belt, the 'soft underbelly' previously identified by pollsters. Despite an energetic push by the SNP in 1974, Labour had retained a firm grip, but now only a moderate shift in votes risked losing it dozens of council seats.[197] There was also the Scottish Labour Party to contend with. Even after its first conference in Stirling had been infiltrated by members of the International Marxist Group suspected by Jim Sillars of being 'useful idiots for MI5 and Special Branch',[198] the party's intervention in a by-election to Strathclyde Regional Council at the end of October 1976 had helped lose Labour another councillor to the SNP.

On polling day Labour experienced a net loss of 130 councillors and the SNP a net gain of 100. Among the casualties was Henry McLeish in Kirkcaldy, his only ever election defeat, and one that still rankled a quarter of a century later.[199] Labour's losses were not necessarily due to peculiarly Scottish factors, being proportionately no greater than those which followed in English elections.[200] But then there were more choices in Scotland. Between 1974 and 1977, Bochel and Denver calculated a swing of 4 per cent from Labour to the Conservatives and 10 per cent from Labour to the SNP.[201] Sillars's breakaway party won a modest three councillors.

Labour's most dramatic losses came in Glasgow district, where sixteen of the seats won in 1974 fell to the SNP and eight to the Conservatives.[202] There followed a clash between the Labour group, which was determined to take control even if it meant an informal pact with the SNP or Conservatives, and Helen Liddell, who had come to the firm 'conclusion that the greatest political advantage to the Party in Scotland would be to push the Tories and the Scottish Nationalist Party into alliance'. After a 'harrowing' three-hour meeting, only Strathclyde Labour leader Dick Stewart's 'very impressive statement' about the dangers of 'coalition and the problems it could cause an administration' decided the matter and the Labour group merely opted to nominate one of their number as provost.[203] The Conservatives duly formed a minority administration.

By the spring of 1977, Labour in Scotland expected to lose up to fifteen seats to the SNP at the next general election, and Liddell stressed to Transport House the necessity for heightened 'activity in Scotland, in particular from Government Ministers, but especially from members of the Cabinet'.[204] There were some glimmers of political hope. In September, a 'disenchanted' Sir Hugh Fraser (the owner of Harrods) expressed a desire to leave the SNP and join Labour. 'Although his money would be very attractive', Liddell remarked, 'his recent bad publicity connected with gambling debts could rub off on the party'.[205]

'HAMMERING THE NATS'

Meanwhile, a battle was raging for political ownership of devolution. Addressing an SNP study group in the wake of February's failed guillotine motion, John P. Mackintosh had annoyed his party by declaring that if Scots wanted devolution, then the 'only hope of getting it was to vote SNP'.[206] In the wake of May's district elections, Labour's Scottish executive lobbied Michael Foot for two bills – one each for Scotland and Wales – and again insisted on a referendum. While David Steel's Liberals made certain demands of the standalone Scotland Bill, Helen Liddell was clear that Labour 'must get the credit for delivering devolution', while in a September 1978 broadcast, Harry Ewing declared that history would 'record the fact that it was Labour who gave the Scottish people a better system of government'.[207]

Nineteen-seventy-eight brought several electoral tests of which party was winning that narrative battle. On 28 April 1978 Geoff Shaw, the convener of Strathclyde Regional Council, died suddenly, as did the Berwick and East Lothian MP John P. Mackintosh on 30 July, both of whom 'could have led the Scottish Assembly with distinction'.[208] Out of Parliament since June 1970, Donald Dewar been selected to fight the Garscadden by-election which followed the death of Willie Small in January 1978. At the Scottish Council's conference in March, Dewar attacked the SNP's attempt to foster a 'girning, whining spirit', adding that Scottish Labour was engaged in a contest for the soul of Scotland.[209]

Strategically, devolution and 'hammering the Nats' had been allied with the economy, something boosted by the government's temporary subsidy for shipbuilding.[210] Chairing the Dunoon conference was the thirty-year-old George Robertson, the Scottish Council's youngest ever chair. His keynote speech boldly attacked nationalisation ('no answer to the arbitrary power of wealth and control') while accusing the SNP of peddling an:

> intoxicating mixture of emotion, seventeenth century chauvinism and cynical self interest to an electorate confused by the failure of the traditional remedies to the lack of jobs, rising prices, urban squalor, slums and insecurity – not one of which is unique to Scotland. They feed on protest, spawning more and more promises of relief, more and more offers of salvation, all to be paid for from the temporary riches of the North Sea.[211]

The Garscadden by-election, meanwhile, had become dominated by a bitter offensive from the Society for the Protection of Unborn Children in a constituency with a substantial Catholic electorate.

Dewar had supported David Steel's Abortion Act 1967, while his by-election opponents, the Conservative Iain Lawson and the SNP's Keith Bovey, remained opposed.[212] There had also been controversy as to whether the issue would be devolved, and Scottish Labour was sufficiently nervous to put 'the record straight' in one of Dewar's campaign news-sheets produced by journalist Julia Langdon and research officer Alf Young, who had succeeded Alex Neil in 1976. This quoted Lord McCluskey (Solicitor General for Scotland) and three Scottish Labour MPs as being content that Dewar was 'a firm opponent of abortion on demand' and thus there 'need be no conflict of conscience for Roman Catholics who wish to vote for Mr Dewar'.[213]

On 13 April 1978 Labour held Garscadden with a substantial majority of 4,552, despite a modest swing to the SNP. Jim Sillars's Scottish Labour Party only managed 583 votes, not many more than the Communist candidate. Party officials grabbed a jubilant Dewar and pushed him outside the count venue with a glass of champagne in hand. 'Those people who said that Labour was dead or dying in west central Scotland haven't been near Garscadden in the last four or five weeks', he declared. 'We have taken the attack to the enemy and we have beaten them out of sight.' The result, Dewar added, 'changes the whole psychological mood of Scottish politics'.[214] The SNP, observed Helen Liddell in her post-mortem, were 'totally demoralised' and 'much less experienced at coping with defeat than we are'. Yet she cautioned Transport House against the assumption 'that our problems in Scotland are all over':

> In Garscadden we were helped by the Budget, by having a good candidate in the face of a totally incompetent S.N.P. opponent, by a sympathetic press, a phenomenon I still don't understand, and by an SNP machine that was less than perfect.[215]

Nevertheless, Garscadden confirmed that Labour's new approach actually worked: taking the fight to the SNP and highlighting what the party believed was its most vulnerable point – the aim of full independence. Even more importantly, the result was no flash in the pan. At regional elections a few weeks later, Labour retained a firm grip on the mighty Strathclyde, the most populous of Scotland's twelve regional and island authorities, and won control of Lothian, the second largest, where the SNP's vice-chairman Stephen Maxwell lost the seat he had gained from

Labour in 1975. Bochel and Denver believed this reflected a general recovery in Labour's position since mid-1977. Given that SNP support was boosted by disappointment with whomever was in government, it followed that when the incumbents were perceived to be doing reasonably well, SNP support would wane accordingly.[216]

Two more by-elections appeared to confirm this analysis. On 31 May 1978 George Robertson held Hamilton by 6,492 votes on a modest swing from the SNP, whose candidate Margo MacDonald failed to repeat her success in Govan five years earlier. 'The main issue will be the endorsement or rejection of the nationalists' policies of separatism', Robertson had observed during the campaign. 'The nationalist tide started in Hamilton, and will end there.'[217] A System Three poll in September found support for Labour in Scotland at its highest level since the previous general election at 52 per cent, with the SNP on just 18 per cent, its lowest level since October 1974.[218]

Finally, at the Berwick and East Lothian by-election caused by the death of John P. Mackintosh, Labour's John Home Robertson held the seat while the SNP's Isobel Lindsay lost her deposit. Helen Liddell had despaired of the candidate ('never around when needed, and interfering when he should have been keeping out of things'), but rejoiced at the extent to which Labour's 'Scottish resurgence was a talking point for journalists and party members alike'.[219] By this point, James Callaghan had decided against an October general election (the *Daily Record* had loaned a journalist in anticipation[220]), although he could at least watch with satisfaction as the once potent threat posed by both the SNP and SLP dissipated. To others, the election of Dewar and Robertson signalled a rightward drift. 'If the last years have been disappointing for the revolutionaries', lamented Neil Williamson of the International Marxist Group, 'they have been a tragedy for the Labour left'.[221]

THE SCOTLAND BILL

On 3 November 1977, the Queen's Speech had confirmed that the government remained 'firmly committed to establishing directly elected assemblies for Scotland and Wales'. Two weeks later MPs debated the second reading of the Scotland Bill, during which Tam Dalyell's 'West Lothian Question' was articulated for the first time.²²² On Burns night 1978 (25 January), the Bill was considered in committee, which is when the trouble started. Eric Heffer (Liverpool Walton) cautioned against any advantage for Scotland at the expense of deprived areas in England, while the Dunfermline-born George Cunningham (Islington South and Finsbury) prepared the legislative coup de grace later christened the 'Cunningham amendment'.

The latter began with a paving amendment tabled by the Canadian-educated lawyer Bruce Douglas-Mann (Mitcham and Morden) to include a stipulation that any post-legislative referendum would require a 33 per cent threshold. When that succeeded, this became a requirement to repeal the legislation if fewer than two-fifths of the Scottish electorate supported a Scottish Assembly.²²³ Cunningham's move was backed by five Scottish Labour MPs, Dalyell, Robin Cook, William Hamilton, Robert Hughes and Peter Doig, 'a strange alliance of right and left'.²²⁴ Helen Liddell (unsuccessfully) lobbied John Smith to have this reversed at report stage. 'If we are not careful in Scotland', she warned, 'then we could end up with 8 S.N.P. representatives because they project themselves as being the only people to care about Scotland.'²²⁵

The government also intended to allow time for a debate on Norman Buchan's long-standing demand for a 'third' referendum question on independence, but in the face of opposition Foot was compelled to withdraw the planned guillotine. A few days later, a bad-tempered Prime Minister made clear his opposition when a Scottish Council delegation called on him at Number 10. Also pushing two questions was research officer Alf Young, who told Callaghan 'just how misguided his approach to the home rule issue had become',²²⁶ while Liddell fretted 'at the cavalier way the Government have changed the Preamble to the [referendum] question to exclude reference to the unity of the United Kingdom'.²²⁷

Perhaps the only pro-devolution Labour MP to emerge with any credit from this period was John Smith, who won:

> glowing compliments, not only from his supporters on devolution but from the Tory Front Bench, for his handling of the Bill. His grasp of the complex detail of the Bill never faltered, and he never failed to defend the right of the Scots to elect the kind of Assembly they wanted, with freedom to act over a wide range of issues within the framework of the UK.²²⁸

Most active in Commons debates, however, were Scottish Labour MPs either opposed to or at least suspicious of the proposed Assembly, particularly Robert Hughes (Aberdeen North) and Robin Cook (Edinburgh Central), although the latter was prepared to accept the Bill on the understanding he would later be free to campaign against it in the referendum. Supporting the government were an eclectic mix: the treacherous (in Labour's eyes) Jim Sillars, still leading what remained of the SLP, the former Conservative front bencher Alick Buchanan-Smith ('a brave heretic') and, as often as not, Norman Buchan, whose hoped-for referendum question on independence had finally been laid to rest.[229]

By March 1978 there remained 'unresolved differences' between Labour's Scottish Council and the government, largely concerning the mechanism by which the UK Parliament might 'override' executive or legislative acts emanating from Edinburgh. Scottish Labour MPs also believed the Scottish Development Agency ought to be 'wholly devolved' rather than awkwardly shared by the Secretary of State and Scottish Executive. Their submission to the government (published in March 1978) suggested transferring the Scottish Secretary's 'nursemaid' functions to an independent commission, legislative disputes to a judicial body and the vice-regal functions of the Secretary of State to appoint and dismiss ministers to an 'impartial' body of Scottish Privy Counsellors.[230]

Little of this made it into the final version of the Bill as it headed back to the Commons from the Lords, where Lord Wilson of Langside, a former Labour Lord Advocate, had made life as difficult as possible for his own government. Finally, the Scotland Act 1978 received Royal Assent on 31 July 1978, just a day after John P. Mackintosh, a consistent champion of devolution for the past 20 years, had died aged just forty-eight.

'A UNITED CAMPAIGN'

At a weekend conference in Kilmarnock the previous November, the Scottish party executive had agreed to fight the referendum with the STUC and Co-operative Party in Scotland in what it hoped would be 'a united campaign for the endorsement of the Bill'. Any party groupings seeking the opposite result would be given no official support or recognition. This 'no collaboration' policy was subsequently endorsed by the Scottish Council conference and communicated to all CLPs in a circular despatched the day after the launch of the 'Labour Movement Yes campaign' chaired by Gordon Brown. This protested that only Labour believed in devolution 'for its own sake' rather than as 'a short-cut' to separation or federalism:

> To share the campaign for a devolved Assembly with those whose declared objectives are so far from our own, would be to compromise totally our own case for devolution. Second, the achievement of an Assembly for Scotland will be ours and it would be wrong to allow our consistent opponents – including those who helped to destroy the last Bill – to claim credit for this constitutional advance ... To associate with the separatists would be to provide our opponents with a major propaganda weapon.

'The history of Labour's fight for devolution', added Helen Liddell in another attempt to rewrite history, 'both for Scotland and for people in general, precedes by a century the rise of the separatists'.[231] At a press conference, she even declared that Labour would not be 'soiling' its 'hands by joining any umbrella Yes group'.[232] Ignoring this instruction was Alex Kitson of the TGWU, a supporter of Liddell's appointment in 1977 and the driving force behind Labour's 1974 devolution U-turn, who joined the cross-party 'Yes for Scotland' campaign.[233]

A Scottish Council publication, *Labour's Scottish Assembly: Our Case*, also attempted to reconcile doctrine with ethos:

> There will be those who will argue that devolution is nothing to do with socialism – and should therefore be opposed. But devolution means more decisions will be made by the people's elected representatives and not by bureaucrats. Aneurin Bevan said that Labour's job was to take power – from private unaccountable groups in our society – to give it away. Devolution is a means of doing precisely this.[234]

Female activists, meanwhile, claimed devolution would provide an 'opportunity to improve the lives of women in Scotland', even while acknowledging the Assembly would lack crucial powers necessary to eliminate sexual discrimination.[235] The Scottish executive's women's section had recently been abolished on the basis that equal pay and sex discrimination legislation had 'brought about sexual equality'.[236]

The Labour Vote No campaign (LVN) had launched in January 1978 and centred on Tam Dalyell. LVN's goal was to make clear that an 'authentic' section of Labour in Scotland believed devolution would lead to 'separation', hence what Miller called an 'audacious and successful bid to associate the Labour name with an anti-Labour policy'.[237] LVN was chaired by Brian Wilson and supported by six of Labour's thirty-nine Scottish MPs, including Robin Cook.[238] As Midwinter et al. later observed, the fact they did not later suffer 'a political penalty for their defiance of party policy' spoke volumes about the party's attitude to devolution.[239]

The referendum date – 1 March 1979 – was announced in the 1978 Queen's Speech. Labour's NEC granted the Scottish Council £50,000 to cover both the referendum campaign and subsequent Assembly elections, but by early 1979 only thirty-six CLPs had active campaign committees.[240] In a pre-referendum broadcast, James Callaghan hoped a 'yes' vote would constitute 'the first and most essential step to putting an end to a controversy that has distracted politics in Scotland intermittently for a century'. The main campaign poster featured an image of the Prime Minister urging Scots to vote 'yes', which to Gordon Brown made devolution 'appear like a diktat from a prime minister based in London with a parliamentary seat in Cardiff'. As Brown and other Scottish Labour MPs knew full well, away from the public gaze Sunny Jim 'could be tough and uncompromising – and unsmiling'.[241]

Brown addressed thirty meetings in the final week of February while preparing a pamphlet setting out the Labour case for the new Assembly and another on what it might do, his aim being to run 'as positive a case as possible on the difference a Scottish Assembly could make to people's lives'.[242] While on 1 March 1979 – St David's Day – a slight majority of Scots endorsed a Scottish Assembly, at 51.62 per cent it fell short of the necessary 40 per cent of the entire Scottish electorate required under the Scotland Act 1978. Brown later blamed the Act – rather than Scottish voters – for being 'deficient' and insufficiently radical.[243]

'THE ECLIPSE OF THE SCOTTISH DIMENSION'

In the House Commons, Callaghan suggested all-party talks on improving the Scotland Act, which struck hardly anyone as either politically or legislatively credible. In his last Commons intervention, William Ross, soon to act as Lord High Commissioner to the General Assembly of the Church of Scotland, wished the Prime Minister well before adding drolly: 'But I hae ma doots.'[244]

At a special Scottish Council conference in Perth on 10 March 1979, an executive statement 'reaffirmed' its commitment to devolution and urged the government to do 'all in its power' to implement the 1978 Act.[245] Gordon Brown argued that 'devolution should be built on the rock of justice' and 'not the shifting sands of nationalism', while Brian Wilson, who opposed the executive statement, declared that 'devolution should be out of the way, finished with!'[246]

In 'great secrecy', meanwhile, Helen Liddell met the Scottish regional secretary of the Communist Party of Great Britain, who assured her of Scottish trade union support.[247] Jimmy Reid, who had contested both 1974 elections on a CPGB platform, had approached Liddell about re-joining Labour in 1977 and was subsequently selected to fight Dundee East. The government faced a motion of no-confidence on 28 March 1979, the first since 1924, and it was supported by the Conservatives and Liberals as well as most SNP MPs, Nationalist 'treachery' which thereafter entered Labour mythology.

In his Edinburgh South address, Gordon Brown tried to move the debate on from devolution, framing the election as a decision on 'the direction in which Scotland and Britain is to move in the years to come – and what programme can ensure a society in which all people have the best chance to achieve their full potential'.[248] Defending Garscadden, meanwhile, Donald Dewar was less circumspect, asserting that Labour remained 'the party for devolution', occupying the 'sensible middle path of devolving democracy within the United Kingdom to the people of Scotland'.[249] Nuffield's general election survey later observed that the 'essential feature' of the 1979 campaign in Scotland was the 'eclipse of the Scottish dimension'.[250] Most Scots, judged *The Economist*, 'were more preoccupied by the ravages of inflation than the relatively academic issues of constitutional reform'.[251]

Six days before the election the Scottish Conservatives, enjoying a modest revival under the leadership of Margaret Thatcher, won a convert in Lord Wilson of Langside, Lord Advocate in Harold Wilson's second government and fresh from chairing

'Scotland Says No'. On polling day, Labour's Scottish vote increased to 41.5 per cent, giving it forty-four seats, double the number of Conservatives. In a surprise gain, John Maxton (a nephew of James) defeated Conservative Teddy Taylor in Glasgow Cathcart, while Jim Sillars licked his wounds and announced his departure from front-line politics. In Drucker's memorable judgement, the breakaway Scottish Labour Party had mistaken 'South Ayrshire for Scotland'.[252]

Two weeks after the election – which gave Mrs Thatcher a comfortable Commons majority of forty-three seats – Donald Dewar predicted that the demand for self-government could only get stronger. 'It may be that many who did vote No, or who abstained', he told his constituents, 'may come to regret the indecisive result of the referendum as Mrs Thatcher's shock troops ride rough-shod ... over Scotland'.[253]

NOTES

1. I. Budge & D. W. Urwin (1966), *Scottish Political Behaviour: A Case Study in British Homogeneity*, London: Longmans, 23.
2. *The Times*, 26 January 1959.
3. R. Davidson & G. Davis (2012), *The Sexual State: Sexuality and Scottish Governance, 1950–80*, Edinburgh: Edinburgh University Press, 61.
4. J. Allison with H. Conroy (1995), *Guilty by Suspicion: A Life and Labour*, Glendaruel: Argyll Publishing, 40.
5. *The Times*, 10 November 1960.
6. M. Keating (1989), 'The Labour Party in Scotland, 1951–1964', in I. Donnachie, C. Harvie & I. S. Wood (eds), *Forward! Labour Politics in Scotland, 1888–1988*, Edinburgh: Polygon, 95.
7. M. Keating (2005), *The Government of Scotland: Public Policy Making after Devolution* (Second Edition), Edinburgh: Edinburgh University Press, 57.
8. M. Fyfe (2020), *Singing in the Streets: A Glasgow Memoir*, Edinburgh: Luath, 153–4.
9. M. Keating (1989), 95.
10. Fyfe, 144–5.
11. HC Deb 24 July 1961 Vol 645 c138.
12. J. Sillars (1986), *The Case for Optimism*, Edinburgh: Polygon, 39.
13. M. Keating & D. Bleiman (1979), *Labour and Scottish Nationalism*, London: Macmillan, 150.
14. F. Bealey (1970), *The Social and Political Thought of the British Labour Party*, London: Weidenfeld and Nicolson, 53.

15. Scottish Council of the Labour Party (1958), *Special Report on Scottish Government of the Executive Committee to the Special Conference*, Glasgow: SCLP, paras 47–51.
16. W. L. Miller (1981), *The End of British Politics?: Scots and English Political Behaviour in the Seventies*, Oxford: Clarendon Press, 65.
17. *Glasgow Herald*, 15 September 1958.
18. Keating and Bleiman, 151.
19. J. Mitchell (2014), *The Scottish Question*, Oxford: Oxford University Press, 115.
20. F. Wood (1989), 'Scottish Labour in Government and Opposition: 1964–79', in I. Donnachie, C. Harvie & I. S. Wood (eds), *Forward! Labour Politics in Scotland 1888–1988*, Edinburgh: Polygon, 105.
21. Keating & Bleiman, 149.
22. Labour Party Scottish Council (1964), *Report of the Executive Committee to the 49th Annual Conference*, Glasgow: SCLP.
23. Wood, 102.
24. *Evening News and Dispatch*, 28 September 1964.
25. Labour Party Scottish Council (1961), *Report of the Executive Committee to the 46th Annual Conference*, Glasgow: SCLP.
26. Labour Party (1963), *Signposts for Scotland*, London: Labour Party, 22–3.
27. Labour Party Scottish Council (1965), *Report of the Executive Committee to the 50th Annual Conference*, Glasgow: SCLP.
28. G. Stott (1991), *Lord Advocate's Diary, 1961–1966*, Aberdeen: Aberdeen University Press, 136–7. Stott was rather detached from his ministerial colleagues, observing after one meeting that like 'other Labour politicians, they suffered from long-windedness and lack of appreciation of what was relevant' (154).
29. A. McPherson & C. D. Raab (1988), *Governing Education: A Sociology of Policy Since 1945*, Edinburgh: Edinburgh University Press, 373.
30. Mitchell, 143.
31. Labour Party Scottish Council (1967), *Report of the Executive Committee to the 52nd Annual Conference*, Glasgow: SCLP. Tom McMillan also held Glasgow Central and Alex Eadie Midlothian.
32. Aberdeen South election address, GD1/1433/1/14/6, Papers of the Dewar Family, Edinburgh: National Records of Scotland.
33. Budge & Urwin, 77.
34. J. G. Kellas & P. Fotheringham (1976), 'The political behaviour of the working class', in A. A. MacLaren (ed.), *Social Class in Scotland: Past and Present*, Edinburgh: John Donald, 155–6.

35. I. McLean (1999[1983]), *The Legend of Red Clydeside*, Edinburgh: John Donald, xxiii.
36. H. Drucker (1978), *Breakaway: The Scottish Labour Party*, Edinburgh: EUSPB, 8.
37. I. G. C. Hutchison (2000), *Scottish Politics in the Twentieth Century*, Basingstoke: Palgrave, 127.
38. Wood, 105.
39. T. Dalyell (1989), *Dick Crossman: A Portrait*, London: Weidenfeld and Nicolson, 224.
40. Keating (1989), 97.
41. Davidson & Davis, 61.
42. J. G. Kellas (1968), *Modern Scotland: The Nation since 1870*, London: Pall Mall Press, 198.
43. Allison, 43.
44. William Hamilton to Harold Wilson, 7 January 1967, and to John Silkin, 23 October 1968, Acc 10951/75, William W. Hamilton Papers, Edinburgh: National Library of Scotland. Hamilton later published *My Queen and I* (1975), in which he branded the Queen 'a clockwork doll', Princess Margaret 'a floozy' and Prince Charles 'a twerp'. Only the Queen Mother – 'a remarkable old lady' – was spared his vitriol.
45. J. McMillan (1969), *Anatomy of Scotland*, London: Leslie Frewin, 99–100.
46. D. Young (1971), *Scotland*, London: Cassell, 136.
47. G. Hassan & E. Shaw (2020), 'The Scottish Labour Party', in M. Keating (ed.), *The Oxford Handbook of Scottish Politics*, Oxford: Oxford University Press, 258.
48. W. H. Marwick (1967), *A Short History of Labour in Scotland*, Edinburgh: Chambers, 113.
49. Young, 135–6.
50. P. Lynch & S. Birrell (2004), 'The autonomy and organisation of Scottish Labour', in G. Hassan (ed.), *The Scottish Labour Party: History, Institutions and Ideas*, Edinburgh: Edinburgh University Press, 181. The requirement for 'the minimum' lasted until 1979.
51. Hutchison (2000), 135.
52. Kellas, 199.
53. T. Dalyell (1977), *Devolution: The End of Britain?*, London: Jonathan Cape, 76–80.
54. Labour Party Scottish Council (1968), *Report of the Executive Committee to the 53rd Annual Conference*, Glasgow: SCLP.
55. Hutchison, 127.
56. Hutchison, 134.
57. Wood, 107.

58. I. McLean & A. McMillan (2005), *State of the Union: Unionism and the Alternatives in the United Kingdom since 1707*, Oxford: Oxford University Press, 161.
59. Miller, 56.
60. A. McInnes (2019), 'Deindustrialisation and Gordon Brown's approach to devolution in Scotland', *Scottish Labour History 54*, 132.
61. H. Drucker & G. Brown (1980), *The Politics of Nationalism and Devolution*, London: Longman, 82–4.
62. A. Marr (1992), *The Battle for Scotland*, London: Penguin, 128.
63. D. Dewar (1970), 'Devolution and local government reform', in N. MacCormick (ed.), *The Scottish Debate: Essays on Scottish Nationalism*, Oxford: Oxford University Press, 79.
64. Crossman considered George Thomson or Dick Mabon potential successors.
65. R. Crossman (1977), *The Diaries of a Cabinet Minister, Volume Three: Secretary of State for Social Services, 1968–70*, London: Hamish Hamilton and Jonathan Cape, 106.
66. J. Sillars (2021), *A Difference of Opinion: My Political Journey*, Edinburgh: Birlinn, 61–2.
67. J. Sillars & A. Eadie (1968), *Don't Butcher Scotland's Future: The Case Against the S.N.P. Together with an Argument for Reform at All Levels of Government*, Ayr: Ayr Labour Party. This reflected the recent creation of a UK Parliamentary Ombudsman.
68. D. Douglas (1968), *Together we Stand: The Case for the UK*, Dundee: Dundee Fabian Society, 10–11.
69. See also A. Hargrave (1969), *Scotland: The Third Choice*, London: Fabian Society.
70. HC Deb 28 October 1969 Vol 790 c12.
71. T. Nairn (1968), 'The three dreams of Scottish Nationalism', *New Left Review* I/49.
72. Scottish Council of the Labour Party (1971), *Commission on the Constitution*, Glasgow: SCLP, 23, 32.
73. Dewar, 73–9.
74. N. Buchan (1971), 'Politics', in D. Glen (ed.), *Whither Scotland? A Prejudiced Look at the Future of a Nation*, London: Victor Gollancz, 86–92.
75. The South Ayrshire by-election took place following the death of Emrys Hughes.
76. Wood, 109–12.
77. *The Times*, 26 March 1970.
78. A. McSmith (1994), *John Smith: A Life*, London: Cornerstone, 42.

79. Herbison's great niece, Karen Whitefield, would later serve as the Labour Member of the Scottish Parliament for Airdrie and Shotts.
80. Anthony Crosland to Donald Dewar, June 1970, GD1/1433/1/11/1, Papers of the Dewar Family. Dewar had come to view Crosland with a degree of cynicism. 'Crosland kept trying to persuade me that various trade unionists had brilliant intellects', Roy Hattersley recalled him remarking, 'when we both knew that was rubbish'. See R. Hattersley (2005), 'As parliamentarian', in W. Alexander (ed.), *Donald Dewar: Scotland's first First Minister*, Edinburgh: Mainstream, 107.
81. William Ross to Donald Dewar, 30 June 1970, GD1/1433/1/11/8, Papers of the Dewar Family.
82. G. Hassan (2002), 'A case study of Scottish Labour: Devolution and the politics of multi-level governance', *Political Quarterly* 73:2, 147.
83. Miller, 57.
84. *The Times*, 2 January 1973.
85. Allison, 171.
86. M. Keating (1988), *State and Regional Nationalism: Territorial Politics and the European State*, Hemel Hempstead: Harvester Wheatsheaf.
87. *Scotsman*, 15 February 1972.
88. G. Brown (2017), *My Life, Our Times*, London: Bodley Head, 77. Dewar was working in Lanarkshire.
89. Keating & Bleiman, 178.
90. Drucker, 20.
91. T. Benn (1989), *Against the Tide: Diaries, 1973–76*, London: Hutchinson, 46, 73.
92. Marr, 137.
93. Dalyell (1977), 94–5.
94. Hutchison, 127.
95. Allison, 171.
96. Hutchison, 129.
97. Miller, 66–7.
98. R. McLean (2001), 'Gallant crusader or cautious persuader? Donald Dewar's role in securing Scotland's parliament', *Scottish Affairs* 34, 5.
99. Marr, 138.
100. A. Eadie, H. Ewing, J. Robertson & J. Sillars (1974), *Scottish Labour and Devolution: A Discussion Paper*, Ayr: Ayr Labour Party.
101. Sillars (1986), 44.

102. B. Donoughue (2005), *Downing Street Diary: With Harold Wilson in No. 10*, London: Jonathan Cape, 156–7.
103. This was at 1 Lynedoch Place in Glasgow and included a Keir Hardie Memorial Library. See Labour Party Scottish Council (1974), *59th Annual Conference, Ayr 1974*, Glasgow: SCLP.
104. Dalyell (1977), 100–1.
105. Drucker & Brown, 92.
106. *The Times*, 24 June 1974.
107. H. Wilson (1979), *Final Term: The Labour Government, 1974–1976*, London: Weidenfeld and Nicolson, 124.
108. T. Dalyell (2016), *The Question of Scotland: Devolution and After*, Edinburgh: Birlinn, 102–3.
109. *The Times*, 26 July 1974.
110. B. Donoughue (2005), 169–70.
111. B. Castle (1980), *The Castle Diaries, 1974–76*, London: Weidenfeld and Nicolson, 153.
112. At the former headquarters of the Scottish Co-operative Wholesale Society, which had had a relationship with Labour in Scotland since the First World War.
113. Dalyell (2016), 104–7.
114. *The Times*, 19 August 1974.
115. J. P. Mackintosh (1974), *A Parliament for Scotland*, Berwick and East Lothian Labour Party, 22.
116. The party had produced separate documents (not called 'manifestos') for Scotland at the 1950, 1959 and 1964 general elections.
117. Drucker, 30, 58.
118. D. Torrance (2006), *The Scottish Secretaries*, Edinburgh: Birlinn, 266.
119. Hutchison, 133–6.
120. J. G. Kellas (1976), 'Reactions to the Devolution White Paper', in M. G. Clarke and H. M. Drucker (eds), *Our Changing Scotland: A Yearbook of Scottish Government 1976–77*, Edinburgh: EUSPB, 12.
121. *Herald*, 6 January 1992.
122. Donoughue (2005), 238, 290.
123. Donoughue (2005), 337, 340.
124. *The Economist*, 29 March 1975.
125. See A. Purves (1978), 'Scottish Labour and British Entry: Labour Movement Attitudes to the European Community at Scottish and UK Levels, 1960–1977', Edinburgh: University of Edinburgh, MPhil thesis.
126. Donoughue (2005), 577–80.
127. J. Phillips, V. Wright & J. Tomlinson (2019), 'Deindustrialization, the Linwood car plant and Scotland's political divergence from

England in the 1960s and 1970s', *Twentieth-Century British History* 30:3, 399–423.
128. Scottish Council of the Labour Party (1977), *An Industrial Strategy for Scotland*, Glasgow: Scottish Council of the Labour Party, 35.
129. Donoughue (2005), 710.
130. Hutchison, 135.
131. McInnes, 129.
132. P. Routledge (1998), *Gordon Brown: The Biography*, London: Pocket Books, 71.
133. Hutchison, 136.
134. G. Brown (ed.) (1975), *The Red Paper on Scotland*, Edinburgh: EUSPB, 8. The front cover of *The Red Paper* included a photograph of a UCS demonstration in 1971 and the back an image of the 1913 Leith dockers' strike.
135. Brown (2017), 55.
136. *The Economist*, 8 February 1975.
137. *The Economist*, 29 March 1975.
138. Donoughue (2005), 148.
139. *The Economist*, 2 August 1975
140. *The Times*, 11 September 1975.
141. *The Times*, 5 November 1975. See also J. P. Mackintosh's 'The case against a referendum' (*Scotsman*, 30 August 1976).
142. Transcript of a press conference to launch 'Our Changing Democracy: Devolution to Scotland and Wales', 27 November 1975.
143. The October 1974 Labour manifesto for Scotland had stated the SDA would 'be responsible to the Secretary of State for Scotland, and when the Assembly is later set up, it may become appropriate to make the Agency responsible to the Assembly'.
144. Kellas (1976), 62.
145. *The Economist*, 6 December 1975.
146. Sillars (1986), 54–5.
147. *The Economist*, 20 December 1975.
148. Fyfe, 171.
149. Donoughue (2005), 635, 655.
150. *The Times*, 8 January 1976.
151. *Scotsman*, 1 November 1975.
152. Bob Brown had been the first Scottish correspondent of *The Times* and the *Guardian* and had first assisted the Scottish Labour MP group with public relations after the 1968 Aberdeen conference.
153. Fyfe, 175.
154. *The Times*, 10 January 1976.
155. Drucker, 10.

156. Norman Buchan later suggested 'Socialism, not Nationalism' would have been more on point (*The Times*, 2 April 1976).
157. *The Times*, 16 January 1976.
158. *The Economist*, 7 February 1976.
159. *The Times*, 4 February 1976.
160. *The Times*, 4 March 1976.
161. *The Times*, 9 March 1976.
162. *The Times*, 27 January 1976.
163. Scottish Council of the Labour Party (1976), *Labour's Analysis of the Economics of Separation*, Glasgow: SCLP, 2–29.
164. One of the most potent myths was that the Labour government withheld projected oil revenues from the Scottish public, when in fact Edmund Dell, the Paymaster General, made a parliamentary statement on 25 February 1975 (HC Deb 25 February 1975 Vol 887 cc290–99 [North Sea Oil (Petroleum Revenue Tax)]).
165. Scottish Council of the Labour Party (1976), *Can Scotland Go it Alone? The Menace of Separation: A Labour Party Analysis*, Glasgow: SCLP, 2–9.
166. *The Times*, 2 April 1976.
167. *The Economist*, 3 April 1976.
168. Dewar, 75.
169. W. Ross (1977), 'Approaching the Archangelic', in H. M. Drucker & M. G. Clarke (eds), *Scottish Government Yearbook 1978*, Edinburgh: Paul Harris, 20.
170. A. Kemp (1993), *The Hollow Drum: Scotland Since the War*, Edinburgh: Mainstream, 140. 'I am certain I did not discuss the name of Willie Ross's successor with him [Mabon]. That was not my practice. Perhaps Harry Ewing approached me at the time but I have no recollection of that' (Lord Callaghan to the author, 18 April 2002).
171. J. P. Mackintosh to Arnold Kemp, 21 March 1978, Mackintosh Papers Acc 13476/53, Edinburgh: National Library of Scotland.
172. *Evening Times*, 5 August 1976. See also R. Ferguson (1983), *Geoff: The Life of Geoffrey M. Shaw*, Gartocharn: Famedram.
173. B. Millan (1978), 'Geoff Shaw – an appreciation', in H. M. Drucker & N. L. Drucker (eds), *Scottish Government Yearbook 1979*, Edinburgh: Paul Harris, 12–14.
174. *Glasgow Herald*, 28 February 1978.
175. *The Times*, 24 August 1976.
176. HC Deb 16 December 1976 Vol 922 cc1735–876.
177. For the fallout from the Conservatives' U-turn on devolution, see D. Torrance (2009), *'We in Scotland': Thatcherism in a Cold Climate*, Edinburgh: Birlinn, 18–19.
178. Miller, 238.

179. *The Times*, 28 February 1977.
180. D. Heald (1976), *Making Devolution Work*, London: Fabian Society, 49.
181. *The Economist*, 20 December 1975.
182. N. Williamson (1978), 'Ten years after – the revolutionary left in Scotland', in H. M. Drucker & N. L. Drucker (eds), *Scottish Government Yearbook 1979*, Edinburgh: Paul Harris, 68.
183. Note dated 18 May 1977, TD 1384/7, Scottish Labour Party Papers, Glasgow: Mitchell Library.
184. H. Drucker (1979), 'The political parties', in D. I. Mackay (ed.), *Scotland: The Framework for Change*, Edinburgh: Paul Harris, 101.
185. Drucker (1979), 99–104.
186. *The Economist*, 20 December 1975.
187. Heald (1976), 49.
188. P. Jones (1992), 'Politics', in M. Linklater & R. Denniston (eds), *Anatomy of Scotland*, Edinburgh: Chambers, 382.
189. Allison, 75.
190. Hutchison, 137.
191. B. Donoughue (2008), *Downing Street Diary, Volume Two: With James Callaghan in No. 10*, London: Jonathan Cape, 152, 187.
192. Note dated 14 November 1977, TD 1384/7, Scottish Labour Party Papers.
193. Notes dated 18–21 April and 10 May 1977, TD 1384/7, Scottish Labour Party Papers.
194. Note dated 17 November 1977, TD 1384/7, Scottish Labour Party Papers.
195. Miller, 239.
196. *The Times*, 14 March 1977.
197. *The Economist*, 23 April 1977.
198. Sillars (2021), 114. Sillars admitted to having no proof.
199. H. McLeish (2004), *Scotland First: Truth and Consequences*, Edinburgh: Mainstream, 23.
200. *The Times*, 5 May 1977.
201. J. M. Bochel & D. T. Denver (1977), 'The District Council elections of May 1977', in H. M. Drucker & M. G. Clarke (eds), *Scottish Government Yearbook 1978*, Edinburgh: Paul Harris, 137.
202. *The Economist*, 7 May 1977.
203. Note dated 5 May 1977, TD 1384/7, Scottish Labour Party Papers.
204. Note dated 30 March–1 April 1977, TD 1384/7, Scottish Labour Party Papers.
205. Note dated 2 September 1977, TD 1384/7, 1977, Scottish Labour Party Papers.

206. H. M. Drucker (ed.) (1982), *John P. Mackintosh on Scotland*, London: Longman, 142.
207. J. Bochel, D. Denver & A. Macartney (eds) (1981), *The Referendum Experience: Scotland 1979*, Aberdeen: Aberdeen University Press, 15, 17.
208. H. M. Drucker & N. L. Drucker (1978), 'Introduction: Towards a Scottish politics', in H. M. Drucker & N. L. Drucker (eds), *Scottish Government Yearbook 1979*, Edinburgh: Paul Harris, 1.
209. *Scotsman*, 18 March 1978.
210. *The Times*, 17 March 1978.
211. Chairman's address, SPA/GR/HC/MP/1/24, George Robertson Collection, Stirling: Scottish Political Archive.
212. *The Economist*, 8 April 1978.
213. *Dewar's Labour Weekly (Extra)*, GD1/1433/1/14/5, Papers of the Dewar Family.
214. *The Times*, 3 August 2023.
215. Notes dated 1–13 and 14 April 1978, TD1384/7, Scottish Labour Party Papers.
216. J. M. Bochel & D. T. Denver (1978), 'The Regional Council elections of May 1978', in H. M. Drucker & N. L. Drucker (eds), *Scottish Government Yearbook 1979*, Edinburgh: Paul Harris, 147–55.
217. *The Times*, 10 May 1978.
218. *The Times*, 12 September 1978.
219. Note dated 8/27 October 1978, TD1384/7, Scottish Labour Party Papers.
220. Harry Conroy, a party member, ostensibly joined Keir Hardie House as a 'volunteer' but 'in reality he is to be paid as usual' (Note dated 23 August 1978, TD1384/7, Scottish Labour Party Papers).
221. Williamson, 69
222. HC Deb 14 November 1977 Vol 939 c87 [Scotland Bill].
223. HC Deb 25 January 1978 Vol 942 cc1424–553 [Referendum].
224. Wood, 125.
225. Notes dated 27 January 1978 and 12–15 February 1978, TD1384/7, Scottish Labour Party Papers.
226. A. Young (2005), 'To see ourselves ...', in W. Alexander (ed.), *Donald Dewar: Scotland's first First Minister*, Edinburgh: Mainstream, 56–7.
227. Note dated 27 January 1978, TD1384/7, Scottish Labour Party Papers.
228. J. Naughtie (1978), 'The Scotland Bill in the House of Commons', in H. M. Drucker & N. L. Drucker (eds), *Scottish Government Yearbook 1979*, Edinburgh: Paul Harris, 33.

229. Naughtie (1978), 24.
230. Labour Party (1978), 'Devolution: The Labour Party position', Rowntree Devolution Conference, 81–91.
231. Bochel et al. (1981), 17.
232. *Daily Record*, 14 November 1978.
233. Wood, 127.
234. Labour Party: Scottish Council (1978), *Labour's Scottish Assembly: Our Case*, Glasgow: SCLP.
235. C. Craig & S. Gilmore (1979), *A Radical Agenda for Scotland: Women and the Scottish Assembly*, Glasgow: Scottish Council of Fabian Societies, 4.
236. G. Hassan (1996), 'New Labour and the politics of a new Scotland', in M. Perryman (ed.), *The Blair Agenda*, London: Lawrence and Wishart, 177.
237. Miller, 113.
238. *Seven Days*, edited by Brian Wilson with mainly Labour movement contributors, was published between October 1977 and May 1978.
239. A. Midwinter, M. Keating & J. Mitchell (1991), *Politics and Public Policy in Scotland*, Edinburgh: Edinburgh University Press, 32.
240. Wood, 126–8.
241. Brown (2017), 57.
242. Brown (2017), 56.
243. Drucker & Brown, 120–30.
244. J. Naughtie (1979), 'The year at Westminster: The Scotland Act brings down the government', in H. M. Drucker & N. L. Drucker (eds), *Scottish Government Yearbook 1980*, Edinburgh: Paul Harris, 49.
245. Miller, 253.
246. *Scotsman*, 12 March 1979.
247. Note dated 15 March 1979, TD1384/7, Scottish Labour Party Papers.
248. McInnes, 138–40.
249. *Labour News (Garscadden 1979)*, GD1/1433/1/14/4, Papers of the Dewar Family.
250. D. Butler & D. Kavanagh (1980), *The British General Election of 1979*, London: Macmillan, 309.
251. *The Economist*, 21 April 1979.
252. Drucker (1978), 141.
253. P. Hetherington (1979), 'The 1979 general election campaign in Scotland', in H. M. Drucker & N. L. Drucker (eds), *Scottish Government Yearbook 1980*, Edinburgh: Paul Harris, 95–100.

5

The Party of Scotland: 1979–1994

The general election result appeared to draw a line under the devolution issue – at least for the time being. Returning to Scotland at the end of 1979 after five years in the Midlands, Mike Watson recalled his Labour activism as being 'shaped by that year's double defeat'. 'The rigged referendum and the installation of the Thatcher government seemed less sinister viewed from Derby than Dundee', he reflected. 'Distance had had a numbing effect which quickly wore off as I absorbed the Scottish political environment.'[1] That included a Scottish National Party which, shocked by its electoral defenestration, turned away from its view of devolution as a desirable 'stepping stone' to full independence. Meanwhile a reductively Marxist analysis of the referendum result – working class 'yes'; middle class 'no' – energised a younger generation of Nationalists who became determined to displace Labour as Scotland's dominant party.[2]

Labour in Scotland eased itself into the 1980s content that it possessed forty-four MPs as well as firm control of most district and regional councils. At the first direct elections to the European Parliament in June, however, the Conservatives managed to come first in vote share (33.7 per cent to Labour's 33) and seats (five to Labour's two). A possible explanation was the financial and political exhaustion of three major campaigns – referendum, Westminster and Europe – in as many months.[3] Much of the Scottish Labour party also opposed the European Economic Community as a 'fundamentally anti-socialist body' which 'imposed colossal burdens on the working population in Scotland'.[4] By May 1980, Labour had once again advanced in district council elections (45.5 per cent of votes cast, its highest yet),[5] while at the Glasgow Central by-election on 26 June 1980, trade unionist Bob McTaggart held the seat despite losing 11 per cent of Labour's general election vote share.

It did not take long for the first Thatcher government to become unpopular amid rising unemployment, an unsuccessful experiment with 'monetarism' and a Prime Minister not yet in full control of her Cabinet. By 1981 opinion polls showed support for Labour in Scotland exceeding 60 per cent, in marked contrast to the performance of the party in most other parts of Great Britain. Now commanded by the emollient George Younger and intellectually impressive Malcolm Rifkind, the Scottish Office set the tone with legislation giving council tenants the 'right to buy' their homes, the opening salvo of a sustained attack on supposedly profligate left-wing local authorities. Considering the Wilson/Callaghan governments had also explored this policy, it made some Scottish Labour MPs squirm. While the former housing minister Hugh Brown called it the 'bribe of the century', he took care to emphasise that he did not oppose sales in all circumstances.[6]

When it came to the Criminal Justice (Scotland) Bill, the Livingston MP Robin Cook scored a notable success with an amendment which finally brought Scotland into line with the Sexual Offences Act 1967 opposed by several of his colleagues in the late 1960s. A similar move to decriminalise homosexual acts between consenting adults in private had failed in the previous Parliament (as had Donald Dewar's attempt to reform Scottish divorce law),[7] but Cook's amendment won an overwhelming majority at the bill's report stage. Dewar, meanwhile, returned to the revived Select Committee on Scottish Affairs, this time as chair. The Scottish Labour MP group innovated by holding elections for its six committee places rather than relying on the 'mysterious workings of the usual channels'.[8] When Dewar was later promoted to Labour's front bench, Aberdeen North MP Robert Hughes succeeded him as chair.

The legislative sequel to the Tenants' Rights, Etc. (Scotland) Act 1980 was an Education Bill to widen 'parental choice' in state education. This met opposition from Cathcart MP John Maxton, nephew of James and a former teacher. The Conservatives used another provision, the Assisted Places Scheme, to accuse Scottish Labour of wishing to restrict educational opportunities for their working-class constituents. And when Dennis Canavan (West Stirlingshire) proposed allowing parents to opt out of corporal punishment in schools, Conservative MPs defended the belt as a necessary deterrent. The government's Commons majority ensured maintenance of the status quo,[9] although Judith Hart, the party's sole Scottish female MP during this period, later helped get the 'Lochgelly Tawse' (and any other form of punishment) banned in 1987.

The breakaway Social Democratic Party (SDP) was formed on 26 March 1981. Robert MacLennan MP (Caithness and Sutherland) joined the party at an early stage and was subsequently joined by Dick Mabon (Greenock and Port Glasgow). Other defectors included Bunty Urquhart, a former assistant Scottish organiser who Jimmy Allison tartly observed had been 'moving to the right all her political life'.[10] Urquhart later rejoined Labour but lost lifelong political friends amid often ferocious attacks, although she remained close to Donald Dewar.[11] The short-lived *Sunday Standard* newspaper caused a brief stir by suggesting that Helen Liddell would jump ship, but this was strenuously denied. Ironically, the architects of the devolution referendum's '40 per cent rule' – Bruce Douglas-Mann and George Cunningham – also joined the new (and essentially pro-devolution) party.

Urquhart played a leading role in the Hillhead by-election, which took place on 25 March 1982. SDP leader Roy Jenkins dramatically entered the Scottish political arena in an almost tailor-made constituency. A marginal seat fought in 1979 by Richard Mowbray (another SDP convert), given its buoyant polling Labour might have seized its forty-fifth MP but instead came third with 26 per cent of the vote. David Wiseman, the Labour candidate, found himself 'mauled' each morning by the press and Scottish party secretary Helen Liddell complained of the 'pro-Jenkins' stance of the *Daily Record* and *Sunday Mail*.[12] The latter title's 'weakened' Labour stance still concerned Liddell at the end of 1984.[13]

Social Democratic elation did not last long, for the Falklands conflict, which began shortly after the by-election, helped transform the Thatcher government's fortunes. In June 1982 there was even a small swing to the Conservatives in the Labour bastion of Coatbridge and Airdrie, which Labour's Tom Clarke nevertheless held comfortably. Several Scottish Labour MPs including Judith Hart, Tam Dalyell, David Marshall and George Foulkes voiced their opposition to the war, and at a meeting of the Parliamentary Labour Party on 29 April George Robertson attacked *Labour Weekly* editor Donald Ross for giving column inches to anti-war views.[14]

In the Commons, the legislative battle moved back to local government with the innocuously titled Local Government (Miscellaneous Provisions) Scotland Bill. Under the bill's provisions, the Secretary of State for Scotland could require any authority whose expenditure was deemed 'unreasonable and excessive' to reduce it. As Drucker put it, Lothian, Dundee and Stirling had been made the 'chief whipping boys of Government action', not because they had 'behaved particularly outrageously' but because their Labour members had 'clothed their actions in the rhetoric of the Left and sought confrontation with central government'.[15]

Despairing of his colleagues' 'extremism', Peter Wilson (a former convener of Lothian Region) defected to the SDP and managed to outpoll Labour at regional elections in May 1982. Labour lost control of four seats in all and relinquished control of Lothian to a Conservative-dominated coalition. By contrast, Labour's vote in Strathclyde rose by 3 per cent, consolidating that vast authority's status as a Labour bastion. Bochel and Denver suggested the Strathclyde result was what might have been expected in 'normal' electoral circumstances, with the other regions' performance explained by a combination of the 'Falklands factor' and local circumstances. Beyond Lothian, the advance of the SDP–Liberal Alliance was almost wholly at the expense of the Conservatives.[16]

'THE BENN FACTOR'

The state of British Labour by May 1982, however, was far from normal, something that had impacted the party's performance in English local government elections to a much greater extent than in Scotland. Not only did polling suggest Michael Foot – who had succeeded James Callaghan in November 1980 – was the most unpopular Leader of the Opposition since the Second World War, but internal constitutional and ideological battles threatened to tear the party apart.

This took a more muted though still destructive form in Scotland. At the Scottish Council conference in March 1980 the Labour Co-ordinating Committee (LCC) formed in 1978 had secured five places on the party executive, including George Galloway, Bill Spiers (deputy general secretary of the STUC) and Mark Lazarowicz (an Edinburgh district councillor). Helen Liddell's weekly communications with party headquarters in London began to describe every Scottish executive meeting as the 'worst' she had ever attended. On 12 January 1980, for example, she recorded complaints about the right to buy, the Scottish Council's firm opposition at odds with the NEC's more 'ambiguous' line, while on 11 June the Scottish media had a field day when the Scottish executive agreed to support a resolution 'calling for the recognition of the P.L.O. as the "sole" representatives of the Palestinian people'.[17]

The British party deputy leadership election on 27 September 1981 further heightened tensions. Although Denis Healey, the incumbent deputy leader, survived a challenge from Tony Benn by a whisker, the contest unleashed a lot of bitterness in a party still reeling from the SDP split. When Michael Foot met with the Scottish party executive in November, Jimmy Allison recalled an 'extremely unpleasant meeting' chaired by George Galloway, who proceeded to 'expound his own views, and not [those] of the executive committee'. Galloway and his supporters were furious that Benn had been denied a Shadow Cabinet place on the basis that he did not accept collective responsibility.[18]

Although Foot 'replied in a full and frank manner', this, in Liddell's account:

> did not stop some members present from sneering at him ... The minutes ... cannot convey the spirit of intolerance that characterised the meeting. At the end, when most members had left, there was a fracas involving Norman Buchan, George Galloway, William Spiers and Archie Drummond. Fearing that violence would ensue, I sent for the Scottish Organiser, who is better able to handle that kind of situation. I witnessed nothing more until a very shaken Norman Buchan came into my office and told me of the treatment he had endured, which could best be described as physical intimidation.[19]

At the AGM of the Scottish Labour MP group a few days later, Liddell found morale 'at an all-time low'.[20] While campaigning in the Coatbridge and Airdrie by-election, she had been depressed to find 'the Benn factor' and 'splits within the Party' raised by 'almost every elector' she spoke to.[21]

Further unhappiness was generated by the mandatory reselection process insisted upon by Walworth Road (Labour's new London HQ), even though parliamentary boundaries were about to be redrawn, which meant in some cases CLPs would have to endure the divisive process twice. Although the LCC were on the left, they were opposed to the Militant Tendency, which sponsored two executive members and intended to challenge several incumbent MPs, including Donald Dewar in Garscadden. Bochel and Denver noted the paradox that despite the left-wing resolutions emanating from the Scottish Council conference, not a single Scottish Labour MP failed to gain reselection, although William Hamilton in Central Fife (who was challenged by Henry McLeish) came close, and Dewar only hung on by seven votes. Even more paradoxically, most of those who survived were on the right of the PLP, with only Ernie Ross (Dundee West), Ron Brown (Leith) and Allan Adams (Paisley) plausible Bennites. In February 1983 they tried but failed to persuade Benn to stand for nomination in the new constituency of Livingston.[22] The Scottish party leadership, therefore, remained 'more united and more obviously respectable than in England'.[23]

When Gordon Brown became vice-chairman of the Scottish Council in 1982, he claimed the executive's Bennite group (by which he meant the LCC) 'persistently tried to thwart' his initiatives,[24] even attempting to prevent him from addressing that year's Scottish conference. Nevertheless, Brown became chairman the following year, supported by the trade unions he had cultivated since the 1970s. The rise of George Galloway, meanwhile, drew attention to Dundee, where aged only twenty-six and already chairman of LCC Scotland, he had recently launched the weekly *Dundee Standard* newspaper. Labour had regained control of the city from the Conservatives in May 1980, and *The Times* did not approve of its actions since:

> Hospitality to Nato ships entering port was withdrawn; the council stoutly refused to sell any council houses even when ordered to do so by the Secretary of State for Scotland; and the rates rose by 150 per cent. Today a delegation from the council is to set off to the Middle East to strengthen the twinning partnership between Dundee and Nablus, a Palestine Liberation Organization stronghold on the Israeli-occupied West Bank.[25]

There were more positive developments when it came to gender. In 1983 Labour's Scottish Women's Committee was elected by women for the first time (rather than by the party as a whole), and by 1985 five 'reserved' women's seats on the Scottish executive had been reinstated, two of which were directly elected by the Scottish Women's Conference, something British party activists had failed to achieve.[26]

'TRYING TO STEAL A MARCH'

Initially, Bochel and Denver noted what they called 'a slow retreat' from Labour's commitment to a Scottish Assembly after 1979, perhaps because polling revealed, as Helen Liddell put it, that the 'most negative factor in the devolution referendum was that the SNP were on the same side as us'.[27] At the 1981 British Labour conference in Brighton no fringe meeting on the subject could be organised while the party's draft 'Programme for 1982' made only a passing reference.[28] John Smith, however, believed the more the party in Scotland debated the issue, the 'firmer' its commitment became, the opposition of the 'older Labour left' having given way to support on 'both left and right among the younger generation'.[29] A Scottish Council discussion paper stated that:

> The Labour Party in Scotland does not believe that an Assembly can provide a panacea for Scotland's ills: indeed, the experience of this Tory Government has reaffirmed our fundamental belief in the necessity to maintain the central struggle for economic and social change at a UK level. Nevertheless, there is now widespread acceptance in the Party and the wider movement in Scotland that the early establishment of a Scottish Assembly by the next Labour Government will represent not only a massive increase in democracy in Scottish life, but can greatly assist in the process of economic regeneration in the UK as a whole.[30]

Mike Watson recalled attending an LCC conference on devolution – journalist Julie Davidson called them Scotland's 'most popular intellectual sport' – at which discussion turned to 'what this new legislature might look like'. When someone declared 'anything but Westminster', this 'won immediate approval from a group confident that not only could we do much better in a Parliament in Scotland, we had to do better'.[31]

At the February 1981 Scottish Council conference, delegates overwhelmingly approved a resolution calling for a Scottish Assembly 'with meaningful powers over the economy of Scotland'.[32] Although vague, it indicated a desire to settle outstanding arguments over fiscal powers. Brian Wilson led the dissenting minority in warning that an Assembly would 'stimulate an image of nationalism and divide the British Labour movement',[33] while the 'Northern group' of Labour MPs demanded a full debate within the British party before the NEC approved the policy.[34]

Some of these tensions were aired at a meeting of the Scottish Labour MP group on 7 April 1981, which was attended by Michael Foot. Tam Dalyell kicked off by claiming that had devolution succeeded in 1979, 'we would have been a long way down the road to the break-up of the United Kingdom', to which George Foulkes responded that there would also be no Assisted Places Scheme in Scotland. Gavin Strang (Edinburgh East) said it would be 'unthinkable' for the party to drop its devolution commitment, while John Smith advocated a pre-legislative referendum which he considered 'inevitable and should, therefore, be made a virtue'. In response, Foot said he regarded himself as 'bound' by the 1979 manifesto, adding that:

> He had met the Northern Group, the North West Group and the Yorkshire Group. The backlash was a reality and strongest in the North East ... The backlash had to be recognised and the English colleagues spoken to. The majority of English Members ... would not consider similar Devolution measures for their Regions as a solution. There was no strong feeling for it but there was a strong feeling that they did not want to be disadvantaged economically vis-a-vis Scotland.

Foot said he would try to prevent the discussion becoming 'injurious to the Party in Scotland' and suggested Scottish Labour MPs work on persuading their English colleagues that 'Scotland was not trying to steal a march on them'.[35]

In stages, Labour in Scotland moved towards a much clearer commitment to a much more powerful form of devolution. In February 1983, an NEC statement committed the next Labour government to the creation of a directly elected Assembly with various revenue-raising and industrial powers, a commitment which subsequently appeared in the 1983 general election manifesto. Even at this stage, Geekie and Levy detected what they called the 'Tartanisation' of Scottish Labour, citing Drucker's comment that 'we are fed up with seeing our laws and our customs overruled as if we were some forgotten colony' as well as others who appeared to have borrowed the rhetoric of 'direct action' from the SNP's failed 'Scottish Resistance' campaign of 1982.[36]

Labour, however, kept its distance from the cross-party Campaign for a Scottish Assembly (CSA) founded in 1980, preferring parliamentary methods to external lobby groups it could not fully control. Labour devolutionists such as Alex Kitson, Dennis Canavan and George Foulkes, however, were active in the CSA and began to articulate the devolution argument through the prism of Thatcherism. Foulkes spoke of 'the consciousness that Thatcher has no mandate in Scotland', an early use of the 'democratic deficit' argument which was yet to be fully embraced by his party.[37] Canavan and Foulkes had been among four Scottish Labour MPs supporting SNP leader Gordon Wilson's attempt to introduce a bill to establish a cross-party 'Scottish Convention' in March 1980.[38]

Ernie Ross, the left-wing Labour MP for Dundee West, was confident Labour could embrace, lead and shape the 'Scottish dimension' while also differentiating itself from the SNP:

> The Scottish nationalism of the Labour movement has recognised the differences in social class in the community, unlike the right-wing leadership of the SNP who tend to ignore this aspect. Part of the traditional message of the Scottish labour movement has always stipulated the need and the demand for Scottish self-government to attack social inequality in Scotland – together with the view that socialism would win the argument in Scotland before it did in England.[39]

Looking ahead to the next election, a former Cabinet minister told *The Scotsman* that although the party would likely 'return even more MPs from Scotland', it would remain out of office 'down here' (Westminster) for another decade. 'We will have to play the nationalist card in Scotland', he added. 'We will have to go for an Assembly with substantial economic power short of independence, but not much short.'[40] John Smith, however, cautioned that a devolution argument which 'expresses itself in such a way that it appears like disguised nationalism' was 'not likely to succeed at Westminster'.[41]

In a pre-election collection of essays edited by Gerald Kaufman, Shadow Scottish Secretary Bruce Millan invoked the closures of the 'car plant at Linwood, the pulp mill at Fort William, the aluminium shelter at Invergordon'. 'The case for devolution does not wax and wane with the rise and fall of the SNP', he added, rather the party was 'picking up a thread that has run through Labour's history, in Scotland for fifty years or more'.[42]

'NO MANDATE'

In January 1983 Gordon Craig identified only five full-time employees at Keir Hardie House, a 'handful' of agents in constituencies and 'weak' party finances. In what he conceded would be a departure from past practice, Craig recommended concentrating on a 'comparatively limited number of defendable and winnable marginal seats' at the forthcoming general election.[43] Indeed, Helen Liddell explored the possibility of letting two floors of Keir Hardie House, as prospects seemed 'grave without capital expenditure'.[44]

Scottish organiser Jimmy Allison, however, considered things to be in reasonably good shape despite the problems faced by the British party, from which he tried to 'distance' Labour in Scotland wherever possible. Harry Conroy, a *Daily Record* journalist, was once again seconded to Keir Hardie House for the duration of the campaign, helping to produce a four-page Scottish 'tabloid' newssheet, 740,000 copies of which were distributed in constituencies.[45] The party's research officer since 1979 had been John Reid, who later became an adviser to Neil Kinnock before entering Parliament in 1987. In Dunfermline East, Gordon Brown was supported by visits from prominent trade unionists including NUM general secretary Lawrence Daly and former Communist Jimmy Reid.[46]

On polling day, Labour lost three seats due to a modest swing to the Conservatives and a respectable showing by the Alliance, which added five MPs to the three it held following defections and a by-election in the previous Parliament. Allison's election report for the Scottish executive and NEC described the result as 'an absolute disaster', for which he was almost disciplined by the British party's national agent. His critique rested upon the party's attachment to public rallies and neglect of the sort of modern television campaigning at which Liberal leader David Steel excelled. 'Regrettably', wrote Allison, 'politics in this day and age is about who comes over best on TV and the Labour Party better start facing up to that unpalatable fact.'[47] The party's Scottish conference had been broadcast live by BBC Scotland since 1981, and Helen Liddell too had noted the need to 'modify our ways of doing things'.[48]

Despite Allison's gloomy analysis, Labour in Scotland had secured a lead of 6.7 per cent vis-à-vis the Conservatives' 17.5 per cent in England and Wales. As Denver noted, this also meant Labour's share of seats was, once again, out of proportion to its share of the vote, largely due to its strength in the Strathclyde region. Housing tenure appeared to be replacing occupation as the best predictor of voting behaviour, with Labour obtaining an absolute majority (53 per cent) of council tenants and the Conservatives almost half of owner-occupiers. No fewer than thirty-eight of the forty-one seats won by Labour had a majority of council tenants.[49]

Labour therefore remained the principal means by which Scottish voters could express their opposition to the Conservatives, although the journalist Chris Baur mused that the party's 'traditional claim on Scottish electoral loyalty' was 'no longer as automatic as it used to be', its 35.1 per cent vote share the worst since the war. If, wrote Baur:

> Labour cannot rebuild in England in a way which makes than look like an alternative government at Westminster, then Labour in Scotland will be sorely tempted to begin looking for alternative means of exercising their political power here in Scotland. The only questions then will be the age-old ones: will the Nationalists be in a position to bid for power by disinheriting Labour? Or will Labour retain power in Scotland by stealing the nationalist mantle?[50]

Labour's Scottish MPs were, noted journalist Jim Naughtie, 'caught in the trap – numerical superiority but relative impotence in the Commons'.[51] Interviewed on the implications of the overall result for Scotland, Helen Liddell confirmed Baur's analysis in complaining to Walworth Road that this had been 'made harder by statements from MPs suggesting Scotland should examine the separatist option'.[52] A week before the election, South Ayrshire MP George Foulkes warned that if the 'Scottish Labour/Westminster Tory arithmetic' remained unaltered then he could foresee 'a major realignment in Scottish politics with Labour MPs and the trade unions forming a breakaway movement'.[53]

This 'no mandate' argument was gaining traction. Although constitutionally weak given that the basis of a government's legitimacy was derived from the 'confidence' (i.e. a majority) of the whole House of Commons rather than a territorial subset (Scotland), it grew stronger in rhetorical and therefore political terms. By the same logic, however, Labour had lacked a 'mandate' to govern England on three occasions since 1964,[54] a point later made by Mrs Thatcher.

Foulkes, Maxton and Dennis Canavan set out their approach in the 'Foulkes memorandum', which included an unofficial referendum on devolution, orchestrated disruption of Parliament (something inspired by Irish nationalists in the late nineteenth century), industrial action to deprive the government of tax revenue and non-cooperation between Labour local authorities and the Scottish Office.[55] Others, in particular Robert Hughes (Aberdeen North) and Norman Buchan (Paisley South), 'winced at the very mention of mandate, and shrank from an argument they believed to be hopelessly misguided'.[56] In his own category was Livingston MP Robin Cook, who did not 'give a bugger if Thatcher has a mandate or not – I will simply do all I can to stop her'.[57]

Shortly after the 1983 election, Cook had co-authored *Scotland: The Real Divide* with Gordon Brown, newly elected in Dunfermline East. He and Norman Godman (Greenock and Port Glasgow) attempted to bridge the gap with the 'Brown–Godman plan', which was put to 'a long and sometimes ill-tempered meeting' of the Scottish Labour MP group. According to Naughtie, this concentrated 'less on a heady campaign of disruption ... than on a painstaking effort to pull suspicious English colleagues into the devolution camp', just as Michael Foot had suggested two years earlier.[58] The more radical Foulkes plan was, for the moment, rejected.

In July 1983, the Scottish Council observed that 'the Tories' had 'no mandate in Scotland', adding that it had 'a clear duty to do what we can to protect the people of Scotland from the worst excesses of the present Tory Government'. It warned, however, that this 'defence of Scotland' must not 'slip into a separatist mould'.[59] Two months later, the Scottish Council,

STUC and Scottish Labour MPs discussed 'the way forward for the Scottish people' at a 'Joint Action Group' (JAG) meeting in Glasgow. Chaired by Gordon Brown, there was the usual constitutional brainstorming. Jimmy Milne (STUC general secretary since 1976) suggested a 'plebiscite' while George Bolton (then chairman of the Communist Party of Great Britain) proposed 'a Convention of the Scottish People' led by the Labour movement.[60] In a paper entitled 'Facing the Future', the JAG argued that 'the discrepancy between the Scottish and English results – now becoming more substantial and wider in congruity than previously – demands that the present constitutional arrangements be altered to reflect this reality'.[61]

This avoided an explicit endorsement of the 'no mandate' argument, most likely for the sake of unity. Instead, the JAG mandated Scottish Labour MPs to press for a Commons debate on devolution, carry the fight into the Scottish Grand Committee (now meeting in Edinburgh's Old Royal High School) and preparation of a Scottish Assembly Bill. Jimmy Milne told *The Times* there was no 'denying that she [Mrs Thatcher] has a mandate. Our job now is not to talk about the problems, but to discuss what action can be taken to fight them.'[62] Milne would soon be succeeded by Campbell Christie, who hailed from a public sector rather than industrial background, and who would adopt a more nationalistic stance. Sometimes described as Scotland's 'Assembly of Labour',[63] the STUC was entering a period in which it was 'much more significant politically' than industrially.[64]

Composite Motion No. 12 at the 1983 British Labour conference in Brighton stated that it was 'now more clearly established than ever before that the Party at a UK level is unequivocally committed to the establishment of an Assembly at the earliest opportunity'. The full text of the resolution attempted to square several circles, repeatedly emphasising the 'majority' of Labour MPs in Scotland, the need for a Scottish Assembly to possess 'significant economic, revenue raising and legislative powers' and authorising, if necessary, co-operation with 'other bodies and organisations' in order to achieve that aim.[65]

At the same conference, the 'dream ticket' of Neil Kinnock and Roy Hattersley succeeded Michael Foot and Denis Healey as leader and deputy leader of the British Labour party. When Bruce Millan retired from the front bench a few weeks later, Kinnock made Donald Dewar Shadow Scottish Secretary, a position he was to hold for the next nine years. The Garscadden MP's capacity for hard graft was enormous, the failure of his marriage a decade earlier having left him a bachelor, albeit one with a wide circle of friends in Glasgow and beyond.[66] Dewar's commitment to the party's devolution policy was also unquestioned, unlike Kinnock, who had been a high-profile opponent in the 1974–9 Parliament.

As Dewar remarked a few months later, he could not 'think of any subject where the party is more united than on the basic principles of devolution',[67] and indeed this was reflected in Labour's devolution Green Paper, published in September 1984 and representing the views of the Scottish Council, STUC and the Co-operative Party in Scotland. By March 1985 the Shadow Scottish Secretary was claiming that an Assembly, had it been established in 1979, would have protected the Scottish people 'from much damaging legislation which does not reflect Scottish priorities'.[68] When John Maxton attempted to introduce the Scottish Assembly Bill agreed by the JAG, however, seven Labour MPs from the north of England voted with the Conservatives to defeat it.[69]

'KEEPING MILITANT AT BAY'

The miners' strike dominated the 1984–5 parliamentary session. Called by the National Union of Mineworkers (NUM) to prevent pit closures, as in the general strike of 1926 Labour found itself treading a fine line between support for industrial action and broader electoral strategy. Donald Dewar echoed Neil Kinnock in reminding Scottish colleagues that supporting the strike was no substitute for an election victory in 1987/8.[70]

In January 1985 the NUM tried to sustain the eight-month-old strike with a rally in Scotland's largest concert hall, although this served to underline the deep divisions in the Labour movement. When NUM president Arthur Scargill obliquely criticised the absence of Neil Kinnock, Dewar and John Smith, who were present, 'gazed into the air'. In response, they stressed the need for a strong, expanding mining industry while Dewar was careful to place the dispute in an industrial rather than a political context.[71]

With defeat came retribution. In Scotland the National Coal Board (NCB) adopted a much tougher line than in England and Wales by refusing to re-employ miners convicted of even relatively trivial offences during the strike. At a Shadow Cabinet meeting on 6 March 1985, Dewar repeated his call at the recent Scottish Council conference for a delegation of Labour MPs to ask NCB chairman Sir Ian MacGregor for a case-by-case review of the sacked miners. MacGregor, however, said he could not condone acts of violence and intimidation, a stance supported by Scottish Secretary George Younger.

The strike also fuelled the Militant Tendency. At the 1984 British Labour conference Kinnock had failed to convince his party to adopt one-person-one-vote for candidate selection, which meant CLP delegates continued to choose potential MPs. Given the paucity of active Labour members in many parts of Scotland, this made some local parties vulnerable to infiltration. But although Labour members were expelled from Pollok, Cathcart, Cumbernauld and Springburn CLPs, Jimmy Allison made efforts to keep these to a minimum.[72] Former rag-and-bone man Jimmy Wray (dubbed 'I. R. Wray' by Private Eye on account of his republicanism) only beat the Militant candidate in Glasgow Provan by one vote, while Dewar once again faced stiff opposition from Jim Mackechnie, a Strathclyde regional councillor and former member of the International Marxist Group. Dewar won comfortably but considered resignation so gruelling was the fight.[73]

One reason Militant failed to secure more of a foothold in Scotland was due to the calming presence of Communist trade union officials who according to Helen Liddell 'were very, very useful in keeping Militant at bay'.[74] According to Liddell's communications with Walworth Road, however, relations between the Scottish Labour MP group and Scottish executive remained poor. At a meeting on 28 February 1984, she came 'under attack' for executive decisions while noting 'very serious tensions' within the Westminster group. Relations between London and Keir Hardie House were also poor. On 19 September 1985, Liddell only found out by 'accident' that Neil Kinnock was soon to visit Glasgow and she and Donald Dewar protested 'in the strongest possible terms'.[75]

'RATES REBELS'

At the May 1984 district elections, Labour built on its already high vote share and won control of authorities responsible for

74 per cent of the Scottish electorate.[76] In the second elections to the European Parliament a month later, Labour reversed its 1979 result by winning five Scottish MEPs, all in the populous central belt. Its share of the vote was 40.7 per cent, higher than the 36.5 per cent secured by Labour across Great Britain.[77]

Politically trickier were the regional council elections of May 1986. While Dick Stewart, an ex-miner and Labour leader of Strathclyde Regional Council, led the opposition to government rate-capping and spending cuts, the Scottish executive deliberated over how far down the road of illegality the official campaign was willing to travel.[78] At the March 1986 Scottish Council conference Neil Kinnock ruffled feathers with an outspoken attack on 'rates rebels' in Edinburgh, Aberdeen and Stirling.[79] This more 'realistic' position appeared to pay off when in May 1986 the Labour vote reached its highest ever level in a regional election. The party now had an absolute majority of seats in four regions (Fife, Lothian, Central and Strathclyde) and was the largest party in two others (Grampian and Tayside).[80]

Just weeks later a row served as a reminder that there still existed a religious divide, particularly in local government. At an Orange rally in Edinburgh, Sam Campbell, convener of Midlothian District Council and a potential candidate for the presidency of the Convention of Scottish Local Authorities, was reported by *The Scotsman* to have made sectarian comments about Catholics. Although Campbell claimed his remarks had been distorted, he resigned as convener and had the whip withdrawn by his Labour group, a decision he subsequently appealed to the NEC. When that body attempted to rehabilitate Campbell following two apologies, the Scottish executive was 'flooded' with resolutions calling for his expulsion. Only in June 1987 did the Midlothian Labour group restore the whip.[81]

One finding of a major survey by Keating, Levy, Geekie and Brand was the strikingly high proportion of Catholics among district and regional Labour councillors in Glasgow. Half their respondents described their religion as Catholic and an additional 11 per cent said they had been raised as such. By contrast, 29.5 per cent described themselves as Protestant or as having been raised in that faith.[82] Councillors from manual working-class occupations had remained remarkably constant over the past two decades, while the proportion of women (12 per cent) was lower than that in England and Wales (19 per cent).

While this had produced a Scottish political elite which shared many characteristics with its base electorate, it also meant MPs who tended to be older at first election and, in Glasgow, a virtual monopoly for former councillors in safe seats. Only when constituencies changed hands, usually at by-elections, did non-councillors stand more of chance.[83]

'DOOMSDAY SCENARIO'

With another general election in sight and evidence of a modest SNP revival in several urban council by-elections, the party revisited its devolution proposals. At the 1986 Scottish Council conference in Perth, Neil Kinnock tried to sweep away residual doubts about his stance by giving delegates an unequivocal commitment to early legislation, while journalists were told this would be included in the next Labour government's first Queen's Speech.[84]

At a devolution rally organised by the Scottish Council, STUC and Scottish Co-operative Party in March 1987, Shadow Foreign Secretary Denis Healey went even further in suggesting an Assembly could be up and running within two years of an election victory.[85] Writing in the magazine *Radical Scotland*, Jack McConnell, a Stirling district councillor and Labour's prospective parliamentary candidate in Perth and Kinross, added a dose of nationalism by suggesting the party had to show 'that the control over their own lives, which Scots have been deprived of for almost three centuries, can be re-established'.[86] When the text of an MPs' 'declaration' drafted by the Campaign for a Scottish Assembly 'failed to acknowledge the need for Scotland to remain within the U.K.', Dewar had it altered to state that: 'any incoming government must, as an urgent priority, establish part of the structure of government in the United Kingdom, a directly elected Legislative Assembly with responsibility for Scotland's domestic affairs'.[87]

McConnell predicted that the first Labour manifesto for that Assembly could be 'a radical attempt to implement socialist ideas in Scotland'.[88] On 11 June 1987, all this proved academic. Although Labour in Scotland once again increased its vote share and number of seats, the Conservatives secured another landslide and Mrs Thatcher embarked upon her third term as Prime Minister.

Donald Dewar's pre-election target of fifty MPs – nine more than in 1983 – had been delivered on 42.4 per cent of the vote. While impressive, Bochel and Denver highlighted the fact Labour's performance in the north of England and in Wales had been even more substantial.[89] Days after the election, Scottish Labour MPs gathered in Glasgow to hear the Shadow Scottish Secretary say he would demand the government establish an Assembly, scrap the planned Community Charge (the 'Poll Tax') and suspend privatisation. And if Dewar did not obtain a 'satisfactory response' to these quixotic demands, Labour would 'initiate a programme of action aimed at making the Government come to terms with their impossible position in Scotland'.[90] Malcolm Rifkind, Scottish Secretary since early 1986, was polite but unmoved.

To a degree, Labour had boxed themselves in with its talk of a 'doomsday scenario' in which the Conservatives would continue to govern Scotland without any MPs. Now the Conservatives had been re-elected with ten Scottish Members, its principal opponents had to match the expectations of radical action they themselves had created. As Susan Deacon, a former chair of Scottish Labour Students, later observed:

> Labour had a choice, with 50 MPs to the Tories' 10 and a virtual monopoly of Scottish Local Government, they could either challenge the Tories' mandate in Scotland and throw away the Westminster rule book; or they could play safe, hang fire and trust that the Scottish people would wait until England voted Labour too.[91]

As the *Glasgow Herald* put it, Scottish Labour now found itself 'the custodian of the devolution consensus and will be expected to advance the cause'.[92]

But how? In August Robin Cook freelanced with the suggestion of establishing an alternative forum to Westminster 'somewhere in Scotland' and inviting 'MPs of other parties to join us there and vote on … Scottish issues',[93] while according to *The Times*, up to fifteen Scottish Labour MPs were contemplating a fully autonomous party in Scotland, the corollary of similar debates within the Scottish Conservative Party.[94] In a Fabian pamphlet, Donald Dewar observed that the election had been:

> a sweeping endorsement for those who recognise that the Scottish dimension must be accommodated in government. If the result means nothing then democracy is in a poor state. It is no answer to say

that the Tories won nationally and the only mandate that matters is that given by the United Kingdom as a whole. This country is a union of distinct interests.

Dewar also stressed that Labour would not fight a 'one issue campaign':

> Labour must do everything possible to put pressure on this administration – a party which has captured an unprecedented 50 Scottish seats has a duty to do exactly that. Labour MPs are not a Scottish pressure group at Westminster, but in moral and electoral terms the real representatives of a real majority. If the government does not recognise that they will be set on a very dangerous course.[95]

They were fine if empty words, directed at restless elements of the party rather than a statement of political reality. Not only did Dewar ensure his friend Sam Galbraith, the newly elected MP for Bearsden and Strathkelvin, replace Dennis Canavan as chair of the Scottish Labour MP group's devolution sub-committee, but he firmly rejected Canavan's proposals for disruption of Commons proceedings. Nevertheless, at the first Scottish Questions of the new Parliament Canavan repeatedly called 'I spy strangers' in protest at the presence of English Conservative MPs. The Speaker was forced to call a division as astonished Conservatives (and journalists in the gallery) watched as Dewar and the Kilmarnock MP Willie McKelvey engaged in a verbal slanging match in front of the Commons Mace. Fifteen Scottish Labour MPs and one Liberal supported Canavan's motion to expel the interlopers,[96] while the SNP's new deputy leader Alex Salmond dubbed his Labour opponents the 'feeble fifty'.

In September 1987, the British Labour conference congratulated the party in Scotland on its election performance, recognising this as a mandate for a Scottish Assembly and calling on it to produce another devolution bill. The STUC initiated a rain-soaked 'Festival for Scottish Democracy' the same month, contrived to unite Scotland's pro-devolution and anti-government forces under an umbrella of Scottish culture. Finally, in November the Labour movement gathered at Edinburgh's Usher Hall to discuss a rather empty eight-page statement of aims from the Scottish party executive. This special conference coincided with publication of the Scotland Bill, which Susan Deacon grandly described as 'a campaigning tool for the whole Party':

We cannot expect it to be passed this time. Neither should the government – or the other parties – expect it to go away. It will remain as a standing reproach to the government for as long as they choose to ignore the wishes of the Scottish people.[97]

Moral sanctimony as well as 'Tartanisation' was coming to dominate Scottish Labour discourse.

George Galloway, whose defeat of Roy Jenkins at Glasgow Hillhead had soon given way to deselection calls concerning his personal life and expenses at War on Want,[98] emphasised that the 'National Question' could be 'a progressive, liberating issue, in no way associated with negative nationalisms',[99] while Donald Dewar conceded it could appear 'a constitutional abstraction'; but 'if you ask people do you want a greater say in your own affairs', he added, 'it becomes different'.[100] It was so far off Neil Kinnock's radar, meanwhile, that he made no mention of a Scottish Assembly in his address to the 1988 Scottish Council conference. Adding insult to injury, when challenged about this omission in a television interview, the Leader of the Opposition said he had not mentioned lots of things, including 'environmental conditions in the Himalayas'.

'A SORT OF DREAMLAND'

In his March 1988 speech, Kinnock had also failed to provide any guidance regarding the so-called Poll Tax, a radical reform of local government 'rates' which, under heavy pressure from the Scottish Office and Scottish Conservative Party, was to be introduced in Scotland ahead of England and Wales. At an Edinburgh press conference the previous month, the Labour leader had attempted to head off calls for a non-payment campaign, something Kinnock described as 'a sort of dreamland' as he was certain not many would refuse to pay.[101] Donald Dewar agreed and secured a Scottish executive vote for purely political opposition to the Poll Tax.[102]

Elements of the party in Scotland, however, were unhappy with such an orthodox response. In March 1988 the Dunfermline West MP Dick Douglas quit as chairman of the Scottish Labour MP group, while in July, Leith MP Ron Brown publicly burned a Scottish Office guide to the Poll Tax in

Edinburgh. In advance of a special Scottish Council conference on 17 September, meanwhile, thirty-two resolutions were submitted backing an illegal campaign. Significantly, the Scottish region of the Transport and General Workers' Union, which had supported Kinnock's moderate line in March, now supported using all means to defeat the Poll Tax 'including non-payment'.[103] In August, the Scottish executive narrowly rejected sanctioning individual Labour members active in non-payment campaigns.[104]

By September 1988, this had become the main dividing line within the Scottish party, with several MPs, including Robin Cook and the rather more blue-blooded John Home Robertson, backing non-payment. Kinnock and Dewar were desperate to avoid Conservative charges of irresponsibility and lawbreaking, not least because the Poll Tax had been a clear Conservative manifesto commitment. This apparently masked broader tensions. Kinnock later recalled Dewar leading a coup attempt with the aim of installing John Smith as Leader of the Opposition.[105]

The Poll Tax battle played out at Govan Town Hall on 17 September, at the conclusion of which the trade union block vote ensured the Kinnock–Dewar position remained party policy by a decisive majority of two-to-one. Furious at what he called this 'pragmatic, timid' stand, John Mulvey, Labour's leader on Lothian Regional Council, announced his departure from local government. 'Labour has not been prepared to take on the issue and see the political potential in leading an extra-parliamentary campaign of civil disobedience', he explained. 'It seems to be more concerned with keeping the lid on protest rather than helping it grow.'[106] At the concurrent SNP conference, Alex Neil stepped up his party's attacks on the 'feeble fifty', highlighting what he considered their hypocritical willingness to break the law at CND demonstrations.[107]

Dissident Scottish Labour MPs and activists then channelled their energy into a so-called 'Committee of 100'. This included John McAllion (Dundee West), Maria Fyfe (Glasgow Maryhill) and Dick Douglas, and by the end of 1988 another five MPs had thrown their weight behind the non-payment campaign alongside clerics, academics and celebrities – McAllion drew parallels with the 'Red Clydesiders' of the 1920s.[108] In the House of Commons, Dennis Canavan disrupted committee proceedings when English Conservative MPs dared to discuss Scottish business and, even more dramatically, Ron Brown picked up, dropped and damaged the Mace during a late-night debate. When he resisted demands by the Speaker for an apology, Brown was suspended for twenty days and lost the Labour whip.[109] Jim Naughtie considered Canavan et al. 'wild boys' whose borderline anti-Englishness was straying 'dangerously close' to a position the Scottish Labour leadership believed would play into the SNP's hands. 'When a Scottish mandate was accepted', asked Naughtie rhetorically, 'where was the case against separation?'[110]

SCOTTISH LABOUR ACTION

In its founding statement, Scottish Labour Action (SLA) – a ginger group launched on the fringe of the 1988 Scottish Council conference – committed itself to:

1. Recognition of the right of the Scottish people to self-determination
2. ... assert that the Tories had no mandate to run Scotland
3. Non-payment of the Poll Tax
4. Labour participation in a Constitutional Convention
5. Non-co-operation at Westminster on Scottish business
6. Greater autonomy for Labour's Scottish organisation[111]

SLA quickly superseded the Labour Co-ordinating Committee to become the Scottish executive's most influential grouping, winning support from MPs like Robin Cook, George Galloway and Dick Douglas. The group's founders, a Glasgow lawyer called Ian Smart and the Edinburgh Labour activist Robert McLean, became minor celebrities on the CLP speaking circuit,[112] where they lectured members 'on non-payment and on the national question'.[113]

Openly critical of Kinnock and Dewar's leadership, SLA noted acidly that after the inevitable defeat of the latest Scotland Bill in the Commons, a 'deathly silence' had fallen, 'punctuated only by the occasional observation that the next election is only four years away'. It also asserted 'Scotland's right to self-determination on such a basis as the people of Scotland themselves decide',[114] language which led Murray Elder, Helen Liddell's successor as Scottish secretary, to brand them:

a quasi-Nationalist organisation, highly critical of the Parliamentary leadership both at national and Scottish levels, and determined to follow a course of action which would lead to making Scotland ungovernable ... there is a great deal of frustration around and it may be that they are working a rich seam.[115]

In another letter to Neil Kinnock's office, Elder admitted that Ian Smart was correct to say most of the Scottish executive would agree with SLA's critique of British Labour policy on the Poll Tax. 'It has been clear for some time', he added, 'that there is an increasing Nationalist tendency amongst the activist membership in Scotland.'[116] Some jokingly dubbed SLA the 'Scottish Liberation Army'.

The group's proposals for a Scottish Parliament – terminology which began to displace the weaker sounding 'Assembly' – were also far in advance of formal Labour policy. SLA advocated devolving everything 'not specifically exempt from the Assembly's remit', 'control over the financial arrangements for Scotland's Parliament', four-year fixed terms, recall powers, smaller constituencies and 'a system of alternative votes within single member constituencies', only some of which later became a reality.[117] Another SLA pamphlet quoted Robin Cook as saying that to 'all intents and purposes Scotland is an occupied country in which the ruling power depends for its support on a power base which is outside the country'.[118] Such sentiments were not far removed from the SNP's more excitable acolytes.

'THE FEEBLE FIFTY'

In October 1988 the former Scottish Secretary Bruce Millan, soon to become one of the UK's two European Commissioners, took the Chiltern Hundreds to force a by-election in his Govan constituency. Scottish party organiser Jimmy Allison immediately sensed a repeat of Hamilton in 1967, when the sudden departure of the incumbent for a 'cushy' job had spectacularly backfired. His instincts were compounded when the candidate chosen was Bob Gillespie, a Glaswegian SOGAT official based at the print union's headquarters in Essex.[119] Not only did Gillespie fudge the Poll Tax question (he would neither pay nor advocate non-payment) but he proved a clumsy campaigner, especially when questioned about the detail of European policy during a memorable Scottish Television debate. His background also generated hostile coverage from the Robert Maxwell-owned and usually Labour-supporting *Daily Record*.[120]

Taunting Gillespie on the campaign trail was Jim Sillars, who had joined the SNP after the failure of his pro-devolution Scottish Labour Party at the 1979 election. In his 1986 book, *Scotland: The Case for Optimism*, Sillars had characterised Scottish independence as the logical conclusion for Labour voters while also reprimanding Nationalists for their sweeping criticisms of the Labour movement. This he still judged:

> the most important institution in the history of the working people ... At the parliamentary and local government level, Labour has been central to the advancement made in housing, education, the welfare services and the creation of an atmosphere in which concern for people can flourish.[121]

Sillars proved the perfect by-election candidate, and while Labour fought the three-week campaign like a general election campaign on national issues against a Conservative enemy, the SNP concentrated on Labour's Poll Tax stance and the 'feebleness' of its elected representatives. On 10 November 1988, Sillars turned a Labour majority of 19,504 into a deficit of 3,554.

To Geekie and Levy, the result was no surprise, for like Dr Frankenstein, Labour politicians in Scotland had 'created' a nationalist 'monster which now threatens to run completely out of control'. It was, they added, 'hardly surprising that the voters of Govan chose the genuine article rather than the Labour imitation when presented with the choice'.[122] Mitchell considered this 'an unsubtle caricature' of what was actually happening, and indeed Geekie and Levy's conclusion (Scottish Labour secession) was less convincing than their analysis. While Sillars announced his intention to seek common ground with what he called the 'nationalist wing of the Labour Party', the Scottish Council of the Labour Party invited post-mortems.

Activist Peter Russell concluded that the SNP's 'feeble fifty' jibe had struck a chord, while Govan CLP was 'a hollow shell':

> We were ill-prepared to expose the emperor's new clothes of independence in Europe, and we could not a produce a candidate who would add to the effectiveness of the existing team at Westminster. We could not command the streets with numbers of workers,

because nobody bothered. We could not consolidate our votes in the district elections because the local branches were too feeble. The sum total was an impression that Labour did not care.[123]

The Scottish Labour Action-aligned Wendy Alexander believed the Govan result demonstrated that Labour had to address the 'Scottish question' with greater urgency:

> it was a mistake for us not to be more upfront in our commitment to devolution, and a Scottish Assembly, and perhaps through the proposed Constitutional Convention ... None of the above mechanisms were the talk of Govan, but they do address the growing desire amongst the Scottish electorate to find some form of distinct political identity within the UK.[124]

Scottish organiser Jimmy Allison took aim at Murray Elder by suggesting the by-election had been lost because of the 'current Leader and new regime at Walworth Road' rather than he and Helen Liddell working 'as a team via our own press and media contacts'. His prognosis was typically gloomy:

> In the event of another Parliamentary By-election in a Labour held seat, how can we stop the SNP from beating us. How can we prevent the SNP bandwagon continuing at Local Government By-elections and the 1989 European Elections followed by the Regional Elections 1990 and possible 1991 General Election.[125]

The final report from the official Govan committee to the National Executive Committee highlighted the need for 'additional resources and staff in Scotland', more 'attention and publicity' to 'Scottish issues and problems', including being 'more up front' in its commitment to a Scottish Assembly and the proposed 'Constitutional Convention'. Finally, it stressed the need to 'expose' the SNP's 'Independence in Europe' stance as well as 'compiling and issuing material geared to exposing the myth that the SNP would be good for Scotland'.[126]

'LIVE A LITTLE DANGEROUSLY'

Although later commentary attributed Labour's embrace of the cross-party Scottish Constitutional Convention to the Govan by-election result, moves in that direction had been afoot since early October.[127] The Campaign for a Scottish Assembly (CSA), hitherto kept at a distance by the Labour Party, had recently produced its 'Claim of Right' which, like Scottish Labour Action, acknowledged the 'sovereign right of the Scottish people to determine the form of Government best suited to their needs'. On 3 October, Donald Dewar had told *The Scotsman* that if there was 'a chance to find common ground which will unite Scottish opinion [then] that is a prize of considerable importance'.[128] He went further in a lecture at Stirling University three weeks later. Dewar declared that:

> The Labour Party must be prepared to negotiate and not simply seek to enforce the devolution package that we already have before the public. Any convention will be based on Scottish MPs, but there may be a case for broadening its membership to include representatives from other bodies ... What we have got to do is to persuade Scotland that fear must be conquered and that canny caution be put on one side. The people must decide if they are prepared to live a little dangerously in order to achieve what they want.[129]

What changed two days after Govan was the Scottish executive's agreement to endorse the Claim of Right and attend preliminary cross-party talks on the establishment of a Convention. This was consistent with a previous executive decision in June 1986 to reassess its rejection of a convention as 'unnecessary' should Labour fail to win the subsequent general election. Govan, judged SLA secretary Susan Deacon, 'concentrated Labour's mind' and offered it a 'prime opportunity' to take the initiative without waiting for a Westminster majority.[130]

Less than a week after the Govan by-election, Campbell Christie told the STUC Women's Conference that once a Scottish Parliament had been secured the people of Scotland could go on to 'examine the option of independence'.[131] Further examples of 'dangerous living' flowed thick and fast. In a television interview Donald Dewar pointedly referred to devolution as 'independence in the UK', while promising constitutional 'entrenchment' to protect a devolved parliament against the future election of a 'hostile' government and a 'reverse block grant'.[132] In Parliament, the hitherto cautious Dewar led every Scottish opposition MP (including the SNP and Democrat) out of the Commons Chamber in protest at the government's refusal to establish a Scottish Affairs Select Committee.[133] 'Independence in the UK' later died a death when, during a visit to Scotland, Gerald Kaufman said it was 'not worthy of the name "idea"', prompting Murray Elder to quietly but firmly remind him that it was Labour policy.[134] The Scottish Labour MEP David Martin also had reservations, cautioning that any convention had to be 'about increased democracy and not independence'.[135]

The first formal cross-party talks on the Scottish Constitutional Convention took place on 27 January 1989 at COSLA's Edinburgh HQ, where some Labour politicians found it difficult to believe they were sitting around a table with SNP leader Gordon Wilson and the treacherous Jim Sillars. At a subsequent press conference, Dewar said there was 'a long hard road ahead' but that there was a 'basis to move forward and to explore common ground'. Within days, however, Wilson and Sillars had jettisoned what they called 'Labour's Convention', something they now believed was a 'rigged' attempt to avoid any discussion of independence.[136]

John MacKay, the Scottish Conservative Party's chief executive, joked that this meant the convention would now constitute 'the Labour Party Conference at prayer'.[137] At the Scottish Council conference in March, Kinnock atoned for past sins by including an unequivocal commitment to devolution in his address, something likely influenced by East Kilbride MP Adam Ingram, his newly appointed PPS.[138] Just days later, almost every Scottish Labour MP put their name to the Claim of Right at the Church of Scotland's General Assembly chamber on the Mound, which was to house the convention and later the Scottish Parliament itself.[139]

Labour had also been compelled to sort out its campaign machine in the event of another Govan-like challenge, something vindicated when the death of MP Bob McTaggart in March 1989 sparked another by-election, this time in Glasgow Central. While the vote of SNP candidate Alex Neil (a longtime a protégé of Jim Sillars) increased by 20 per cent on the 1987 result, the former LCC activist and trade union official Mike Watson romped home with 54.6 per cent of the vote. Suddenly, everything seemed to be going right for Labour in Scotland. Not only had Keir Hardie House pulled out all the stops in the wake of Govan, but on the constitution the party 'was not now seen, as had been the case in the 1970s, to be endorsing Home Rule merely as a response – made under pressure and with marked reluctance – to political exigencies'.[140] And by supporting the Claim of Right and taking the Scottish Labour Party into the Scottish Constitutional Convention, Donald Dewar had impressed by moving 'beyond narrow party interests' and embracing 'a wider consensus'.[141]

Coinciding with the Glasgow Central by-election had been the third elections to the European Parliament. Keating has observed that as the European Community developed its 'regional' dimension (Bruce Millan became Regional Policy Commissioner), Labour in Scotland began to accommodate Europe within its alternative vision for the UK.[142] At the same time, Labour fought the 1989 campaign as a referendum on the Conservative government's handling of the Poll Tax, unemployment, industrial policy and the NHS, something for which they were rewarded with seven out of eight Scottish Euro constituencies. As Bochel and Denver concluded, it was clear Labour was 'best in tune with Scottish attitudes and aspirations', and so long as it maintained that position it was 'likely to remain the major political force'.[143]

In 1989 the Scottish Militant activist Tommy Sheridan was expelled from Labour for 'bringing the party into disrepute', an NEC-ordered inquiry into Militant infiltration of Glasgow Pollok CLP having begun the previous year. The process was 'long and tedious' and briefly held up by an interim interdict.[144] Centrism remained the order of the day in local government, where Militant was yet to intrude, although former Edinburgh District Council leader Alex Wood had recently established a short-lived 'Scottish Socialist Party' to campaign for an independent socialist Scotland.[145] The Labour vote held up at district elections in May 1988,[146] although at the regional tier Labour-led authorities like Lothian continued to court illegality by defying statutory limits on Poll Tax rates. Keeping within the law meant retaining the last resort of a warrant sale, the optics of which were unwelcome at Keir Hardie House.[147]

As Hutchison observed, Labour's success in local government during the 1980s was 'a bonus', for through its dominance of COSLA and alliance with the STUC it was able to create a 'united front of opposition to Conservative policy', an option it did not have in the rest of the country.[148] In 1990, Jack McConnell became the youngest council leader in Scotland, and despite Bob Thomson of Unison describing him as the 'Ken Livingstone of Scotland', the former maths teacher froze council tax, introduced a 'customers' charter', women's officers and crèches. As his biographer observed, McConnell wanted to 'send a signal that he was not a Labour Party tax-and-spend leader but one who could deliver better services without landing taxpayers ... a greater bill'.[149]

Six weeks out from the May 1990 regional elections, Labour in Scotland also innovated by unveiling its alternative to the Poll Tax, a largely property-based charge quickly dubbed a 'roof tax' by Scottish Conservative chairman Michael Forsyth, an epithet gobbled up by the media.[150] When Forsyth demanded figures, Donald Dewar offered £470 while Charles Gray, the Labour leader of Strathclyde Region, said it would be more like £550. 'Donald where's yer figures', asked Conservative campaign posters, while a MORI poll suggested more Scots approved of the Poll Tax than Labour's alternative.[151] Jimmy Allison blamed Murray Elder, Dewar and particularly Wendy Alexander for the policy, which she had first mooted at the Scottish executive's policy sub-committee.[152]

Such was Labour's electoral strength that days of negative publicity did not prevent it remaining the majority party in Fife, Lothian, Central and Strathclyde, as well as regaining a plurality of seats in Grampian and Tayside.[153] Fife councillor David Rougvie had been 'terrified' the SNP would successfully use its opposition to the Poll Tax to take Labour 'apart'.[154] The roof tax was finally laid to rest a few months later when the Scottish executive announced the 'interim measure' of a return to domestic rates should it win the next election. By 1990, meanwhile, Labour considered its attitude to local government more generally, something driven by its increasingly enthusiastic support for a devolved Scottish Parliament. A 1990 report entitled *The Future of Local Government in Scotland* argued that the existing two-tier system was confusing and that all-purpose authorities might 'assist in the development of local government as an enabling coordinator'. By 1992 the Scottish Labour manifesto declared that local government reform could only 'be effectively undertaken within the framework of constitutional change' and following the recommendations of an independent commission.[155]

'NEW-STYLE POLITICS OVER THE OLD GUARD'

The roof tax also provided an unlikely impetus for personnel changes at Keir Hardie House. When Jimmy Allison's critical report on the regional elections was leaked to the *Sunday Times*, this provided a pretext for early 'retirement' after fourteen years as Scottish organiser. While Allison resented being included within the 'cloth cap image of the Labour Party',[156] journalist Peter Jones described 'a clash of personalities, and a victory for new-style politics over the old guard'. Murray Elder, the Scottish party secretary and Allison's bête noire, was close to Donald Dewar, John Smith and Gordon Brown, his 'cool intellect' having helped convince the party to embrace the Constitutional Convention.[157]

And although Susan Deacon found it 'paradoxical that a party committed to the transference of power from Westminster finds it difficult to contemplate devolving control from Walworth Road',[158] British Labour continued to reject greater autonomy for the party in Scotland. Nevertheless, the tendency of the Scottish Council and its executive to pass left-wing resolutions in defiance of national policy was generally indulged by the London-based leadership. In February 1990, for example, the executive unanimously defied an NEC ban on inviting a Palestine Liberation Organisation representative to speak at its annual conference,[159] while later that year it maintained its long-standing commitment to the 'unilateral removal of all nuclear weapons and bases from British soil and waters in the lifetime of the next Labour government'.[160] The 1991 conference also pledged Scottish Labour to 'promoting debate on uniting Ireland'.[161]

Initially, it appeared Labour in Scotland was also on a collision course when it came to proportional representation for a Scottish Parliament. British deputy leader Roy Hattersley said he was opposed, while Alistair Darling, one of the 1987 Scottish MP intake, argued that if the devolved parliament was elected under first-past-the-post then 'some people felt Labour was likely to be in power for ever and a day'.[162] The STUC agreed with the Scottish executive, while the Scottish Council rejected first past the post but declined to endorse PR.[163] The British Labour conference then established a working party on electoral reform for its planned Scottish, Welsh and English regional assemblies, local government and the House of Commons.

Momentum grew in Scotland for the German-style Additional Member System (AMS), although the May 1991 Scottish Council conference did not specify a model beyond rejecting, once again, the status quo. Donald Dewar made this a virtue, declaring that those who depicted Labour as 'a deeply conservative body incapable of change' had 'not looked at what is happening', while Pat Lally (Labour leader of Glasgow District Council) and George Foulkes warned of a slippery slope, with PR being adopted for every election in the UK.[164] The party had also grown nervous about moves in the Convention to 'entrench' individual powers of the Scottish Parliament, something Scottish secretary Murray Elder now considered 'unnecessary and overcomplex'.[165] Labour representatives also insisted that references to a reduced number of Scottish MPs at Westminster once devolution was achieved were removed from a Convention document.[166]

'SOME KIND OF ACTIVE RESENTMENT'

Only occasionally, or so it seemed, did Labour in Scotland discuss anything other than the constitution. In early 1990 the MPs George Foulkes and Anne McGuire attempted to address the perceived 'ideas deficit' in the Scottish party by establishing the John Wheatley Centre, although this was hamstrung by a lack of funds and activist engagement.[167] In 1991, however, the Centre published Bernard Crick and David Millar's 'Standing Orders for a Scottish Parliament' on behalf of the Constitutional Convention, which later proved influential. 'Labour Scotland', as the party styled itself between 1990 and 1994, also published its own policy documents on rural affairs and Scottish education.[168]

At Westminster, Scottish Labour MPs opposed Conservative plans to transform the Scottish Development Agency (a Labour creation) into the more Tory-friendly 'Scottish Enterprise', a 'single door' agency for job training and state assistance of which even the STUC approved. Detecting a muted response to the closure of the Ravenscraig steelworks, there was also no pledge to re-nationalise should Labour win the next election.[169] Hostilities in the Middle East, meanwhile, led to the formation of Scottish Labour Against the Gulf War which attracted support from between eight and fifteen Scottish MPs but severe reservations on the part of Shadow Cabinet members such as Robin Cook.[170] Since 1979, the number of Scots in the Shadow Cabinet had steadily increased, peaking at five out of fifteen, an over-representation vis-à-vis the Scottish party's strength in the PLP (which was around 20 per cent) and a dramatic turnaround from the position between 1951 and 1974.

As the 1992 general election loomed into view, Strathclyde councillor Charles Gray predicted that if Labour lost another election then 'young people ... might spearhead a breakaway from the Labour movement' while the Scottish people 'would be galvanised into some kind of active resentment'.[171] In April 1990 Dick Douglas had resigned the Labour whip and established a one-man Independent Labour Party in the Commons, eventually joining the SNP that October. When a major opinion poll in February 1992 found that more than 50 per cent of Scots now favoured independence (including half of Labour supporters) and only a quarter devolution, Labour managed to hold its nerve.[172] At the March 1992 Scottish Council conference, Neil Kinnock reiterated a commitment to the speedy passage of devolution legislation, something SLA founder Ian Smart told a fringe meeting would be the most radical change to the UK constitution since 1707, perhaps leading to a 'federal system' both in parliament and 'inside the Labour Party'.[173]

On 9 April 1992, the SNP's vote increased by more than twice the decrease in Labour's – 7.4 to 3.4 per cent – with the Nationalist vote-share having risen in every one of the forty-four seats Labour had defended. Even so, Labour lost just one of its fifty MPs, and the SNP failed to retain either Dick Douglas or Jim Sillars. Clark and Berridge noted three 'unusual' seats in which the Labour vote fell by more than average: 19.7 per cent in Glasgow Pollok, where Scottish Militant Tommy Sheridan had conducted his campaign from prison; 15.1 per cent in Edinburgh Leith, where the deselected Ron Brown had stood as an Independent Labour candidate; and 15.9 per cent in Glasgow Govan where Labour was nevertheless relieved to have reversed its humiliating by-election loss.[174]

As the Conservatives embarked upon a fourth term many of its Scottish MPs had not expected to see, Bochel and Denver posited that the 'chance of a Labour government at Westminster seems as far away as ever and the danger for Labour is that in these circumstances voters will seek solutions elsewhere'.[175] The Scottish Office minister Michael Forsyth was even more certain Labour in Scotland would soon 'disintegrate, and those who have been fanning the flames of nationalism will join the nationalists, and the rest will pay the price of Labour having abandoned a Unionist position'.[176] Malcolm Chisholm, the new

MP for Edinburgh Leith, told Tony Benn he was 'not a separatist' but 'did think things had gone badly wrong'.[177]

Indeed, within weeks, MPs like Brian Wilson, Norman Hogg and John McFall were expressing serious doubts regarding the party's devolutionary emphasis during the general election campaign. Hogg urged a return to the 'bread and butter issues' of jobs, the economy, housing and health instead of what journalist Iain Macwhirter called the 'constitutional metaphysics of mandate, legitimacy and claim of right'.[178] Even Jack McConnell had 'no doubt' Conservatives had successfully 'tapped into concerns about devolution'.[179] Charles Gray channelled Donald Dewar's 1988 remarks by saying Scots would now 'have to live a little dangerously', which he again suggested might include some form of civil disobedience.[180] Towards the end of May, George Galloway led several Scottish Labour MPs into the 'Scotland United' campaign, which also encompassed senior members of the STUC and pop singers such as Pat Kane (Hue and Cry) and Ricky Ross (Deacon Blue). Murray Elder denounced them for 'flying kites' rather than discussing 'Scotland's situation' within the appropriate Labour Party forums.[181]

Galloway and other Members allied with Scotland United were briefly suspended after disrupting a meeting of the Scottish Grand Committee on the now standard pretext that it was 'stacked' with backbench English Conservative MPs.[182] While Donald Dewar said he was confident the 'vast majority' of the party both in the country and in Parliament would not want to adopt 'a quasi-nationalist position', John McAllion asserted that a 'significant number' of Labour MPs now rejected the 'sovereignty of Westminster', although he took care to add that he opposed independence and supported 'home rule within the UK'.[183] On 12 December 1992 thousands of demonstrators demanded constitutional change on the streets of Edinburgh and Labour MPs among them were bounced into signing a 'Declaration of Scottish Sovereignty' which troubled the Scottish Labour leadership.[184] Later, George Robertson warned that those 'of us who want to give real and practical life to a parliament in Scotland have to see beyond the bus tops', a pejorative reference to Scotland United campaign methods.[185]

'A SCOTTISH MAFIA'

On 18 July 1992 John Smith was elected British Labour leader and became Leader of the Opposition, with his close friend Murray Elder swiftly translated from Scottish party secretary at Keir Hardie House to political fixer at Walworth Road. Smith's victory consolidated the hold of what some called the 'Scottish mafia' over the British party, with Gordon Brown (Treasury), the Fettes-educated Tony Blair (Home Office), Robin Cook (trade and industry) and Donald Dewar (now shadowing social security), among its presbyterian godfathers. Smith's leadership was welcome to most sections of the Scottish Labour movement, not least because he was more trusted on devolution than Kinnock. Smith famously called it his (and Scotland's) 'unfinished business'.[186]

Succeeding Dewar as Shadow Scottish Secretary was the Monklands West MP Tom Clarke, whose main claim to fame had been piloting the Disabled Persons (Services, Consultation and Representation) Act 1986 through Parliament. Shortly after his appointment to the front bench, however, Clarke was diagnosed with chronic fatigue syndrome, which kept him away from the Commons until early 1993 and deprived him of the chance to stamp his authority on what remained a fractious Scottish Labour MP group. Clarke's most effective lieutenant was Henry McLeish, a former professional footballer and the MP for Central Fife, who kept up pressure on the Conservatives over water privatisation, Rosyth and an acrimonious dispute at the Timex factory in Dundee.[187] In his memoirs, McLeish reflected on what he called the party's 'insidious' factionalism:

> It should not matter if you are Catholic or Protestant – but in too many constituencies it [did]. I could not be pigeon-holed as either and had a varied group of friends, which some found baffling. I did not go to Glasgow University, so was not an automatic member of the inner circle, which included John Smith, Donald Dewar and their fellow alumni. Nor did I come from the west of Scotland, so was not part of the Glasgow/Lanarkshire power grouping which seemed to think it had some kind of hereditary right to control Scottish Labour.

Instead of enjoying 'a party of fraternity', McLeish found it 'hard to believe some of the things that were done and said by colleagues, about colleagues'.[188]

McLeish might have been referring to Clarke, for upon his return to Westminster, the Shadow Scottish Secretary found himself caught between Scotland United and his group's more unionist Members. In March 1992 the SNP unwittingly handed Labour a lifeline by voting with John Major's government on the Maastricht Treaty in return for some additional places on the largely irrelevant European Committee of the Regions. With the taunt of 'tartan Tories' back in vogue, at the subsequent Scottish Labour conference Clarke was able to call off cross-party talks on devolution and return to the less problematic forum of the Constitutional Convention without any political damage.[189]

Media and party criticism of Clarke, however, continued, something his ally Jimmy Hood said was motivated by 'jealousy and political snobbery',[190] and for which Clarke partly blamed Donald Dewar, whom he considered a 'hard-hearted, miserable, mean misanthrope'.[191] The April 1993 Scottish conference offered him an opportunity to reassert himself with a passionate rallying call to fight for Scotland's growing underclass. 'Let them hear our angry voices', declared Clarke. 'Let them know that our intolerance of poverty is absolute.' He also drew on the party's favoured mythology, observing that it was:

> Sixty years since the Clydeside MPs descended on parliament with a dream to build the fair society. Today the task is as urgent, as necessary, as demanding as ever. As we seek to lead the people of Scotland into a new century, we can build the society of which our pioneers dreamed a fair society, built on needs not greed.[192]

In attendance was Tony Benn, who approvingly detected 'just a flavour of the old radicalism'.[193]

At the same conference, calls to 'devolve' Scottish party organisation from Walworth Road prompted an outburst from Aberdeen North MP Robert Hughes against being 'dragged down the alleys of stupid, silly little constitutional issues'.[194] The concept of a more autonomous party had drawn support from Scotland United, particularly George Galloway, and had been a cornerstone of Scottish Labour Action's agenda since its formation in 1988. In essence, SLA believed Labour had to make the transition from 'Scottish Council' to a fully-fledged 'Scottish Labour Party' if it was to retain the support of the Scottish people.[195] Such calls had been fuelled by tensions over

Labour's stance on water privatisation, which the party in Scotland opposed but on which Tom Clarke appeared equivocal. This, according to SLA's Robert McLean, highlighted the need to have policies which reflected the 'political consensus in Scotland' as well as for 'a leader who has the authority of being elected by the party in Scotland'.[196]

In October 1992 Labour had appointed Jack McConnell 'general secretary' of the Labour Party in Scotland, a change in nomenclature supported by British Labour's then general secretary, Larry Whitty. A leading light in Scottish Labour Action – the former Stirling Council leader confessed to having been an SNP member before he 'grew up' – McConnell now jettisoned his previous belief in party autonomy.[197] The recruitment process, described by Glasgow MEP Janey Buchan as 'sexist, shitty, and stupid', had not only been held in Blackpool to accommodate the interview panel's presence at the Trades Union Congress, but two capable women candidates had been passed over despite Labour's promise to address its male dominance.[198] Making matters worse was the Scottish executive's decision later in 1993 to drop a proposal for women-only shortlists under pressure from the NEC, a move which outraged the increasingly influential Scottish Labour Women's Caucus.

'VENTILATING LOCAL PARTY DEMOCRACY'

It must have been a source of some grief for John Smith that his short leadership of the party often seemed to be dominated by a row involving his Monklands constituency. The allegations were threefold: first, that Labour councillors from mainly Catholic Coatbridge had kept control of nearly all the top jobs on Monklands District Council (MDC) at the expense of those in mainly Protestant Airdrie; second, that major spending projects had been disproportionately allocated to Coatbridge on the same basis, including the loss-making Time Capsule sports complex; and third, that MDC operated a two-tier system for job applications, or at the very least did not follow standard recruitment practices.

The dispute began in August 1992 when four dissident Airdrie Labour councillors (all of whom were Catholic) revealed the existence of green job application forms – apparently only available to councillors – and pink forms for everyone else. All were subsequently suspended by the party. It was a good story, and indeed by November the *Daily Record* was devoting a growing number of column inches to the allegations. At around the same time the Scottish party finally set up an inquiry into MDC's recruitment and selection procedures, although Jack McConnell made a point of defending the decision of Smith and Tom Clarke (whose constituency also fell within MDC) not to intervene. It was, he said, an internal Labour Party matter which had to be dealt with in the usual way.[199] Later, McConnell reflected that Smith was 'genuinely torn between sympathy for those who had been loyal to him locally for many years, and the obvious need to investigate the charges'. Smith, however, had ultimately (and correctly in McConnell's account) opted to 'put the public and party interest first'.[200]

In early 1993 Clarke – a former Monklands provost – chose publicly to defend the conduct of Coatbridge councillors in his constituency, which simply served to highlight the continuing silence of Smith. In his memoirs, he dismissed the whole affair as 'one of the silliest and most time-wasting pieces of wholly invented nonsense in recent British political history'.[201] In March 1993, Labour's inquiry recommended a major overhaul of MDC's recruitment procedures but was accused by the media of a 'whitewash' in relation to the 'jobs for the boys' and infrastructure spending allegations. Inquiry chair Anne McGuire called it an attempt to 'ventilate local party democracy' even though its only real criticism was directed at the *Airdrie and Coatbridge Advertiser* for having gone 'beyond reasonable bounds' in its coverage of the affair.[202]

The nadir came the following month when Smith's monthly constituency surgery was targeted by forty Labour protestors and filmed by a Scottish Television camera crew.[203] The BBC reporter Michael Crick also ventured north to pointedly ask the Leader of the Opposition if he viewed Monklands as 'a model for how a Labour Government would operate'.[204] Scottish Office minister Allan Stewart went for the jugular, telling journalists that 'John Smith preaches about Christian socialism but actions speak louder than words – and his silence on Monklands speaks volumes'.[205] In this as well as other respects, judged *Scotland on Sunday*, Smith's 'otherwise admirable Scottishness' could prove a weakness. Not only did he lack daily contact through his constituency or family residence (which was in Edinburgh's

Morningside) with peculiarly English problems, but Scottish Labour had been so dominant for so long that both it and Smith failed 'to realise the extent of the alienation in middle and southern England that still exists between the Labour Party and the electorate'.[206]

In October 1993, an obviously unhappy Tom Clarke was moved from shadowing the Scottish Office to international development in a front bench reshuffle. George Robertson took over as Shadow Scottish Secretary and remained in post until the 1997 general election. In his memoirs, Henry McLeish credited Robertson with 'a significant return to common sense in the Scottish Labour Party'.[207] In March 1994, Strathclyde Regional Council held a postal referendum of residents on water and sewerage privatisation, which had been one of the issues troubling Clarke. Turnout was high and, though not sanctioned by the government or legally binding, 97 per cent voted against.

'THE NATIONAL PARTY OF SCOTLAND'

Just weeks after Robertson's appointment, the results of an internal Labour Party consultation were obtained by *Scotland on Sunday*. This revealed that Scottish members wanted a distinct party organisation to contest seats in a Scottish Parliament albeit without a 'complete split' from Walworth Road. 'The manifesto should be prepared in Scotland and agreed in Scotland', said a sympathiser, 'without a veto from London'. Once cleared by a joint meeting of the Scottish executive and NEC, the rule changes were to be submitted to the next Scottish party conference for approval.[208]

Activists had already been invited to suggest a new party name as part of an internal review Jack McConnell hoped might rejuvenate an organisation 'lacking the level of activity you would associate with the largest political party in Scotland'. Until recently, it had continued to apply 'the minimum', a 1,000-member affiliation rule which had ceased to be a formal requirement back in 1979.[209] When actual membership began to be reported in the early 1990s, the figure dropped from 74,000 to a more realistic 20,000, half the English recruitment ratio.[210] Informally, meanwhile, journalists and MPs already used the term 'Scottish Labour Party', in part because 'Scottish Council of the Labour Party' was a bit of a mouthful. As Bennie, Brand

and Mitchell observed, despite the formal constitutional position the Scottish Council had often acted reasonably autonomously, a tension between the formal and informal constitutions which resembled that 'in the constitution of the state itself'.[211]

At the Dundee conference in March 1994, delegates voted by three to one formally to become the 'Scottish Labour Party', thereby ridding themselves, as *The Scotsman* noted, 'of the spectre of the 1976 split over devolution' led by Jim Sillars.[212] The nomenclature also evoked Keir Hardie's party in the late ninteenth-century, although the Scottish executive had preferred 'Labour Party Scotland'. Labour, however, could now stake its claim to be 'the national party of Scotland, a small semantic difference but a big ideological gulf away from claiming to be the nationalist party of Scotland'.[213] Flanked by a pipe band and wearing a tartan tie, George Robertson drove home this point by saying Scots could celebrate their identity without turning 'to the dangerous separatism of the Nationalists in order to express it'. By voting for the Scottish Labour Party, he added, 'they are voting not only for a party that is distinctly Scottish but one that can get rid of the Tories'. SNP leader Alex Salmond was unimpressed. The Scottish people, he predicted, would 'see through the sham of Labour's pathetic attempt to repackage themselves with a tartan wrapper'.[214]

The change of name was largely symbolic. Staff at Keir Hardie House continued to be appointed and paid for by Walworth Road, although Scottish views were considered to a greater degree than in the past.[215] Tommy Sheppard, the former deputy leader of Hackney Council, returned to Scotland as Jack McConnell's deputy, while the party planned new offices throughout Scotland, an activism network, a full-time youth officer and glitzy fund-raising dinners, even though the previous year's £100-a-plate affair with John Smith had prompted criticism from Mike Watson and others in the LCC.[216] Mohammed Sarwar had recently joined the Scottish executive, becoming the first millionaire to join the party leadership as well as its first non-white representative.[217]

'THE SETTLED WILL'

During 1993 and 1994, the Scottish Labour group of MPs had bitterly opposed Conservative plans for local government reorganisation even though the party was increasingly in sympathy with the principle of single-tier authorities. They vowed to oppose implementation and, if necessary, reverse it once in government. Ostensibly, Labour's stance stemmed from the failure to advance change in the context of a devolution, although the fact the new boundaries were in several cases politically determined by the government masked any contradictions.[218] The Local Government (Scotland) Act 1994 – which created twenty-nine mainland and three island unitary authorities – would not receive Royal Assent until November 1994, and in the interim John Smith fudged the issue by pledging an independent commission to inform a Scottish Parliament's view on restructuring.[219]

Local government continued to cause headaches beyond Monklands. In January 1994 a group of eight rebel Edinburgh District councillors who had defied the Labour whip to support a Conservative vote of no confidence in the council's chief executive were suspended by the NEC,[220] a decision they tried to get overturned at the Court of Session.[221] Their legal action came just days after what turned out to be Scotland's final regional elections on 5 May, at which Labour's vote share dropped slightly to 41.8 per cent, losing the party a trio of councillors. The SNP's rose by 5 per cent to 26.8, securing the party an additional thirty-one regional councillors, albeit without very much to do.

A week later, on 12 May 1994, John Smith died from a heart attack. Paying tribute in the Commons, Dennis Canavan recalled Smith's efforts to get devolution onto the statute book, trusting that soon 'the fruits' of those 'labours will be there to be seen'.[222] Smith had recently called devolution 'the settled will of the Scottish people' and the 'cornerstone' of his 'plans for democratic renewal' in the UK.[223] At his funeral in Edinburgh, the former Labour leader was eulogised by three close friends, James Gordon, Derry Irvine and, most eloquently, Donald Dewar. 'The people know they have lost a friend, someone who was on their side', he said. 'They know it, and they feel it.'[224] Following a reception at Edinburgh's Parliament House – custom built as the Old Scots Parliament in the seventeenth century – Smith's coffin was taken by road and ferry to be laid to rest on the Hebridean island of Iona. It was, as many commentators noted, the traditional burial ground of Scottish kings.

NOTES

1. M. Watson (2001), *Year Zero: An Inside View of the Scottish Parliament*, Edinburgh: Polygon, xi.
2. See D. Torrance (2009), 'The journey from the 79 Group to the modern SNP', in G. Hassan (ed.), *The Modern SNP: From Protest to Power*, Edinburgh: Edinburgh University Press, 162–76.
3. L. Bennie, J. Brand & J. Mitchell (1997), *How Scotland Votes: Scottish Parties and Elections*, Manchester: Manchester University Press, 52.
4. *The Times*, 10 March 1980.
5. J. M. Bochel & D. T. Denver (1980), 'Parties' progress: The District Council elections of May 1980', in H. M. Drucker & N. L. Drucker (eds), *Scottish Government Yearbook 1981*, Edinburgh: Paul Harris, 237–52.
6. J. Naughtie (1980), 'The year at Westminster', in H. M. Drucker & N. L. Drucker (eds), *Scottish Government Yearbook 1981*, Edinburgh: Paul Harris, 35–6.
7. R. Cook (1977), 'Parliament and the Scots conscience: Reforming the law on divorce, licensing and homosexual offences', in H. M. Drucker & M. G. Clarke (eds), *Scottish Government Yearbook 1978*, Edinburgh: Paul Harris, 108–12.
8. D. Dewar (1980), 'The Select Committee on Scottish Affairs', in H. M. Drucker & N. L. Drucker (eds), *Scottish Government Yearbook 1981*, Edinburgh: Paul Harris, 13–14.
9. J. Naughtie (1981), 'The year at Westminster', in H. M. Drucker & N. L. Drucker (eds), *Scottish Government Yearbook 1982*, 5–7.
10. J. Allison with H. Conroy (1995), *Guilty by Suspicion: A Life and Labour*, Argyll Publishing, 84–5.
11. *Herald*, 13 November 2001. On one occasion Dewar rescued Urquhart 'from a splenetic Sam Galbraith in the middle of Glasgow Airport'.
12. Note dated 3/26 March 1982, TD 1384/7, Scottish Labour Party Papers, Glasgow: Mitchell Library.
13. Note dated 13 December 1984, TD 1384/7, Scottish Labour Party Papers.
14. Allison, 95.
15. H. Drucker (1982), 'The curious incident: Scottish party competition since 1979', in D. McCrone (ed.), *Scottish Government Yearbook 1983*, Edinburgh: University of Edinburgh, 20.
16. J. M. Bochel & D. T. Denver (1983), 'Towards a four party system? The regional elections of May 1982', in D. McCrone (ed.), *Scottish Government Yearbook 1983*, Edinburgh: University of Edinburgh, 77–80.

17. Notes dated 12 January, 27 February and 11 June 1981, TD 1384/7, Scottish Labour Party Papers.
18. Allison, 94.
19. Note dated 14 November 1981, TD 1384/7, Scottish Labour Party Papers. The 'altercation' concerned an advert in *Labour Student* about the PLO.
20. Note dated 24/25 November 1981, TD 1384/7, Scottish Labour Party Papers.
21. Note dated 4–25 June 1982, TD 1384/7, Scottish Labour Party Papers.
22. *The Times*, 25 February 1983.
23. Bochel & Denver (1983), 25–7.
24. G. Brown (2017), *My Life, Our Times*, London: Bodley Head, 60–3.
25. *The Times*, 28 March 1981.
26. F. Mackay (2004), 'Women and the Labour Party in Scotland', in G. Hassan (ed.) (2004), *The Scottish Labour Party: History, Institutions and Ideas*, Edinburgh: Edinburgh University Press, 116.
27. Note dated 18 September 1979, TD1384/7, Scottish Labour Party Papers. The poll was published in the *Sunday Mail* which, noted Liddell, 'continues to be most helpful to us'.
28. Bochel & Denver (1983), 26.
29. Anonymous (1981), 'John Smith: Portrait of a devolutionist', *Bulletin of Scottish Politics* 2, 45.
30. 'Discussion Paper on Devolution', 19 January 1982, Acc.10951/124, William W. Hamilton Papers, Edinburgh: National Library for Scotland.
31. Watson, 28.
32. *The Economist*, 21 February 1981.
33. *The Times*, 16 March 1981.
34. *The Times*, 18 March 1981.
35. Minutes of Scottish Labour Group meeting, 7 April 1981, Acc.10951/124, William W. Hamilton Papers.
36. J. Geekie and R. Levy (1989), 'Devolution and the tartanisation of the Labour Party', *Parliamentary Affairs* 42:3, 5–6.
37. A. Marr (1992), *The Battle for Scotland*, London: Penguin, 183.
38. HC Deb 4 March 1980 Vol 980 cc256–64 [Government Of Scotland (Scottish Convention)]. The others were David Lambie and John Home Robertson.
39. E. Ross (1983), 'Devolution', in J. Lansman & A. Meale (eds), *Beyond Thatcher: The Real Alternative*, London: Junction Books, 191.

40. *Scotsman*, 28 July 1982.
41. *Radical Scotland*, February–March 1983.
42. B. Millan (1983), 'Scotland', in G. Kaufman (ed.), *Renewal: Labour's Britain in the 1980s*, London: Penguin, 139–44.
43. Gordon Craig, 25 January 1983, TD 1384/11/1, Scottish Labour Party Papers.
44. Note dated 15 August 1983, TD 1384/7, Scottish Labour Party Papers.
45. Allison, 101–2.
46. A. McInnes (2019), 'Deindustrialisation and Gordon Brown's approach to devolution in Scotland', *Scottish Labour History* 54, 143.
47. Allison, 101–3.
48. Note dated 11 March 1981, TD 1384/7, Scottish Labour Party Papers.
49. D. T. Denver (1983), 'The 1983 general election in Scotland', in D. McCrone (ed.), *Scottish Government Yearbook 1984*, Edinburgh: University of Edinburgh, 8–17.
50. C. Baur (1983), 'The election conundrum', in D. McCrone (ed.), *Scottish Government Yearbook 1984*, Edinburgh: University of Edinburgh, 26.
51. J. Naughtie (1982), 'The year at Westminster', in D. McCrone (ed.), *Scottish Government Yearbook 1983*, Edinburgh: University of Edinburgh, 12.
52. Note dated 10 June 1983, TD 1384/7, Scottish Labour Party Papers.
53. *Glasgow Herald*, 1 June 1983.
54. In the 1964–6, February–October 1974 and 1974–9 Parliaments.
55. *The Scotsman* (28 July 1982) called them Scottish Labour's 'Gang of Four' (John Maxton, John Home Robertson, George Foulkes and David Marshall).
56. J. Naughtie (1983), 'The year at Westminster', in D. McCrone (ed.), *Scottish Government Yearbook 1984*, Edinburgh: University of Edinburgh, 32.
57. *Radical Scotland*, June/July 1984.
58. Naughtie (1983), 33.
59. Scottish Council statement, July 1983, Acc.10951/124, William W. Hamilton Papers.
60. Report of Joint Action Group, 16 September 1983, Acc.10951/124, William W. Hamilton Papers.
61. McInnes, 142–4.
62. *The Times*, 17 September 1983.
63. J. Craigen (1989), 'The Scottish T.U.C. – Scotland's Assembly of Labour', in I. Donnachie, C. Harvie & I. S. Wood (eds) (1989),

     Forward! Labour Politics in Scotland, 1888–1988, Edinburgh: Polygon, 133.
64. K. Aitken (2001), *The Bairns o' Adam: The Story of the STUC*, Edinburgh: Polygon, 2.
65. 1983 British Labour conference resolution, SPA/GF/CSA/1, George Foulkes Collection, Stirling: Scottish Political Archive.
66. J. Naughtie (1984), 'The year at Westminster', in D. McCrone (ed.), *Scottish Government Yearbook 1985*, Edinburgh: University of Edinburgh, 28.
67. *Glasgow Herald*, 1 March 1984.
68. *Glasgow Herald*, 1 March 1985.
69. Geekie & Levy, 409.
70. M. Dowle (1985), 'The year at Westminster', in D. McCrone (ed.), *Scottish Government Yearbook 1986*, Edinburgh: University of Edinburgh, 13.
71. *Guardian*, 4 January 1985.
72. Allison, 67.
73. *Guardian*, 2 January 1986.
74. G. Hassan & E. Shaw (2012), *The Strange Death of Labour Scotland*, Edinburgh: Edinburgh University Press, 289–90.
75. Notes dated 28 February 1984 and 21 September 1985, TD 1384/7, Scottish Labour Party Papers.
76. J. Bochel & D. Denver (1984), 'The district elections of 1984: A 1+3 party system', in D. McCrone (ed.), *Scottish Government Yearbook 1985*, Edinburgh: University of Edinburgh, 6–16.
77. J. Bochel & D. Denver (1984), 'The 1984 European election in Scotland', in D. McCrone (ed.), *Scottish Government Yearbook 1985*, Edinburgh: University of Edinburgh, 20–2.
78. *Guardian*, 28 October 1985.
79. Dowle, 13.
80. J. Bochel & D. Denver (1986), 'Labour predominance reasserted: The regional elections of 1986', in D. McCrone (ed.), *Scottish Government Yearbook 1987*, Edinburgh: University of Edinburgh, 27–31.
81. Allison, 140–3.
82. M. Keating, R. Levy, J. Geekie & J. Brand (1989), *Labour Elites in Glasgow*, Glasgow: University of Strathclyde, 19.
83. Keating et al., 7–23.
84. *Guardian*, 10 March 1986.
85. *Financial Times*, 14 March 1987.
86. *Radical Scotland*, February/March 1987.
87. John Home Robertson to Scottish Labour MPs, 19 March 1987, Acc.10951/124, William W. Hamilton Papers.
88. *Radical Scotland*, February/March 1987.

89. J. Bochel & D. Denver (1987), 'The 1987 general election in Scotland', in D. McCrone & A. Brown (eds), *Scottish Government Yearbook 1988*, Edinburgh: University of Edinburgh, 27.
90. *Financial Times*, 16 June 1987.
91. S. Deacon (1989), 'Adopting conventional wisdom – Labour's response to the national question', in A. Brown & R. Parry (eds), *Scottish Government Yearbook 1990*, Edinburgh: University of Edinburgh, 63.
92. *Glasgow Herald*, 13 June 1987.
93. *Glasgow Herald*, 31 August 1987.
94. *The Times*, 11 August 1987.
95. D. Dewar (1987), *Scotland: The Way Forward*, London: Fabian Society, 10.
96. M. Dowle (1987), 'The year at Westminster: all change?', in D. McCrone & A. Brown (eds), *Scottish Government Yearbook 1988*, Edinburgh: University of Edinburgh, 16–17.
97. Deacon, 63–4.
98. *Guardian*, 19 September 1987.
99. *Radical Scotland*, October/November 1987.
100. *Guardian*, 22 January 1988.
101. *Financial Times*, 3 February 1988.
102. *Financial Times*, 30 January 1988.
103. *Guardian*, 15 August 1988.
104. *Guardian*, 23 August 1988.
105. A. Seldon (2022), 'Neil Kinnock reflects', in K. Hickson (ed.), *Neil Kinnock: Saving the Labour Party?*, London: Routledge, 17.
106. *Guardian*, 17 September 1988.
107. *Guardian*, 19 September 1988.
108. *Guardian*, 10 December 1988.
109. P. Hannam (1988), 'The year at Westminster', in A. Brown & D. McCrone (eds), *Scottish Government Yearbook 1989*, Edinburgh: University of Edinburgh, 14–17.
110. J. Naughtie (1989), 'Labour 1979 to 1988', in I. Donnachie, C. Harvie & I. S. Wood (eds) (1989), *Forward! Labour Politics in Scotland, 1888–1988*, Edinburgh: Polygon, 162.
111. J. Mitchell (2014), *The Scottish Question*, Oxford: Oxford University Press, 46.
112. I. Macwhirter (1989), 'After Doomsday: The Convention and Scotland's constitutional crisis', in A. Brown & R. Parry (eds), *Scottish Government Yearbook 1990*, Edinburgh: University of Edinburgh, 24.
113. Marr, 200.
114. Marr, 200

115. Murray Elder to Larry Whitty, 4 March 1988, SPA/JMC/SN/SLA/8, Jack McConnell Collection, Stirling: Scottish Political Archive. How this material came to form part of Jack McConnell's papers is a mystery.
116. Murray Elder to Charles Clarke, 4 March 1988, SPA/JMC/SN/SLA/7, Jack McConnell Collection.
117. Scottish Labour Action (1989), *Proposals for Scottish Democracy: A Scottish Labour Action Discussion Document*, Edinburgh: SLA, 4–16.
118. Scottish Labour Action (1989), *Real Power for Scotland: Scottish Labour Action's Response to the Constitutional Convention's Consultative Document – 'A Parliament for Scotland'*, Whitburn: SLA, 8.
119. Allison, 183.
120. Liddell was by this point working for Robert Maxwell, having left Keir Hardie House in 1988.
121. J. Sillars (1986), *Scotland: The Case for Optimism*, Edinburgh: Polygon, 25.
122. Geekie & Levy, 400–11.
123. Peter Russell, 'Govan by-election 1988', 15 December 1988, TD 1384/11/7, Scottish Labour Party Papers. 'The bizarre notion of getting more self-determination from Brussels or Strasbourg than from Westminster', added Russell, 'should be exposed as the fantasy it is'.
124. Wendy Alexander, undated, TD 1384/11/7, Scottish Labour Party Papers.
125. James Allison, 13 November 1988, TD 1384/11/7, Scottish Labour Party Papers.
126. Govan Committee report, undated, TD 1384/11/7, Scottish Labour Party Papers.
127. For a full analysis, see A. McFadyen (2011), 'Agents and Institutions: Donald Dewar and the Politics of Devolution', Edinburgh: University of Edinburgh, PhD thesis.
128. *Scotsman*, 3 October 1988.
129. L. Paterson (ed.) (1998), *A Diverse Assembly: The Debate on a Scottish Parliament*, Edinburgh: Edinburgh University Press, 172–3.
130. Deacon, 68.
131. *Glasgow Herald*, 17 November 1988.
132. Deacon, 70–3.
133. *The Times*, 21 December 1988.
134. Macwhirter (1989), 21.
135. D. Martin (1989), 'The democratic deficit', in O. Dudley Edwards (ed.), *A Claim of Right for Scotland*, Edinburgh: Polygon, 85.

136. See D. Torrance (2015), *Salmond: Against the Odds* (Third Edition), Edinburgh: Birlinn, 77–9.
137. Macwhirter (1989), 27–32.
138. P. MacMahon (1989), 'The year at Westminster', in A. Brown & R. Parry (eds), *Scottish Government Yearbook 1990*, Edinburgh: University of Edinburgh, 16.
139. It has commonly been asserted that every Scottish Labour MP except Tam Dalyell put their name to the Claim, but not all of them were present on 30 March 1989.
140. I. G. C. Hutchison (2000), *Scottish Politics in the Twentieth Century*, Basingstoke: Palgrave, 151.
141. M. Smith (2005), 'An unconventional politician', in W. Alexander (ed.), *Donald Dewar: Scotland's first First Minister*, Edinburgh: Mainstream, 73.
142. M. Keating (2015), 'The European dimension to Scottish constitutional change', *Political Quarterly* 86:2, 2.
143. J. Bochel & D. Denver (1989), 'The 1989 European elections in Scotland', in A. Brown & R. Parry (eds), *Scottish Government Yearbook 1990*, Edinburgh: University of Edinburgh, 96–9.
144. Allison, 70.
145. *Glasgow Herald*, 12 January 1989.
146. J. Bochel & D. Denver (1988), 'The Scottish district elections of 1988', in A. Brown & D. McCrone (eds), *Scottish Government Yearbook 1989*, Edinburgh: University of Edinburgh, 20–31.
147. *Guardian*, 21 November 1989.
148. Hutchison (2000), 149.
149. L. Davidson (2005), *Lucky Jack: Scotland's First Minister*, Edinburgh: Black & White, 47–8.
150. Labour Scotland (1990),*The Property Tax: Overall a Fairer Tax for Scotland*, Glasgow: SCLP.
151. I. Macwhirter (1990), 'The year at Westminster', in A. Brown & D. McCrone (eds), *Scottish Government Yearbook 1991*, Edinburgh: University of Edinburgh, 17–19.
152. Allison, 202.
153. J. Bochel & D. Denver (1990), 'The regional elections of 1990', in A. Brown & D. McCrone (eds), *Scottish Government Yearbook 1991*, Edinburgh: University of Edinburgh, 132.
154. David Rougvie to William Hamilton, 15 July 1990, Acc.10951/124, William W. Hamilton Papers.
155. M. McVicar, G. Jordan & G. Boyne (1994), 'Ships in the night: Scottish political parties and local government reform', *Scottish Affairs* 9, 91.
156. For a full account see Allison, 226.

157. P. Jones (1993), 'Politics', in M. Linklater & R. Denniston (eds), *Anatomy of Scotland*, Edinburgh: Chambers, 385–6.
158. Deacon, 73.
159. *Guardian*, 27 February 1990.
160. Press Association, 23 October 1990.
161. Labour Party (1994), *Report '94*, Glasgow: Labour Scotland.
162. *Independent*, 8 March 1990.
163. *Independent*, 11 March 1990.
164. *Independent*, 26 May 1991.
165. 'Note to Scottish Executive Committee', 4 May 1990, TD 1384/13, Scottish Labour Party Papers.
166. *Scotsman*, 9 December 1991.
167. Hassan & Shaw, 59. The John Wheatley Centre published *European Unity and the Democratic Deficit* (1990) and *European Union: The Shattered Dream?* (1993), both by Labour MEP David Martin. It was later renamed the Centre for Scottish Public Policy.
168. See *A Future for Rural Scotland: Policy Document* and *A New Approach – Scottish Education in the 1990s: Policy Document*.
169. Macwhirter (1990), 15–24.
170. I. Macwhirter (1991), 'The political year in Westminster', in L. Paterson & D. McCrone (eds), *Scottish Government Yearbook 1992*, Edinburgh: University of Edinburgh, 22.
171. *The Economist*, 6 April 1991.
172. *Herald*, 27 February 1992. It was a rogue poll, with subsequent surveys placing support at 30–35 per cent. By April 1992, another poll showed 55 per cent of Labour voters supporting devolution and only 27 per cent independence.
173. *Herald*, 14 March 1992.
174. I. Clark & J. Berridge (1992), *Scotland Votes: The General Election 1992 in Scotland*, Aberdeen: Grampian Television.
175. J. Bochel & D. Denver (1992), 'The 1992 general election in Scotland', *Scottish Affairs* 1, 26.
176. *Independent*, 11 April 1992.
177. T. Benn (2002), *Free at Last! Diaries, 1991–2001*, London: Hutchinson, 116.
178. I. Macwhirter (1993), 'The road to nowhere: Scotland in Westminster, Parliamentary Session 1992/3', *Scottish Affairs* 4, 112.
179. *Scotland on Sunday*, 6 September 1998.
180. *The Economist*, 11 April 1992.
181. *Guardian*, 26 May 1992.
182. *Herald*, 17 June 1992.

183. *Herald*, 5 June 1992. This was self-evidently contradictory.
184. Macwhirter (1993), 118.
185. *Scotland on Sunday*, 7 November 1993. Speakers at one rally (including Nicola Sturgeon) had orated from an open-top double decker bus.
186. Bennie et al., 58.
187. Macwhirter (1993), 113.
188. Henry McLeish (2004), *Scotland First: Truth and Consequences*, Edinburgh: Mainstream, 32.
189. Macwhirter (1993), 119–20.
190. *Guardian*, 5 March 1993.
191. Clarke, 425.
192. *Scotsman*, 22 April 1993.
193. Benn, 166.
194. *Scotsman*, 22 April 1993.
195. J. Clark (1993), 'An autonomous Scottish Labour Party', *Scottish Affairs* 2, 126.
196. *Herald*, 18 February 1993.
197. *Herald*, 13 October 1992.
198. *Scotsman*, 15 February 1993.
199. M. Stuart (2005), *John Smith: A Life*, London: Politico's, 351–7.
200. *Scotland on Sunday*, 6 September 1998.
201. Tom Clarke (2025), *To Be Honest … The Story of My Life* (Kindle edition), Glasgow: Baxter Jardine, 299.
202. *Scotland on Sunday*, 7 March 1993 and Scottish Council of the Labour Party (1993), *Report of the Monklands Committee*, Glasgow: SCLP.
203. Stuart, 351–7.
204. Stuart, 361.
205. *Guardian*, 3 August 1993.
206. *Scotland on Sunday*, 24 October 1993.
207. McLeish, 53.
208. *Scotsman*, 25 November 1993.
209. P. Lynch & S. Birrell (2004), 'The autonomy and organisation of Scottish Labour', in G. Hassan (ed.), *The Scottish Labour Party: History, Institutions and Ideas*, Edinburgh: Edinburgh University Press, 181.
210. *Guardian*, 24 September 1993.
211. Bennie et al., 48–9.
212. *Scotsman*, 14 March 1994.
213. *Herald*, 14 March 1994.
214. *Guardian*, 12 March 1994.
215. The Scottish party executive had entered negotiations with the NEC in 1989 regarding the 'responsibility of the Scottish Party

to appoint to Scottish posts' (see Statement from SEC to 1989 conference, TD1384/3/1/5, Scottish Labour Party Papers).
216. *Scotsman*, 21 April 1994.
217. *Herald*, 15 March 1994. See also M. Sarwar with B. Wylie (2016), *My Remarkable Journey: The Autobiography of Britain's First Muslim MP*, Edinburgh: Birlinn, 126.
218. McVicar et al., 95.
219. Press Association, 12 March 1994.
220. *Herald*, 8 January 1994.
221. *Scotsman*, 9 May 1994.
222. HC Deb 12 May 1994 Vol 243 c436 [Mr John Smith (Tributes)].
223. *Herald*, 3 June 1994.
224. *The Times*, 21 May 1994.

6

The Scottish Labour Party: 1994–2011

During its eighteen years in opposition, the Scottish Labour Party had come to dominate Scotland's representation at Westminster and in most of its major local authorities. It became, in effect, 'a quasi-establishment party, blurring the line between the state and civil society'.[1] John Smith's leadership of British Labour had consolidated this dominance, and thus his premature death was to 'reawaken fears that the leadership in London could not be trusted', particularly when it came to devolution.[2]

As British Labour embarked upon the election of a new leader for the second time in as many years, the party in Scotland concentrated on elections to the European Parliament – in which it lost north-east Scotland to the SNP[3] – and the by-election in Monklands East necessitated by Smith's death. This, as *The Times* observed, was 'one of the dirtiest by-election campaigns of recent times',[4] and one which highlighted Scottish Labour's failure to draw a line under charges of sectarianism that had first arisen in 1992.

Helen Liddell, who had left Keir Hardie House in 1988 to work for media tycoon Robert Maxwell, was selected to fight what was, on paper, a safe seat. It also represented a proactive attempt to address the embarrassing paucity of female Scottish Labour MPs, only three out of forty-nine since the 1992 election.[5] In essentially a straight fight with the SNP's Kay Ullrich, Liddell began the campaign by dismissing allegations of impropriety at Monklands District Council as 'tittle tattle'. When she later wrote to the chief executive asking for a detailed explanation of 'apparent disparities' in council expenditure,[6] Tom Clarke, the MP for Monklands West and a former Shadow Scottish

Secretary, was furious. Although Liddell won on 30 June 1994, Smith's majority of nearly 16,000 was reduced to just 1,640. In her acceptance speech, the new MP accused the Conservative and SNP candidates of having 'played the Orange card' during the campaign, something both furiously denied. Outside the count, a thin line of policemen had to keep apart chanting SNP and Labour factions.[7]

The Monklands affair rumbled on until June 1995 when a statutory inquiry repudiated many of the wilder allegations. Party general secretary Jack McConnell nevertheless promised never to 'allow this situation to develop in the Scottish Labour Party ever again'.[8] Usefully from Labour's point of view, in a subsequent boundary review the name 'Monklands' was erased from both parliamentary constituencies: Tom Clarke's Monklands West seat became Coatbridge and Chryston and Helen Liddell's Monklands East was reconstituted as Airdrie and Shotts.

'OUT-DATED SOCIALIST BAGGAGE'

A few weeks after the by-election on 21 July, Tony Blair was elected British Labour leader. As the journal *Scottish Affairs* observed:

> The problems posed to the Scottish Labour Party by the new leadership will need careful handling. It's not just Blair's perceived 'Englishness' (despite his Scottish origins) that might alienate a lot of Scottish Labour voters. There is the bonfire of socialist nostrums too. Labour is in the throes of 'modernisation' under Tony Blair ... [but] the point about this 'out-dated socialist baggage' is that the Scottish electorate rather liked much of it.[9]

That last assertion was questionable, but while the Scottish Labour Party no longer had the ear of Blair as it had Smith's, Scots continued to be well represented on the opposition front bench. Donald Dewar, whom Blair considered 'superb ... a real discovery',[10] became the party's chief whip while John McAllion, not exactly a loyalist, was added to George Robertson's Scottish frontbench team.

In September, the Shadow Scottish Secretary urged Scottish Labour MPs to 'move on' the devolution debate by 'enthusing' voters with a 'flavour of how Scotland will be different and better with a Labour government and with a Scottish parliament'.[11] While the party attracted some unlikely recruits – long-standing SNP activist Isobel Lindsay joined in July, much to the bafflement of associates – almost half the Scottish Labour executive told *Scotland on Sunday* they were 'concerned' at the new economic strategy outlined by Blair and Shadow Chancellor Gordon Brown.[12] By October, some Scottish Labour members had established the Campaign for Socialism. Its goal was to retain Clause IV of the party's constitution – the common ownership clause – which was within Blair's modernising sights.[13]

Jack McConnell believed that by the early 1990s this Labour shibboleth was 'hopelessly out of date, with no mention of equality, basic freedoms or the environment'. But while in England there was 'no effective internal opposition' to its reform, in Scotland, reflected McConnell, 'naturally, it was the other way around'. He also believed it a 'myth' that Scotland was 'the most Labour-ite part of Britain':

> The real industrialised, working-class parts of Britain then were the north-east of England, some bits of the north-west, and south Wales. Scotland is actually a modern, cosmopolitan country, where people do have individualistic aspirations to get their children a decent education and a secure job. While Scotland's community spirit lives on, collectivist aspirations were becoming a thing of the past.[14]

On 10 March 1995 the Scottish Labour Party gathered in Inverness for its annual conference. Improvising his speech due to a broken autocue, Blair said the question voters would ask at the next election was:

> 'Do we trust Labour?' I believe it is essential, for that trust to be won, that we are clear about the values we hold dear. We need the people with us ... The only thing that stands between us and government is trust. Trust will be gained, not by clinging to icons for fear of thinking anew, but by seizing the spirit without which all thought is barren.

Following a passionate debate in which a delegate from Glasgow Maryhill caused a minor sensation with a passionate argument against change, the Scottish conference narrowly backed reform. McConnell recalled hugging Blair backstage.[15] In his memoirs, Blair reflected that if 'we could win ... in Scotland where traditional thought was strong ... then we could win in most places, and even in the unions'.[16] Dennis Canavan later mocked 'erstwhile lefties' such as John Reid and Gordon Brown for supporting the new Clause IV. 'It was the day that Labour lost its socialist soul', he said of the Inverness conference, 'and it has never recovered'.[17]

By the end of 1995, Blair's first full year as Leader of the Opposition, the Scottish Labour Party had 28,466 members compared with a British membership of 363,460. Scottish Labour constituted 18 per cent of the Parliamentary Labour Party but only 8 per cent of its national membership.[18] Although this represented an improvement on historically low individual membership levels, the Scottish party remained curiously ramshackle. In April 1995, Paisley North MP Irene Adams had alleged infiltration of her CLP by drugs gangsters and a party inquiry was later widened to cover every branch in three Renfrewshire constituencies.[19] This spilled over into May's local government elections, when a major split over candidate selection based on what McConnell called 'factionalism and personality clashes' led to expulsions and an electoral boost to the local SNP.[20] Two months later, the entire Labour group on the soon-to-be-abolished Strathclyde Regional Council was suspended following allegations of nepotism and religious discrimination.[21] Despite two visits from Blair to support Gordon Brown protégé Douglas Alexander (a fellow son of the manse) in the Perth and Kinross by-election, meanwhile, the SNP's Roseanna Cunningham took the once safe Conservative seat with more than 40 per cent of the vote.

In July 1995, Scottish Labour women activists had also expressed shock when Blair jettisoned John Smith's policy of all-female shortlists. The Scottish Labour Party later rejected this by a large majority,[22] and it took an industrial tribunal ruling that under the Sex Discrimination Act 1975 (introduced by a Labour government) such shortlists would be illegal.[23] Three Scottish candidates already chosen under the policy – Sandra Osborne in Ayr, Anne McGuire in Stirling and Anne Begg in Aberdeen South – were unaffected. By this point, the campaign for greater gender balance among candidates and elected representatives had become intermeshed with ongoing planning – via the Scottish Constitutional Convention (SCC) – for the precise shape of a devolved Scottish Parliament, particularly within the

Scottish Labour Women's Caucus. George Robertson resisted moves to devolve control of elections to a Scottish Parliament, instead proposing the compromise of a post-election review. This, as he told Blair, would 'take the sting out of the gender debate without conceding anything'.[24]

This spoke to a tightening of constitutional policy under Blair, in contrast to the 1988–92 period in which the cross-party SCC had been allowed to set the agenda.[25] In August 1995, Labour and the Liberal Democrats agreed to abandon Dewar's idea of a 'reverse block grant' (or 'assigned revenue'), while the following month Robertson and Scottish Liberal Democrat leader Jim Wallace bypassed the SCC completely to agree the parliament would elect 129 members, a compromise the STUC called 'unacceptable'.[26] Writing in *The Scotsman*, the Shadow Scottish Secretary hailed Blair's 'firm and personal imprint' on the party's devolution pledge and attacked the SNP. 'They know that devolution will kill stone-dead the rump separatist desire, but they cannot oppose it because it is so popular.'[27] It was the first use of a phrase that would later come back to haunt Robertson.

Writing in March 1996, the Scottish Labour activist and commentator Gerry Hassan reflected upon the party's epic 'revisionism', which now saw it presenting its devolution commitment as 'a historical link running unbroken through Scottish Labour from Keir Hardie to John Smith and today'. He also identified a lack of dialogue between the Scottish and British parties, Scottish Labour invoking 'popular sovereignty, entrenchment, and electoral reform, while the British party is concerned about parliamentary sovereignty and the West Lothian question'.[28] This was reflected in deputy general secretary Tommy Sheppard's concern that depicting a Scottish Parliament as being 'inside and strengthening the United Kingdom' would leave the party 'vulnerable to attack' from the SNP. He proposed in its place 'something along the lines of a Scottish parliament as part of a new Labour Britain'.[29]

At his first British party conference as leader, Blair repeated Neil Kinnock's pledge to legislate in the first year of a Labour government while attacking the SNP:

> We are drawing strength, and I don't believe the people of Scotland will ever be taken in by the SNP. Because, however you dress it up, whatever language they try to employ, you can never find the true

nature of the SNP, narrow nationalism that has nothing whatever to do with the principles of democratic socialism.[30]

Summoning up the ghost of Keir Hardie, Jack McConnell rebuked internal and external critics by linking Blairite realism with Hardie's Victorian socialism, arguing that New Labour had 'not been about throwing away the roots and principles of the party founded here in Scotland'.[31] Gordon Brown was fond of telling a joke about the 1918 Scottish Labour manifesto: 'We promised home rule, proportional representation and the prohibition of alcohol. And in more than seventy years we have managed to secure none of them.'[32]

During 1996, meanwhile, the Scottish Militant convener Tommy Sheridan helped establish the Scottish Socialist Party – another name which evoked Labour's long history – as an antidote to New Labour.[33] Polling, however, suggested no significant disaffection among Labour's traditional supporters in Scotland,[34] although in March 1996 the Scottish executive passed one of its habitual resolutions to scrap Trident, this time in direct defiance of an appeal from Blair. At that year's Scottish conference, five members of the Campaign for Socialism, which continued as a left-wing pressure group having lost its fight over Clause IV, won election to the Scottish executive, including Cathy Peattie, Cathy Jamieson and Marilyn Glen, all future Labour MSPs. Jack McConnell attempted to argue that conference had demonstrated a 'new maturity' in diluting its position on unilateralism, not stipulating a figure for the planned minimum wage and pulling back from calling for the renationalisation of privatised utilities,[35] but there were obvious tensions as a general election approached.

'UNFINISHED BUSINESS'

No matter how many times Tony Blair restated his commitment to the 'unfinished business' of devolution, some in the Scottish Labour Party remained uneasy, perhaps because his lack of enthusiasm was obvious. By February 1996, the Leader of the Opposition had already resolved to alter that policy in a way which infuriated Scottish activists at the time, but within a few years had come to be seen as a sensible and even pro-devolution move.

On first learning of Blair's thinking – not only a pre-legislative referendum but an additional question on tax powers and a 'clear' expression of Westminster's continuing sovereignty – media adviser Alastair Campbell was concerned by an apparent lack of necessary 'political groundwork' involving George Robertson and Donald Dewar, the latter considering it a 'dangerous' and 'totally unnecessary' course. Blair reasoned that 'every home-rule effort up to now had failed because of overambition or overemotionalism. We had to be hard-headed.' Gradually, Robertson et al. came round to the referendum and tax elements but not that regarding sovereignty, even though Blair insisted this 'was a statement of the obvious, power devolved, but power retained'. A supportive Jack McConnell, meanwhile, was summoned to London to 'get things in motion'. 'It was clearly going to be a big deal up there', acknowledged Campbell in his diary, 'and probably fasten seat belts time'.[36]

That was an understatement. At a press conference in Glasgow on 27 June 1996, the Shadow Scottish Secretary announced that after years of insisting the election of a Labour government would constitute a sufficient 'mandate' to create a Scottish Parliament, the party was now advocating a referendum to be held a few months after the next general election. Furthermore, this would ask not one but two questions, the first to test opinion on the general principle of devolution itself and the second on whether it ought to have modest tax-varying powers. Conscious of the likely reaction, Robertson was flanked by chief whip Donald Dewar, shadow chancellor Gordon Brown and shadow foreign secretary Robin Cook, all of whom had long championed devolution. Aware of lingering resentment caused by the 'Cunningham amendment', they made it clear that on this occasion a simple majority for both questions would suffice.

The Scottish media, later described by Alastair Campbell as 'unreconstructed wankers', reacted very badly, not least because details of the U-turn had first appeared in the London-based *Independent*. There was also a major backlash from members of the Scottish Labour Party, which had long considered itself in primary control of devolution policy, and more broadly from stakeholders in the Scottish Constitutional Convention, who already felt sidelined by bilateral political deals.

What explained the change in policy? As journalist Peter Jones later observed in his detailed account of the episode, Robertson had not adequately explained the motivation at his press conference. Late the previous year, he had persuaded Labour's NEC, policy committee and new policy forum to accept the model of devolution as formulated by the Convention, after which the Shadow Cabinet began to consider how it might fit into its first legislative programme. The detail was delegated to the Shadow Lord Chancellor, Lord Irvine of Lairg, a close friend of the late John Smith and Blair's former law chambers boss. Significantly, the experience of those involved with the devolution legislation of 1975–8 was sought, including the former Scottish Office minister Harry (now Lord) Ewing, now co-chair of the SCC. Meanwhile, the referendum device had been suggested by Alasdair McGowan, Robertson's researcher, as a way of 'clearing the ground' before a new Scotland Bill was introduced to Parliament.[37] No one appeared to remember that John Smith had proposed something similar back in 1983, also a consequence of his experience in the late 1970s.[38]

Lord Irvine's committee quickly concluded the arguments for a pre-legislative referendum were overwhelming, and that if Labour did not commit now it would likely be forced to by the Commons, as in the 1970s. Irvine later reflected that in 1996 there was no 'expectation of the huge majority that was to come', while Labour remained 'high vulnerable' to its perceived 'tax and spend' image, i.e. Michael Forsyth's repackaged 'tartan tax'. Finally, it was felt necessary to 'diminish the salience of devolution as a general election issue'. A referendum meant 'the Scottish people' would take the devolution decision for themselves, but *after* a general election.[39] Blair, meanwhile, told UK Liberal Democrat leader Paddy Ashdown the policy would head off 'English nationalists' in his party, especially northern Labour MPs, whom Blair told Ashdown he feared 'most of all'.[40] The Scottish media ('a disaster area' according to Campbell) were, however, briefed that the idea had come exclusively from Robertson.[41]

Following the announcement, there were two resignations, Lord Ewing as co-chair of the SCC and, the following day, Scottish affairs spokesman John McAllion, who believed Labour had 'lost control of its own policy'.[42] 'Well done comrade', wrote the STUC's Bill Spiers in response, 'it's just a pity those shitbags made it necessary'.[43] Scottish Labour Action's Ian Smart was more pragmatic in accepting the case for a referendum, although he believed there was 'no justification at all for the manner in which established policy was abandoned or … the proposal to separate out the taxation powers from the rest of the package'.[44] In private correspondence, George Robertson accepted the optics of the announcement 'left much to be desired' but protested that to have done nothing 'would have been a genuine betrayal of the historic project which is creating the first Scottish Parliament for the Scottish people in three hundred years'.[45]

Never afraid of a fight with his own party, Blair was nothing if not evangelical in response. After defending the referendum in an Edinburgh speech, he spent three hours debating the referendum policy with largely hostile members of the Scottish Labour executive. Chairman Davie Stark told Blair the 'party felt they were being pushed too far', while Bob Thomson of Unison asked why a Labour government did not just create a thousand new peers to get legislation through the Lords. Eventually, however, the executive endorsed a two-question ballot by sixteen votes to twelve following an assurance it would be consulted on the wording of the second question. Blair told Campbell he 'never thought we would do as well as that. It was quite a triumph in its own way.'[46]

A consultation later revealed that a majority of Scottish Labour members supported the two-question plan, although this did not prevent critics campaigning for a single-question referendum. One pamphlet by Bill Speirs called it the worst wrecking device since George Cunningham's '40 per cent rule', while Margaret Curran, convener of the Scottish Labour Women's Caucus, said the 'sense of retreat was real'.[47] When the thirty-nine members of the Scottish Labour executive gathered in Stirling for another special meeting on 31 August, the balance looked to be narrowly against. Even after Blair personally lobbied waverers, the party remained split and only agreed (by twenty-one to eighteen) when George Robertson conceded that the taxation power would only be activated following *another* referendum. The Scottish media once again went on the attack and five days later Robertson publicly U-turned. 'The cause of Scottish devolution to me is more important', he explained, 'than an individual committee decision.'[48]

Although undeniably messy, Peter Jones rightly concluded that 1996 was the year in which 'serious Westminster politicians re-engaged with Scottish political thinking':

They gave thought, for the first time since the Scotland Act 1978, on how Scotland could get what was wanted. They found that it wasn't going to be easy, and decided the people will need to say 'yes' in a referendum. If the Scottish parliament does arrive in Edinburgh this side of the millennium it will be because of that forethought. What many were anxious to portray as a sell-out is almost certainly the exact opposite.[49]

The experience clearly left Blair with a degree of cynicism as regards the Scottish press corps, whom he dubbed the 'Scottish media establishment', obsessed by the detail of devolution and wrong to assume the argument had already been won. Devolution, he told reporters, was not the 'only thing that matters to the people':

> It is simply tedious for people to go on about the Scottish Constitutional Convention has done this or that. The SCC was a very good initiative. Well, fine. But in the end, the convention can't deliver devolution. Only the Westminster Parliament can.[50]

In his memoirs, Blair recalled being asked:

> Isn't having a referendum vote just a way of denying Scotland its due and proper Parliament? I would say: Er, but the Scots are the ones voting. Ah, they [Scottish journalists] would say, but suppose they vote no? Well, I would say, in that case I assume they don't want one. And so on.[51]

Eventually, things settled down, punctuated by the SNP's Alex Neil comparing George Robertson to Nazi collaborator Lord Haw-Haw,[52] and further media excitement when Blair referred to 'my proposal' (the referendum) before quickly adding 'the proposal that I agreed to'.[53] By November 1996 Scottish party members revealed themselves as enthusiastic as those in England when asked formally to endorse 'New' Labour's draft programme for government.[54]

In December, the SNP published the leaked findings of a System Three survey of floating voters' attitudes towards Blair and his party. Usefully, this reflected Nationalist attack lines such as New Labour being indiscernible from the Conservatives, backtracking on devolution, a 'smarmy' and 'English' Labour leader and a Shadow Scottish Secretary perceived as taking instructions from London. It later emerged the polling had been stolen from the car of Tommy Sheppard, deputy general secretary of the Scottish Labour Party. Awaiting a delayed flight to Glasgow, Blair remarked to Alastair Campbell and Pat McFadden (a former member of Scottish Labour Action) that 'our entire programme could be fucked because of the commitment to the Scottish Parliament and still they [Scottish Labour members] whine that we're not doing enough for them'.[55] Publicly, Blair made light of the document, saying 'I am what I am' and promising to carry Labour's message into 'middle and lower Scotland' as well as 'middle and lower England'. 'I am very proud of being born in Scotland', he added. 'I live in England and my family have been brought up there. I speak with an English accent: so what?'[56]

Within weeks, Sheppard had quit Keir Hardie House in an 'amicable agreement', the details of which were subject to a confidentiality agreement.[57] He later blamed Robertson and said Jack McConnell 'could have done more' to prevent his removal.[58] Sheppard was replaced by Mike Donnelly, who 'immeasurably improved' general election planning.[59] There was better news when McConnell announced that Scottish Labour had virtually doubled its membership to 30,371,[60] something Cunninghame North MP Brian Wilson said tended to confirm that 'most of what is written about Scotland's views of Tony Blair is nonsense'.[61] Equally impatient with lazy analysis was *The Scotsman*'s Peter Jones:

> If Blair is the wrong Labour leader for Scotland, why did Scottish party members vote for him so overwhelmingly? If the Scottish party is so enthused by old-style socialism, why did only one Scottish constituency party vote to keep the Clause IV nationalisation commitment in the party's constitution? If Blair is a complete turn-off to Scots, why has party membership nearly doubled over the last four years to around 30,000? ... The reason that this kind of evidence is dismissed is that the Old Labourites have bought too much nationalist mythology. This mythology contends that the Scots differ from the English in almost every regard.[62]

Indeed, a study of British political culture by Miller et al. had recently concluded that differences between Scottish and English voters were generally small, although Scots were 10 per cent more favourable to the socially disadvantaged.[63]

'AN UNDERLYING FRAGILITY'

At around this time a new group called 'Network' emerged, its aim being to 'mainstream New Labour policy ideas' within the Scottish party as well as 'extensions of democracy in party structures', in other words shift policy-making away from the Scottish executive and annual conference. Leading figures included Jim Murphy, a former president of the National Union of Students in Scotland, Rosemary McKenna, a Lanarkshire councillor and former president of the Convention of Scottish Local Authorities, and Jim Stevens.[64] At the March Scottish conference the Blairites won seven of the eight executive places Network had targeted.[65] Two left-wing Scottish Labour MPs, John McAllion and Dennis Canavan, complained of a 'witch hunt' against those who had opposed the referendum U-turn,[66] while George Robertson implored Scottish Labour members to 'end the self-indulgence of wrangling over internal issues in public'.[67]

The focus then shifted to modernisation of the Scottish party: one-member-one-vote elections for the Scottish executive, the 'drastic pruning' of its size, proper policy sub-groups and more open policy debates at constituency level. The aim, judged *The Scotsman*, was to make the party 'look and sound like a modern, democratic political force and not the leftover Stalinist oligarchy it so often appears to be'.[68] Not for the first time, party officials at Millbank – the British party's new headquarters – had looked on in horror as reports emerged of an expenses scandal involving the Glasgow City Council Labour group.[69] Fearing another Monklands, the NEC ordered an inquiry while the Scottish party bluntly warned the councillors in question that without urgent changes it would 'not give money to maintain inefficiencies or to allow people to fly round the world at public expense'.[70]

In a long memorandum to Tony Blair written at the beginning of 1997, George Robertson painted a nuanced picture of the Scottish political scene as that Parliament drew to a close. There was, he said, an 'underlying fragility' in which Labour/SNP switching was 'too easy for comfort', something fuelled by 'a constant questioning of Labour['s] commitment to Scotland which appears to be affecting our level of trust amongst voters'. The Shadow Scottish Secretary was also concerned that any 'slippage' might mobilise a Tory 'onslaught on middle England' à la the surprisingly effective fight of premier John Major to 'save the Union' in 1992. Thus Scottish Labour's objective, wrote Robertson, was to be the 'real national Party of Scotland', win 'at least' five additional seats, 'markedly' increase its poll, 'marginalise and permanently reduce the credibility of the SNP' and 'further erode the performance of the Scottish Tories'. In policy terms, he conceded 'remaining holes in policy', including housing which, 'given the very high public housing domination' in Scotland, was 'a big worry'. In conclusion, Robertson told Blair that:

> The constant attacks on our integrity, trustworthiness and our Scottishness have an effect and can lead to sudden swings of opinion. The preference for 'independence' is remarkably and worryingly high even among Labour voters, and far higher than those who want the SNP to deliver it. But the fact that it is there and that the SNP can command so much lasting attention adds to the sheer unpredictability of events. [But] I believe we have the ideas, and the same will and determination which has kept us ahead in spite of all last year's troubles, to make sure that Scotland plays its full part in securing, and not hindering, an overall victory.[71]

Because of the proximity of the election, the 1997 Scottish Labour conference was truncated to a one-and-a-half-day rally. But rather than being 'full of self-belief, confidence, and energy', Gerry Hassan detected 'a sense of unease and foreboding', something he attributed to the referendum U-turn and trepidation at 'what sacred cows might next be sacrificed by a Blair Government'.[72]

This was misplaced. In March the *Scottish Sun* reverted to supporting the party after a five-year Nationalist interlude, while Creation Records' Alan McGee boosted Scottish Labour's election fighting fund with a £50,000 donation. A tartan clad Scottish manifesto was unveiled the following month and at a press conference Blair spoke of 'traditional Scottish values' like community, decency and respect having been 'squeezed out of national life' by the Conservatives.[73] George Robertson, meanwhile, made it clear the Scottish Trades Union Congress would 'play no part in influencing Labour Party policy or the decisions made by Labour in government'.[74]

Just weeks before the election, and despite the 'fragility' identified by George Robertson, Blair fell victim to what journalist

John Rentoul called his 'Anglo-centrism' with a loosely worded interview with *The Scotsman*.[75] Asked how he might justify the 'fairness' of devolution (given the West Lothian Question) to voters in his Sedgefield constituency, Blair replied:

> I will say to them, we are going to devolve these matters to a Scottish Parliament but as far as, you know, we are concerned, the sovereignty rests with me as an English MP and that's the way it that will stay ... I think that England understands that provided it is not breaking the essential sovereignty of a Westminster parliament, that these are things the Scots can decide.

And asked about the tax-varying power which was to be the subject of a second referendum question, Blair added, even more clumsily, that:

> it's like any local authority, powers which are constitutionally there, they can be used but the Scottish Labour party has plans to raise income tax rates ... but no, of course, a Scottish Parliament once the power is given it's like the smallest English parish council, it's got the right to exercise it.[76]

While both points were constitutionally accurate, journalist Brian Taylor thought the reaction 'out of all proportion to the remarks and, indeed, misrepresented them'.[77] Blair was defended in print by Gordon Brown, who denied his leader was watering down the parliament's proposed powers ('Far too often on the football field Scotland has snatched defeat from the jaws of victory'),[78] while Blair himself likened the minutiae of devolution to 'dancing on the head of a pin' during a phone-in on eight Scottish commercial radio stations.[79] At the end of April a Glasgow councillor defected to the SNP, but that was it. Labour's sheer momentum papered over any cracks.

The Govan constituency, meanwhile, had been at the centre of a gruelling year-long candidacy battle between incumbent Glasgow Central MP Mike Watson and cash-and-carry millionaire Mohammad Sarwar. Watson had won the initial CLP ballot by a single vote, but when Sarwar appealed to the NEC alleging the vote had been 'fixed in favour of a white man to stop a Muslim getting to Parliament', he eventually secured a re-run, which Watson lost.[80] It was the first time an incumbent Scottish Labour MP had been deselected. On 2 May 1997, Sarwar became the UK's first Muslim MP, although a police investigation into possible voting fraud was already under way. Again, all this was lost amid an extraordinary Labour landslide. Labour had smashed George Robertson's target, winning 45.6 per cent of the vote in Scotland and an additional seven MPs.

'NEW LABOUR, NEW SCOTLAND'

The first Labour government in eighteen years naturally fell victim to unrealistic expectations. With George Robertson a surprise appointment at the Ministry of Defence, Tony Blair's natural choice as Secretary of State for Scotland was Donald Dewar. A long-standing supporter of devolution, he quickly set out a 'formidable' timetable: a White Paper in July, a pre-legislative referendum in September and a Scotland Bill early the following year.[81] Even so, *The Scotsman* complained that while the new government had 'hit the ground sprinting, the Scottish Office was strolling'.[82]

Meanwhile there were Scottish Labour MPs galore in other departments: Robin Cook at the Foreign Office, Gavin Strang at Transport and of course Gordon Brown at the Treasury, as were Alistair Darling (Chief Secretary) and Helen Liddell (Minister of State). Although not an MP, Derry Irvine became Lord High Chancellor of Great Britain. Those with long memories would have noted the irony of Irvine and Dewar sharing a Cabinet table given that Alison McNair had left Dewar for Irvine in the early 1970s. The Lord Chancellor would later confess to a 'strong sense of guilt' over what had happened.[83] Malcolm Chisholm, a junior Scottish Office minister, only lasted a few months before resigning over single parent benefit cuts. When a 1998 Scottish conference motion later described this policy as 'economically inept, morally repugnant and spiritually bereft', the Chancellor was furious.[84]

The weeks between Labour taking office and publication of its devolution white paper were not inactive: Dewar extended a moratorium on compulsory competitive tendering for local government (later replaced with 'Best Value') while Scottish health minister Sam Galbraith authorised several hospitals to be built under the private finance initiative, a policy Labour had attacked before the election. This created tension with the STUC, although as Unison's Matt Smith later observed, the fact Dewar 'was with us and we with him on the creation of a Scottish Parliament' papered over any cracks.[85]

There were also party matters. At Edinburgh City Council a modernising faction led by David Begg and Susan Dalgety ousted two councillors from key positions, while on 28 July 1997 the Paisley South MP Gordon McMaster committed suicide. He left a note blaming Renfrewshire West MP Tommy Graham and Labour peer Lord Dixon for smearing him. Graham was subsequently suspended.[86] In Jack McConnell's account, McMaster had ended up holding 'the jackets, in that old west of Scotland phrase' amid a boundary review, something that had created huge tension between Renfrewshire's three incumbent MPs. Tommy Graham was later cleared of direct involvement in McMaster's death but expelled for bringing the party into disrepute.[87]

'SCOTLAND'S PARLIAMENT'

As if to make good on repeated pledges by successive British Labour leaders, the Referendums (Scotland and Wales) Bill was the first piece of legislation introduced to the new Parliament on 15 May 1997. Publication of the *Scotland's Parliament* White Paper on 27 July, meanwhile, rolled the pitch for the once-controversial referendum six weeks later. An original civil service draft had not been to Dewar's liking, but over a busy weekend it was knocked into shape by Wendy Alexander (sister of Douglas) and Murray Elder, his special advisers. As health was to be devolved, it followed that abortion would be too, but on that issue 'principle gave way to pragmatism'. As the Scottish Office minister Lord Sewel later recalled:

> The political problem had to do with the salience of abortion for the Roman Catholic Church and the correlation between Labour voting and Roman Catholicism, especially in the west of Scotland ... Dewar canvassed the views of his junior ministerial colleagues in the Scottish Office and decided in favour of reservation.[88]

On 6 August Labour and SNP politicians met to plan a mutual political campaign for the first time since the abortive Scottish Constitutional Convention discussions almost a decade earlier. Nationalists had only recently extracted themselves from an 'independence – nothing less' stance adopted in 1979, so the welcome given to Alex Salmond et al. by the Scotland FORward umbrella group was not shared by some members of the Scottish Labour executive. Jim Stevens called it 'a cross-party campaign too far', adding that the White Paper ought to be 'the graveyard of Scottish separatism' and be promoted on that basis.[89]

Although in Linlithgow angry party members threatened Tam Dalyell with deselection if he did not break the habit of his career and support a Scottish Parliament,[90] the only significant event which disrupted campaigning was the death of Diana, Princess of Wales on 31 August. On a surprisingly low turnout (60.18 per cent), almost three quarters of Scottish voters backed the principle of devolution and 63.5 per cent tax-raising powers. 'A Nation Again' was *The Scotsman*'s headline on 12 September 1997, while the Prime Minister told Alastair Campbell that Labour 'must get the message out loud and clear that there must be no pandering to nationalism, and we must stress that it's good for the UK, not just for Scotland'.[91] Dewar paid tribute to:

> all those who have carried the devolution torch through its darkest days and to those who helped build the cross party consensus in the Scottish Constitutional Convention. In particular I would like to mention George Robertson whose decision to hold the referendum has been so spectacularly vindicated and the Prime Minister, Tony Blair whose commitment to delivering a Scottish Parliament has never wavered.[92]

'ENGLAND AND SCOTLAND TOGETHER ON EQUAL TERMS'

The Scottish Secretary moved the second reading of the Scotland Bill on 12 January 1998. 'In years to come', Dewar told MPs, 'people will look back on it as a decisive step in the fight to modernise our constitution.'[93] Later in the bill's consideration, he described the provisions for the Scottish Parliament to be elected via proportional representation as 'the best example of charitable giving this century in politics'.[94]

Dewar, meanwhile, had been disappointed to find that Blair was 'not as good' a Prime Minister as he had expected. The Labour peer Giles Radice recorded a visit from the Secretary of State in August 1998:

He says that Cabinet government is not really working and that even Cabinet Committees are not all that important: 'The Blair government is mostly government by bilateral meeting' – and he means the meetings between Blair and Brown ... He is a bit worried by Blair's authoritarianism. He always wants, according to Donald, to discipline or get rid of people. He thinks that Tony is not really in favour of devolution.[95]

Dewar's suspicion was not entirely misplaced. As Blair later confessed, he had never been 'a passionate devolutionist': 'It is a dangerous game to play', he observed in his memoirs. 'You can never be sure where nationalist sentiment ends and separatist sentiment begins.'[96] And while Blair did not regret the legislation (as with Freedom of Information), he did consider it a 'mistake' not to have found 'ways of culturally keeping England, Scotland and Wales very much in sync with each other'.[97]

Dewar, meanwhile, was obviously tired, admitting to the broadcaster Fiona Ross (daughter of Willie) that he lacked John Smith's 'killer instinct' when it came to dealing with troublemakers. 'He was paralysed by indecision', Ross later recalled, 'totally convinced that everyone against him – government colleagues at Westminster, activists in Scotland, the media and even his closest friends and advisers'. In Ross's recollection, Dewar even toyed with not standing for the Scottish Parliament and taking another UK portfolio, if not quitting politics altogether.[98]

Meanwhile, no serious impediment to the Scotland Bill presented itself, although Conservatives in the Commons and Lords cautioned that without explicit statutory restrictions the legality of a future independence referendum might become what one Tory peer called a 'festering issue'.[99] The Scotland Act 1998 received Royal Assent on 19 November 1998, twenty years after its ill-fated predecessor. Dewar treasured a copy on which Blair wrote: 'it was a struggle; it may always be hard but it was worth it. England and Scotland together on equal terms!'

'A POLITICAL WITCH HUNT'

Weighing on Dewar's mind was an ongoing process to select Labour's candidates for the new Scottish Parliament. The Scottish party executive had assigned responsibility for this to a newly formed Scottish Selection Board comprising five members appointed by the SEC from within its own ranks, five prominent but 'independent' party members and five others appointed by the NEC who were deemed to have 'a reasonable connection with or knowledge of Scottish politics'.

The Board was chaired by the newly elected MP Rosemary McKenna (Cumbernauld and Kilsyth), a former convenor of COSLA. She spoke of sweeping away 'the cronyism, the smoke-filled rooms and the mutual scratching of backs' which had often characterised Labour's selection contests in favour of a more professional 'criteria-led selection'.[100] A second objective was recruiting what Dewar called 'able and talented people' who had not been active in party politics,[101] while a third was equal representation of men and women. In Shaw's analysis, the third objective was realised (half the Labour MSPs elected in 1999 were women), the second was not (most had been long active in politics), while the first was hotly disputed. Critics alleged an 'ideological cull ... a political witch hunt'.[102]

The most controversial case was the incumbent Falkirk West MP Dennis Canavan. Long disliked by Dewar and Blair, it was naturally difficult for some to believe this had played no part in an ostensibly 'criteria-led' process. Others eliminated at an early stage included Esther Roberton, chief executive of the Campaign for a Scottish Assembly, Mark Lazarowicz, a former leader of Edinburgh City Council (he became an MP in 2001), Tommy Sheppard, Jeane Freeman (later a special adviser), Mary Picken of the STUC, Isobel Lindsay of the SCC (and formerly of the SNP), two other MPs (Ian Davidson and Mike Connarty) and even Murray (later Lord) Elder, a former Scottish party secretary and aide to John Smith. Susan Deacon of Scottish Labour Action was also initially dropped but senior colleagues ensured she was reinstated on appeal.[103]

Canavan was particularly incensed when Dewar reportedly told a fundraising dinner that he had been excluded not because of his left-wing politics but because he was 'simply not good enough'.[104] But as journalist Douglas Fraser later observed, the Scottish Secretary also did remarkably 'little to shape an experienced and loyal team with which to lead the transition to devolution', with no apparent effort even to find friends like Murray Elder and John Sewel candidacies.[105] Very few incumbent Scottish Labour MPs, meanwhile, chose to run, even ostensibly passionate devolutionists; only Dewar, Sam Galbraith, Henry McLeish and Malcolm Chisholm swapped Westminster for Edinburgh.

It appeared the divide between Scottish MPs identified by Keating in 1975 endured, those who desired a 'Scottish' career and those who preferred a UK path. In one particularly bitter contest for the Motherwell and Wishaw candidacy, former general secretary Jack McConnell narrowly defeated AEEU official Bill Tynan amid suggestions of sectarianism.[106]

Another party matter was rather more harmonious. British Labour had established a National Policy Forum as its principal policy development body (Scottish Labour had twelve of its 180 members) and its counterpart in Scotland was the Scottish Policy Forum (SPF) created in 1998. The SPF would come to comprise ninety-four members, with thirty-two constituency representatives, twenty trade unionists, five national policy people and four Young Labour members, all elected by their own groups, as well as seventeen MPs, MSPs, MEPs and councillors. The manifesto, meanwhile, was to be drafted by a Joint Policy Committee drawn equally from the Scottish executive and a committee of whomever constituted the Scottish Labour MP Group. According to Gerry Hassan, however, the SPF was 'widely seen by party members as a top-down process, involving greater centralisation and management by the party leadership'.[107]

Following consultation, the party's women's sections were abolished, as were women's seats on the Scottish executive on the basis that new 50:50 quotas made them redundant. Under these rules, out of the seven key posts in each Constituency Labour Party (chair, secretary, treasurer, two vice-chairs, women's officer and youth officer) at least three had to be women. Most staff at Keir Hardie House, meanwhile, were female, the career trajectory of Lesley Quinn, who rose from office junior to become general secretary in 1999, providing 'a striking personal illustration of this process of feminisation'.[108]

The 1998 Scottish Labour conference also considered the executive's proposals to adapt its 'rules, structures, and procedures – indeed the whole culture of our party – to prepare for government and for devolution', many of which mirrored those approved at the British Labour conference in 1997. The 'old, unwieldy' conference model was to give way to 'greater participation by delegates and a wider range of agenda items'; the size of the 'too large' Scottish executive was to be reduced (and include MSPs); 'devolution in the party' implemented when it came to policy making; and a system established for the election of the 'person who will be our leader in the Parliament and in Scotland at large'.[109] Donald Dewar, of course, became the first directly-elected leader of the Labour Party in Scotland on 19 September 1998.

Journalist Murray Ritchie noted that Dewar still looked annoyed whenever someone asked why Millbank did not grant the Scottish Labour Party further autonomy, and would accuse questioners of 'following a Nationalist agenda'.[110] In November 1997, Scottish Labour Action's final publication (written by Tommy Sheppard) had proposed giving the SLP autonomy over policy, organisation and campaigning in devolved areas:

> If the party does not devolve and is seen as having its Scottish policy run from London, it will put itself at a considerable disadvantage compared to its competitors. In time, the Scottish people will want their parties home grown, and Labour will have to change or leave the political stage to others.[111]

At the 1999 Scottish conference, Bob Thomson also used his final report as treasurer to complain about Labour being the 'least devolved of the British parties' and called for a complete decentralisation of the party structure, sentiments which were warmly applauded from the conference floor.[112]

Paradoxically, Scottish Labour was during this period at its organisational peak. The key seats strategy for the 1997 general election and preparations for the first Scottish elections in 1999 had seen the recruitment of communications specialists, researchers and regional organisers, while a further expansion in 1998–9 took its total staff to twenty-six.[113] Following a March 1998 trip to Scotland, Blair demanded changes at both the Scottish Office and Keir Hardie House. Two new special advisers were imposed on the Scottish Secretary, including the former STV and *Daily Record* journalist David Whitton as Dewar's official spokesman.

These proved rather more enduring than the party's director of communications. Paul McKinney, another former STV journalist (and researcher for Gordon Brown), was appointed in April 1998 but left just a few weeks later, despite clear ability, an affinity with the Scottish press (not generally shared by the party) and a Blairite view there were serious presentational problems in Scotland. 'Senior Labour sources' briefed that

McKinney had voted for the SNP in 1997 because Blair was 'taking the party too far to the right and could not be trusted to deliver on devolution'. Lorraine Davidson (yet another journalist and later a biographer of Jack McConnell) was appointed in July 1998 and lasted until the first devolved election in May 1999, although the Prime Minister was reportedly irritated by her exclusion of television cameras from a speech in Glasgow.[114]

In September 1998 the Scottish Labour Party moved out of Keir Hardie House, its Park Circus home since 1974, and into Delta House, which Davidson described as 'a soulless, modern city-centre office block'.[115] That weekend was also the anniversary of Gordon McMaster's suicide, and party officials were shocked to learn that McConnell, who had recently quit as general secretary, intended *Scotland on Sunday* to serialise his political memoirs. Journalist Iain Martin recorded recollections over two days at an Edinburgh hotel and the first instalment ran on 6 September. Although McConnell called them 'positive articles commenting on significant changes in Scottish Labour over recent years', colleagues took a dim view, with Irene Adams calling it 'pathetic' and a party spokesperson 'an error of judgement'.[116] Serialisation ceased and as a quid pro quo McConnell avoided removal from Scottish Labour's list of approved candidates for the Scottish Parliament.[117]

'THE DEATH KNELL FOR SEPARATISM'

In a December 1995 television interview, the then Shadow Scottish Secretary George Robertson had insisted Labour's devolution policy would kill moves towards independence 'stone dead', adding that the party's scheme was 'integrationist and the death knell for separatism'.[118] By April 1998, however, polling suggested Labour and the SNP had drawn level on 40 per cent, while by June the Nationalists even claimed a fourteen-point lead. It was not clear if the referendum had (as some feared) 'legitimised' Alex Salmond and his party, or if some voters considered them a logical next step now that Labour had (almost) delivered a Scottish Parliament. Whatever the case, the polling was baffling to a party which in the rest of Britain was still basking in record approval ratings.[119]

In a pre-election pamphlet entitled *New Scotland, New Britain*, Gordon Brown and Douglas Alexander argued that the real battle in May 1999 would:

> be between those who put the politics of social justice first, and those who practice the politics of national identity above and before anything else. There is and always has been more to Scottish politics than identity politics. Solidarity – and working together – offers Scotland more than separation – and splitting ourselves apart. That is why a politics based on the expansive vision of social justice will defeat the narrow divisiveness of Nationalism.[120]

But as Hassan later observed, for those like him who had 'grown up with Scottish Labour's championing of the Scottish dimension in the 1980s', this new strategy came as 'a bit of a shock: a hard, abrasive, populist anti-Scottish Nationalist message'.[121] The Chancellor also addressed himself to the challenge of remaking the case for the Union in New Labour terms. Brown understood Britishness:

> as being outward-looking, open and inter-nationalist, a commitment to democracy and tolerance, to creativity and enterprise and to public service, and to justice or, as we often put it, to fair play … The case for Britain is straightforward – that we achieve more working together than working apart … unity comes not from uniformity, but from celebrating diversity.

'With a vacuum where the Tories used to be', observed *Observer* columnist Andrew Rawnsley, 'Labour was becoming the Unionist Party.'[122]

By February 1999, Labour had regained a firm lead over the SNP. When the SNP pledged to reverse the Chancellor's recent penny cut in income tax via the new parliament's tax-varying power, Brown 'pounded away with it, bargaining that the Scots were actually just as averse to tax increases as the English'. Alex Salmond and his party, meanwhile, were presented as a threat to the integrity of the UK, not to be trusted on defence and fiscally reckless. Apocalyptic broadcasts also depicted the UK literally breaking apart;[123] the pollster Philip Chalmers was credited with devising the accompanying slogan: 'Divorce is an expensive business'. And when Salmond described NATO's bombing of Serbia as of 'dubious legality' and 'unpardonable folly', Foreign Secretary Robin Cook relished branding the SNP leader the 'toast of Belgrade'.[124]

Uncomfortable with this sort of rough and tumble, Donald Dewar was despatched on a bus tour of Scotland, his aides having failed, by the Scottish Secretary's own admission, to 're-create' his image, although as even Blairites had come to appreciate, Dewar's 'unflashy decency' was an asset. Labour presented him as the 'wise and moderate father of the nation to be contrasted favourably with smart-Alex Salmond', and polls indicated that even non-Labour supporters believed the sixty-one-year-old Scottish Secretary would make the best First Minister of Scotland.[125] Even so, Alastair Campbell recorded that he and Blair had 'both pretty much lost confidence in DD, who had virtually collapsed'. This meant relying on their 'own instincts' and occasional input from Gordon Brown, but they did not consider Scottish Labour's campaign to be 'in good shape'. Demoralised after one visit to Scotland, Blair felt 'something had changed irreversibly', which made him 'question the whole policy of devolution'. On the flight home, the Prime Minister had relaxed, believing 'we could turn it around but ... it was going to be difficult and it would be a big blow to the government as a whole if it went to the SNP'.[126]

That Blair even considered an SNP victory possible was revealing. Scottish Labour's election pledges, meanwhile, were uninspiring, a hospital building programme, improved schools, a new Drug Enforcement Agency, 200 more police officers and new industrial apprenticeships. The manifesto launched on 12 April was also what Murray Ritchie called 'a rehash of old policies, all carefully worded', prompting journalists to point out there was nothing in it 'which could not be ordered by the Secretary of State for Scotland without any need for a Scottish Parliament'.[127] Nevertheless, Ritchie observed that:

> Labour thoroughly deserves to prosper in this election because its victory two years ago in the General Election paved the way for the successful Referendum and the Scotland Act and, now, the Scottish general election. You have to give Labour due credit for keeping its word on devolution and doing so promptly, even if the motivating force for all of this is the threat from Scottish nationalism.

But if this was the best Labour could manage, Ritchie wondered presciently:

> when it is running the most popular government in history, two years into its term of office, what will happen in a Scottish Parliament

election when Labour is deeply unpopular, a circumstance which must come about one day? No party wins all of the elections all of the time, even in Scotland. The SNP's time will surely come.[128]

'THIS IS ABOUT WHO WE ARE'

By the end of the twentieth century, observed Macdonald:

> Labour dominance in Scotland – while some way from being the hegemonic creed of turn-of-the-century Liberalism – was treated as a given and accepted as a fundamental feature of the political landscape in most political discussions, even though the party had never secured more than 50 per cent of the vote in a general election.[129]

At the first elections to the Scottish Parliament on 6 May 1999, this fundamental feature began to weaken. In the constituency vote, Labour secured 38.8 per cent and in the regional PR element 33.6. This produced fifty-six Members of the Scottish Parliament (MSPs), nine short of the sixty-five necessary for an overall majority. This was no surprise, for this act of 'charitable giving', as Donald Dewar had called it, had been intended not, as some later claimed, to deprive the SNP of a majority, but to deprive *any* party of parliamentary hegemony.

The Scottish National Party had not done badly, securing 28.7 and 27.3 per cent respectively, giving it thirty-five MSPs and the transformative status as the new parliament's principal opposition party. Two other straws in the wind were the election of Scottish Socialist Party leader Tommy Sheridan via the Glasgow list and Dennis Canavan, who in the face of a determined campaign to oust him had nevertheless trounced Labour's official candidate in Falkirk West. Caveats aside, the Scottish Labour Party was relieved. 'We have held all the seats we took from the Tories in 1997', wrote Henry McLeish, 'we have returned 4 Labour MSPs from the Highlands and Islands, and the key SNP battlegrounds have stayed Labour'.[130]

Perfect gender balance had been achieved through 'twinned' constituencies, while age-old notions about 'serving your time' were upended by a raft of thirty-something MSPs, many of whom became ministers. 'Thanks to Labour', beamed McLeish, 'Scotland asserts its claim to be the most modern, progressive and representative democracy in the world'.[131] There was also a discernible shift towards more middle-class representatives, as only two Labour MSPs (as opposed to fourteen Labour MPs) came from manual working-class backgrounds. In other respects, old party habits died hard: twenty-three of the fifty-six had local government backgrounds, including ten former council leaders.[132] Denver and MacAllister found that Labour's vote was no longer significantly related to the percentage of manual workers in certain constituencies, partly because Labour was now in competition with the SNP rather than the Conservatives.[133]

Donald Dewar, the First Minister-elect, had been embarrassed during the election by a story to the effect that a 'power-sharing pact' had already been agreed by Blair, Robin Cook and Liberal Democrat leader Paddy Ashdown in 1996.[134] This was not quite true, although Ashdown's diaries clearly demonstrate that he, Blair and Gordon Brown were fully involved after the 1999 election.[135] Henry McLeish linked Keir Hardie's commitment to 'Home Rule' with the similarly 'long and proud' goal of the Liberals: 'Both Parties co-operated to win the Parliament through the Constitutional Convention, in the Referendum campaign, on the Scotland Act and in the Constitutional Steering Group because of this shared history'.[136] Sharing devolved government was the logical next step.

As coalition negotiations between Labour and the Liberal Democrats got under way, the Scottish Parliamentary Labour Party (SPLP) met for the first time. This was presented with a full Partnership Agreement on 9 May, but there was grumbling from some Labour MSPs about a lack of consultation. Patricia Ferguson (later a deputy presiding officer) and Pauline McNeill instinctively supported a minority administration but realised some sort of partnership was necessary for legislative stability. In Greenock and Inverclyde, Duncan McNeil's concern was more partisan, for the senior Liberal Democrat Ross Finnie had presented a strong challenge. But he too conceded 'partnership was the best way of making the Parliament work for the next four years'.[137]

The coalition agreement was signed at the Museum of Scotland on 28 June 1999 and saw Jim Wallace, Scottish Liberal Democrat leader since 1992, become Deputy First Minister. Dewar's first (and indeed only) Cabinet had a strong Scottish Labour Action tenor with Jack McConnell at finance, Susan Deacon at health and Wendy Alexander at communities. Sarah

Boyack, whose father Jim had been the driving force behind the Campaign for a Scottish Assembly, became transport minister, Henry McLeish got the enterprise and lifelong learning brief and Sam Galbraith – perhaps Dewar's closest friend in the Scottish Parliament – education. Galbraith hated the 'briefing' culture which existed in the party at that time, particularly among members of the new Cabinet.[138]

An eloquent speech from Dewar ensured the royal opening of the Scottish Parliament on 1 July 1999 was a memorable and happy occasion. 'This is a moment', he said, 'anchored in our history':

> Today, we reach back through the long haul to win this Parliament, through the struggles of those who brought democracy to Scotland, to that other Parliament dissolved in controversy nearly three centuries ago ... This is about more than our politics and our laws. This is about who we are, how we carry ourselves. In the quiet moments today, we might hear some echoes from the past: The shout of the welder in the din of the great Clyde shipyards; The speak of the Mearns, with its soul in the land; The discourse of the enlightenment, when Edinburgh and Glasgow were a light held to the intellectual life of Europe; The wild cry of the Great Pipes; And back to the distant cries of the battles of Bruce and Wallace. The past is part of us.[139]

Robert McLean of Scottish Labour Action noted the 'difference in tone' from that struck by the 'cautious reformer of the late 1960s', something he suggested reflected 'the changes in Scottish society, and Donald Dewar's perspective, over the past thirty years'.[140]

'WHOEVER GETS TO THE FLAG FIRST ...'

The briefing culture so disliked by Sam Galbraith did not take long to manifest itself. Just a fortnight after the election, former Fife Council leader Alex Rowley resigned as Scottish Labour's general secretary after only a year in post. Close to Chancellor Gordon Brown and steeped in the trade union movement, he had faced complaints on two fronts: first, that he was Brown's man rather than Scottish Labour's and, second, that he 'simply was not up to the job'. On concluding that he had lost the confidence of Millbank and British party general secretary Margaret McDonagh, Rowley chose to quit, making plain as he did so that the party in Scotland 'must be given more discretion to run its own affairs'.[141]

Once the devolved Scottish Executive had been formed, meanwhile, Dewar appointed John Rafferty – who had navigated the party's Poll Tax strategy in the late 1980s – his principal special adviser and reappointed David Whitton his official spokesman. As the civil service was at this time still regulated under the royal prerogative, an Order in Council allowed Dewar to appoint up to twelve 'SpAds', two of whom were to work with Liberal Democrat ministers. But when Rafferty emerged as the source of inaccurate press reports, he resigned, swiftly followed by comms adviser Philip Chalmers after a tabloid exposé of convictions for drink-driving in Glasgow's red-light area. When Whitton was recorded by a journalist blaming Rafferty for the Chalmers story, he was reprimanded by the First Minister but kept his job after issuing an 'unreserved apology'.[142]

In June 1999 there was a slight electoral knock at elections to the European Parliament, with Scottish Labour winning only three (rather than five) MEPs on 28.7 per cent of an admittedly low poll. Denver and MacAllister posited that when 'unconstrained by the first-past-the-post system' the Scottish electorate was 'less strongly Labour-inclined than might have been anticipated'.[143] Could it also have been concluded that voters were beginning to tire of a party that had dominated Scottish politics for so long? There was certainly a vagueness of political purpose now that the Scottish Parliament – the focus of party energy for a decade – had been established.

Gerry Hassan had anticipated this as early as March 1996, chastising Labour for spending more time on 'the detail of Standing Orders' than the 'areas people care about': education, health, housing, transport, the environment. He said:

> The nightmare scenario is a Scottish parliament arriving – and no-one having any idea what to do it with it, of how it should make a difference, of how it would improve the quality of life of people in Scotland. The existing anti-Tory consensus, with its romantic and radical images of Scotland, aids this divorce between practical politics and dreaming.[144]

What policy there was had been emerged from coalition bargaining with the Liberal Democrats, for example local government electoral reform and the graduate endowment, but of any distinct Labour thinking there was little sign. All Jack McConnell could offer was moving 'onto the next stage of modernisation ... reappraising the left's message in light of the complexities and uncertainties of the modern world'.[145] In a party where the 'left' and 'right' categories of the 1980s and 1990s had become largely redundant, there was a platitudinous void. The risk for Labour was that it would be filled by nationalism. As Donald Dewar reportedly remarked to Steven Purcell, then a young Glasgow councillor: 'Whoever gets to the flag first, it is their values that will dominate this new Scotland'.[146]

'THE DEFECTS IN ALL THIS DEVOLUTION STUFF'

There were other problems regarding policy which went beyond a lack of ideas. In a *Guardian* article by Matthew Taylor of the Institute for Public Policy Research (a former assistant general secretary of the British Labour Party), he declared that to suggest devolution meant Scottish Labour politicians had 'free rein to redesign the party's values and core policies' was 'to deny the very definition of a political party'.[147]

Although this represented a remarkably reductive view of devolution, Taylor was not alone. The coalition negotiations in May 1999 had produced a remarkable exchange between Tony Blair and Paddy Ashdown regarding tuition fees, a UK-wide policy introduced in 1998, and which the Scottish Liberal Democrats had insisted was scrapped or at least modified in Scotland:

> TB: You can't have Scotland doing something different from the rest of Britain.
> PA: Then you shouldn't have given the Scots devolution, including, specifically, the power to be different on this issue. You put yourself in a ridiculous position if, having produced the legislation to give power to the Scottish Parliament, you then say it is a matter of principle that they can't use it.
> TB (laughing): Yes, that is a problem. I am beginning to see the defects in all this devolution stuff.[148]

The Liberal Democrats had kept Labour 'on the back foot' throughout the election campaign on an issue Mike Watson was sure had 'cost Labour votes in middle-class areas the length and breadth of Scotland'.[149] With every party bar the Conservatives committed to abolition, Dewar was compelled to agree to what became the Graduation Endowment and Student Support (Scotland) Act 2001.

Another senior Labour figure who had failed to grasp the realities of devolution was John Reid, a former research officer at Keir Hardie House and member of the Communist Party of Great Britain whose political journey had taken him into Cabinet as the first post-1999 Secretary of State for Scotland. The renamed Scotland Office had lost an empire but not yet found a role, and relations between it and the Scottish Executive were tested when Kevin Reid, John's lobbyist son, was recorded boasting of having access to Labour ministers. Although Dewar defended Reid senior, during the British Labour conference in Bournemouth there was a public slanging match between the two, the First Minister having floated a standards investigation. A few days later, Reid and Dewar were all smiles as they launched devolution concordats intended to act as non-statutory 'ground rules' for relations between the two governments.[150]

Journalists did not have to try very hard to find unreconstructed Scottish Labour MPs. At the Scottish conference in March 2000, Jimmy Hood (Clydesdale) criticised the UK government for having 'given away' power in Scotland and jettisoning first past the post, an electoral system he said had 'served Labour well'.[151] Tom Harris recalled Commons tearoom jokes about amending the Scotland Act 1998: 'Line 1, between "There shall" and "be a Scottish Parliament", insert "not".'[152] In his memoirs, Henry McLeish alluded to 'residual ill will at Westminster', with many Scottish Labour MPs believing the 'new Parliament has undermined their position and curtailed their media exposure'.[153]

Even when the Scottish Executive acted in unison with Westminster there were problems. Wendy Alexander's intention to repeal clause 2a of regulations issued under the Local Government Act 1988 – those which prohibited the 'promotion' of homosexuality in schools – tested Scotland's apparent progressiveness. It sparked a furious backlash from the media, businessman Brian Soutar (who funded a private referendum to 'keep the clause') and Cardinal Winning, who was openly supported by several Scottish Labour MPs and MSPs. Mike Watson suggested his colleagues believed they 'were acting as conduits for the continuance of good relations between the Church and the party'.[154] Dewar, to his credit, stood firm, telling the 2000

British Labour conference: 'We won. In Scotland we did not keep the clause; section 28 is no more.'[155]

Only proposals to write off Glasgow City Council's £1 billion housing debt in return for stock transfer stood out as an innovative – if controversial – piece of policy making associated with the Dewar era.[156] In a 1998 St Andrew's Day lecture, he had warned that the next decade 'must not be one long embittering fight over further constitutional change', but rather one focused on 'what we do with our Parliament not what we do to it'.[157] Fine words, but in truth the First Minister was not terribly interested in ideas. At the Scottish Office between 1997 and 1999, Brian Wilson had pushed hard on land ownership, which eventually materialised in Scottish Parliament legislation on a community right to buy and abolition of feudal ownership. Journalist Peter Jones believed this, together with housing stock transfer, justified the description of Dewar as 'a radical' and even 'as a moderniser'.[158] But Frank McAveety was not alone in reflecting that:

> It did seem that the problem was what to do next. He had fought hard for his position and he deserved it but, in the end, there was a feeling that his work was done. Perhaps he did feel that reaching that stage was an end in itself.[159]

Section 28 and a row over Scottish exam results deepened cynicism towards the Scottish media, most vociferously from ex-*Mirror* journalist Alastair Campbell. He claimed that in the first ten weeks of 2000 clause 2a and 'sleaze' had accounted for a total of forty-seven front page stories, while education scored four and the economy just two.[160] Blair, Gordon Brown, George Robertson, Derry Irvine, Dewar and Alistair Darling were all reportedly 'implacably opposed' to a separate 'Scottish Six' news programme on the BBC, a stance which succeeded in offending Scotland's media establishment.[161]

Meanwhile the estimated cost of the new Scottish Parliament building continued to rocket, Dewar having rashly included a £40 million estimate in the 1997 White Paper. As Carol Craig later observed, once decisions were reached about its location and design concept, 'Donald's interest seemed to wane'.[162] Chancellor Gordon Brown told Alastair Campbell there was 'a real sense that Donald was just drifting, there was no real drive so it was no wonder they [the Scottish Executive] were attacked the whole time'.[163] Some Westminster colleagues were openly critical. Glasgow Pollok MP Ian Davidson told the BBC that Dewar's leadership 'was reminiscent of the worst days of John Major', while George Galloway (Glasgow Kelvin) called for the First Minister to be replaced. 'Maybe there's a need for someone younger, hungrier, leaner and fitter', he told the BBC. 'He's a parliamentary operator of great experience, but he seems to have lost the plot.'[164] In March 2000 Labour lost the first by-election of the new parliament when Ian Welsh resigned in Ayr, claiming there was not enough to do, while the following month enough Labour MSPs were 'pulled to the left' by arguments to abolish poindings and warrant sales. Tommy Sheridan's member's bill to that end led to the Executive's first significant defeat.[165]

Just a few weeks after the 2000 Scottish Labour conference, the First Minister underwent a three and a half-hour operation to replace a leaking aortic valve. Jim Wallace took over as Acting First Minister. 'It's not just Scotland which needs you', wrote Home Secretary Jack Straw, 'but the whole of the UK!'[166] The Prime Minister also paid a private visit to Glasgow Royal Infirmary while in the city for a health summit with the devolved administrations. Dewar returned to work in late June, cautioned squabbling Cabinet colleagues in July and returned to the Scottish Parliament in early September. But after a bad-tempered First Minister's Questions on 5 October Dewar looked visibly tired and, five days later, he tripped on the steps outside his official residence, which caused internal bleeding to his brain. On 11 October 2000 the first First Minister of Scotland was pronounced dead aged just sixty-three. 'Donald's achievement is much more than a Parliament', said Gordon Brown at his funeral. 'It is that he ennobled the very idea of service and by his pursuit of a just society, he gave moral purpose to our public life.'[167] The *Daily Record* later helped raise money for a statue which later stood on Glasgow's Sauchiehall Street.

'TURF WARS BETWEEN THE EXECUTIVE AND THE GOVERNMENT'

In many ways, the emergence of Dewar as the first leader of a devolved Labour-led Scottish government had been surprising. He had no locus in the trade union movement (unlike Gordon Brown) or record in local government (unlike Jack McConnell) but was a middle-class lawyer from the West End of Glasgow, something confirmed by a will which revealed an extensive bequest of properties, pictures and investments. Glasgow University contemporary Menzies Campbell later recalled a conversation with Dewar ten days before he died. 'The Labour Party in Scotland hasn't understood me for the past thirty years', he remarked when Campbell asked how Labour colleagues would react to Dewar's support for his bid to become Commons Speaker. 'I see no reason to try to change that now.'[168]

Nevertheless, the loss of Dewar was deeply felt by a party which had also lost John Smith just six years earlier. By coincidence, in the week of Dewar's death the Scottish Labour Party moved to its third headquarters in as many years. Not only was the party to share the AEEU's office on Glasgow's West Regent Street, but it was to be called 'John Smith House', a reminder, thought journalist Douglas Fraser, 'that Scottish Labour was closer to the values of Tony Blair's predecessor'.[169] After a period in which the party nearly avoided a contest at all ('It's got to be Henry', screamed the *Daily Record*), the Scottish Labour Parliamentary Group and Scottish Labour executive combined in a mini-electoral college to elect Henry McLeish leader. There had been no left or right; rather McLeish stood for 'Labour establishment continuity' while Jack McConnell 'embraced a pro-autonomy, modernising agenda'.[170]

Polling showed McLeish to have a plurality of support among Labour supporters (29 per cent) and the electorate (24 per cent), and indeed he was also London's – or rather Gordon Brown's – preferred candidate, as well as every member of the Scottish front bench and most of the Scottish party executive. McConnell, meanwhile, had a clear majority of backbench MSPs, though not among contemporaries in Scottish Labour Action. The Campaign for Socialism-aligned Cathy Jamieson was elected unopposed as deputy leader, while *Scotsman* journalist Peter MacMahon replaced David Whitton as official spokesman.

During his brief period as First Minister, Trench identified three ways in which McLeish attempted to assert himself: institutional innovation, policy innovation and symbolic politics.[171] The first was exemplified by the suggestion in January 2001 that the term 'Scottish Executive' be changed to 'Scottish Government'. The hostile reaction from London was brutal, particularly Scottish

Secretary John Reid. 'They can call themselves the White Heather Club if they want', said a source later identified as Brian Wilson, 'but they will never be a government'.[172] McLeish protested that the Prime Minister was 'not in the least bothered' by his proposal, but the damage had been done. 'Because Labour had not been encouraged to think about these things', he reflected in his memoirs, 'we were accused of being nationalists or fellow-travellers'.[173]

On the second, policy innovation, the new First Minister also incurred significant wrath from Westminster colleagues. A Royal Commission on long-term care for the elderly had recommended in March 2000 that the cost of all nursing and personal care should be met by the state. In October 2000, Donald Dewar had followed London's lead in rejecting full implementation on cost grounds, but his successor embraced a clear piece of policy divergence from the UK Labour government. McLeish believed there now had to be 'a wider vision and a view of Scotland that was beyond managing and delivering services', and that free personal care provided 'a statement of a country that was compassionate'.[174] In a calculated rebuke, Alistair Darling, the Edinburgh MP, former member of the International Marxist Group and now Work and Pensions Secretary, withheld £23 million in attendance allowance (a reserved benefit), which forced the Scottish Executive to meet the cost from within its own block grant. 'Our opponents will say this is £23m taken from Scotland and spent on increasing benefits to people in England', the First Minister warned Darling, as well as giving succour to 'those who oppose the devolution settlement' or 'argue that conflict between Westminster and Edinburgh is inevitable within the current settlement'.[175]

Thirdly, when it came to symbolic politics McLeish designated a Minister for European Affairs despite it being a reserved matter, signed the Flanders Declaration on regional representation in Europe, lobbied for a Scottish Executive presence at the UK embassy in Washington DC and took part in New York City's 'Tartan Day' celebrations in April 2001, a trip which included a rather gauche meeting with President Bush at the White House. Indeed, the First Minister's poor parliamentary performances – which were in curious contrast to his more assured Westminster style – attracted much negative briefing from anonymous colleagues as well as generating material for sketch-writers and commentators; the term 'McCliches' was coined to describe his verbal infelicities.[176] Henry had not turned out to be the safe pair of hands – or tribune for Gordon Brown – many had expected.

At the Scottish conference in March 2001 Tony Blair rallied activists in advance of the UK general election, telling them they ought to be 'proud of what we've done and humble about what we've still to do!'[177] The 2001 Scottish manifesto referred, slightly disingenuously given recent events, to the 'growing maturity of the devolution settlement delivered by Labour'.[178] On polling day, Labour held all its fifty-six Scottish seats despite a modest dip in vote share, while nationally the party was rewarded with another landslide.[179] David Cairns had only just been able to contest Inverclyde after legislation removed an historic bar on ordained clergy.[180]

Six of Labour's ten Glasgow MPs, meanwhile, were ex-councillors and only one, Ann McKechin, a woman. By the election, however, former Scottish party secretary Helen Liddell had succeeded John Reid (whom McLeish called a 'patronising bastard' within range of a live microphone the day after the election) as the first female Secretary of State for Scotland.[181] She later recalled that much of her role had been to 'avert or defuse turf wars between the Executive and the Government'. McLeish, she reflected, 'seemed to perceive the Secretary of State as a threat rather than a colleague who could fight their corner'.[182]

In October 2001 questions began to surface concerning McLeish's undeclared Westminster expenses. To journalist Iain Macwhirter, the resulting 'Officegate' affair was a kind of metaphor for Scottish civic culture, 'a dense coagulation of Labour politicians, their clients and apparatchiks'.[183] Although the subletting of his Fife constituency office involved no illegality – the First Minister referred to 'a muddle not a fiddle' – it was clumsily handled and given the deterioration in relations between the party in Scotland and London, the usual New Labour 'support system' was conspicuous by its absence. As McLeish later reflected:

> With notable exceptions in the [Scottish] Parliament, the trade unions and the general secretary Lesley Quinn, the attitude in the Scottish Labour Party was disappointing. Some colleagues believed

what they were reading, others were creating mischief and reinforcing the warped propaganda by briefing the press, and the rest had their heads down ... Indeed, some who clearly saw opportunity for advancement under a new leader joined in the feeding frenzy.[184]

Despite its messy end, it remains possible to mount a defence of McLeish's approach to devolved government. Institutionally, the SNP's Alex Salmond later won acclaim for his 'Scottish Government' rebranding; in terms of policy, McLeish correctly judged that devolution could not simply mean 'tartanised' versions of policy emanating from London, indeed Rhodri Morgan as First Minister of Wales made a virtue of putting what he called 'clear red water' between his devolved government and New Labour orthodoxy.[185]

'DOING LESS BETTER'

To Gerry Hassan, the election of Jack McConnell with no open contest in November 2001 revealed even more 'significant faultlines' within Scottish Labour. Initially, Wendy Alexander offered her candidacy with the support of Chancellor Gordon Brown, only to withdraw when British party chairman Charles Clarke intervened to ensure the election was conducted under one-member-one-vote.[186] Iain Macwhirter called it a 'Lanarkshire lock-out, the kind of politics that flourishes in the badlands of Labour local government in west central Scotland',[187] although McConnell's badlands were in Stirling rather than Lanarkshire. Accompanied by his wife Brigid, one of the new leader's first acts was to head off potential tabloid trouble by admitting to an extra-marital affair with a former Scottish Labour employee.

Significantly, McConnell was the first First Minister without any Westminster provenance, but although regarded as a Blairite, his relationship with the Prime Minister had in fact 'deteriorated slowly and quietly over the years'.[188] He also had solid credentials on the party's nationalist wing as a founder member of Scottish Labour Action, although he had moderated much of this on becoming general secretary in 1992. Nevertheless, Gordon Brown was apparently worried 'Jack would flirt with neo-nationalism',[189] the two having fallen out in 1994 when McConnell supported Blair for the British party leadership.[190] McConnell certainly wanted a clean sweep, sacking several ministers and prompting another, Susan Deacon, to jump before she was pushed. Only Wendy Alexander survived from Dewar's first Cabinet. It was, judged Hazell, 'a signal of his determination to impose his authority on the Executive in a manner that neither of his predecessors had succeeded in doing'.[191]

In came perceived left-wingers such as Cathy Jamieson at education, Malcolm Chisholm at health and Mike Watson at culture and sport. Finance went to former council leader Andy Kerr. Mike Donnelly, a contemporary of McConnell's from Stirling University (and Council), joined as policy adviser while a civil servant (Andrew Baird) was appointed official spokesman. The new First Minister maintained free personal care but admitted defeat on attendance allowance, while embracing an environmental agenda based on renewable energy,[192] but there was at the time a sense he was holding back until equipped with his own electoral mandate. McConnell's slogan was 'doing less better', and his aim to make Scotland the 'best small country in the world'.

Electoral reform in local government was an early test of McConnell's modernising credentials, and one he ultimately embraced. Despite the recommendations of the McIntosh (1999) and Kerley (2000) reports, many in Scottish Labour were bitterly opposed to yet another act of charitable giving. In December 2001 the First Minister set out a timetable for reform which prompted Dan Carrigan, Scottish secretary of the AEEU, to attack what he called 'nauseating' talk of introducing PR to 'clean up local councils', something he considered 'an insult' to swathes of Labour councillors in largely corruption-free authorities.[193]

Otherwise, by 2002 Hassan believed Scottish Labour had 'increasingly become a conservative party, and the political establishment'.[194] It seemed Wendy Alexander, who resigned from the Scottish Executive in May 2002, agreed. In a private email to Jim Sillars later leaked to newspapers, she observed that:

> Perhaps one of the last times the Labour Movement in Scotland made a real intellectual contribution to the UK Labour Party was around the rapid growth of the ILP following the establishment of the Forward newspaper in 1906 ... We have often spent so long obsessing about our constitutional choices that we have spent too little time reflecting on the sort of nation we wish to create.[195]

Scottish Labour's lack of input into reserved policy matters came to head when on 20 March 2003 a US-led force (including UK troops) invaded Iraq, a military initiative which could be traced back to the events of 9/11. With much of the party opposed, the recent Scottish Labour conference had been potentially hazardous. Several resolutions critical of the anticipated UK intervention had been submitted, although Millbank intervened to remove the whole issue from the conference agenda. Under pressure from trade union affiliates, however, conference – chaired by the future leader Richard Leonard – was given the right to discuss Iraq but not hold a vote.[196] A senior Labour MSP later claimed that 'McConnell was virtually told to back Blair over Iraq',[197] while in the Scottish Parliament on 13 March, six Labour MSPs supported an anti-war stance. When the following day an anti-war motion was defeated in the House of Commons, seventeen Scottish Labour MPs were among 139 rebels.

These divisions arguably benefitted the Liberal Democrats, who had set themselves against Iraq adventurism from day one. According to an audit of the Scottish Executive's first term, the Scottish Liberal Democrats had been responsible for almost 70 per cent of coalition policies which had not featured in either party's 1999 manifesto, something Roddin believed was, in part, due to a 'lack of Labour initiatives'.[198] Keating noted that while Scottish Labour had the right to make its own policy on devolved issues via the Scottish Policy Forum and annual conference, in practice this had 'ceased to be an important source of new ideas'. Long notorious for infighting and division, by 2003 this tended to concern 'power and factionalism rather than competing visions of social democracy'.[199]

'A DISTINCTIVE CONCEPT OF DEVOLUTION'

At the second elections to the Scottish Parliament in May 2003, Scottish Labour saw its vote share drop and a net loss of six seats, continuing a trend evident at the three elections (Scottish, council and European) of 1999. The Liberal Democrats gained on the constituency vote which meant Scottish Labour lost proportional strength to their junior coalition partners. Denver suggested this represented a 'wake-up' call to both Labour and the SNP, the latter having also lost votes under the leadership of John Swinney.²⁰⁰ Alluding to a 10 per cent 'gap' between support for the party in Scotland and in the rest of Britain, McConnell said there 'are many people in Scotland who prefer London Labour to Scottish Labour, and we need to tackle that'.²⁰¹ At its annual congress during the campaign, the STUC had only narrowly endorsed a motion calling on its members to vote Labour. It was opposed by Unison, Scotland's largest trade union.

In concurrent local government elections, Labour received 32.6 per cent of the vote and took 41.7 per cent of council seats. But here too electoral support was less entrenched than it had been historically, with the party maintaining overall majority in thirteen out of thirty-two unitary authorities, two fewer than in 1999. Allan McConnell believed Labour's support showed signs of being eroded by the Scottish Socialist Party, particularly in Glasgow where Tommy Sheridan's party came second in eighteen out of seventy-nine wards.²⁰² The Local Governance (Scotland) Act 2004 received Royal Assent the following year and was to take effect at the next council elections in 2007, bringing an end to first-past-the-post elections.

Beyond local government, Finlay observed that:

> for all the talk of Scotland being more radical than England and of the nation being predisposed towards left-of-centre redistributive politics, these characteristics have not really manifested themselves in any meaningful way. There is little to differentiate between the policies pursued at Holyrood and those pursued at Westminster.²⁰³

Hopkin and Bradbury concluded that all Labour First Ministers had been 'comfortable with the Blairite New Labour agenda',²⁰⁴ although Keating believed Scottish Labour had adopted a more collectivist, traditionally social democratic stance on key policy issues.²⁰⁵ Mooney and Poole pointed to health, the NHS in Scotland and England having clearly diverged when it came to private sector involvement.²⁰⁶ But was this proactive or passive? Wendy Alexander believed any divergences had arisen through 'a failure to follow an English example rather than as a result of pioneering new ideas'.²⁰⁷ Keating also observed that Jack McConnell carefully avoided 'criticism or comment where things were done differently in England', while 'maintaining a strict ban on ministers making their views known on reserved matters'.²⁰⁸

There was certainly no attempt by any Labour First Ministers to choose between Keating and Harvey's two ideal-type economic models, either market-liberalism based on low taxes, flexibility and deregulation, or social investment with higher taxes and greater regulation.[209] Labour proved itself unable to marry a constitutional vision with a set of economic and social policies to show how devolution could be used to improve Scotland's growth and apparent commitment to 'social justice'.[210] In his 2004 memoirs, Henry McLeish warned that unless Scottish Labour articulated 'a distinctive concept of devolution' it risked being 'out-manoeuvred as both the Scottish National Party and the Liberal Democrats seize the opportunities being offered by a changing world'.[211]

Out of office, Wendy Alexander emphasised a growth agenda. In *Chasing the Tartan Tiger: Lessons from a Celtic Cousin?*, she looked to post-independence Ireland for lessons in crafting 'a new Scottish story' with the business community at its core. Even in 2003, Alexander was conscious that public and economic discourse in Scotland was stymied by being 'a proxy for constitutional agendas'. 'We may have anticipated the political change home rule would bring', she concluded, 'but are only starting to explore the emotional, cultural and economic consequences'.[212]

Policy did occasionally intrude. At the 2005 UK general election, the divergence in health policy noted above dogged the Labour campaign in Scotland, chiefly a Commons vote on removing proposals for 'foundation' hospitals from the Health and Social Care (Community Health and Standards) Bill. Although the government defeated the amendment, it had relied on the support of forty-two Scottish and twenty-five Welsh MPs representing parts of the country where the policy would not apply. A slight majority of English MPs had voted against the government. This was the West Lothian Question of which Tam Dalyell – who left the Commons at that election – had long warned and which privately troubled Tony Blair.

The 2005 result once again 'flattered' Labour in Scotland due to the majoritarian electoral system, masking the fact its vote share had declined to its lowest level since 1983. As a delayed quid pro quo for devolution, Scotland's seventy-two constituencies had been reduced to fifty-nine, resulting in often radically altered constituency boundaries, although only three incumbent Labour MPs had failed to become candidates as a consequence.[213]

Back in 1995, Blair had fretted to Paddy Ashdown about this long-planned change on the basis that 'Scotland was overwhelmingly Labour' and that it would 'in future reduce Labour's ability to get a majority'.[214] This was misplaced, for Blair had just secured his third term in government.

Jack McConnell, meanwhile, built on his predecessor's symbolic differentiation with international aid for Malawi, a country with colonial ties to the Church of Scotland. This inhabited the no man's land between reserved and devolved matters but was largely tolerated by Labour colleagues at Westminster, as was the Fresh Talent Scheme launched in 2005, a bespoke graduate visa which allowed international students leaving Scottish universities to continue working for up to two years after graduation. There was populist (and to some, punitive) legislation to tackle anti-social behaviour while the First Minister hosted a sectarianism 'summit' amid important shifts in the political allegiances of Scotland's Catholic community. In 2006, Cardinal Keith O'Brien even made it known he would be 'happy' if Scots voted for independence.[215] McConnell also addressed another shibboleth by recommending Elish Angiolini for appointment as Lord Advocate, the first woman and solicitor to take up the historic post.

If anything, by 2006 the Scottish Executive was considered a little boring, with a growing feeling (as found in a YouGov poll) that Scottish Labour had 'been in power too long in Scotland' and that it was therefore 'time for a change'. That summer Ipsos-MORI placed the SNP two points ahead of Labour in voting intentions for the next Scottish Parliament election, with later surveys showing the parties at least neck and neck. The SNP, once again led by Alex Salmond with Nicola Sturgeon as his deputy, were back in contention. In February 2006, Labour's Catherine Stihler had also lost the Dunfermline and West Fife Westminster by-election to Liberal Democrat Willie Rennie.

Scottish Labour's reaction was to dust off its 1999 playbook. At a Press Fund lunch in Glasgow soon after becoming Scottish Secretary in May 2006, Douglas Alexander (brother of Wendy) attacked the SNP for peddling the politics of 'grudge and grievance'. 'The essential difference between myself and the Nationalists is this', he added, 'they believe that what scars Scotland is the border with England. I believe that what scars Scotland is poverty, inequality and injustice.'[216] Alexander and

Gordon Brown expanded on this theme in a Fabian pamphlet entitled *Stronger Together: The 21st Century Case for Scotland and Britain*. The Anglo-Scottish Union in its 300th year, they concluded, was clearly founded on 'social justice ... We pool our wealth to ensure that every part of the Union has the resources it needs to meet its social, economic and geographical demands'.[217]

This was the attempt to develop a UK-wide identity which Blair now regretted not having pursued earlier, as well as the beginning of Gordon Brown's later 'pooling and sharing' argument which he deployed during the 2014 independence referendum. The main themes of Scottish Labour's 2007 campaign were clear from its Oban conference in November 2006. Proceedings were dominated by vehement attacks on the SNP from Blair, Brown and John Reid; the last even claimed independence would hinder the fight against terrorism. Jack McConnell attempted a more positive policy agenda centred on education, while towards the end of the campaign he rather clumsily floated council tax reform but came unstuck when pressed for details.

But what had worked in 1999 would not necessarily work in 2007. 'We started to feel as if we were swimming against a tide', reflected McConnell a few years later. '[The SNP] ran with a very positive campaign and we ended up on the other side of that, sounding negative.'[218] Not only had the fallout from the 2003 invasion of Iraq dented British Labour's credibility, but Alex Salmond had skilfully neutralised the independence question by promising, in a move reminiscent of Labour's in 1996, that it would only happen following a referendum. A decision to renew the UK's nuclear deterrent also played into the SNP's narrative that Scottish Labour could not function 'without remote control from their London masters'.[219] Curtice et al. found that opposition to the Iraq War (64 per cent), building more nuclear stations (51 per cent) and the replacement of Trident (42 per cent) all ultimately depressed the Labour vote in Scotland.[220] On the eve of polling, former adviser John McLaren denigrated 'doing less, better' as a strategy, observing that initiatives such as the smoking ban and Fresh Talent stood alone rather than as 'part of a coherent narrative on health or on economic development'.[221]

When it came to the campaign itself there were obvious tensions between London and Glasgow. Campaigners sent from

England to assist their Scottish counterparts were apparently aghast to discover that in most of Labour's Scottish seats there were no canvass returns from previous elections. 'No work had been done', one official was quoted as saying. 'We basically had to start from scratch finding out who our voters were.' As in 1999, it was decided that Blair and Brown would dominate the campaign, although Jack McConnell also fronted the launch of a document entitled *Economic Stability at Risk*, which attacked the SNP's sums. Anticipating what was to come in 2014, one Labour campaigner told *The Scotsman* that 'after 10 years in government, it is fear, not hope, that will win'.[222]

McConnell was also less popular than Alex Salmond while at UK level there was little evidence the impending appointment of Gordon Brown as Prime Minister did much to sway voting intentions.[223] The outgoing Chancellor asked Blair to go a few weeks earlier, 'believing that the simple fact of there being a Scottish prime minister would help us win power in Scotland', while Brown clearly resented being depicted by the SNP as 'a London and Westminster politician' despite his family home being in North Queensferry.[224]

The result was painfully close. Initially it looked as if Labour had won four seats and the SNP none in the Highlands and Islands region, which would have given the largest incumbent party forty-seven seats and the opposition forty-five. But when the SNP demanded a recalculation, the result was three Labour and the SNP two. Salmond's party had a plurality of just one MSP, leading Labour in the constituency vote by just 0.7 per cent and on the regional list by the slightly more substantial 1.8 per cent. Given the SNP had begun the campaign with a five to six-point poll lead, Peter Jones concluded that Labour's assault on independence *had* worked. Where Labour had mounted last-minute constituency support it had held seats it was expected to lose, while it appeared the SNP had benefitted more from the self-destruction of the Scottish Socialist Party.[225]

But the first rule of politics, to quote Lyndon Johnson, is 'to be able to count'. The SNP had a plurality of seats in a system contrived to prevent any single party dominating the devolved parliament. And when Salmond shrewdly depicted this as an unequivocal win, the political ball entered his court. 'Scotland has changed for good and forever', said Salmond, after arriving by helicopter at Prestonfield House on the outskirts of

Edinburgh. 'There may well be Labour governments and Labour First Ministers in the decades to come, but never again will we see the Labour Party assume that it has a divine right to rule Scotland.'[226]

'BRING IT ON'

Writing in 1999, Gerry Hassan had predicted it would come as a:

> complete shock to Scottish Labour to find that one day it is not running the Scottish Parliament ... a defining moment for the new Scotland and Scottish Labour, where it will not be able to blame its predicament on others, but will have to begin a painful and long overdue process of renewal and modernisation. This will be a point where Scottish Labour grows up.[227]

In May 2007 this shock was compounded by the anticipated recalibration of local government given the change to single transferable vote elections. Scottish Labour's share of seats fell to 28.5 per cent and it was left with control of just two out of thirty-two authorities, Glasgow and North Lanarkshire. Hassan and Shaw concluded that by inflating party support for so long, first-past-the-post had created few incentives for the party to strengthen its membership base or reinvigorate political engagement.[228] Figures presented to the 2008 Scottish conference showed that half Scotland's CLPs had fewer than 300 members and fourteen fewer than 200. Henry McLeish bluntly described his Fife constituency party as resembling 'a poorly attended social club'.[229]

Although Gordon Brown tried to persuade UK Liberal Democrat leader Menzies Campbell to 're-form our coalition' they were reluctant, a 'loss of nerve' he believed had 'allowed Alex Salmond to capitalise'.[230] This was an heroic analysis given the two parties had only sixty-two seats between them, three short of even a workable majority. When SNP–Liberal Democrat negotiations also floundered over an independence referendum, Salmond formed a minority administration – an option considered but rejected by Scottish Labour MSPs back in 1999. Tony Blair was acutely conscious that once Alex Salmond 'got his feet under the table' it would be 'far harder to remove him than to stop him in the first place'.[231]

Now in opposition to the soon-to-be-rebranded 'Scottish Government', Scottish Labour ratcheted up its unionism while the UK Labour government launched a belated campaign for Britishness as a 'civic nationalist' project, which ironically echoed Salmond's own successful recasting of Scottish nationalism.[232] Now the first female leader of the Scottish Labour Party, Wendy Alexander used a St Andrew's Day speech to set out the case for a cross-party review of Holyrood's existing powers. She considered a priority 'strengthening' its 'financial accountability' by moving to a mixture of 'assigned and devolved taxes' while retaining 'financial transfers within the UK ... to ensure that areas with greater spending needs have the resources to fund them'. Alexander continued:

> The priorities of the people of Scotland remain the same as others in countries across the world – health, education, law-and-order, housing. But if the only reform alternative people can see is one of separatism they can be forgiven for assuming that this is their only choice. It is up to us to offer a better alternative. A new Scottish Constitutional Commission will allow us to do just that.[233]

In her 2008 Scottish conference speech, meanwhile, Alexander expanded upon what she saw as defining lines between Labour and the SNP:

> Scotland is a country I love to the core of my being. However, 'Scotland' is not a political philosophy. 'Scotland' can just as easily be Adam Smith as it can be John Smith. The world over, politics comes down to a choice: right versus left, conservatives versus progressives, nationalists versus internationalists.[234]

A few weeks later, Alexander boldly challenged the SNP government to 'bring it on', suggesting that she (and more to the point Westminster) would sanction an independence referendum as she did not 'fear the verdict of the Scottish people'. It quickly became clear, however, that this had been inadequately cleared with the Scottish party and its Westminster MPs. According to Hassan and Shaw, a paper contemplating the move was circulated to Brown and Blair with only the latter indicating enthusiasm. Impatient with the delay, Alexander made her move.[235] When Gordon Brown appeared less than enthusiastic on being challenged by Conservative leader David Cameron in the Commons,[236] the Scottish Labour leader's authority was dealt a severe blow. This was further eroded by a contrived row over donations to Alexander's leadership campaign and she resigned on 28 June 2008.

Iain Gray took over as acting leader while the SNP's narrow victory in the Glasgow East Westminster by-election on 24 July instigated a fuller debate within Scottish Labour about its relationship with the British party. Former Health Minister Andy Kerr called for the next leader to have greater control in Scotland, including authority over the party's thirty-eight Scottish MPs. One of his backers, former Holyrood Finance Minister Tom McCabe, accused those MPs of being 'arrogant' and 'in denial' as to the scale of the party's difficulties.[237] Gray, who was confirmed as leader in September, did not appear to share their analysis. His East Lothian party was then embroiled in a messy battle over incumbent MP Anne Moffat, whom the CLP wished to deselect. A motion of no confidence to that end led to suspension by the NEC and was only upheld following a long war of attrition in March 2010.[238]

In June 2009 the Calman Commission initiated by Wendy Alexander recommended greater fiscal and welfare autonomy for the Scottish Parliament which was later enacted via the Scotland Act 2012. Meanwhile the 2008 Glenrothes and 2009 Glasgow North East by-elections (the latter sparked by Speaker Michael Martin's resignation) reinforced Scottish Labour's belief that its Westminster hegemony remained intact and its opposition status at Holyrood was merely temporary. This appeared to be vindicated when Labour held all its forty-one MPs at the 2010 UK general election and increased its Scottish vote share to 42 per cent despite a 6.2 per cent reduction across Britain as a whole.

In the British Labour leadership contest that followed Gordon Brown's defeat and resignation, it emerged that Scottish party membership had fallen to 13,135 from a peak of more than 30,000 in 1998 and 18,800 in March 2006. Despite this, Iain Gray geared up for the 2011 Holyrood election reasonably confident of once again achieving a plurality of MSPs. His March 2011 Scottish conference speech invoked wartime Scottish Secretary Tom Johnston, drew upon his experience as a community activist in Wester Hailes, and declared that Scottish Labour 'values' had made the 'lives of millions better, given hope to the dispossessed and made the weak stronger'.²³⁹ The Scottish Labour manifesto, meanwhile, was a product of what the party breathlessly called 'the most exciting and ambitious policy process that Labour has ever embarked on'.²⁴⁰

The campaign opened with Gray buoyed by polls giving Scottish Labour a mighty fifteen-point lead over the SNP, something which concerned even the usually optimistic Alex Salmond. The party had also modernised its campaigning machinery since 2007, using database software to target potential Labour voters. Soon, however, the polls dramatically shifted. As voters in Scotland moved out of the previous year's Westminster mindset and on to Holyrood, they appeared increasingly convinced by the SNP's slick 'team, record, vision' campaign. Not only did Gray lack voter recognition (in stark contrast to Alex Salmond),²⁴¹ but his campaign was dominated by gaffes, including an ambush by protestors at Glasgow Central Station. On the eve of the election, and in an apparent act of desperation, Scottish Labour U-turned on its opposition to a council tax freeze and 'free' university tuition, both Scottish Government policies.²⁴²

Even more damagingly, there was evidence voters doubted Scottish Labour's commitment to an extension of the devolution settlement, despite its role in establishing the Calman Commission.²⁴³ This was underscored by Gray's attack on independence:

> [Salmond] says that a second term gives him the moral authority to pursue independence ... Five more years of his constant obsession with independence. Is that what you want? Is that what the country wants? is that something that Scotland can afford?²⁴⁴

Although turnout was extremely low – 50.4 per cent – a plurality of voters ignored Gray's dark warning and equipped the SNP with something that was supposed to be impossible, an overall majority. Scottish Labour had badly misread the nature of the campaign, which in the wake of the financial crisis and a Conservative-led government at Westminster concerned which party was best placed to 'stand up for Scotland'. This had once clearly been the Scottish Labour Party, now it was unequivocally the SNP. Alex Salmond's long campaign to situate his party in the 'mainstream' of Scottish political opinion while challenging Labour's dominance in west-central Scotland had finally come to pass, a mere 21 years after the fledgling party leader had first promised his supporters precisely that.[245]

NOTES

1. G. Hassan (2002), 'A case study of Scottish Labour: Devolution and the politics of multi-level governance', *Political Quarterly* 73:2, 155.
2. L. Bennie, J. Brand & J. Mitchell (1997), *How Scotland Votes: Scottish Parties and Elections*, Manchester: Manchester University Press, 58.
3. P. Lynch (1994), 'The 1994 European elections in Scotland: Campaigns and strategies', *Scottish Affairs* 9, 24–44.
4. *The Times*, 1 July 1994.
5. They were Maria Fyfe (Glasgow Maryhill), Irene Adams (Paisley North) and Rachel Squire (Dunfermline West).
6. *Independent*, 22 June 1994.
7. *Herald*, 1 July 1994.
8. *Herald*, 20 June 1995.
9. I. Macwhirter (1994), 'The year at Westminster: Parliamentary Session 1993–1994', *Scottish Affairs* 8, 122.
10. P. Ashdown (2000), *The Ashdown Diaries, Volume I: 1988–1997*, London: Allen Lane, 385.
11. *Scotsman*, 14 September 1994.
12. *Scotland on Sunday*, 2 October 1994.
13. *Scotsman*, 20 October 1994.
14. *Scotland on Sunday*, 6 September 1998.
15. J. Rentoul (2013), *Tony Blair: Prime Minister*, London: Faber and Faber, 259–60.
16. T. Blair (2010), *A Journey*, London: Hutchinson, 86.
17. D. Canavan (2009), *Let the People Decide: The Autobiography of Dennis Canavan*, Edinburgh: Birlinn, 227–8.
18. Bennie et al., 64.
19. *Herald*, 24 April 1995.
20. *Scotland on Sunday*, 6 September 1998.
21. Press Association, 28 June 1995.
22. *Herald*, 4 October 1995.
23. *Scotsman*, 9 January 1996.
24. George Robertson to Tony Blair, 1 September 1995, SPA/GR/SN/PARL/1/7, George Robertson Collection, Stirling: Scottish Political Archive.
25. P. Lynch (1996), 'The Scottish Constitutional Convention, 1992–5', *Scottish Affairs* 15, 12–13.
26. Press Association, 4 October 1995.

27. *Scotsman*, 11 September 1995.
28. *Herald*, 9 March 1996.
29. Tommy Sheppard to George Robertson, 21 February 1995, SPA/GR/SN/PARL/1/1, George Robertson Collection.
30. Press Association, 2 October 1995.
31. *Scotland on Sunday*, 24 September 1995.
32. T. Brown & H. McLeish (2007), *Scotland: The Road Divides – New Politics, New Union*, Edinburgh: Luath, 1.
33. *Herald*, 15 January 1996.
34. *Daily Record*, 15 April 1996.
35. *Scotsman*, March 11, 1996.
36. A. Campbell & B. Hagerty (eds) (2010), *The Alastair Campbell Diaries, Volume 1: Prelude to Power, 1994–1997*, London: Hutchinson, 477–80. Campbell had suffered the beginning of a nervous breakdown while covering Scottish Labour's 1986 conference for *Today*.
37. P. Jones (1997), 'Labour's referendum plan: Sell-out or act of faith?', *Scottish Affairs* 18, 1–11.
38. See p. XXX [author – please complete at proofs].
39. D. Irvine (2005), 'A skilful advocate', in W. Alexander (ed.), *Donald Dewar: Scotland's first First Minister*, Edinburgh: Mainstream, 126.
40. Ashdown (2000), 441–2.
41. Peter Jones's account in *Scottish Affairs* accepted this version of events.
42. SPA/JMA/RES/12, John McAllion Collection, Stirling: Scottish Political Archive. McAllion was succeeded as Scottish spokesman by Malcolm Chisholm.
43. Bill Spiers to John McAllion, 3 July 1996, SPA/JMA/RES/5/1, John McAllion Collection.
44. Ian Smart to John McAllion, 28 June 1996, SPA/JMA/RES/35, John McAllion Collection.
45. George Robertson to John Henderson, 21 August 1996, SPA/JMA/RES/11, John McAllion Collection.
46. Campbell (2010), 481–4.
47. *Herald*, 29 August 1996.
48. *Scotsman*, 7 September 1996.
49. Jones (1997), 16.
50. *Herald*, 10 September 1996.
51. Blair, 252–3.
52. *Herald*, 27 September 1996.
53. Press Association, 1 October 1996.
54. *Scotsman*, 5 November 1996.
55. Campbell (2010), 582–3

56. *Scotsman*, 6 December 1996.
57. Press Association, 10 January 1997.
58. L. Davidson (2005), *Lucky Jack: Scotland's First Minister*, Edinburgh: Black and White, 87.
59. 'Scottish Labour's Political strategy', 31 January 1997, SPA/GR/SN/PARL/1/10, George Robertson Collection.
60. P. Cairney & N. McGarvey (2013), *Scottish Politics* (Second Edition), London: Palgrave Macmillan, 32.
61. *Scotsman*, 3 January 1997.
62. *Scotsman*, 14 January 1997.
63. W. L. Miller, A. Mae Timpson & M. Lessnoff (1996), *Political Culture in Contemporary Britain: People and Politicians, Principles and Practice*, Oxford: Clarendon Press.
64. *Scotland on Sunday*, 19 January 1997.
65. Press Association, 7 March 1997.
66. *Independent*, 2 February 1997
67. *Daily Record*, 20 January 1997.
68. *Scotsman*, 10 March 1997.
69. Davidson, 82.
70. Note of meeting with Glasgow City Council representatives, 17 February 1997, George Robertson Collection.
71. 'Scottish Labour's Political strategy', SPA/GR/SN/PARL/1/10, George Robertson Collection.
72. *Herald*, 6 March 1997.
73. Press Association, 4 April 1997.
74. *Scotsman*, 14 April 1997.
75. Rentoul, 306.
76. *Scotsman*, 5 April 1997.
77. B. Taylor (1999), *The Scottish Parliament*, Edinburgh: Edinburgh University Press, 150.
78. *Scotland on Sunday*, 6 April 1997.
79. *Scotsman*, 14 April 1997.
80. M. Sarwar with B. Wylie (2016), *My Remarkable Journey: The Autobiography of Britain's First Muslim MP*, Edinburgh: Birlinn, 132–3.
81. *Scotsman*, 6 May 1997
82. *Scotsman*, 13 May 1997.
83. 'Lord Irvine's guilt over Dewar's wife', BBC News online, 2 December 1998 <http://news.bbc.co.uk/1/hi/uk_politics/226251.stm>
84. J. Naughtie (2001), *The Rivals: The Intimate Story of a Political Marriage*, London: Fourth Estate, 204.
85. M. Smith (2005), 'An unconventional politician', in W. Alexander (ed.) (2005), *Donald Dewar: Scotland's first First Minister*, Edinburgh: Mainstream, 74.

86. D. Stenhouse (2004), *How the Scots Took Over London*, Edinburgh: Mainstream, 43. Gordon McMaster had been elected at a by-election in November 1990.
87. Graham sat on the opposition benches until he left the Commons in 2001 (*Scotland on Sunday*, 6 September 1998).
88. J. Sewel (2005), 'Getting the Act together', in W. Alexander (ed.), *Donald Dewar: Scotland's first First Minister*, Edinburgh: Mainstream, 132–4.
89. *Scotsman*, 6 August 1997.
90. *Irish Times*, 12 August 1997.
91. A. Campbell & B. Hagerty (eds) (2011), *The Alastair Campbell Diaries, Volume 2: Power and the People, 1997–1999*, London: Hutchinson, 148.
92. Scottish Labour Party (1997), *Referendum 97*, Glasgow: SLP.
93. HC Deb 12 January 1998 Vol 304 c34 [Scotland Bill].
94. HC Deb 6 May 1998 Vol 311 c803 [Review Of Role Of Scottish Members Of House Of Commons].
95. G. Radice (2004), *Diaries: From Political Disaster to Election Triumph*, London: Weidenfeld and Nicolson, 422.
96. Blair, 251.
97. *The Times*, 2 September 2015.
98. F. Ross (2005), 'As a friend', in W. Alexander (ed.), *Donald Dewar: Scotland's first First Minister*, Edinburgh: Mainstream, 46.
99. HL Deb 21 July 1998 Vol 592 c853 [Scotland Bill].
100. *Scotsman*, 25 May 1998.
101. *Scotsman*, 21 August 1997.
102. *Scotsman*, 12 May 1998.
103. E. Shaw (2003), 'Paper presented to the Annual Conference of the Elections, Public Opinion and Party Group of the Political Studies Association', Cardiff: University of Cardiff (online).
104. Canavan, 242.
105. D. Fraser (2005), 'New Labour, new Parliament', in W. Alexander (ed.), *Donald Dewar: Scotland's first First Minister*, Edinburgh: Mainstream, 135.
106. Davidson, 102–3.
107. Hassan (2002), 148.
108. F. Mackay (2004), 'Women and the Labour Party in Scotland', in G. Hassan (ed.), *The Scottish Labour Party: History, Institutions and Ideas*, Edinburgh: Edinburgh University Press, 109, 117.
109. Scottish Labour Party (1998), *A Modern Scottish Labour Party: Rule Changes Proposed by the Scottish Executive Committee*, Glasgow: SLP.

110. M. Ritchie (2000), *Scotland Reclaimed: The Inside Story of Scotland's First Democratic Parliamentary Election*, Edinburgh: Saltire Society, 51.
111. T. Sheppard (1997), *A New Scottish Labour Party*, Scottish Labour Action, 24.
112. Ritchie, 51.
113. P. Lynch & S. Birrell (2004), 'The autonomy and organisation of Scottish Labour', in G. Hassan (ed.), *The Scottish Labour Party: History, Institutions and Ideas*, Edinburgh: Edinburgh University Press, 179.
114. P. Schlesinger, D. Miller & W. Dinan (2001), *Open Scotland? Journalists, Spin Doctors and Lobbyists*, Edinburgh: Polygon, 168–72.
115. Davidson, 99.
116. *Scotsman*, 7 September 1998.
117. *Scotland on Sunday*, 13 September 1998.
118. *Scotsman*, 4 December 1995.
119. Ritchie, 29.
120. G. Brown & D. Alexander (1999), *New Scotland, New Britain*, Glasgow: Smith Institute, 47.
121. G. Hassan & E. Shaw (2012), *The Strange Death of Labour Scotland*, Edinburgh: Edinburgh University Press, 96.
122. A. Rawnsley (2000), *Servants of the People: The Inside Story of New Labour*, London: Penguin, 252.
123. Rawnsley, 251–3.
124. P. Jones (1999), 'The 1999 Scottish Parliament elections: From anti-Tory to anti-Nationalist politics', *Scottish Affairs* 28, 6.
125. Rawnsley, 53.
126. Campbell (2011), 644, 675–6.
127. Ritchie, 81, 92.
128. Ritchie, 145.
129. C. M. M. Macdonald (2009), *Whaur Extremes Meet: Scotland's Twentieth Century*, Edinburgh: John Donald, 225.
130. H. McLeish (1999), 'The negotiation diaries: Diary of Scottish Labour Party negotiator: Henry McLeish MSP', *Scottish Affairs* 28, 56.
131. McLeish (1999), 57.
132. G. Hassan (2002), 'The paradoxes of Scottish Labour: Devolution, change and conservatism', in G. Hassan & C. Warhurst (eds), *Tomorrow's Scotland*, London: Lawrence and Wishart, 36.
133. D. Denver & I. MacAllister (1999), 'The Scottish Parliament elections 1999: An analysis of the results', *Scottish Affairs* 28, 29.
134. Ritchie, 127–8.

135. P. Ashdown (2000), 439–58.
136. McLeish (1999), 60.
137. M. Watson (2001), *Year Zero: An Inside View of the Scottish Parliament*, Edinburgh: Polygon, 4–5, 135.
138. J. Baillie (2016), 'The Holyrood years', in G. Teasdale (ed.), *Remembering Sam: The Life and Times of Sam Galbraith*, Edinburgh: Birlinn, 142.
139. D. Torrance (2011), *Great Scottish Speeches*, Edinburgh: Luath, 186–8.
140. R. McLean (2001), 'Gallant crusader or cautious persuader? Donald Dewar's role in securing Scotland's parliament', *Scottish Affairs* 34, 10.
141. Taylor, 153–6.
142. Schlesinger et al., 174–9.
143. D. Denver & I. MacAllister (2000), 'The 1999 European Parliament election in Scotland', *Scottish Affairs* 30, 140.
144. *Herald*, 9 March 1996.
145. J. McConnell (1999), 'The modernisers', in G. Hassan & C. Warhurst (eds), *A Different Future: A Modernisers' Guide to Scotland*, Glasgow: Big Issue, 69.
146. *Herald*, 30 December 2016.
147. *Guardian*, 11 May 1999.
148. P. Ashdown (2001), *The Ashdown Diaries, Volume II: 1997–1999*, London: Allen Lane, 446.
149. Watson, 80.
150. D. Torrance (2006), *The Scottish Secretaries*, Edinburgh: Birlinn, 348.
151. Watson, 4.
152. T. Harris (2018), *Ten Years in the Death of the Labour Party*, London: Biteback, 107.
153. McLeish (2004), 83.
154. Watson, 158.
155. M. Elder (2005), 'As Scottish Labour leader', in W. Alexander (ed.), *Donald Dewar: Scotland's first First Minister*, Edinburgh: Mainstream, 91.
156. The 1983 Grieve Inquiry concluded that Glasgow needed to transfer at least 40 per cent of its housing stock.
157. G. Brown (2005), 'As a colleague', in W. Alexander (ed.), *Donald Dewar: Scotland's first First Minister*, Edinburgh: Mainstream, 79.
158. P. Jones (2005), 'The modernising radical', in W. Alexander (ed.), *Donald Dewar: Scotland's first First Minister*, Edinburgh: Mainstream, 163.
159. *The Dewar Years* (2001), Glasgow: Scottish Television.

160. A. Campbell & B. Hagerty (eds) (2011b), *The Alastair Campbell Diaries, Volume 3: Power and Responsibility, 1999–2001*, London: Hutchinson, 257.
161. Schlesinger et al., 180.
162. C. Craig (2005), 'His finest hour', in W. Alexander (ed.), *Donald Dewar: Scotland's first First Minister*, Edinburgh: Mainstream, 101. According to Neil Findlay, Dewar arranged for the ashes of Mick McGahey, a long-time supporter of a Scottish Parliament who died in January 1999, to be scattered in its foundations. See N. Findlay with J. Holmes (2023), *Hope and Despair: Lifting the Lid on the Murky World of Scottish Politics*, Edinburgh: Luath, 98.
163. Campbell (2011b), 257.
164. *Holyrood* (2000), Glasgow: BBC Scotland, 5 March 2000.
165. Fraser, 140.
166. Jack Straw to Donald Dewar, 30 April 2000, GD1/1433/1/11/14, Papers of the Dewar Family, Edinburgh: National Records of Scotland.
167. M. Elder (ed.) (2000), *Donald Dewar: A Book of Tribute*, Edinburgh: HMSO, 41.
168. M. Campbell (2008), *Menzies Campbell: My Autobiography*, London: Hodder and Stoughton, 161.
169. Fraser, 127.
170. Hassan (2002), 37.
171. A. Trench (ed.) (2001), *The State of the Nations, 2001: The Second Year of Devolution in the United Kingdom*, Exeter: Imprint Academic, 52–70.
172. *Daily Telegraph*, 10 January 2001. Wilson maintains the second part of his quotation was an embellishment by then SNP leader Alex Salmond.
173. McLeish (2004), 130–8.
174. McLeish (2004), 132–3.
175. *Herald*, 14 June 2008.
176. R. Hazell (ed.) (2003), *The State of the Nations, 2003: The Third Year of Devolution in the United Kingdom*, Exeter: Imprint Academic, 120.
177. Campbell (2011b), 547.
178. Scottish Labour Party (2001), *Forward not Back*, Glasgow: SLP, 10.
179. D. Denver & I. MacAllister (2003), 'Constituency campaigning in Scotland at the 2001 general election', *Scottish Affairs* 42, 128–30.
180. House of Commons (Removal of Clergy Disqualification) Act 2001.

181. Liddell had anticipated this in her 1990 novel *Elite* (London: Century), which depicted the career of Scottish Labour MP Ann Clarke against the backdrop of a Scotland 'becoming ever more politically and strategically important for its oil revenues'.
182. Torrance (2006), 351.
183. I. Macwhirter (2002), 'The new Scottish political classes', in G. Hassan & C. Warhurst (eds), *Anatomy of the New Scotland: Power, Influence and Change*, Edinburgh: Mainstream, 27–30.
184. McLeish (2004), 182.
185. M. Keating (2005), *The Government of Scotland: Public Policy Making after Devolution* (Second Edition), Edinburgh: Edinburgh University Press, 62.
186. Hassan (2002), 37.
187. Macwhirter (2002), 31.
188. Davidson, 250.
189. Campbell (2011b), 430.
190. Naughtie, 360.
191. Hazell, 122.
192. Macwhirter (2002), 30–3.
193. *Daily Telegraph*, 19 December 2001.
194. Hassan (2002), 43.
195. Hazell, 124–6.
196. F. Simpkins (2018), 'The conflicting loyalties of the Scottish Labour Party', in E. Avril & Y. Béliard (eds), *Labour United and Divided from the 1830s to the Present*, Manchester: Manchester University Press, 265.
197. M. Laffin, E. Shaw & G. Taylor (2007), 'The new subnational politics of the British Labour Party', *Party Politics* 13:1, 21–2.
198. E. Roddin (2004), 'Has the Labour Party or the Liberal Democrats proved more successful in the partnership for Scotland coalition, 1999–2003? An initial assessment', *Scottish Affairs* 48, 46.
199. Keating, 59.
200. D. Denver (2003), 'A "wake up!" call to the parties? The results of the Scottish Parliament elections 2003', *Scottish Affairs* 44, 52.
201. *Scotsman*, 26 August 2003.
202. A. McConnell (2004), *Scottish Local Government*, Edinburgh: Edinburgh University Press, 139–41.
203. R. Finlay (2004), *Modern Scotland, 1914–2000*, London: Profile, 393.
204. J. Hopkin & J. Bradbury (2006), 'British statewide parties and multilevel politics', *Publius: The journal of federalism*, 36:1, 144.
205. M. Keating, L. Stevenson, P. Cairney & K. Taylor (2003), 'Does devolution make a difference? Legislative output and policy divergence in Scotland', Stirling: University of Stirling (online).

206. G. Mooney & L. Poole (2004), '"A land of milk and honey"? Social policy in Scotland after devolution', *Critical Social Policy* 24:4, 476.
207. W. Alexander (2005), 'Foundations, frustrations and hopes', in W. Alexander (ed.), *Donald Dewar: Scotland's first First Minister*, Edinburgh: Mainstream, 222–3.
208. M. Keating (2005), 'Policy convergence and divergence in Scotland under devolution', *Regional Studies* 39:4, 127.
209. M. Keating & M. Harvey (2014), *Small Nations in a Big World: What Scotland Can Learn*, Edinburgh: Luath.
210. Keating et al. (2003).
211. McLeish (2004), 215–17.
212. W. Alexander (2003), *Chasing the Tartan Tiger: Lessons from a Celtic Cousin?* Glasgow: Smith Institute.
213. N. McEwen (2005), 'Adapting to multi-level politics: the political parties and the general election in Scotland', *Scottish Affairs* 53, 124–32.
214. Ashdown (2000), 353.
215. J. Mitchell (2014), *The Scottish Question*, Oxford: Oxford University Press, 262.
216. Torrance (2006), 359.
217. G. Brown & D. Alexander (2007), *Stronger Together: The 21st Century Case for Scotland and Britain*, Fabian Society, 1–2, 25.
218. D. Torrance (2010), *Salmond: Against the Odds*, Edinburgh: Birlinn, 239.
219. D. Torrance (2017), 'Scotland's progressive dilemma', *Political Quarterly* 88:1, 54.
220. J. Curtice, D. McCrone, N. McEwen, M. Marsh & R. Ormiston (2009), *Revolution or Evolution? The 2007 Scottish Elections*, Edinburgh: Edinburgh University Press, 104–21.
221. Mitchell, 259.
222. P. Jones (2007), 'The smooth wooing: The SNP's victory in the 2007 Scottish Parliament elections', *Scottish Affairs* 60, 6–21.
223. R. Johns, D. Denver, J. Mitchell & C. Pattie (2010), *Voting for a Scottish Government: The Scottish Parliament Election of 2007*, Manchester: Manchester University Press, 54–6.
224. G. Brown (2017), *My Life, Our Times*, London: Bodley Head, 398.
225. Jones (2007), 20–1.
226. Torrance (2011), 197–9.
227. G. Hassan (1999), *Redesigning the State: The New Scotland*, London: Fabian Society, 27.
228. Hassan & Shaw, 164.
229. McLeish (2004), 216.

230. Brown, 398.
231. Blair, 651.
232. Keating, 62.
233. D. Torrance (ed.) (2013), *Great Scottish Speeches: Volume II*, Edinburgh: Luath, 180–2.
234. G. Hassan (2009), 'The auld enemies: Scottish Nationalism and Scottish Labour', in G. Hassan (ed.), *The Modern SNP: From Protest to Power*, Edinburgh: Edinburgh University Press, 157.
235. Hassan & Shaw, 309.
236. HC Deb 7 May 2008 Vol 475 cc695–96 [Prime Minister].
237. *Daily Telegraph*, 3 August 2008.
238. Hassan & Shaw, 293–4.
239. I. Gray (2011), Scottish Labour conference speech, 19 March 2011.
240. Scottish Labour Party (2010), *Report of the Scottish Policy Forum*, Glasgow: SLP.
241. *Scotsman*, 18 February 2011.
242. F. Simpkins (2013), 'The 2011 Scottish Labour campaign: changing tactics?', *Numéros 5* (online).
243. C. Carman, R. Johns & J. Mitchell (2014), *More Scottish than British: The 2011 Scottish Parliament Election*, London: Palgrave Macmillan, 103.
244. Press Association, 25 April 2011.
245. D. Torrance (2011), 'A tale of two elections', *Scottish Affairs* 76, 25–32.

7

The Strange Death of Labour Scotland?
2011–2026

The 2011 Scottish Parliament election was Labour's worst result in Scotland since October 1931. What made it more painful was the expectation for much of the campaign that a plurality of seats was in prospect. According to journalist Joe Pike, on polling day plans were:

> still being finalised for a four-strong team to lead coalition negotiations. Scottish Labour had even drawn up a grid of the party's first 100 days in government, mapping out policy announcements, speeches and ministerial visits. But on the day set aside for power brokering, the party's beleaguered Scottish leader Iain Gray announced his resignation.[1]

The party had lost seven seats, leaving it with only fifteen constituency MSPs and twenty-two regional Members, the latter a commensurate increase due to the constituency losses. Four former Labour ministers including Andy Kerr and Tom McCabe were among the casualties. Nine SNP-held constituencies had been targeted of which Scottish Labour won none.[2]

Long-standing cleavages loosened dramatically. Labour trailed the SNP by 14 per cent among Scots who identified as working class, while the Nationalists were also the party of choice for trade unionists and those identifying as Catholic.[3] The groundbreaking gender balance achieved in 1999 also slipped, with seventeen out of Labour's thirty-seven MSPs women, a reduction of 4 per cent on 2007. Kenny and Mackay feared a return to the party's past tradition of decentralised constituency-based selection and the 'privileging' of 'favourite sons'.[4]

Ed Miliband, British Labour leader since September 2010, ordered a review of Scottish party structure which was led by Jim Murphy MP and Sarah Boyack MSP. Their recommendations, which were endorsed by both the British and Scottish conferences, included:

- The creation of the new post of 'Leader of the Scottish Labour Party' rather than leader *in* the Scottish Parliament
- The right of all Labour parliamentarians elected in Scotland to stand for the post of leader provided they pledged to seek election as an MSP
- The rearrangement of constituency Labour parties on Scottish Parliament rather than Westminster boundaries
- Procedural responsibility for the selection of all Labour candidates in Scotland to rest with the Scottish party executive
- The establishment of a political strategy board and new political base in Edinburgh[5]

The Scottish leader, meanwhile, was still to be chosen by a three-tier electoral college comprising ordinary members, trade unions and MPs/MSPs, a structure which gave Scottish Labour's forty MPs a proportionately greater say than its thirty-seven MSPs.[6] Under this system (which echoed that of the British party), Johann Lamont was elected the first leader of the *entire* Labour Party in Scotland on 17 December. A former teacher and Scottish Executive minister, Lamont possessed a deeply grounded analysis of politics, particularly social justice and women's rights. She had voted 'no' to devolution in 1979, perceiving the 'politics of nationalism as a diversion from more central aims', but had later come to see a Scottish Parliament 'as a vehicle for democratic change in Scotland'.[7] Anas Sarwar, whose father Mohammad had become the UK's first Muslim MP in 1997, was elected Lamont's deputy.

In her victory speech, Lamont made a point of acknowledging that Labour appeared to voters 'a tired old politics machine which was more about itself than it was about them'. 'If anyone has ever deluded ourselves into thinking that Scotland was really a Labour country', she added, 'last May must have finally shaken us out of that delusion'. The only way to change Scotland was by 'changing the Scottish Labour Party'.[8] At a speech in October, Douglas Alexander had also conceded that 'some of the old Labour "hymns" were increasingly unfamiliar to an audience without personal knowledge of the tunes'.[9]

The first electoral test of the old hymns and indeed the new leadership came at local government elections in May 2012, the second conducted under STV. Although there were swings to both the SNP and Labour, the former became the largest party with 32.3 per cent of the vote to Labour's 31.4. Labour now controlled two more authorities than in 2007.[10] To its surprise, Labour retained control of Glasgow, to which the former MSP and minister Frank McAveety returned as a councillor.[11] In Edinburgh, Labour formed an unlikely alliance with the SNP which was to last a decade and survive two referendums and five Westminster/Holyrood elections.

INDEPENDENCE REFERENDUM

By May 2012 the long campaign for an independence referendum had already begun, the UK Conservative–Liberal Democrat coalition government having conceded that the SNP's unprecedented overall majority had provided it with a 'mandate' to make good on its manifesto pledge. As that aspect of the constitution remained a reserved matter (something disputed by the Scottish Government), this required legislation, the parameters of which were enshrined in the Edinburgh Agreement agreed in October 2012.

Ed Miliband, meanwhile, attempted to situate Labour's unionism within an historical frame:

> The story of the Scotsman, the Englishman, and the Welshman is not just the start of a good joke. It is the history of social justice in this country. It was a Scotsman, Keir Hardie, who founded the Labour party a hundred and twelve years ago. An Englishman, Clement Attlee, who led the most successful Labour Government in history. And a Welshman, Nye Bevan, who pioneered that Government's greatest legacy, our National Health Service. These are the achievements of our nations working together.[12]

A year into her leadership, Johann Lamont attracted considerable criticism for an 'almost Blairite' speech in which she attacked Scotland's 'something for nothing' culture,[13] while her relations with Miliband deteriorated over the choice of a candidate to succeed MP Eric Joyce, who resigned following a violent altercation in a Westminster bar. When the Unite trade union was accused of trying to rig the outcome, British Labour's

National Executive Committee placed Falkirk CLP under special measures.[14]

It had been agreed, meanwhile, that the 'No' campaign would be funded by Conservative donors but fronted by Labour and to a lesser extent the Liberal Democrats. The then Chancellor George Osborne later described what followed as an 'eye opener':

> We all thought [the] Labour machine in Scotland was this incredible force [but] it was a bit like that scene in the Wizard of Oz when we pulled back the curtain and realised that there was nothing much to Scottish Labour behind it. We suddenly thought, 'my God we're placing a lot of trust in this operation which doesn't really exist'.[15]

'It wasn't until I got involved with this [campaign]', remarked one Liberal Democrat, 'that I realised how dysfunctional the Labour Party was – some of the relationships are toxic and go back generations'.[16]

Amid SNP charges that Labour preferred 'Tory government to self-government', the 'Better Together' campaign (the words 'Union' or 'Unionist' were absent) launched at Edinburgh' s Napier University on 25 June 2012.[17] A fringe group called 'Labour for Independence' was also established, although Anas Sarwar dismissed this as an 'SNP front'. Two supporters of independence, Jamie Maxwell and Owen Dudley Edwards, argued that while the independence cause was not 'purely Socialist' it would be 'the best and surest way of Scotland becoming Socialist'.[18] Former First Minister Henry McLeish repeatedly hinted at support for independence but did not follow through.

Anas Sarwar explained that:

> Constitutional politics brings together people who wouldn't normally be on the same side and we will continue to work with the Better Together campaign. But the Labour movement has a different view of Scotland's future from the Conservatives and Liberals.

Other parts of the Scottish Labour movement disagreed. Dave Watson of Unison said 'most' had 'a huge difficulty with any campaign that includes the Tories'. Mary Lockhart, chair of the Labour-aligned Scottish Co-operative Party, quit after calling it 'insulting' and 'offensive'. For a while it also looked as if the STUC was flirting with support for independence, although ASLEF, USDAW and Community all ultimately swung behind political as well as industrial unity.[19] Increasing such unease was the fact Alistair Darling had received an ovation during a fringe meeting at the Scottish Conservative conference. The SNP called him the 'Darling of the Tory conference'.[20]

Scottish Labour's standalone 'no' campaign, 'United with Labour', was therefore an attempt to put some distance between the two parties. This was led by Gordon Brown, a convenient way of involving the former Prime Minister without getting in Darling's way, their relationship having broken down during the 2008–9 financial crisis. Brown privately favoured a 'third option' on the referendum ballot offering a 'more powerful Scottish Parliament as a positive alternative to both independence and the status quo' while his book, *My Scotland, Our Britain*, explored what the former Chancellor called a 'pooling and sharing' Union, including the intriguing suggestion it was 'not an English imposition but a Scottish invention'.[21]

Pauline Bryan (later a Jeremy Corbyn-nominated peer), Tommy Kane and MSP Neil Findlay promoted what they called 'radical federalism' via the Red Paper Collective, 'retaining a redistributive system of taxation and the Barnett formula but with double devolution to regions and communities'.[22] The collective's name evoked Brown's 1975 edited volume while its constitutional programme deliberately looked beyond the referendum to equip Scottish Labour with a vision capable of competing with the increasingly hegemonic SNP.[23]

Findlay therefore took a dim view of Johann Lamont's Scottish Labour Devolution Commission, which reported in March 2014. *Powers for a Purpose* spoke of a 'sharing union ... underpinned by political union, economic and social union' as 'the ultimate safeguard and guarantor of the Welfare State'.[24] Neil Findlay believed opposition from Shadow Chancellor Ed Balls had led to a 'convoluted' proposal to devolve only 40 per cent of income tax and the whole package he judged 'weak, unenthusiastic and limited'.[25] Findlay had been present a few weeks earlier when the Scottish shadow cabinet had warning from Iain McNicol, British Labour's general secretary, that the party risked 'sleepwalking towards independence'.[26]

Increasingly, Labour and the other unionist parties appeared to be losing legitimacy through well-targeted attacks from Alex Salmond et al. In his Judith Hart Memorial Lecture, Shadow Foreign Secretary Douglas Alexander warned that the referendum campaign could descend into a 'battle for standing': 'We need vision, not viciousness, as we make our choice'.[27] The former MP Maria Fyfe, meanwhile, marshalled several Scottish Labour women to make the 'positive' case against independence.[28] The anti-devolution Tam Dalyell diplomatically refused to do any media interviews in the closing days of the campaign as he was reluctant to 'cause any problems' for his party.[29]

At the SNP's April 2014 conference, Salmond claimed independence would 'be good for Scottish Labour'. 'The Labour Party, freed from Westminster control', he added, 'will have the chance to return to its core values: many of which we in this party agree with and share'.[30] Salmond cleverly took up old battle cries associated with Labour's long campaign for a Scottish Parliament, chiefly that independence would promote economic growth and social democracy. As the Scottish Labour MP Tom Harris later observed: 'Scottish Labour found itself the target of the same arguments deployed by Donald Dewar in the '80s and '90s: if the Conservatives had been anti-Scottish for opposing devolution then, weren't Labour anti-Scottish for opposing independence now?[31]

Polls had long shown substantial (though minority) support among Scottish Labour voters for independence, although this had been 'hidden' by the party's devolutionary nationalism of the 1980s and 1990s. But during the 2012–14 referendum campaign, in which a central part of the Yes campaign's strategy was peeling these voters away with promises of 'social justice', they were pushed into choosing between that vision and their traditional party allegiance. This had little to do with coherent policy, including a tenuous claim that a 'no' vote would lead the NHS in Scotland to be privatised. Neil Findlay was not alone in being depressed that 'good people on the left' had 'totally abandoned their capacity to critically analyse what the Yes side tell us, and have a view that because it is from them it must be true'.[32] Former Labour MP Brian Wilson protested that the SNP's professed 'utilitarian nationalism' was a 'pose' to cover up what was, at root, the 'existential' variety.[33]

Conscious of this and determined to mitigate it, Labour hit back on points of detail – often good ones – but ended up looking as if it no longer believed its own story that Scotland was more left-wing, more egalitarian, anti-Tory than the rest of Britain;[34] neither 'comfortable unionists', in the words of Anas Sarwar, nor 'comfortable nationalists'.[35] It did not help that the referendum campaign had led to a 'broadening out' of the term 'unionist' to reflect a range of views, straddling federalism (Liberal Democrats), further devolution (Labour and the Conservatives) and a minority who supported no change or a return to the pre-1999 settlement. The terms 'Unionist' and 'unionism' (other than trade) were accordingly expunged from Labour speeches, publications and even general discourse.[36]

In its place, as Brown Swan has shown, Labour adopted three interconnected discursive strategies: first, an attempt to speak to the UK as 'One Nation', in which a British identity comfortably encompassed regional and sub-state identities; second, an attempt to ignore the independence issue in favour of a broader social solidarity; and third, an instrumental argument in favour of the Union on the basis of welfare and economic benefit.[37] A concept of 'Britishness' was rarely elaborated, perhaps because that was considered the preserve of the Conservative Party.[38]

Having ploughed a lonely furrow via United with Labour, in the closing stages of the referendum campaign Gordon Brown suddenly became front and centre as a YouGov poll gave 'Yes' a narrow lead. Speaking at the Loanhead Miners' Welfare and Social Club on 8 September 2014, the former Prime Minister (with the authority of the current) set out 'a tight timetable with tough deadlines … for delivery and a roadmap to our goal'. He added:

> Labour since Keir Hardie has been the party of Home Rule for Scotland within the United Kingdom so the plan for a stronger Scottish Parliament we seek agreement on is for nothing else than a modern form of Scottish Home Rule within the United Kingdom, published by St Andrew's Day on November 30, with the draft laws around January 25.[39]

And on 17 September, just a day before the referendum, Brown emphasised his unionist themes of 'comradeship', 'solidarity' and 'sharing' in a barnstorming thirteen-minute speech.[40] 'I was convinced that in addition to focusing on the benefits of the Union and on exposing the economic risks of independence,' he reflected in his memoirs, 'we also had to make people feel proud about voting No.'[41]

While on 18 September 2014 there was a comfortable 55–45 per cent vote in favour of the status quo, what worried Labour was the number of heartland seats that had unequivocally

backed independence, particularly in Glasgow and Dundee.⁴²
Neil Findlay recalled a shadow cabinet meeting on 20 September
resembling 'a wake with members quiet, down and sombre'.
Johann Lamont reminded them No had beaten Yes by more
than 10 per cent, that Alex Salmond 'was gone' and that
Scottish Labour's task was to get back to the 'everyday issues
that matter to people, such as the NHS, jobs, low pay and public
services'. Branding Better Together an 'appalling idea', Findlay
was blunter:

> I called for a return to class politics with a radical agenda that
> puts clear red water between ourselves and the SNP. The problem
> we have is No won in SNP areas like Aberdeenshire, yet we lost
> traditional Labour areas like Glasgow. We have huge political and
> organisational problems.⁴³

Ironically, on 24 June the shadow cabinet had discussed post-referendum tactics, including how to prevent the SNP claiming 'victory in defeat'. 'This is absolutely vital', Findlay had written in his diary, 'if Labour fails on this we are in real trouble'.⁴⁴

From the day after the referendum, however, polling registered a substantial shift in voting intentions, a major realignment of party preferences across both Holyrood and Westminster in which more than 95 per cent of Labour–SNP switchers had voted 'yes' on 18 September.⁴⁵ Giving them an extra nudge had been David Cameron's post-referendum promise to deliver 'English votes for English laws', something Alistair Darling and others cautioned against while emotions were still raw. The Prime Minister, according to David Laws, said he would let 'Labour sort it out' as Scotland was no longer his 'problem'.⁴⁶

On 17 October Johann Lamont was informed by Ed Miliband's chief of staff that Ian Price, whom she herself had appointed general secretary of the Scottish party in 2013, had been sacked.⁴⁷ She resigned a week later, attacking as 'dinosaurs' both the SNP ('nationalists who can't accept they were rejected by the people') and Scottish Labour MPs at Westminster ('who think nothing has changed'). But Lamont's most stinging observation related to the long-standing issue of party autonomy: 'Just as the SNP must embrace that devolution is the settled will of the Scottish people, Labour must recognise that the Scottish party has to be autonomous and not just a branch office of a party based in London.'⁴⁸

This validation of a wounding SNP attack line infuriated sections of the Scottish Labour Party. 'Her resignation could have been constructed by SNP headquarters', one source told Joe Pike. 'It was fashioned to cause maximum damage to the party she claims to love.' Lamont's broadside coincided with the party's annual fundraising dinner in Glasgow, at which Ed Miliband was the star guest. Not only was this targeted by anti-Labour protestors ('We're not in government in Scotland', exclaimed MSP Graeme Pearson, 'we're not in government in the UK, but we still have protestors outside!'[49]) but at a private meeting beforehand Neil Findlay recorded 'member after member' of the Scottish Labour MSP group savaging Miliband 'like a lost puppy'.[50]

On 13 December 2014, the former Secretary of State for Scotland Jim Murphy was elected leader of the Scottish Labour Party with a promise it would hold all its forty-one MPs at the forthcoming general election.[51] 'This is a fresh start for the Scottish Labour Party', he declared. 'Scotland is changing and so too is Scottish Labour.'[52] Kezia Dugdale was elected deputy leader and fulfilled a similar role to that of Nicola Sturgeon between 2004 and 2007, leading the party (in Murphy's absence from Holyrood) at First Minister's Questions. Once again, the party refused to reveal membership numbers, although Murphy claimed the figure was 'about 20,000'. Other reports suggested it had fallen as low as 8,000. The final opinion poll of 2014 put Scottish Labour seventeen points behind the SNP.[53] Scottish voters, reflected Neil Findlay, 'can't wait to give us a kicking!'[54] Early in 2015, Murphy made a point of rejecting the term 'unionist'. 'As a family of Irish Catholic immigrants, we're not unionists', he explained. 'I grew up in a family of trade unionists, but we're not political unionists.' Kezia Dugdale agreed, saying 'it's not what shapes my politics'.[55]

At a one-day conference in March 2015 Jim Murphy proposed a new Clause IV for the Scottish Labour Party, which was endorsed despite leadership nerves and some trade union opposition.[56] This now stated that it was 'a democratic socialist party rooted in social justice' which would work 'for the patriotic interest of the people of Scotland'. Sixteen years after the devolution of power, meanwhile, final decisions on devolved policy were to rest with the party in Scotland rather than the NEC in London.[57]

With the UK general election fixed for May, polling and focus groups suggested a 'hung' Parliament in which Labour and a much-enlarged group of SNP MPs might hold the balance of power.[58] David Cameron called this a 'coalition of chaos', and indeed the SNP became the perfect bogeyman with which the Conservatives could keep hold of their own voters and attract others.[59] Despite Jim Murphy's energy and optimism, however, the Scottish Labour Party moved towards a damage limitation strategy. According to BBC journalist Iain Watson, Labour summoned a regional organiser from Yorkshire to try and save Douglas Alexander's Paisley constituency, while Murphy's East Renfrewshire seat was also targeted with resources usually reserved for a by-election. Only in Edinburgh South did Ian Murray have reason to be hopeful, with polling suggesting he would attract non-Labour voters who did not like the SNP.[60]

Yet on paper Scottish Labour's campaign was in good shape. There were fifty-five full-time members of staff in the field, while resources and literature were not in short supply. On 13 March 2015, however, a distillation of internal polling and focus groups showed none of this to have had any effect. This decline had 'been happening for ten years', pollster James Morris informed party workers. 'You can't turn it round in seven weeks.' The independence referendum had 'unlocked the door' to voters supporting the SNP at Westminster as well as Holyrood elections.[61]

According to journalist Joe Pike, younger Labour candidates were conscious that some long-serving MPs had never bothered campaigning. 'It's 1997 again', declared Coatbridge MP and former Shadow Scottish Secretary Tom Clarke with astonishing complacency. 'We'll sweep the board.' By polling day (7 May), Jim Murphy had decided to remain leader even if he lost his seat, something party rules if not political reality would not prevent. The following day, and as the scale of Scottish Labour's defeat became clear, its general secretary Brian Roy was heard being physically sick in the toilets at party HQ.[62] 'In the 117-year history of the party', wrote Neil Findlay in his diary, 'it's difficult to think of a more depressing moment'.[63]

2015 AFTERMATH

The Scottish Labour vote fell from 42 per cent in 2010 to just 24.3 per cent, while the SNP's more than doubled from 19.9 to just shy of 50 per cent. And just as first-past-the-post had long inflated Labour support in Scotland, it now cruelly deflated it, leaving the party with just one seat, Ian Murray in Edinburgh South, hardly Scotland's 'reddest' constituency. Jim Murphy reflected that:

> The party that had traditionally been the tireless champion of the underdog now finds itself in the position of being the underdog. But the Scottish Labour Party has been around for more than a century and, 100 years from tonight, we'll still be around. Scotland needs a strong Labour Party, and our fightback starts tomorrow morning.[64]

Just over a week later Murphy narrowly survived a no-confidence vote but resigned anyway with a parting shot at his leading critic, Len McCluskey of the Unite union. Observing that Scottish Labour was the 'least modernised part of the Labour movement, he also urged that his successor be elected under a one-member-one-vote.[65] As the party now had only one MP, Baroness (Meta) Ramsay, a former diplomat, foreign policy adviser to John Smith and opposition Scottish spokesperson in the Lords, became the PLP's representative on the Scottish party executive. Descending on the House of Commons, meanwhile, the SNP's fifty-six MPs used their maiden speeches that evoked the 'Red' Clydesiders of 1922. Typical was that of Mhairi Black, who had unseated Douglas Alexander in Paisley:

> I, like so many SNP Members, come from a traditional socialist Labour family, and I have never been quiet in my assertion that I feel it is the Labour party that left me, not the other way about. The SNP did not triumph on a wave of nationalism; in fact, nationalism has nothing to do with what has happened in Scotland. We triumphed on a wave of hope – hope that there was something different from and better than the Thatcherite, neo-liberal policies that are produced from this Chamber, and hope that these representatives could genuinely give a voice to those who do not have one.[66]

There were the usual post-mortems. Gordon Brown told Neil Findlay, 'quite remarkably', that Labour should 'expose the failings of neo-liberalism',[67] while Jack Straw, never a fan of devolution, suspected there would have to be 'a distinctive party', the 'run from London' argument having become 'increasingly potent'.[68]

In June 2015 the Scottish Labour Party adopted the same system of one-member-one-vote leadership elections initiated by the British party in February 2014.[69] This meant not only Scottish Labour Party members and affiliates would have a vote but also 'registered' supporters who had paid as little as £3. On this basis, Kezia Dugdale was elected leader on 15 August with 72 per cent of the vote. A few weeks later, and much to the horror of most Labour MPs, Jeremy Corbyn also became Leader of the Opposition following the same electoral system.

The long-standing Member for Islington had no obvious interest in the constitution beyond republicanism and support for a united Ireland, for his platform was predicated upon class rather than identity. 'Corbyn can't even spell devolution', one Scottish Labour politician remarked, 'much less understand or care about it'. The new leader's Scottish supporters, notably Richard Leonard and Neil Findlay, viewed Corbyn's state-centred programme of nationalisation and redistribution as a route back to power in Scotland.[70] A membership surge following his election in September 2015 took Scottish Labour back to almost 30,000, 3,285 of whom were registered supporters. The party and Corbyn were at least in synch when it came to Trident renewal, which the Scottish Labour conference overwhelmingly rejected later that year.[71]

Following an agreement in October 2015, the Scottish Labour Party gained even more autonomy, including the selection of Westminster and European candidates and the right for its conference to formulate positions on reserved matters. Dugdale hailed a 'more federal' party which was 'now on track to become fully autonomous'.[72] This was a clear attempt to lay the 'branch office' charge to rest in advance of the May 2016 Holyrood elections. What Dugdale called the 'most radical Labour manifesto ever' was an attempt to outflank the SNP on the left and park the constitutional argument. Early in the campaign, meanwhile, Dugdale was 'outed' as having a female partner (an SNP MSP) in an interview with the *Fabian Review*.[73]

Another unexpected feature of the campaign was Scottish Conservative leader Ruth Davidson's unconventional pitch, not for power but to become the principal opposition party in the Scottish Parliament. This she bolstered by depicting her party as the main 'unionist' voice in the land, something aided by Dugdale's initially equivocal statements on independence. For once, Scottish Tory strategy worked. While the Conservatives more than doubled their number of MSPs from fifteen to thirty-one, Labour's fell from thirty-eight to twenty-four, even though its constituency vote share remained just ahead of the Conservatives at 22.6 per cent. Even a more autonomous Scottish Labour Party had 'suffered again from its association with its parent/UK party', not least persistent charges of anti-Semitism.[74]

To the Corbynite MSP Richard Leonard, the message was clear: 'We need to stop dividing people on the basis of nationality, and start uniting them on the basis of class',[75] while Scottish Labour MEP David Martin suggested a middle way:

> If properly articulated, Labour's position on the constitution is where the majority of Scottish people are. They do not want unbridled Unionism or Nationalism. They want for Scotland: 'maximum power with maximum security'. Labour the Party of Home Rule should have no difficulty in promising such an outcome.[76]

As ever, it was not entirely clear what 'Home Rule' actually meant.

BREXIT AND THE 2017 ELECTION

The June 2016 referendum on the UK's membership of the European Union further disrupted the constitutional status quo and traditional party allegiances. There was to be no Better Together redux. Senior Labour figures like Harriet Harman and Gordon Brown believed that had been such a disaster that 'no cross-party' vehicle 'could ever work again'. In Scotland, the official Leave campaign mustered former Scottish Labour MPs Tom Harris and Nigel Griffiths, while Brown also reprised the 'revivalist-preacher style of oratory' he had deployed apparently to good effect in the closing days of the independence referendum campaign.[77]

It did not work. Although 52 per cent of those voting across the UK backed Brexit, the fact a majority in Scotland and Northern Ireland had supported the status quo reignited the independence question in Scotland, eventually collapsed Northern Ireland's power-sharing institutions and led to turmoil within the British Labour Party. Kezia Dugdale joined the chorus of criticism as there was a determined attempt by the PLP to jettison Corbyn on the basis he had been insufficiently pro-European. Despite swathes of Shadow Cabinet resignations, this also did not work, although by the end of that year the British party's NEC had expanded to include two extra members nominated by the Scottish and Welsh Labour leaders, both at that point 'Corbynsceptics'.[78]

Already struggling to navigate Scotland's polarised constitutional terrain, Scottish Labour now had to find some way of tailoring its political message to an electorate comprising a majority of Unionist *and* Remain voters. Dugdale outlined her plan for a 'federal solution' in a speech at the Institute for Public Policy Research in London. This was fleshed out by former Lord Chancellor Lord Falconer and, together with a 'people's constitutional convention',[79] endorsed by the Scottish Labour conference in February 2017. That same month Scottish Labour MSPs voted overwhelmingly against triggering Article 50 of the Treaty of the European Union, contrary to Corbyn's position at Westminster (where the power rested) but calculated to further emphasise the Scottish party's newfound autonomy.

Prime Minister Theresa May then bounced the UK Parliament into an early election to be held in June 2017. That March, Scottish First Minister Nicola Sturgeon had announced her plan for another independence referendum, and Corbyn incensed the Scottish party by saying he would be 'absolutely fine' with a second ballot. This directly contradicted Dugdale's careful positioning. Ian Murray, the sole Scottish Labour MP, tweeted: 'Often asked why I resigned from shadow Cabinet. Ladies & Gentlemen I give u Jeremy Corbyn.'[80]

The Scottish Labour manifesto instead included attacks against both the SNP and Conservative governments. Awan-Scully detected less of a 'nationalist' tone than that deployed by Welsh Labour, which had been in devolved government for almost two decades.[81] In his last television interview, former Welsh First Minister Rhodri Morgan suggested Scottish politics had allowed itself to become polarised along nationalist/unionist lines without leaving room for a 'devolutionist' third way, 'a belief', as Morgan put it, 'that the British constitution is much healthier for having devolution since 1999'.[82]

Then, towards the end of the general election campaign, something unexpected occurred: 'Corbynmania' spread north, perhaps appealing to some of the same instincts ignited by the independence referendum. Sensing this groundswell, Nicola Sturgeon said her party would sustain Corbyn – hitherto depicted by the SNP as unelectable – on an issue-by-issue basis if there was to be a hung Parliament. 'If you want a Labour Government in Westminster', ran the opportunistic pitch, 'you should vote SNP'.[83]

As with its Corbyn-induced membership boost, Scottish Labour was not complaining when it attracted 27.1 per cent of the vote – a slight improvement on 2015 but still putting it third behind the SNP and Conservatives – and seven MPs instead of one. And, usefully for a recovering party, where once the SNP had boasted five-figure majorities, there were now dozens of Labour candidates within one or two thousand votes of retaking certain constituencies. The Scottish Labour Party could now see a path to electoral recovery, although it remained uneasy about that involving either Jeremy Corbyn or a decisive shift to the left.[84] Earlier that year, five members of the Campaign for Socialism – now allied with the Corbynite Momentum – had won places on the Scottish Labour executive.

Nevertheless, when Kezia Dugdale said the time had come to 'pass on the baton' to someone else ahead of the next Holyrood election (colleagues had been assured of a long-term commitment to the leadership) there was a general expectation that former trade union organiser Richard Leonard would succeed her. The press made much of his being English born and privately educated (Pocklington, on a scholarship), the latter a provenance shared by his opponent Anas Sarwar (Hutchesons' Grammar), for whom the extension of this privilege to his children dominated his campaign. 'There is a certain irony in the party turning to a Yorkshireman', observed one Sarwar supporter, 'to combat Scottish Nationalism'.[85]

Leonard was elected Scottish Labour leader on 18 November 2017 with 56.7 per cent of the vote, but never really made an impact. While party membership stood at 25,836 by January 2018, within twelve months it had fallen to 21,162. As Jeremy Corbyn became further embroiled in Brexit battles and charges of anti-Semitism, Leonard told the 2018 Scottish conference it was clear to him that 'we cannot only call for the amelioration of deepening poverty and widening inequality: we must also win power to transform the system that creates it in the first place'.[86]

In truth, Leonard and Corbyn were in a similar position, mandated by their respective party memberships but at odds with their parliamentary parties. During 2018 Neil Findlay recorded several 'all-out' attacks on Leonard during shadow cabinet meetings.[87] Sarwar, meanwhile, pursued a case against South Lanarkshire councillor Davie McLachlan for allegedly telling him 'Scotland wouldn't vote for a brown Muslim Paki', although his complaint was dropped by Labour's National Constitutional Committee on a technicality.[88] In July 2019 the Airdrie councillor Ian McNeil also attracted criticism when he became executive officer of the Grand Orange Lodge of Scotland.[89] Later, in a leaked WhatsApp message, Shadow Scottish Secretary Ian Murray said the party was full of 'thugs and incompetents', angered at it having reneged on a promise to fully fund Kezia Dugdale's legal costs in a defamation battle against pro-independence blogger Stuart Campbell (she won, although it cost the party £80,000).[90] There were rumours early in 2019 that Ian Murray planned to join a breakaway Labour party, although that did not transpire.[91]

The UK's last European Parliament election on 27 May 2019 stimulated more criticism of Leonard when Scottish Labour lost both its MEPs, attracting just 9.3 per cent of the vote and coming fifth behind the SNP, Brexit Party, Liberal Democrats and Scottish Conservatives. Neil Findlay suggested there were actually 'two Labour parties':

> one is socialist, grassroots-based, working-class, grounded in the trade union movement, critical of the EU and in favour of much more powers for the Scottish Parliament with a belief Better Together was a disaster. The other is economically liberal, socially woke, middle-class, Pro EU and hard-line unionist with a hatred of the SNP and belief Better Together was a triumph. These two sides coexist very uncomfortably in times of relative calm and break into open warfare at other times.[92]

On 8 October 2019, Kezia Dugdale – whom Findlay presumably placed in the second group – quit Labour over Brexit, adding for good measure that she had not backed it at the recent European elections. Another early UK election in December 2019 offered no respite, with Scottish Labour slipping to 18.6 per cent and losing all six MPs it had regained in 2017. Henderson et al. concluded that Labour's independence stance, its leader (Corbyn) and lack of reputation for sound economic management had all contributed to the Scottish party's poor performance.[93] Although Corbyn finally fell on his sword, Richard Leonard resisted growing pressure from MSPs to resign. Justice spokesman James Kelly warned that Scottish Labour faced 'catastrophic defeat' at Scottish Parliament elections due in May 2021.[94]

STARMERISM/SARWAR

Sir Keir Starmer, who was elected leader of the British Labour Party on 4 April 2020, did not view Leonard as part of his recovery 'project'. His Lanarkshire-based adviser Morgan McSweeney called his blueprint for revival in Scotland 'Project Lazarus' and, according to journalists Patrick Maguire and Gabriel Pogrund, considered Leonard's leadership 'a period piece: heavy on nostalgia for a lost world of Red Clydeside, trade unions and heavy industry. These were not Starmer's politics, nor those of the Scottish public'.

Fearful of a backlash, Starmer initially suggested Leonard be put on 'a performance improvement plan' as if he were 'a sales rep who had failed to meet his targets'. The end came in December 2020 when Starmer enlisted the GMB to push the Scottish Labour leader out, donors having reportedly threatened to withhold funds unless Leonard quit.[95] A former Director of Public Prosecutions, Sir Keir took his cue from Gordon Brown in describing the Union as 'a force for social justice and a moral force for good in the world ... We are all stronger because we choose to pool our resources to share the risks and rewards'.[96] The UK's departure from another union, however, continued to cause problems. At the end of 2020 Scottish Labour supported the SNP in refusing to provide legislative consent for a Brexit deal at Holyrood while British Labour supported it at Westminster. 'All hell broke loose', noted Neil Findlay in his diary, 'with party members appalled by what is going on and the SNP having a field day at this contradictory position'.[97] Scottish Labour general secretary Michael Sharpe was also 'forced out by a cabal of self-entitled right wingers who made his job impossible'[98] and succeeded by former Labour MSP Drew Smith in an acting capacity.

On his second attempt, meanwhile, Anas Sarwar was elected Scottish Labour leader on 27 February 2021, the first Muslim to lead a political party in the UK. Local government elections in May 2022 suggested a modest recovery, with the Labour vote increasing to 21.8 per cent and an additional twenty councillors meaning Labour was once again the second party in Scottish local government. Despite winning six fewer councillors than the SNP in Edinburgh, Labour severed its ten-year alliance and Cammy Day instead formed a minority administration with Conservative and Liberal Democrat support. Two Labour councillors who refused to endorse the administration were suspended for eight weeks.[99]

A few days after becoming leader, Sarwar had told Neil Findlay he would not be taking a 'hard unionist line',[100] but the following month Kelvin candidate Hollie Cameron was dropped for supporting another independence referendum.[101] A year later Scottish Labour replaced its red rose emblem with a red and purple thistle while Sarwar admitted he had not quite grasped how 'hollowed out' the party was 'as an organisation'. He pointed to the fact that in the twelve months before he became leader Scottish Labour had fundraised just £250.[102] By the end of 2023, meanwhile, that 'hollowed out' organisation moved to 'Donald Dewar House' in Glasgow's Laurieston.

The Scottish Fabians, meanwhile, cautioned against another 'auction of powers', suggesting that any constitutional discussions had to begin 'with a shared understanding of the purpose of the United Kingdom as a multinational, devolved state'.[103] Gordon Brown's Commission on the UK's Future took a more holistic approach, locating a devolved Scotland within a reformed second chamber ('an Assembly of the Nations and Regions') while proposing a statutory Sewel Convention, enhanced parliamentary privilege for Holyrood and directly elected mayors for Scotland's major cities.[104] Although endorsed by Starmer, only Sewel and privilege survived in the 2024 Labour manifesto. Contributing more to a change in Scotland's political temperature were the Supreme Court's unanimous rejection of Holyrood's power to hold a second independence referendum in November 2022 and Nicola Sturgeon's resignation as SNP leader and First Minister in February 2023.

The Rutherglen and Hamilton West by-election of October 2023 provided Scottish Labour with a Garscadden-like fillip when its candidate Michael Shanks took the seat from the SNP with almost 60 per cent of the vote. Sarwar ally Gordon McKee considered the victory celebrations an important confidence boost. 'Almost everyone in that room had been through the really difficult times and we'd had ten years of real misery', he recalled. 'It was the first proper celebration that I'd ever had in the Scottish Labour Party.'[105] Visibly elated, Sir Keir Starmer exclaimed: 'Rutherglen, you did it. You blew the doors off!'[106] Mitchell recalled Alex Salmond's mockery of the 'feeble fifty' in the late 1980s. 'But have the 80 per cent of SNP MPs returned in 2019 been any more effective in opposition', he asked, 'or the 95 per cent of SNP MPs returned in 2015?'[107]

Anas Sarwar took care to differentiate the Scottish and British Labour parties, most notably with a commitment to scrap the two-child benefit cap which Starmer now wanted to retain. And when the Leader of the Opposition vacillated over his support for an end to the conflict in Gaza, Sarwar broke ranks to call for a ceasefire alongside London Mayor Sadiq Khan and Greater Manchester metro mayor Andy Burnham. In February 2024 the Scottish Labour leader made it clear he supported neither independence nor another referendum, although leaked figures suggested 30 per cent of Scottish Labour members disagreed on the second point.[108]

During the 2024 UK general election campaign, Scottish Labour's pitch was cleverly distilled into 'we can't just send a message in this election, we must send a government'. According to one account, during early campaign planning there existed 'tension' within Starmer's team 'over whether Scotland was worth the effort'. Sir Keir and his adviser Morgan McSweeney (whose wife Imogen Walker was a candidate) argued that it was.[109] The Labour Together think tank bankrolled Labour candidates to the tune of £100,000 and, on 4 July, seventeen of them were elected along with twenty others in a dramatic reversal of the party's 2015 losses. Among them were Blair McDougall and others who bore the scars of the independence referendum almost a decade earlier. Joani Reid, a former Lewisham councillor and granddaughter of Jimmy, was returned for East Kilbride and Strathaven, as was Imogen Walker in Hamilton and Clyde Valley. Her husband believed that with another 100 activists in the field Labour 'could have won even more'.[110]

The overall result was significant yet shallow. With 35.3 per cent of the Scottish vote, just five points separated Labour from an SNP firefighting on several fronts, suggesting that the main driver had been the negative urge to oust the Conservative government rather than a positive vote for Starmer as Prime Minister. It was not long before Coll McCail, a former member of the Scottish party executive, complained that instead of 'standing up to Starmer' as Sarwar had promised, Labour's thirty-six new Scottish MPs had fallen into line on the two-child benefit cap and means-testing the winter fuel payment. 'Rather than leveraging the Westminster group to illustrate Scottish Labour's independence', he wrote, 'Scotland's Labour MPs have done the opposite'.[111] At the British Labour conference Sarwar admitted the story of Scottish Labour's revival was 'only half-written'.[112] More positively, Blair McDougall believed his colleagues now viewed devolution as 'an opportunity rather than a threat'.[113]

By February 2025, polling suggested Scottish Labour's performance remained volatile, with barely more than 10 per cent of those surveyed planning to back Labour on Holyrood's list vote and just 13.8 per cent at constituency level in May 2026. Psephologist Sir John Curtice declared 'the worst thing that ever happened to Anas Sarwar was Keir Starmer becoming Prime Minister'.[114] An indication of Scottish Labour nerves came when Sarwar and his deputy, veteran Dumbarton MSP Jackie Baillie, expressed regret over their support for the Scottish Government's Gender Recognition Reform Bill, which had been vetoed by the previous UK Conservative government with minimal political fallout. 'Anas does not owe apologies to women like me', remarked former Scottish Labour leader Johann Lamont. 'He owes them to women who lobbied MSPs, who turned up at surgeries, who wrote letters, who demonstrated – and who were ignored as they said the things we now see to be true.'[115]

There was better news when the UK government invested £200 million in the troubled Grangemouth oil refinery. 'That is the difference a Labour government can make', declared Starmer, the funding having reportedly followed intense lobbying by Scottish Secretary Ian Murray.[116] He was later sacked from the Cabinet and succeeded by Douglas Alexander, who returned to the Scotland Office almost 20 years after his first appointment. Alloa and Grangemouth MP Brian Leishman, meanwhile, emerged as the rebel of the Scottish Labour MP group, particularly over planned disability benefit cuts,[117] a policy which also prompted former MSP Neil Findlay to quit the party after thirty-five years of membership.[118] 'If the [Holyrood] election is framed as a chance to make a judgment on Keir Starmer's government ... then that is really challenging for us', a senior Scottish Labour figure admitted to Politico. 'We have to make it about what we would do differently from the SNP.'[119]

The June 2025 Hamilton, Larkhall and Stonehouse by-election, meanwhile, was viewed as 'the most important by-election of devolution' by journalist Paul Hutcheon.[120] Despite a sustained media narrative that the SNP would hold the Holyrood seat amid a Reform surge – a Scottish Labour councillor even defected to Nigel Farage's party during the campaign[121] – it turned out to be a convincing gain for Labour's Davy Russell. There was breathless talk about it having been 'the most sophisticated campaign in Scotland's political history',[122] but it certainly represented a huge fillip to a party not exactly used to good news.

Anas Sarwar declared that the voters of Hamilton had 'led the way to a change of government'[123] and increasingly framed the 2026 Holyrood election as 'straight choice':

> John Swinney or me, the SNP or Scottish Labour, the NHS in decline with them or fixed with Labour. Our education standards in decline with them or a new direction for our young people with me. Safety and security on our streets with us or a continuation of people feeling unsafe, not able to see a police officer with the SNP. An addiction to wasting people's money, billions of pounds lost with the SNP, or respect of public money with me – that's the choice.

The electoral contest, added Sarwar, would be the 'most consequential in the history of devolution'.[124]

NOTES

1. J. Pike (2015), *Project Fear: How an Unlikely Alliance Left a Kingdom United but a Country Divided*, London: Biteback, 4–5.
2. F. Simpkins (2013), 'The 2011 Scottish Labour campaign: Changing tactics?', *Numéros 5* (online).
3. When the Scottish Parliament later voted on same-sex marriage, Catholic Labour MSP Neil Findlay expected 'a lot of heat from

the church' given his support but was surprised when 'opposition' was in fact 'limited'. See N. Findlay with J. Holmes (2017), *Socialism and Hope: A Journey Through Turbulent Times*, Edinburgh: Luath, 42.
4. M. Kenny & F. Mackay (2011), 'In the balance: Women and the 2011 Scottish Parliament elections', *Scottish Affairs* 76, 75–85.
5. Scottish Labour Party (2011), *Review of the Labour Party in Scotland*, Glasgow: SLP. The party in Glasgow moved to new premises on Bath Street in October 2012.
6. Simpkins, 'The 2011 Scottish Labour campaign'.
7. M. Watson (2001), *Year Zero: An Inside View of the Scottish Parliament*, Edinburgh: Polygon, 28.
8. 'Johann Lamont named new Scottish Labour leader', BBC News online, 17 December 2011.
9. D. Alexander (2011), 'A Better Nation', John Williamson Memorial Lecture, Stirling University, 13 October 2011.
10. D. Denver, H. Bochel & M. Steven (2012), 'Mixed messages for (some) parties: The Scottish Council elections of 2012', *Scottish Affairs* 80, 1–19.
11. McAveety became Labour leader of Glasgow City Council in 2015.
12. C. Brown Swan (2022), '"We're socialists not nationalists": British labour and the national question(s)', *Nations and Nationalism* 29:2, 467–81.
13. *Herald*, 25 September 2012.
14. Pike, 90–3.
15. *Inside The Room: The Scottish Independence Referendum* (Part 1: The vote is granted), Political Currency podcast, 25 November 2024.
16. D. Torrance (2013), 'Referendum debate: Year two', *Scottish Affairs* 84, 27–8.
17. D. Torrance (2012), 'Better Together or Yes Scotland? Year one in the battle of Britain', *Scottish Affairs* 80, 69–87.
18. J. Maxwell & O. Dudley Edwards (eds) (2014), *Why Not? Scotland, Labour and Independence*, Edinburgh: Luath, 11.
19. Torrance (2013), 29.
20. 'Labour's Darling delivers pro-Union message', BBC News online, 8 June 2013.
21. G. Brown (2017), *My Life, Our Times*, London: Bodley Head, 401–2.
22. Findlay (2017), 30.
23. P. Bryan & T. Kane (2013), *Class, Nation and Socialism: Red Paper on Scotland 2014*, Glasgow: Glasgow Caledonian University.

24. Scottish Labour Party (2014), *Powers for a Purpose – Strengthening Accountability and Empowering People*, Glasgow: SLP.
25. Findlay (2017), 50–4.
26. Findlay (2017), 37.
27. D. Alexander (2013), 'Ideas and Ideals: Not a Battle for Standing', The Judith Hart Memorial Lecture 2013, 3 May 2013.
28. M. Fyfe (ed.) (2014), *Women Saying NO: Making a Positive Case Against Independence*, Edinburgh: Luath.
29. Findlay (2017), 111.
30. D. Torrance (2015), *Salmond: Against the Odds* (Third Edition), Edinburgh: Birlinn, 238.
31. T. Harris (2018), *Ten Years in the Death of the Labour Party*, London: Biteback, 113.
32. Findlay (2017), 55.
33. *Scotsman*, 5 December 2012.
34. D. Torrance (2017), 'Scotland's progressive dilemma', *Political Quarterly* 88:1, January–March 2017, 52–9.
35. *Sunday Politics Scotland* (BBC Scotland), 8 May 2016.
36. M. Rosie & E. Hepburn (2015), '"The essence of the Union ... ": Unionism, nationalism and identity on these disconnected islands', *Scottish Affairs* 24:2, 141–62.
37. Swan, 469.
38. A. Aughey (2007), *The Politics of Englishness*, Manchester: Manchester University Press, 88.
39. *New Statesman*, 8 September 2014.
40. 'Gordon Brown's speech at the "Love Scotland Vote No" rally in Glasgow', Office of Gordon and Sarah Brown website, 17 September 2014.
41. Brown, 404.
42. E. Bort (2015), 'The annals of the parish: Referendum year 2014', *Scottish Affairs* 24:1, 1–21.
43. Findlay (2017), 115.
44. Findlay (2017), 86.
45. A. Henderson, R. Johns, J. M. Larner & C. J. Carman (2022), *The Referendum that Changed a Nation: Scottish Voting Behaviour, 2014–2019*, London: Palgrave Macmillan, 125.
46. D. Laws (2016), *Coalition: The Inside Story of the Conservative–Liberal Democrat Coalition Government*, London: Biteback, 512–13.
47. T. Harris (2018), *Ten Years in the Death of the Labour Party*, 116.
48. *Daily Record*, 24 October 2014.
49. Pike, 187–93.

50. Findlay (2017), 126.
51. Neil Findlay ran as the Campaign for Socialism candidate.
52. 'MP Jim Murphy named Scottish Labour leader', BBC News online, 13 December 2014.
53. Pike, 206.
54. Findlay (2017), 157.
55. *The Times*, 17 January 2015.
56. Findlay (2017), 175.
57. 'New Scottish Labour Clause IV passes at one-day conference', LabourList website, 7 March 2015.
58. Pike, 214.
59. E. Bort (2017), 'The annals of the parish: 2015–2016. From referendum to referendum to ... referendum?', *Scottish Affairs* 26:1, 69–102.
60. I. Watson (2015), *Five Million Conversations: How Labour Lost an Election and Rediscovered its Roots*, Edinburgh: Luath, 180–2.
61. Pike, 200–65.
62. Pike, 200–65.
63. Findlay (2017), 194. It is not clear how Findlay was calculating the age of the Scottish party.
64. 'Election 2015: Scottish Labour leader Murphy loses seat to SNP', BBC News online, 8 May 2015.
65. 'Scottish Labour leader Jim Murphy to resign', BBC News online, 16 May 2015.
66. HC Deb 14 July 2015 Vol 598 c776 [Commons Chamber].
67. Findlay (2017), 191.
68. *The Times*, 11 June 2015.
69. G. Pogrund & P. Maguire (2020), *Left Out: The Inside Story of Labour Under Corbyn*, London: Bodley Head, 17–18.
70. Swan, 472.
71. 'Scottish Labour votes to scrap Trident', BBC News online, 1 November 2015.
72. *Financial Times*, 21 September 2016.
73. *Fabian Review*, 1 April 2016. Dugdale later claimed this had been against her wishes.
74. P. Cairney (2016), 'The Scottish Parliament election 2016: Another momentous event but dull campaign', *Scottish Affairs* 25:3, 277–93.
75. 'how we will rebuild Scotland by redistributing power and wealth', Scottish Labour Party website, 24 September 2018.
76. D. Martin, 'Radical home rule', *Labour Hame*, 9 May 2016.
77. T. Shipman (2016), *All Out War: The Full Story of Brexit*, London: William Collins, 74, 363.

78. Pogrund & Maguire, 239.
79. 'Scottish Labour conference delegates back federal UK motion', BBC News online, 24 February 2017.
80. Harris, 264.
81. R. Awan-Scully (2018), *The End of British Party Politics?* London: Biteback, 99.
82. *Rhodri Morgan – The Last Interview* (ITV Wales), 19 June 2017.
83. T. Ross & T. McTague (2017), *Betting the House: The Inside Story of the 2017 Election*, London: Biteback, 335–7.
84. The new Welsh First Minister Mark Drakeford, by contrast, described himself as a Corbynite.
85. *The i paper*, 19 November 2017.
86. Scottish Labour Party (2018), *Real Change: Conference Guide and Annual Report*, Glasgow: SLP.
87. N. Findlay (2023), *Hope and Despair: Lifting the Lid on the Murky World of Scottish Politics*, Edinburgh: Luath, 64–5.
88. Dumfries councillor Jim Dempster was also suspended in 2018 after making 'offensive and terrible' comments about then SNP transport minister Humza Yousaf. He quit the party four years later (*Daily Record*, 28 February 2022).
89. *Herald*, 29 July 2019.
90. *Herald*, 5 May 2019.
91. *The Herald* reported on 4 September 2020 that footage existed of Murray rehearsing a branded Change UK speech.
92. Findlay (2023), 120.
93. A. Henderson, R. Johns, J. Larner & C. Carman (2020), 'Scottish Labour as a case study in party failure: Evidence from the 2019 UK general election in Scotland', *Scottish Affairs* 29:2.
94. *Guardian*, 2 September 2020.
95. P. Maguire & G. Pogrund (2025), *Get In: The Inside Story of Labour Under Starmer*, London: Bodley Head, 137, 213.
96. 'A socially just Scotland in a modern United Kingdom', LabourList website, 21 December 2020.
97. Findlay (2023), 213.
98. Findlay (2023), 211.
99. *Edinburgh Evening News*, 28 June 2022.
100. Findlay (2023), 224.
101. Findlay (2023), 255.
102. 'Sarwar: "I didn't grasp how hollowed out Scottish Labour was"', STV News, 14 February 2022.
103. Scottish Fabians (2021), *A Voice for the Future: How Labour can Shape the Next 20 Years of Devolution*, London: Fabian Society, 96.

104. Labour Party (2022), *A New Britain: Renewing our Democracy and Rebuilding our Economy – Report of the Commission on the UK's Future*, Newcastle: Labour Party.
105. T. Ross & R. Wearmouth (2024), *Landslide: The Inside Story of the 2024 Election*, London: Biteback, 261.
106. Maguire & Pogrund, 319.
107. *Holyrood*, 15 January 2024.
108. *National*, 1 February 2022.
109. Ross & Wearmouth, 258–9.
110. Ross & Wearmouth, 264.
111. *Herald*, 17 November 2024.
112. 'Scotland is being "held back" by the SNP, Anas Sarwar says', STV News, 23 September 2024.
113. *Daily Record*, 24 September 2024.
114. *Herald*, 1 February 2025.
115. *Sunday Times*, 23 February 2025.
116. 'Scottish Labour's Keir Starmer problem', Politico, 24 February 2025.
117. *The i paper*, 18 March 2025.
118. 'Former Labour MSP quits party over welfare cuts', BBC News online, 19 March 2025.
119. 'Scottish Labour's Keir Starmer problem', Politico.
120. *Daily Record*, 15 April 2025.
121. *Daily Record*, 2 June 2025.
122. *Sunday Times*, 8 June 2025.
123. 'Two Cheers for Hamilton', Scottish Labour Left website, 13 June 2025.
124. *Evening Standard*, 7 May 2025.

Conclusion
Whither Scottish Labour?

During the 2015 UK general election campaign, one Scottish Labour MP described the mood in Scotland as resembling 'the last days of Rome', just 'without sex, or wine. In fact, with none of the fun bits.' And when on polling day the electoral map of Scotland turned from red to yellow with just a speck of blue in the south, red in the east and orange in the north, Jim Murphy, the leader of the once-mighty Scottish Labour Party, spoke of having been 'overwhelmed by history and circumstance'.[1]

How did the Labour Party in Scotland reach that moment? This study has attempted to account for both the period before that political 'tsunami', during which it advanced to become the dominant 'party of Scotland' between the 1920s and 1990s, as well as that following the 2015 election, which Hassan and Shaw – borrowing from Dangerfield – called the 'strange death of Labour Scotland'. And while the 2024 general election suggested reports of the party's demise had been greatly exaggerated, polling at the time of writing indicates not. Such are the fluctuations of early twenty-first-century Scottish – and indeed wider – politics.

As with the Scottish Conservative Party, the subject of a previous volume in this series, there have been many attempts to account for Labour decline. Most have focused on its traditional 'pillars' of support: the urban working class, trade unions, local government, council housing and Catholicism, all of which began to weaken some time before the party in Scotland started to lose votes.[2] Others have concentrated on what Drucker termed 'doctrine and ethos', with Knox suggesting that as Scottish Labour was transformed from 'an alliance of the white, Protestant skilled workers and the petty bourgeoisie' into what Hassan suggested was a 'less misogynist and less sectarian' party, it was at the expense of 'a commitment to greater social and economic equality'.³

THE 'BRANCH OFFICE' PARADOX

One striking feature to have emerged from this study is the long-standing weakness of Labour Party organisation in Scotland. This has been true during periods in which it was electorally successful, while even when organisation appeared to be in better shape it performed poorly. There is no clear correlation. Even in the 1920s when the Independent Labour Party (ILP) lent Scottish Labour much of its energy and campaigning prowess, local parties were geographically concentrated – with few beyond Scotland's central industrial belt – and often small and dysfunctional. Only in extreme cases such as the ILP's disaffiliation in 1932 can one detect a concerted effort to organise, and in that case impressively so.

Later, in the 1960s and 1980s when Labour dominated local and general elections in Scotland, individual membership was lower than in equivalent English Constituency Labour Parties, although this was masked for several decades by 'the minimum', a reporting fiction in which CLPs claimed 1,000 members even when their true strength was barely a fifth of that number. This increased the Scottish party's financial and administrative dependence on London, and indeed the British organisation was often compelled to intervene to suspend, disband or rejuvenate local parties, usually in Glasgow where, paradoxically, Labour was strongest electorally.

What accounts for this surprising fact? One explanation is that given the party's electoral success for much of the twentieth century, there was no real impetus to improve or maintain its organisational machinery. Hassan and Shaw have convincingly argued that a post-1945 'highpoint of class identity, social solidarity, and tenacious party allegiances' reduced the need for 'active campaigning and mobilization'. Furthermore, the party possessed a 'cadre' of activists, councillors, trade union officials and MPs who 'were well-connected, much-respected and had deep roots in their communities'.⁴ Even well past its heyday, for example, large crowds were drawn to the oratory of the ILP's James Maxton.

Like Maxton, many of Labour's Scottish leaders were surprisingly middle class, some by background and others having acquired 'either through marriage, the labour movement, individual endeavour, or by inheritance, petit bourgeois status', which to Knox included most of those prominent between 1918 and 1939.[5] From the 1960s and 1970s this remained true in a slightly different way. Some were sons or daughters of the manse – Gordon Brown and the Alexanders (Wendy and Douglas) – others the privately educated children of Scottish professionals or businesspeople, such as Donald Dewar and, more recently, Iain Gray and Anas Sarwar.

This mixed class composition helped give Labour in Scotland a broader electoral appeal as well as, in the eyes of left-wing critics, a deadening hand in ideological terms. The long-standing influence of the Catholic Church in Scotland – something that persisted into the early 2000s – also meant the party was not always as socially progressive as it liked to think it was, although for much of that period neither was Scottish society.

First-past-the-post elections significantly benefitted Labour in Scotland. As Hassan and Shaw have also argued, the party mistook the resulting 'dynamics and distortions' as a true indication of its real-world popularity and breadth of support.[6] This instilled a certain hubris and feeling of invincibility. While the urban central belt was the most populous, it did not represent all of Scotland, and indeed Labour in other parts of the UK was consistently even more successful, not just in the north of England but in its major cities and in Wales, where it regularly exceeded a majority of the popular vote in post-war elections, something never managed by Scottish Labour or indeed most other parties in Scotland.

Another striking conclusion is that tensions arising from a lack of organisational autonomy were baked into the Labour Party almost from the beginning. It was clear to McKibbin, for example, that the attempt in 1915 to extend 'local autonomy while at the same time increasing central over-all direction was everywhere as much likely to fail as to succeed, and in the conditions of Scotland more likely to fail'.[7] Over the next century this was a persistent complaint from the Labour Party in Scotland in good times and in bad. In some respects, the constraints imposed by the party in London were absurd – the conference of the Scottish Council of the Labour Party (SCLP) could not even consider non-Scottish motions until 1972.

On the other hand, this meant the SCLP could devote perhaps a disproportionate amount of attention to the question of Scottish autonomy and governance which in many respects mirrored that concerning the party itself. Yet there is also a sense that such questions appeared more important to Scottish party officials and leaders than they were to voters, who were unlikely to be familiar with Labour's rules or constitution beyond Clause IV. Therefore, Scottish Labour often looked in on itself, convinced that from constitutional reform – party or state – would flow radical, vote-winning ideas. Again, the empirical evidence suggests otherwise. In the interwar period and again in the 1960s, Labour in Scotland produced transformative policies when the party was at its least autonomous, while by the early twenty-first century Scottish Labour had gained considerable autonomy yet had ceased producing ideas of any consequence. One might call this the 'branch office' paradox.

LABOUR AND SCOTTISH NATIONALISM

Implicit in this is the elephant in the room: nationalism. Labour in Scotland existed on the basis of class and social solidarity, yet during the latter half of the twentieth century it had to adapt to a discourse increasingly dominated my constitutional matters, chiefly what Mitchell called the 'Scottish Question' – how Scotland was to be governed within the framework of the United Kingdom.

Scottish Labour's response to that question was inconsistent and often incoherent, constitutionally, politically and philosophically. Originally carried over from the old Scottish Liberal Party, the early party's commitment to 'Home Rule' – which generally meant legislative devolution but, on occasion, Dominion status – was more an article of constitutional and nationalist faith than a carefully developed programme. As Gordon Brown observed:

> No theorist attempted in sufficient depth to reconcile the conflicting aspirations for home rule and a British socialist advance. In particular, no one was able to show how capturing power in Britain – and legislating for minimum levels of welfare, for example-could be combined with a policy of devolution for Scotland.

The 'real problem for Scottish Labour', concluded Brown, 'was that it wanted to be Scottish and British at the same time'.[8]

There was always a fear, whether articulated by ILP Scottish organiser John Paton in the 1920s[9] or Tony Blair in the 1990s, that the fine line between patriotism and nationalism would prove difficult to maintain, and so it proved in the 2010s. Labour's 'nationalist unionism' took several forms. The first phase borrowed heavily from Scottish Liberalism, support for 'Home Rule' within the British Empire and a recalibrated United Kingdom, together with the idea that 'radical' or 'progressive' Scotland was being held back by 'Tory' England. The second embraced the 'administrative devolution' promoted by the Scottish Unionists and disdained anything more; the third reluctantly accepted legislative devolution and sold it on the basis that Keir Hardie would have approved. As the party frankly admitted in the late 1970s:

> This nationalism has always been an element in all Scottish political parties; it was strong among the founders of the Labour Party in Scotland and remained so, but the growth of the Scottish National Party both confused and reduced the support within the Labour Party for the idea of devolution. The SNP is identified by the Labour Party with the most negative aspects of nationalism, with chauvinism, hostility to England and above all with selfishness and greed in their claims on North Sea oil.[10]

The fourth phase, nevertheless, took the once grudging support for legislative devolution and pitched it to voters with purposeful moral force relating to Scotland's 'distinct' (and it was posited) superior political culture, not to mention its institutional autonomy, which needed defending from the 'anti-Scottish' actions of 'alien' Conservative governments at Westminster. But just as Scottish Unionists had created trouble for themselves by framing Scottish political discourse in such terms, so too did the Labour Party during the 1980s and 1990s. Geekie and Levy spoke of it having created a Frankenstein's Monster, which would one day turn upon its creator. The inevitable corollary of 'standing up for Scotland' was the accusation of 'talking Scotland down', to which Labour fell prey in the 2010s.

It was the Thatcher era which prompted the Scottish Labour Party to throw caution to the wind, what Tom Harris called the 'fruitful – but ultimately disastrously self-defeating – strategy of portraying the Conservative government as undemocratic, even un-Scottish, for opposing devolution'.[11] The trio of factors which Bealey suggested explained Labour Party doctrine were all recognisable.[12] First, the party's long years in opposition during the Thatcher era (its 'situation within the polity') pushed the Scottish party, particularly after the 1983 and 1987 elections, in a more nationalist direction; second, the state of the economy persuaded it that devolution would both protect the 'old' economy (heavy industry) while also encouraging the new; and third, the 'experience and ideas' of those outside the Labour movement ('externality') impacted party strategy, not only pressure from the Scottish Trades Union Congress – long ahead of the devolutionary curve – but also the Scottish National Party, particularly as its support grew in the late 1980s.

To paraphrase Gordon Brown, by the end of the twentieth century Labour wanted to be nationalist and unionist at the same time, talking of the 'sovereignty of the Scottish people' and even, albeit briefly, 'independence in the UK', when devolution did not, and arguably could not, satisfy such rhetoric. Scottish Labour was caught in a chicken-and-egg situation: to contain what it saw as the 'bad' sort of nationalism, it had to promote the 'good' variety, but as Keating observed as early as 1989, 'it was not until Labour had raised the Scottish issue for its own purposes that the nationalists were able to exploit it; and that could only be done if Labour were seen to fail'.[13]

Much like the British Conservative Party, Labour possessed its own 'territorial code', although this was inconsistently applied: in 1958, the 'centre' informed the 'periphery' that its historic commitment to Home Rule had been abandoned, while in 1974 London (Labour's National Executive Committee) instructed Glasgow (the party's Scottish Council) to reverse its opposition and support legislative devolution. Did Labour in Scotland have any choice? Tam Dalyell and Brian Wilson both consistently warned of the dangers, as they saw them, of embracing legislative devolution, the Member for West Lothian in terms of dismantling the Union and Wilson more in terms of its destructive impact upon the Labour movement in Scotland. By 1997, however, Dalyell had become wildly unrealistic, convinced all Tony Blair had to do was reform local government, while Wilson realised the party had little choice but to deliver. On one level, this was a great achievement: successive British Labour leaders had promised speedy legislation to create a Scottish Parliament and that is exactly what happened. SNP leader Alex Salmond once remarked that Labour could not deliver a pizza let alone a parliament, but he was wrong. Its much-criticised referendum policy also turned out to be a masterstroke, not to mention Labour's act of 'charitable giving' when it came to the PR electoral system.

On another level, devolution was a failure, at least judged against the arguments which Labour itself made. In a memorable inaugural speech, Donald Dewar looked forward to: 'the days ahead when this Chamber will sound with debate, argument and passion. When men and women from all over Scotland will meet to work together for a future built from the first principles of social justice'.

But did that happen? To Mitchell, the reality as opposed to the theory of devolved government 'exposed the extent to which Scottish leftist politics was based on rhetoric'. Jack McConnell, he suggested, 'encapsulated' yet another Scottish Labour paradox:

> The young radical council leader and Scottish Labour Action founder might have been expected to have carved out a distinct Scottish policy agenda. There was no lack of money to experiment and develop a different Scotland. But when the curtain was drawn back, Labour in Scotland under Mr McConnell was exposed to be no different from the party in London. It mimicked the best and worst of the government in London. There was no alternative Scottish strategy. There was no critique of the growing income inequality that might have been expected from the Scottish party of old.[14]

Brian Wilson reckoned the debilitating factor was a 'fault line' between what he called 'conveners', practical politicians who 'thought they were creating a modern, devolved parliament' within the UK in the 'interests of good government for Scotland', and 'reconveners' who saw the Scottish Parliament as an 'interim arrangement' on the long road to independence. The competing causes of 'progressive government and the constitution' became entangled, and not in a way that benefitted Labour. Rather the 'pre-eminent consequence of the Scottish Parliament's creation was to build a platform for the constitutional issue to dominate Scottish politics'.[15]

This was perhaps not pre-ordained. During his brief period in office Henry McLeish developed what Mitchell called 'a different understanding of devolution' which combined nation-building symbolism with policy differentiation.[16] What if McLeishism had been sustained and presented with more panache? The Welsh experience showed this to be possible, although with the caveat that an initially weaker National Assembly for Wales focused Labour's nationalist-unionist energies on a broadly consensual extension of that body's powers, thus maintaining its post-1922 dominance in that part of the United Kingdom.

There was something of the 1920s in the experience of Scottish Labour almost a century later. The Liberals, once Scotland's dominant party, had long sustained themselves on the basis of delivering Irish Home Rule, yet almost as soon as that was partially fulfilled with devolution for Northern Ireland and Dominion status for the Free State, the party went into decline, to be displaced by Labour as the main progressive alternative to the Conservatives. Almost as soon as the Scottish Parliament was up and running Labour lost support, at a trio of elections in 1999 and consolidated in 2007 when the SNP assumed minority office for the first time. The conceit that Labour alone 'stood up for Scotland' was necessary but not wholly sufficient for continued electoral success.

For a while first-past-the-post lulled Scottish Labour into a false sense of Westminster if not Holyrood security, but then the independence referendum of 2012–14 forced many naturally nationalist Labour supporters to choose between actually delivering 'independence' or continuing to support a party which had now set itself against radical constitutional change having once been the leading proponent of it. As Keating observed, the party then reverted to a 'strong unionist tone', less concerned with class solidarity, state control and centralised planning as it had been after the Second World War, and now largely preoccupied with economic self-interest.[17] Ironically, Labour figures such as George Foulkes and George Galloway who in the 1980s had been seen as nationalist rebels came to be viewed as ultra-unionists.

MYTHOLOGY

Karl Marx was alive to the power of mythology, what he called the anxious conjuring up of past 'spirits' to the service of those in the present, 'borrowing from them names, battle slogans, and costumes' in order to present a 'new scene in world history in time-honored disguise and borrowed language'. Most political parties, particularly old ones, are fuelled by myths, but perhaps Scottish Labour has more than most.

The most enduring is that of its own radicalism. As Midwinter et al. observed in 1991, 'Red Clydeside' was 'nurtured to present the party as a crusading movement, well to the left of the party in England'. Although it was an exaggeration to say (as Midwinter went on to claim) that for much of its history Scottish Labour had sustained itself by 'patronage and ward-heeling',[18] the consistency of this particular myth is striking, surfacing frequently in manifestos, speeches and pamphlets. But what all its myth-makers appeared to forget was that it related to the Independent Labour Party (ILP) rather than the Labour Party itself, as well as the fact the ILP had seceded from the Scottish Labour movement in 1932, causing it much pain and trauma in the process.

Furthermore, as has been consistently charted, the evidence for this apparent radicalism is remarkably thin. As McLean observed, if Glasgow was ripe for revolution in January 1919 why 'had it just sent fourteen Coalition M.P.s to Westminster, only one Labour, and none from any point further left?'[19] Even in 1922, when Scotland's largest city did send a large band of representatives to the Imperial Parliament, most of the ILP's own contemporary chroniclers stressed the group's ideological orthodoxy and spectrum of views. In 1922 the forces of reactionary Liberalism and National Liberals still managed twenty-seven seats in Scotland, while the even more reactionary Scottish Unionists (which boasted more robust organisation in Glasgow than any other party) secured ten more seats than Labour in 1924.

As Knox and Mackinlay have argued, by the 1940s and 1950s the Labour Party in Scotland was defined more by the economic turbulence of the 1930s than any 'historical memory' of the ILP tradition, yet still Red Clydeside endured as a 'mobilizing symbol of the collective power of the Scottish working class'. As Christopher Grieve (Hugh MacDiarmid) put it, it was a party 'educated not in class struggle but in administrative patience', and striving not 'for social equality, but for the betterment of the workers'.[20] As Gordon Brown noted of the 1929 Scottish Labour group of MPs, they were the 'voice of labour, not socialism'.²¹ It is curious that Fife, which elected a Communist MP until 1950, possessed no comparable hold on the party's imagination.

But what is not in dispute is the importance of that myth to Scottish Labour's 'understanding of itself'.²² As early as 1918 Labour Scotland was presented as 'progressive in political thought and action' while England showed 'a marked disposition to conservatism',²³ and four decades later the party still boasted of 'roots' which lay 'deep in the history of Scottish radicalism'. Although by the 1970s it seemed unlikely any more than a few scholars were genuinely familiar with the political thought of Keir Hardie, his Scottish Labour Party was presented in 1958 as 'the parent of the political party we know today'.²⁴ The myth of Red Clydeside, meanwhile, imperceptibly morphed into a broader narrative of 'radical Scotland'.

As a consequence, Labour often chose curious heroes. As Mitchell has noted, even the more right-wing elements in the Scottish Labour Party 'played along' with this myth of radical Scotland. Gordon Brown wrote a glowing biography of the largely performative James Maxton, and while Tom Johnston had admirable achievements to his name he became deified to a much greater degree than the practically forgotten Willie Ross, who was 'no Labour member's hero despite bringing considerable money to the Scottish Office, the key measure of success in post-war Scottish politics'.²⁵ Bruce Millan, creator of the interventionist Scottish Development Agency and architect of Europe's regional policy was also marginalised. Ramsay MacDonald, meanwhile, was disdained as much by the Scottish as British party, which was not inclined to celebrate his extraordinary rags-to-riches story or hard graft in making Labour a party of government.

The ghost of Keir Hardie was also mobilised to disguise Labour's fluctuating support for Scottish self-government, what Wood called 'self-created myths about its uninterrupted commitment' to 'Home Rule' or devolution from 1888 to 1988 and beyond. As she observed, Liberals and Communists in Scotland had been rather more consistent.²⁶ Norman Buchan was a rare dissenter in the early 1970s, highlighting the uncomfortable truth that the implications of that commitment were 'never thought through' and had been quickly overtaken by economic events. It was curious, Buchan added, to:

notice how the exponents of the constitutional panacea have been invoking the names of Keir Hardie and John Maclean in that one context – while ignoring in both of them their real radical content. Their priorities, too, were socialism first and devolution second.[27]

Another myth was that of SNP treachery, present in nascent form during the 1920s owing to Nationalist interventions which deprived Labour of by-election gains, sustained as a result of attacks from the Scottish Covenant Association and Winnie Ewing, and turbo-charged by the party's decision to vote with Conservatives and Liberals against a Labour government at the tail end of the 1970s. For years, the Scottish Labour MP Norman Hogg would write an annual letter to a Scottish newspaper marking the anniversary of SNP MPs 'collaborating' with Margaret Thatcher by supporting her motion of no confidence.[28] It mattered not that James Callaghan's government was worn out, lacking a majority and rapidly approaching the end of its parliamentary shelf-life, the SNP made convenient scapegoats.

In time, Scottish Labour fell victim to the SNP's own mythology. The most persistent held that John Smith, Donald Dewar et al. had only supported devolution under 'pressure' from – or electoral fear of – the Scottish National Party. Although that was largely true of its 1974 conversion, by the mid-to-late 1980s fear had clearly given way to conviction. Not only were there fewer SNP MPs breathing down Labour's neck than in the 1974–9 Parliament, but even before the 1988 Govan by-election Labour in Scotland was headed towards a Scottish Constitutional Convention from which the SNP ultimately remained aloof. Few remember that between 1979 and 1997 the only two political parties in Scotland formally opposed to devolution were the Conservatives and SNP, though each for very different reasons. Labour delivered devolution in 1997–9, not the SNP. And while Alex Salmond played a spirited part in the cross-party 'yes' campaign of September 1997, it seems inconceivable the result would have been significantly different without his input.

Even more damagingly for Labour, the SNP purposefully coopted *its* myths and heroes. At SNP conferences Alex Salmond invoked lost comrades such as Jimmy Reid and Campbell Christie, while during the independence referendum he managed to persuade Ravenscraig shop steward Tommy Brennan that a 'yes' vote would revitalise Scotland's long-dormant heavy industry.

The First Minister even displayed Tom Johnston's portrait at Bute House, while promoting his constitutional vision in precisely the terms Labour had once championed devolution, as a means by which Scotland's innately 'social democratic' ethos could be sustained and protected against the advance of neoliberal England. By 2024 Hassan noted the irony that in many respects the SNP had 'ended up reproducing the same sort of conceits and language' Labour had when running Scotland.[29] All the same, the SNP had undeniably and skilfully acquired the 'standing up for Scotland' mantle worn by Labour since the late 1950s. And it obviously hurt.

DOCTRINE AND ETHOS

How much did Scottish Labour's rise, hegemony and fall have to do with its doctrine and to what extent was it related to the party's ethos? The former, as we have already seen, was largely more orthodox than mythology would suggest. For much of the party's history, policy in Scotland followed closely that in the rest of Britain, not least because its structure concentrated policy-making power with the British Labour conference and National Executive Committee in London.

This study has already quoted Wendy Alexander's private observation that the main intellectual contribution made by the Labour movement in Scotland had been 'around the rapid growth of the ILP following the establishment of the Forward newspaper in 1906'. This, however, did Scottish Labour a disservice. Not only was policy underdeveloped in 1906 (not least because the party was nowhere near any level of government) but within two decades the ILP MP John Wheatley had pioneered State-financed council housing, often of considerable quality, while during the Second World War Tom Johnston (anther ILPer) laid the groundwork for the NHS in Scotland and brought hydroelectricity to the Highlands. In the 1960s and 1970s, meanwhile, Willie Ross transformed the Scottish Office into a significant lobbying machine and raised public spending in Scotland to significantly higher levels. These were not insignificant, and some, like children's panels and social work departments, still exist today. As Brian Wilson has observed, many of these police achievements are now 'forgotten' despite being the ones 'most beneficial to millions'.[30]

Where Wendy Alexander had a point was in her observation that Labour had spent so long 'obsessing' about Scotland's constitutional future that it had 'spent too little time' reflecting on the sort of nation it wished to create.[31] This mirrored the internal debate regarding party autonomy – in both cases process and institutional models occupied almost all the party's bandwidth to the extent it often thought about little else. And even once various extensions to the devolution settlement had played out and the party had achieved virtual autonomy, what Hassan called a 'political void' remained, a 'missing *instrumental* case for devolution, as opposed to the *intrinsic* case for the Scottish Parliament'.[32]

Or, as Keating put it, Labour proved itself incapable of marrying a constitutional vision with a set of economic and social policies to show how devolution could be used to improve Scotland's economic growth and apparent commitment to 'social justice'.[33] Even when it came to defending the union – as Labour was required to do more proactively after 2007 – the party appeared defensive and unwilling to make an argument which had existed in some form since the early 1960s. In 1963 *Signposts for Scotland* had confidently asserted Scotland's 'fairer sharing of both benefits and burdens' on the basis of 'relatively greater needs', while warning that cutting Scotland off from the rest of the UK would 'give Scotland the worst of both worlds'.[34] It took the independence referendum and Gordon Brown to revive this discourse as 'pooling and sharing' and Scotland having the 'best of both worlds' as part of the UK. As the left-wing MSP Neil Findlay observed in 2015, 'UK-wide redistribution' was 'central to creating a fairer society',[35] yet Scottish Labour rarely made that case.

Yet even beyond doctrine, the party appeared to have a problem with its ethos. This, as Hassan and Shaw have argued, was by the 1980s an asset as well as a hindrance, sustaining Scottish Labour through a turbulent decade but depriving it of any desire for a deep 'rethinking'.[36] At the same time, critics urged the party to 'change' and 'adapt' but never quite said how. Some hinted that it should support independence and promote itself within that new constitutional order. But with the SNP claiming to inhabit the same doctrinal space, that seemed a risky strategy, not to mention a U-turn too far. Perhaps the Scottish Labour Party wanted to be too many things: Scottish *and* British, nationalist *and* unionist, autonomous *and* one part of a wider movement. To paraphrase Dean Acheson, by the early twenty-first century it appeared to have lost an empire but not yet found a role. The irony was that the party had itself helped bring about that evidently uncomfortable state of affairs.

NOTES

1. *Guardian*, 21 May 2015.
2. D. McTavish (ed.) (2016), *Politics in Scotland*, London: Routledge, 59–60.
3. W. W. Knox (2006), 'Review: the Scottish Labour Party: History, institutions and ideas', *Scottish Historical Review* 85:1, 174.
4. G. Hassan & E. Shaw (2012), *The Strange Death of Labour Scotland*, Edinburgh: Edinburgh University Press, 258.
5. W. W. Knox (ed.) (1984), *Scottish Labour Leaders, 1918–39: A Biographical Dictionary*, Edinburgh: Mainstream, 21.
6. Hassan & Shaw, 1.
7. R. McKibbin (1974), *The Evolution of the Labour Party, 1910–1924*, Oxford: Clarendon Press, 43.
8. G. Brown (1981), 'The Labour Party and Political Change in Scotland, 1918–1929: The Politics of Five Elections', Edinburgh: University of Edinburgh, PhD thesis, 527.
9. J. Paton (1936), *Left Turn! The Autobiography of John Paton*, London: Secker and Warburg, 181–2.
10. Labour Party (1978), 'Devolution: the Labour Party position', Rowntree Devolution Conference, 80.
11. T. Harris (2018), *Ten Years in the Death of the Labour Party*, London: Biteback, 105.
12. F. Bealey (1970), *The Social and Political Thought of the British Labour Party*, London: Weidenfeld and Nicolson, 2.
13. M. Keating (1989), 'The Labour Party in Scotland, 1951–1964', in I. Donnachie, C. Harvie & I. S. Wood (eds) (1989), *Forward! Labour Politics in Scotland, 1888–1988*, Edinburgh: Polygon, 98.
14. J. Mitchell (2014), *The Scottish Question*, Oxford: Oxford University Press, 267.
15. *Scotsman*, 28 September 2024.
16. Mitchell, 258.
17. M. Keating (2005), *The Government of Scotland: Public Policy Making after Devolution* (Second Edition), Edinburgh: Edinburgh University Press, 62.
18. A. Midwinter, M. Keating & J. Mitchell (1991), *Politics and Public Policy in Scotland*, Edinburgh: Edinburgh University Press, 30.

19. I. McLean (1999), *The Legend of Red Clydeside*, Edinburgh: John Donald, 1.
20. W. W. Knox & A. Mackinlay, 'The re-making of Scottish Labour in the 1930s', in I. Donnachie, C. Harvie & I. S. Wood (eds) (1989), *Forward! Labour Politics in Scotland, 1888–1988*, Edinburgh: Polygon, 193.
21. Brown, 484.
22. L. Bennie, J. Brand & J. Mitchell (1997), *How Scotland Votes: Scottish Parties and Elections*, Manchester: Manchester University Press, 54.
23. D. Howell (1986), *A Lost Left: Three Studies in Socialism and Nationalism*, Manchester: Manchester University Press, 208.
24. Labour Party (1958), *Let Scotland Prosper: Labour Plans for Scotland's Progress*, London: Labour Party, 1.
25. Mitchell, 267.
26. F. Wood (1989), 'Scottish Labour in government and opposition: 1964–79', in I. Donnachie, C. Harvie & I. S. Wood (eds) (1989), *Forward! Labour Politics in Scotland, 1888–1988*, Edinburgh: Polygon, 124.
27. N. Buchan (1971), 'Politics', in D. Glen (ed.), *Whither Scotland? A Prejudiced Look at the Future of a Nation*, London: Victor Gollancz, 86–92.
28. See, for example, *Scotland on Sunday*, 27 March 1994.
29. 'Where stands the SNP and independence?', Bella Caledonia website, 2 September 2024.
30. *Scotsman*, 28 September 2024.
31. R. Hazell (ed.) (2003), *The State of the Nations 2003: The Third Year of Devolution in the United Kingdom*, Exeter: Imprint Academic, 124–6.
32. G. Hassan (2023), 'From Donald Dewar to Humza Yousaf: The role of Scotland's First Ministers and the importance of political leadership', *Political Quarterly* 94:4, October/December 2023, 560.
33. M. Keating, L. Stevenson, P. Cairney & K. Taylor (2003), 'Does Devolution Make a Difference? Legislative Output and Policy Divergence in Scotland', Stirling: University of Stirling (online).
34. Labour Party (1963), *Signposts for Scotland*, London: Labour Party, 22–3.
35. N. Findlay with J. Holmes (2017), *Socialism and Hope: A Journey through Turbulent Times*, Edinburgh: Luath, 176.
36. Hassan & Shaw, 14.

Appendix 1 – Party Leaders

SCOTTISH SECRETARY (SCOTTISH ADVISORY COUNCIL/ SCOTTISH COUNCIL OF THE LABOUR PARTY)

Benjamin Shaw (1914–32)
Arthur Woodburn (1932–9)
John Taylor (1939–51)
William Marshall (1951–77)
Helen Liddell (1977–88)
Murray Elder (1988–92)

GENERAL SECRETARY (SCOTTISH COUNCIL/SCOTTISH LABOUR PARTY)

Jack McConnell (1992–8)
Alex Rowley (1998–9)
Lesley Quinn (1999–2008)
Colin Smyth (2008–12)
Ian Price (2013–14)
Brian Roy (2014–19)
Michael Sharpe (2020)
James Kelly (2021–3)
John Paul McHugh (2023–4)
Kate Watson (2024–)

SECRETARIES OF STATE FOR SCOTLAND (INCLUDING SHADOWS)

William Adamson (1924–31)
Thomas Johnston (1941–5)
Joseph Westwood (1945–7)
Arthur Woodburn (1947–50)
Hector McNeil (1950–1)
Tom Fraser (1951–62)
Willie Ross (1962–76)
Bruce Millan (1976–83)
Donald Dewar (1983–92)
Tom Clarke (1992–3)
George Robertson (1993–7)
Donald Dewar (1997–9)

LEADER OF THE LABOUR PARTY IN THE SCOTTISH PARLIAMENT

Donald Dewar (1999–2000)
Henry McLeish (2000–1)
Jack McConnell (2001–7)
Wendy Alexander (2007–8)
Iain Gray (2008–11)

LEADER OF THE SCOTTISH LABOUR PARTY

Johann Lamont (2011–14)
Jim Murphy (2014–15)
Kezia Dugdale (2015–17)
Richard Leonard (2017–21)
Anas Sarwar (2021–)

Appendix 2 – Election Results

WESTMINSTER ELECTION RESULTS, 1892–2024

Election year	Vote share %	Number of MPs	Seats contested	Total no. of seats
1892	0.9 (SLP)	0	5	72
1895	0.8 (ILP)	0	7	72
1900	0.6 (SWRC)	0	1	72
1906	2.3 (LRC/SWRC)	2	9	72
1910 (Jan)	5.1	2	12	72
1910 (Dec)	3.6	3	5	72
1918	22.9	6	39	74 (including 3 university seats)
1922	32.2	29	43	74
1923	35.9	34	48	74
1924	41.0	26	63	74
1929	42.3	36	66	74
1931	32.6	7	57	74
1935	36.8	20	63	74
1945	47.9	37	68	74
1950	46.2	37	71	71 (university seats abolished)
1951	47.9	35	71	71
1955	46.7	34	71	71
1959	46.7	38	71	71
1964	48.7	43	71	71
1966	49.9	46	71	71
1970	44.5	44	71	71
1974 (Feb)	36.6	40	71	71
1974 (Oct)	36.3	41	71	71

Election year	Vote share %	Number of MPs	Seats contested	Total no. of seats
1979	41.5	44	71	71
1983	35.1	41	72	72
1987	42.4	50	72	72
1992	39.0	49	72	72
1997	45.6	56	72	72
2001	43.3	55	71	72
2005	38.9	40	58	59 (Scottish seats reduced)
2010	42.0	41	59	59
2015	24.3	1	59	59
2017	27.1	7	59	59
2019	18.6	1	59	59
2024	35.3	37	57	59

Sources: House of Commons Library (1918–2024); various sources (1892–1910).

SCOTTISH PARLIAMENT ELECTION RESULTS, 1999–2021

Election year	Constituency vote %	Regional vote %	Number of MSPs	Total no. of seats
1999	38.8	33.6	56	129
2003	34.6	29.3	50	129
2007	32.1	29.2	46	129
2011	31.7	26.3	37	129
2016	22.6	19.1	24	129
2021	21.6	17.9	22	129

Sources: House of Commons Library.

Bibliography

PRIMARY SOURCES

Records of James Carmichael and Neil Carmichael, Glasgow: Mitchell Library
Papers of the Dewar Family, Edinburgh: National Records of Scotland
George Foulkes Collection, Stirling: Scottish Political Archive
William W. Hamilton Papers, Edinburgh: National Library of Scotland
John McAllion Collection, Stirling: Scottish Political Archive
Jack McConnell Collection, Stirling: Scottish Political Archive
Ramsay MacDonald Papers, London: The National Archives
John P. Mackintosh MP papers, Edinburgh: National Library of Scotland
George Mathers Papers, Edinburgh: National Library of Scotland
George Robertson Papers, Stirling: Scottish Political Archive
Scottish Home Department Papers, Edinburgh: National Records of Scotland
Scottish Labour Party Papers, Glasgow: Mitchell Library

SECONDARY SOURCES

Aitken, K. (2001), *The Bairns o' Adam: The Story of the STUC*, Edinburgh: Polygon.
Alexander, W. (2003), *Chasing the Tartan Tiger: Lessons from a Celtic Cousin?*, Glasgow: Smith Institute.
Alexander, W. (ed.) (2005), *Donald Dewar: Scotland's first First Minister*, Edinburgh: Mainstream.
Allison, J. & H. Conroy (1995), *Guilty by Suspicion: A Life and Labour*, Argyll Publishing.

Anonymous, *The Scottish Socialists: A Gallery of Contemporary Portraits*, London: Faber and Faber.
Ashdown, P. (2000), *The Ashdown Diaries, Volume I: 1988–1997*, London: Allen Lane.
Ashdown, P. (2001), *The Ashdown Diaries, Volume II: 1997–1999*, London: Allen Lane.
Aughey, A. (2007), *The Politics of Englishness*, Manchester: Manchester University Press.
Avril, A. & Y. Béliard (eds) (2018), *Labour United and Divided from the 1830s to the Present*, Manchester: Manchester University Press.
Awan-Scully, R. (2018), *The End of British Party Politics?*, London: Biteback.
Barr, J. (1948), *Lang Syne: Memoirs of The Rev. James Barr*, Glasgow: William Maclellan.
Bealey, F. (1970), *The Social and Political Thought of the British Labour Party*, London: Weidenfeld and Nicolson.
Benn, T. (1989), *Against the Tide: Diaries, 1973–76*, London: Hutchinson.
Benn, T. (2002), *Free at Last! Diaries, 1991–2001*, London: Hutchinson.
Bennie, L., J. Brand & J. Mitchell (1997), *How Scotland Votes: Scottish Parties and Elections*, Manchester: Manchester University Press.
Blair, T. (2010), *A Journey*, London: Hutchinson.
Bochel, J., D. Denver & A. Macartney (eds) (1981), *The Referendum Experience: Scotland 1979*, Aberdeen: Aberdeen University Press.
Breitenbach, E. & E. Gordon (eds) (1992), *Out of Bounds: Women in Scottish Society, 1800–1945*, Edinburgh: Edinburgh University Press, 156–8.
Brown, A. & D. McCrone (eds) (1988), *Scottish Government Yearbook 1989*, Edinburgh: University of Edinburgh.
Brown, A. & R. Parry (eds) (1989), *Scottish Government Yearbook 1990*, Edinburgh: University of Edinburgh.
Brown, A. & D. McCrone (eds) (1990), *Scottish Government Yearbook 1991*, Edinburgh: University of Edinburgh.
Brown, G. (ed.) (1975), *The Red Paper on Scotland*, Edinburgh: EUSPB.
Brown, G. (1986), *Maxton*, Edinburgh: Mainstream.
Brown, G. (2017), *My Life, Our Times*, London: Bodley Head.
Brown, G. & D. Alexander (1999), *New Scotland, New Britain*, Glasgow: Smith Institute.
Brown, G. & D. Alexander (2007), *Stronger Together: The 21st century Case for Scotland and Britain*, Fabian Society.

Brown, K. D. (ed.) (1985), *The First Labour Party, 1906–1914*, London: Croom Helm.
Brown, T. & H. McLeish (2007), *Scotland: The Road Divides – New Politics, New Union*, Edinburgh: Luath.
Bryan, P. & T. Kane (2013), *Class, Nation and Socialism: Red Paper on Scotland 2014*, Glasgow: Glasgow Caledonian University.
Budge, I. & D. W. Urwin (1966), *Scottish Political Behaviour: A Case Study in British Homogeneity*, London: Longmans.
Burns, T. (1937), *Plan for Scotland*, London: London Scots Self-Government Committee.
Burns, T. (1939), *The Real Rulers of Scotland*, London: London Scots Self-Government Committee.
Butler, D. & D. Kavanagh (1980), *The British General Election of 1979*, London: Macmillan.
Cairney, P. & N. McGarvey (2013), *Scottish Politics* (Second Edition), London: Palgrave Macmillan.
Cameron, E. A. (2010), *Impaled Upon a Thistle: Scotland Since 1880*, Edinburgh: Edinburgh University Press.
Campbell, A. & B. Hagerty (eds) (2010), *The Alastair Campbell Diaries, Volume 1: Prelude to Power, 1994–1997*, London: Hutchinson.
Campbell, A. & B. Hagerty (eds) (2011), *The Alastair Campbell Diaries, Volume 2: Power and the People, 1997–1999*, London: Hutchinson.
Campbell, A. & B. Hagerty (eds) (2011b), *The Alastair Campbell Diaries, Volume 3: Power and Responsibility, 1999–2001*, London: Hutchinson.
Campbell, M. (2008), *Menzies Campbell: My Autobiography*, London: Hodder and Stoughton.
Canavan, D. (2009), *Let the People Decide: The Autobiography of Dennis Canavan*, Edinburgh: Birlinn.
Carman, C., R. Johns & J. Mitchell (2014), *More Scottish than British: The 2011 Scottish Parliament Election*, London: Palgrave Macmillan.
Castle, B. (1980), *The Castle Diaries, 1974–76*, London: Weidenfeld and Nicolson.
Checkland, S. & O. Checkland (1989), *Industry and Ethos: Scotland, 1832–1914*, Edinburgh: Edinburgh University Press.
Chrimes, S. B. (ed.) (1950), *The General Election in Glasgow February, 1950: Essays by Members of the Staff of the University of Glasgow*, Glasgow: Jackson, Son and Company.
Clark, I. & J. Berridge (1992), *Scotland Votes: The General Election 1992 in Scotland*, Aberdeen: Grampian Television.

Clarke, T. (2025), *To Be Honest ... The Story of My Life* (Kindle edition), Glasgow: Baxter Jardine.
Clarke, M. G. & H. M. Drucker (eds) (1976), *Our Changing Scotland: A Yearbook of Scottish Government, 1976–77*, Edinburgh: EUSPB.
Colville, J. (1986), *The Fringes of Power: Downing Street Diaries, Volume One: 1939 –October 1941*, London: Sceptre.
Conservative and Unionist Central Office (1955), *The Campaign Guide 1955: The New Political Encyclopædia*, London: CUCO.
Coupland, R. (1954), *Welsh and Scottish Nationalism: A Study*, Glasgow: Collins.
Craig, C. & S. Gilmore (1979), *A Radical Agenda for Scotland: Women and the Scottish Assembly*, Glasgow: Scottish Council of Fabian Societies.
Crick, M. (1986), *The March of Militant*, London: Faber and Faber.
Crossman, R. (1977), *The Diaries of a Cabinet Minister, Volume Three: Secretary of State for Social Services, 1968–70*, London: Hamish Hamilton and Jonathan Cape.
Curtice, J., D. McCrone, N. McEwen, M. Marsh & R. Ormiston (2009), *Revolution or Evolution? The 2007 Scottish Elections*, Edinburgh: Edinburgh University Press.
Dalyell, T. (1977), *Devolution: The End of Britain?*, London: Jonathan Cape.
Dalyell, T. (1989), *Dick Crossman: A Portrait*, London: Weidenfeld and Nicolson.
Dalyell, T. (2016), *The Question of Scotland: Devolution and After*, Edinburgh: Birlinn.
Darling, W. Y. (1945), *King's Cross to Waverley*, London: William Hodge.
Davidson, L. (2005), *Lucky Jack: Scotland's First Minister*, Edinburgh: Black and White.
Davidson, R. & G. Davis (2012), *The Sexual State: Sexuality and Scottish Governance, 1950–80*, Edinburgh: Edinburgh University Press.
Dewar, D. (1987), *Scotland: The Way Forward*, London: Fabian Society.
Donnachie, I., C. Harvie & I. S. Wood (eds) (1989), *Forward! Labour Politics in Scotland, 1888–1988*, Edinburgh: Polygon.
Donoughue, B. (2005), *Downing Street Diary: With Harold Wilson in No. 10*, London: Jonathan Cape.
Donoughue, B. (2008), *Downing Street Diary, Volume Two: With James Callaghan in No. 10*, London: Jonathan Cape.

Bibliography

Dorey, P. (2008), *The Labour Party and Constitutional Reform: A History of Constitutional Conservatism*, London: Palgrave Macmillan.

Douglas, D. (1968), *Together we Stand: The Case for the UK*, Dundee: Dundee Fabian Society.

Drucker, H. (1978), *Breakaway: The Scottish Labour Party*, Edinburgh: EUSPB.

Drucker, H. (1979), *Doctrine and Ethos in the Labour Party*, London: HarperCollins.

Drucker, H. (ed.) (1982), *John P. Mackintosh on Scotland*, London: Longman.

Drucker, H. & G. Brown (1980), *The Politics of Nationalism and Devolution*, London: Longman.

Drucker, H. M. & M. G. Clarke (eds) (1977), *Scottish Government Yearbook 1978*, Edinburgh: Paul Harris.

Drucker, H. M. & N. L. Drucker (eds) (1978), *Scottish Government Yearbook 1979*, Edinburgh: Paul Harris.

Drucker, H. M. & N. L. Drucker (eds) (1979), *Scottish Government Yearbook 1980*, Edinburgh: Paul Harris.

Drucker, H. M. & N. L. Drucker (eds) (1980), *Scottish Government Yearbook 1981*, Edinburgh: Paul Harris.

Drucker, H. M. & N. L. Drucker (eds) (1981), *Scottish Government Yearbook 1982*.

Dyer, M. (1996), *Capable Citizens and Improvident Democrats: The Scottish Electoral System, 1884–1929*, Aberdeen: Scottish Cultural Press.

Eadie, A., H. Ewing, J. Robertson & J. Sillars (1974), *Scottish Labour and Devolution: A Discussion Paper*, Ayr: Ayr Labour Party.

Edwards, O. Dudley (ed.) (1989), *A Claim of Right for Scotland*, Edinburgh: Polygon.

Elder, M. (ed.) (2000), *Donald Dewar: A Book of Tribute*, Edinburgh: HMSO.

Ewan, E., S. Innes & S. Reynolds (2007), *The Biographical Dictionary of Scottish Women: From the Earliest Times to 2004*, Edinburgh: Edinburgh University Press.

Ferguson, R. (1983), *Geoff: The Life of Geoffrey M. Shaw*, Gartocharn: Famedram.

Ferguson, W. (1978), *Scotland: 1689 to the Present*, Edinburgh: Oliver and Boyd.

Findlay, N. (2023), *Hope and Despair: Lifting the Lid on the Murky World of Scottish Politics*, Edinburgh: Luath.

Findlay, N. with J. Holmes (2017), *Socialism and Hope: A Journey Through Turbulent Times*, Edinburgh: Luath.
Finlay, R. (1994), *Independent and Free: Scottish Politics and the Origins of the Scottish National Party, 1918–1945*, Edinburgh: John Donald.
Finlay, R. (2004), *Modern Scotland, 1914–2000*, London: Profile.
Fraser, W. H. (2000), *Scottish Popular Politics From Radicalism to Labour*, Edinburgh: Polygon.
Fyfe, M. (ed.) (2014), *Women Saying NO: Making a Positive Case Against Independence*, Edinburgh: Luath.
Fyfe, M. (2020), *Singing in the Streets: A Glasgow Memoir*, Edinburgh: Luath.
Galbraith, R. (2018), *Without Quarter: A Biography of Tom Johnston*, Edinburgh: Birlinn.
Glen, D. (ed.) (1971), *Whither Scotland? A Prejudiced Look at the Future of a Nation*, London: Victor Gollancz.
Gordon, E. (1991), *Women and the Labour Movement in Scotland, 1850–1914*, Oxford: Clarendon Press.
Grigg, J. (1985), *Lloyd George: From Peace to War, 1912–1916*, London: Methuen.
Gunnin, G. C. (1987), *John Wheatley, Catholic Socialism, and Irish Labour in the West of Scotland, 1906–1924*, USA: Routledge.
Hamilton, W. (1975), *My Queen and I*, London: Quartet.
Hargrave, A. (1969), *Scotland: The Third Choice*, London: Fabian Society.
Harris, T. (2018), *Ten Years in the Death of the Labour Party*, London: Biteback.
Harvie, C. (1999), *Travelling Scot*, Glendaruel: Argyll Publishing.
Harvie, C. (2016), *No Gods and Precious Few Heroes: Scotland, 1900–2015* (Fourth Edition), Edinburgh: Edinburgh University Press.
Hassan, G. (1999), *Redesigning the State: The New Scotland*, London: Fabian Society.
Hassan, G. (ed.) (2004), *The Scottish Labour Party: History, Institutions and Ideas*, Edinburgh: Edinburgh University Press.
Hassan, G. (ed.) (2009), *The Modern SNP: From Protest to Power*, Edinburgh: Edinburgh University Press.
Hassan, G. & E. Shaw (2012), *The Strange Death of Labour Scotland*, Edinburgh: Edinburgh University Press.
Hassan, G. & C. Warhurst (eds) (1999), *A Different Future: A Modernisers' Guide to Scotland*, Glasgow: Big Issue.

Hassan, G. & C. Warhurst (eds) (2002), *Anatomy of the New Scotland: Power, Influence and Change*, Edinburgh: Mainstream.

Hassan, G. & C. Warhurst (eds) (2012), *Tomorrow's Scotland*, London: Lawrence and Wishart.

Hazell, R. (ed.) (2003), *The State of the Nations 2003: The Third Year of Devolution in the United Kingdom*, Exeter: Imprint Academic.

Heald, D. (1976), *Making Devolution Work*, London: Fabian Society.

Henderson, A., R. Johns, J. M. Larner & C. J. Carman (2022), *The Referendum that Changed a Nation: Scottish Voting Behaviour, 2014–2019*, London: Palgrave Macmillan.

Hickson, K. (ed.) (2022), *Neil Kinnock: Saving the Labour Party?*, London: Routledge.

Holford, J. (1988), *Reshaping Labour: Organisation, Work and Politics – Edinburgh in the Great War and After*, London: Croom Helm.

Howell, D. (1986), *A Lost Left: Three Studies in Socialism and Nationalism*, Manchester: Manchester University Press.

Hughes, E. (1956), *Keir Hardie*, London: George Allen and Unwin.

Hutchison, I. G. C. (1986), *A Political History of Scotland, 1832–1924: Parties, Elections and Issues*, Edinburgh: John Donald.

Hutchison, I. G. C. (2000), *Scottish Politics in the Twentieth Century*, Basingstoke: Palgrave.

Independent Labour Party (1893), *Report of the First General Conference*, Glasgow: Labour Literature Society.

Johns, R., D. Denver, J. Mitchell & C. Pattie (2010), *Voting for a Scottish Government: The Scottish Parliament Election of 2007*, Manchester: Manchester University Press.

Johnston, T. (1934), *The Financiers and the Nation*, London: Methuen.

Johnston, T. (1952), *Memories*, London: Collins.

Kaufman, G. (ed.) (1983), *Renewal: Labour's Britain in the 1980s*, London: Penguin.

Keating, M. (1988), *State and Regional Nationalism: Territorial Politics and the European State*, Hemel Hempstead: Harvester Wheatsheaf.

Keating, M. (2005), *The Government of Scotland: Public Policy Making after Devolution* (Second Edition), Edinburgh: Edinburgh University Press.

Keating, M. (ed.) (2020), *The Oxford Handbook of Scottish Politics*, Oxford: Oxford University Press.

Keating, M. & D. Bleiman (1979), *Labour and Scottish Nationalism*, London: Macmillan.

Keating, M. & M. Harvey (2014), *Small Nations in a Big World: What Scotland Can Learn*, Edinburgh: Luath.
Keating, M., R. Levy, J. Geekie & J. Brand (1989), *Labour Elites in Glasgow*, Glasgow: University of Strathclyde.
Kellas, J. G. (1968), *Modern Scotland: The Nation Since 1870*, London: Pall Mall Press.
Kemp, A. (1993), *The Hollow Drum: Scotland Since the War*, Edinburgh: Mainstream.
Kenefick, W. (2007), *Red Scotland! The Rise and Fall of the Radical Left, c. 1872 to 1932*, Edinburgh: Edinburgh University Press.
Kirkwood, D. (1935), *My Life of Revolt*, London: George G. Harrap and Co.
Knox, W. (ed.) (1984), *Scottish Labour Leaders, 1918–39: A Biographical Dictionary*, Edinburgh: Mainstream.
Labour Party (1937), *Central Scotland: Report of the Labour Party's Commission of Enquiry into the Distressed Areas*, London: Labour Party.
Labour Party (1946), *Scottish Local Government Handbook*, London: Labour Party and Glasgow: Scottish Co-operative Wholesale Society.
Labour Party (1958), *Let Scotland Prosper: Labour Plans for Scotland's Progress*, London: Labour Party.
Labour Party (1963), *Signposts for Scotland*, London: Labour Party.
Labour Party (1978), 'Devolution: The Labour Party Position', Rowntree Devolution Conference.
Labour Party (1994), *Report '94*, Glasgow: Labour Scotland.
Labour Party (2022), *A New Britain: Renewing our Democracy and Rebuilding our Economy – Report of the Commission on the UK's Future*, Newcastle: Labour Party.
Labour Party Scottish Council (1923), *Report of the Eighth Annual Conference*, Glasgow: SCLP.
Labour Party Scottish Council (1926), *Report of the Eleventh Annual Conference*, Glasgow: SCLP.
Labour Party Scottish Council (1948), *Report of the Executive Committee to the Annual Conference*, Glasgow: SCLP.
Labour Party Scottish Council (1953), *Programme for the Highlands and Islands*, Glasgow: SCLP.
Labour Party Scottish Council (1956), *Report of the Executive Committee to the 41st Annual Conference*, Glasgow: SCLP.
Labour Party Scottish Council (1957), *Report of the Executive Committee to the 42nd Annual Conference*, Glasgow: SCLP.

Labour Party Scottish Council (1958), *Report of the Executive Committee to the 43rd Annual Conference*, Glasgow: SCLP.
Labour Party Scottish Council (1961), *Report of the Executive Committee to the 46th Annual Conference*, Glasgow: SCLP.
Labour Party Scottish Council (1964), *Report of the Executive Committee to the 49th Annual Conference*, Glasgow: SCLP.
Labour Party Scottish Council (1965), *Report of the Executive Committee to the 50th Annual Conference*, Glasgow: SCLP.
Labour Party Scottish Council (1967), *Report of the Executive Committee to the 52nd Annual Conference*, Glasgow: SCLP.
Labour Party Scottish Council (1968), *Report of the Executive Committee to the 53rd Annual Conference*, Glasgow: SCLP.
Labour Party Scottish Council (1970), *Report of the Executive Committee to the 55th Annual Conference*, Glasgow: SCLP.
Labour Party Scottish Council (1974), *59th Annual Conference, Ayr 1974*, Glasgow: SCLP.
Labour Party Scottish Council (1978), *Labour's Scottish Assembly: Our Case*, Glasgow: SCLP.
Labour Scotland (1990), *The Property Tax: Overall a Fairer Tax for Scotland*, Glasgow: SCLP.
Lansman, J. & A. Meale (eds) (1983), *Beyond Thatcher: The Real Alternative*, London: Junction Books.
Laws, D. (2016), *Coalition: The Inside Story of the Conservative-Liberal Democrat Coalition Government*, London: Biteback.
Linklater, M. & R. Denniston (eds) (1993), *Anatomy of Scotland*, Edinburgh: Chambers.
Lowe, D. (1919), *Souvenirs of Scottish Labour*, Glasgow: W. and R. Holmes.
Lyman, R. W. (1957), *The First Labour Government*, London: Chapman and Hall.
Lynch, M. (ed.) (1993), *Scotland, 1850–1979: Society, Politics and the Union*, London: The Historical Association.
MacCallum, R. B. & A. Readman (1947), *The British General Election of 1945*, Oxford: Oxford University Press.
McConnell, A. (2004), *Scottish Local Government*, Edinburgh: Edinburgh University Press.
MacCormick, N. (ed.) (1970), *The Scottish Debate: Essays on Scottish Nationalism*, Oxford: Oxford University Press.
McCrone, D. (ed.) (1982), *Scottish Government Yearbook 1983*, Edinburgh: University of Edinburgh.

McCrone, D. (ed.) (1983), *Scottish Government Yearbook 1984*, Edinburgh: University of Edinburgh.
McCrone, D. (ed.) (1984), *Scottish Government Yearbook 1985*, Edinburgh: University of Edinburgh.
McCrone, D. (ed.) (1985), *Scottish Government Yearbook 1986*, Edinburgh: University of Edinburgh.
McCrone, D. (ed.) (1986), *Scottish Government Yearbook 1987*, Edinburgh: University of Edinburgh.
McCrone, D. & A. Brown (eds) (1987), *Scottish Government Yearbook 1988*, Edinburgh: University of Edinburgh.
Macdonald, C. M. M. (2001), *The Radical Thread: Political Change in Scotland, Paisley Politics, 1885–1924*, East Linton: Tuckwell Press.
Macdonald, C. M. M. (2009), *Whaur Extremes Meet: Scotland's Twentieth Century*, Edinburgh: John Donald.
MacDonald, J. R. (1921), *The History of the ILP: Notes for Lecturers and Class Leaders*, London: ILP Information Committee.
MacDougall, I. (ed.) (1965), *An Interim Bibliography of the Scottish Working-Class Movement, and of other Labour Records held in Scotland*, Edinburgh: Scottish Committee, Society for the Study of Labour History.
MacDougall, I. (ed.) (1978), *Essays in Scottish Labour History: A Tribute to W. H. Marwick*, Edinburgh: John Donald.
MacDougall, I. (ed.) (1978), *A Catalogue of some Labour Records in Scotland and some Scots Records outside Scotland*, Edinburgh: Scottish Labour History Society.
MacDougall, I. (1985), *Labour in Scotland: A Pictorial History from the Eighteenth Century to the Present*, Edinburgh: Mainstream.
McGovern, J. (1960), *Neither Fear Nor Favour*, London: Blandford Press.
Mackay, D. I. (ed.) (1979), *Scotland: The Framework for Change*, Edinburgh: Paul Harris.
McKibbin, R. (1974), *The Evolution of the Labour Party, 1910–1924*, Oxford: Clarendon Press.
McKinlay, A. & R. J. Morris (eds) (1991), *The ILP on Clydeside, 1893–1932: From Foundation to Disintegration*, Manchester: Manchester University Press.
Mackintosh, J. P. (1974), *A Parliament for Scotland*, Berwick and East Lothian Labour Party.
MacLaren, A. A. (ed.) (1976), *Social Class in Scotland: Past and Present*, Edinburgh: John Donald.

McLean, I. (1978), 'Labour Elites and Electorates in Glasgow', ESRC study 1007, University of Essex.

McLean, I. ([1983] 1999), *The Legend of Red Clydeside*, Edinburgh: John Donald.

McLean, I. & A. McMillan (2005), *State of the Union: Unionism and the Alternatives in the United Kingdom since 1707*, Oxford: Oxford University Press.

McLean, R. (1991), *Labour and Scottish Home Rule: Part 1: Mid Lanark to Majority Government, 1888–1945*, Whitburn: Scottish Labour Action.

McLean, R. (1991), *Labour and Scottish Home Rule: Part II: Unionist Complacency to Crisis Management, 1945–1988*, Whitburn: Scottish Labour Action.

McLeish, H. (2004), *Scotland First: Truth and Consequences*, Edinburgh: Mainstream.

McMillan, J. (1969), *Anatomy of Scotland*, London: Leslie Frewin.

MacNeill Weir, A. (1945), *Highland Plan: An Outline of Labour Policy for the Highlands*, Glasgow: Scottish Council Labour Party.

McPherson, A. & C. D. Raab (1988), *Governing Education: A Sociology of Policy Since 1945*, Edinburgh: Edinburgh University Press.

McSmith, A. (1994), *John Smith: A Life*, London: Cornerstone.

Maguire, P. & G. Pogrund (2025), *Get In: The Inside Story of Labour under Starmer*, London: Bodley Head.

Marr, A. (1992), *The Battle for Scotland*, London: Penguin.

Marwick, W. H. (1950), *Scottish Devolution: A Study to Further Discussion*, London: Fabian Society.

Marwick, W. H. (1967), *A Short History of Labour in Scotland*, Edinburgh: Chambers.

Maxwell, J. & O. Dudley Edwards (eds) (2014), *Why Not? Scotland, Labour and Independence*, Edinburgh: Luath.

Middlemas, K. (1965), *The Clydesiders: A Left Wing Struggle For Parliamentary Power*, London: Hutchinson.

Midwinter, A., M. Keating & J. Mitchell (1991), *Politics and Public Policy in Scotland*, Edinburgh: Edinburgh University Press.

Miller, W. L. (1981), *The End of British Politics?: Scots and English Political Behaviour in the Seventies*, Oxford: Clarendon Press.

Miller, W. L., A. Mae Timpson & M. Lessnoff (1996), *Political Culture in Contemporary Britain: People and Politicians, Principles and Practice*, Oxford: Clarendon Press.

Mitchell, J. (1990), *The Myth of Dependency*, Glasgow: Scottish Centre for Economic and Social Research.
Mitchell, J. (1996), *Strategies for Self-government: The Campaigns for a Scottish Parliament*, Edinburgh: Polygon.
Mitchell, J. (2014), *The Scottish Question*, Oxford: Oxford University Press.
Moran, M. (2017), *The End of British Politics?*, London: Palgrave Macmillan.
Morgan, K. O. (1985), *Labour in Power, 1945–1951*, Oxford: Oxford University Press.
Naughtie, J. (2001), *The Rivals: The Intimate Story of a Political Marriage*, London: Fourth Estate.
Paterson, L. (ed.) (1998), *A Diverse Assembly: The Debate on a Scottish Parliament*, Edinburgh: Edinburgh University Press.
Paterson, L. & D. McCrone (eds) (1991), *Scottish Government Yearbook 1992*, Edinburgh: University of Edinburgh.
Paton, J. (1936), *Left Turn! The Autobiography of John Paton*, London: Secker and Warburg.
Pentland, G. (2017), *The Autobiography of Arthur Woodburn (1890–1978): Living with History*, Woodbridge: Boydell and Brewer.
Perryman, M. (ed.) (1996), *The Blair Agenda*, London: Lawrence and Wishart.
Petrie, M. (2019), *Popular Politics and Political Culture in Urban Scotland, 1918–1939*, Edinburgh: Edinburgh University Press.
Pike, J. (2015), *Project Fear: How an Unlikely Alliance Left a Kingdom United but a Country Divided*, London: Biteback.
Pogrund, G. & P. Maguire (2020), *Left Out: The Inside Story of Labour Under Corbyn*, London: Bodley Head.
Radice, G. (2004), *Diaries: From Political Disaster to Election Triumph*, London: Weidenfeld and Nicolson.
Rawnsley, A. (2000), *Servants of the People: The Inside Story of New Labour*, London: Penguin.
Rentoul, J. (2013), *Tony Blair: Prime Minister*, London: Faber and Faber.
Ritchie, M. (2000), *Scotland Reclaimed: The Inside Story of Scotland's First Democratic Parliamentary Election*, Edinburgh: Saltire Society.
Ross, T. & T. McTague (2017), *Betting the House: The Inside Story of the 2017 Election*, London: Biteback.
Ross, T. & R. Wearmouth (2024), *Landslide: The Inside Story of the 2024 Election*, London: Biteback.

Routledge, P. (1998), *Gordon Brown: The Biography*, London: Pocket Books.
Sarwar, M. & B. Wylie (2016), *My Remarkable Journey: The Autobiography of Britain's First Muslim MP*, Edinburgh: Birlinn.
Schlesinger, P., D. Miller & W. Dinan (2001), *Open Scotland? Journalists, Spin Doctors and Lobbyists*, Edinburgh: Polygon.
Scottish Council of the Labour Party (1940), *Report of the Executive Committee presented to the Annual 25th Conference*, Glasgow: SCLP.
Scottish Council of the Labour Party (1958), *Special Report on Scottish Government of the Executive Committee to the Special Conference*, Glasgow: SCLP.
Scottish Council of the Labour Party (1965), *Golden Jubilee, 1915–1965: Labour Party Scottish Council*, Glasgow: SCLP.
Scottish Council of the Labour Party (1971), *Commission on the Constitution*, Glasgow: SCLP.
Scottish Council of the Labour Party (1976), *Labour's Analysis of the Economics of Separation*, Glasgow: SCLP.
Scottish Council of the Labour Party (1976), *Can Scotland Go it Alone? The Menace of Separation: A Labour Party Analysis*, Glasgow: SCLP.
Scottish Council of the Labour Party (1977), *An Industrial Strategy for Scotland*, Glasgow: Scottish Council of the Labour Party.
Scottish Council of the Labour Party (1993), *Report of the Monklands Committee*, Glasgow: SCLP.
Scottish Fabians (2021), *A Voice for the Future: How Labour Can Shape the Next 20 Years of Devolution*, London: Fabian Society.
Scottish Labour Action (1989), *Proposals for Scottish Democracy: A Scottish Labour Action Discussion Document*, Edinburgh: SLA.
Scottish Labour Action (1989), *Real Power for Scotland: Scottish Labour Action's Response to the Constitutional Convention's Consultative Document – 'A Parliament for Scotland'*, Whitburn: SLA.
Scottish Labour Party (1997), *Referendum 97*, Glasgow: SLP.
Scottish Labour Party (1998), *A Modern Scottish Labour Party: Rule Changes Proposed by the Scottish Executive Committee*, Glasgow: SLP.
Scottish Labour Party (2001), *Forward not Back*, Glasgow: SLP.
Scottish Labour Party (2010), *Report of the Scottish Policy Forum*, Glasgow: SLP.

Scottish Labour Party (2011), *Review of the Labour Party in Scotland*, Glasgow: SLP.
Scottish Labour Party (2014). *Powers for a Purpose – Strengthening Accountability and Empowering People*, Glasgow: SLP.
Scottish Labour Party (2018), *Real Change: Conference Guide and Annual Report*, Glasgow: SLP.
Sheppard, T. (1997), *A New Scottish Labour Party*, Scottish Labour Action.
Sheridan, D. (ed.) (1986), *Among You Taking Notes: The Wartime Diary of Naomi Mitchison, 1939–1945*, Oxford: Oxford University Press.
Shipman, T. (2016), *All Out War: The Full Story of Brexit*, London: William Collins.
Sillars, J. & A. Eadie (1968), *Don't Butcher Scotland's Future: The Case Against the S.N.P. Together with an Argument for Reform At All Levels of Government*, Ayr: Ayr Labour Party.
Sillars, J. (1986), *The Case for Optimism*, Edinburgh: Polygon.
Sillars, J. (2021), *A Difference of Opinion: My Political Journey*, Edinburgh: Birlinn.
Smout, T. C. (1986), *A Century of the Scottish People, 1830–1950*, London: Collins.
Smyth, J. J. (2000), *Labour in Glasgow, 1896–1936: Socialism, Suffrage, Sectarianism*, Edinburgh: John Donald.
Stenhouse, D. (2004), *How the Scots Took Over London*, Edinburgh: Mainstream.
Stewart, W. (1925), *J. Keir Hardie*, London: Cassell.
Stott, G. (1998), *Q.C.'s Diary, 1954–1960*, Edinburgh: Mercat Press.
Stott, G. (1991), *Lord Advocate's Diary, 1961–1966*, Aberdeen: Aberdeen University Press.
Stuart, C. (ed.) (1975), *The Reith Diaries*, London: HarperCollins.
Stuart, M. (2005), *John Smith: A Life*, London: Politico's.
Tanner, D., P. Thane & N. Tiratsoo (eds) (2000), *Labour's First Century*, Cambridge: Cambridge University Press.
Taylor, B. (1999), *The Scottish Parliament*, Edinburgh: Edinburgh University Press.
Teasdale, G. (ed.) (2016), *Remembering Sam: The Life and Times of Sam Galbraith*, Edinburgh: Birlinn.
Torrance, D. (2006), *The Scottish Secretaries*, Edinburgh: Birlinn.
Torrance, D. (2009), *'We in Scotland': Thatcherism in a Cold Climate*, Edinburgh: Birlinn.
Torrance, D. (2010), *Salmond: Against the Odds*, Edinburgh: Birlinn.

Torrance, D. (ed.) (2011), *Great Scottish Speeches*, Edinburgh: Luath.
Torrance, D. (ed.) (2013), *Great Scottish Speeches: Volume II*, Edinburgh: Luath.
Torrance, D. (2015), *Salmond: Against the Odds* (Third Edition), Edinburgh: Birlinn.
Torrance, D. (2020), *'Standing Up for Scotland': Nationalist Unionism and Scottish Party Politics, 1884–2014*, Edinburgh: Edinburgh University Press.
Torrance, D. (2022), *A History of the Scottish Liberals and Liberal Democrats*, Edinburgh: Edinburgh University Press.
Torrance, D. (2024), *The Wild Men: The Remarkable Story of Britain's First Labour Government*, London: Bloomsbury Continuum.
Torrance, D. (2024), *A History of the Scottish Conservative and Unionist Parties*, Edinburgh: Edinburgh University Press.
Trench, A. (ed.) (2001), *The State of the Nations 2001: The Second Year of Devolution in the United Kingdom*, Exeter: Imprint Academic.
Walker, G. (1988), *Thomas Johnston*, Manchester: Manchester University Press.
Watson, I. (2015), *Five Million Conversations: How Labour lost an Election and Rediscovered its Roots*, Edinburgh: Luath.
Watson, M. (2001), *Year Zero: An Inside View of the Scottish Parliament*, Edinburgh: Polygon.
Wheatley, Lord (1987), *One Man's Judgment: An Autobiography*, London: Butterworths.
Wilson, H. (1979), *Final Term: The Labour Government, 1974–1976*, London: Weidenfeld and Nicolson.
Winter, B. (2023), *The ILP: Past and Present, Part 1*, Leeds: Independent Labour Publications Trust.
Worley, M. (ed.) (2017), *Labour's Grass Roots: Essays on the Activities of Local Labour Parties and Members, 1918–45*, London: Routledge.
Young, D. (1949), *Labour Record on Scotland, 1945–1949*, Glasgow: Scottish Secretariat.
Young, D. (1971), *Scotland*, London: Cassell.

JOURNAL ARTICLES

Anonymous (1981), 'John Smith: Portrait of a devolutionist', *Bulletin of Scottish Politics* 2, 44–54.
Bochel, J. & D. Denver (1992), 'The 1992 general election in Scotland', *Scottish Affairs* 1, 14–26.

Bort, E. (2015), 'The annals of the parish: Referendum year 2014', *Scottish Affairs* 24:1, 1–21.
Bort, E. (2017), 'The annals of the parish: 2015–2016. From referendum to referendum to ... referendum?', *Scottish Affairs* 26:1, 69–102.
Breitenbach, E. (2016), 'For workers' rights and self-determination? The Scottish labour movement and the British empire from the 1920s to the 1960s', *Scottish Labour History* 51, 113–33.
Cairney, C. (2016), 'The Scottish Parliament election 2016: Another momentous event but dull campaign', *Scottish Affairs* 25:3, 277–93.
Cameron, E. A. (2024), 'The Bulletin, "Londonisation" and Scottish politics in the 1940s and 1950s', *Scottish Historical Review* 1:261, 156–77.
Carrigan, D. (2016), 'Patrick Dollan and the Glasgow labour movement: A reappraisal', *Scottish Labour History* 51, 134–53.
Clark, J. (1993), 'An autonomous Scottish Labour Party', *Scottish Affairs* 2, 124–6.
Denver, D. (2003), 'A "wake up!" call to the parties? The results of the Scottish Parliament elections 2003', *Scottish Affairs* 44, 31–53.
Denver, D. & I. MacAllister (1999), 'The Scottish Parliament elections 1999: An analysis of the results', *Scottish Affairs* 28, 10–31.
Denver, D. & I. MacAllister (2000), 'The 1999 European Parliament election in Scotland', *Scottish Affairs* 30, 130–40.
Denver, D. & I. MacAllister (2003), 'Constituency campaigning in Scotland at the 2001 general election', *Scottish Affairs* 42, 127–43.
Denver, D., H. Bochel & M. Steven (2012), 'Mixed messages for (some) parties: The Scottish council elections of 2012', *Scottish Affairs* 80, 1–19.
Finlay, R. & C. Wood (2013), 'A house divided? The impact of the First World War on the Scottish Liberals and Labour', *History Scotland*, May/June 2013.
Gallagher, T. (2010), 'Scottish Catholics and the British left, 1918–1939', *Innes Review* 34:1, 17–42.
Geekie, J. & R. Levy (1989), 'Devolution and the tartanisation of the Labour Party', *Parliamentary Affairs* 42:3, 399–411.
Harvie, C. (1981), 'Labour and Scottish government: The age of Tom Johnston', *Bulletin of Scottish Politics* 2, 1–20.
Harvie, C. (1983), 'Labour in Scotland during the Second World War', *Historical Journal* 26:4, 921–44.
Hassan, G. (2002), 'A case study of Scottish Labour: Devolution and the politics of multi-level governance', *Political Quarterly* 73:2, 144–57.

Henderson, A., R. Johns, J. Larner & C. Carman (2020), 'Scottish Labour as a case study in party failure: Evidence from the 2019 UK general election in Scotland', *Scottish Affairs* 29:2, 127–40.

Hopkin, J. & J. Bradbury (2006), 'British statewide parties and multilevel politics', *Publius: The Journal of Federalism* 36:1, 135–52.

Hughes, A. (2013), '"A clear understanding of our duty": Labour women in rural Scotland, 1919–1939', *Scottish Labour History* 48, 136–57.

Jones, P. (1997), 'Labour's referendum plan: Sell-out or act of faith?', *Scottish Affairs* 18, 1–17.

Jones, P. (1999), 'The 1999 Scottish Parliament elections: From anti-Tory to anti-Nationalist politics', *Scottish Affairs* 28, 1–9.

Jones, P. (2007), 'The smooth wooing: The SNP's victory in the 2007 Scottish Parliament elections', *Scottish Affairs* 60, 6–21.

Keating, M. (1983), 'Labour and Scottish Nationalism: An update', *Cencrastus* 12, 29–31.

Keating, M. (2005), 'Policy convergence and divergence in Scotland under devolution', *Regional Studies* 39:4, 453–63.

Keating, M. (2015), 'The European dimension to Scottish constitutional change', *Political Quarterly* 86:2, 201–8.

Keating, M., L. Stevenson, P. Cairney & K. Taylor (2003), 'Does devolution make a difference? Legislative output and policy divergence in Scotland', Stirling: University of Stirling (online).

Kellas, J. G. (1964), 'The Mid-Lanark by-election (1888) and the Scottish Labour Party (1888–1894)', *Parliamentary Affairs* XVIII:3, 321–4.

Kenny, M. & F. Mackay (2011), 'In the balance: Women and the 2011 Scottish Parliament elections', *Scottish Affairs* 76, 75–85.

Knox, W. W. (1988), 'Religion and the Scottish Labour movement, c. 1900–39', *Journal of Contemporary History* 23:4, 609–30.

Knox, W. W. (2006), 'Review: The Scottish Labour Party: History, institutions and ideas', *Scottish Historical Review* 85:1, 172–4.

Knox, W. W. & A. Mackinlay (1995), 'The re-making of Scottish Labour in the 1930s', *Twentieth Century British History* 6:2, 174–93.

Laffin, M., E. Shaw & G. Taylor (2007), 'The new subnational politics of the British Labour Party', *Party Politics* 13:1, 88–108.

Levitt, I. (1998), 'Britain, the Scottish Covenant movement and devolution, 1946–50', *Scottish Affairs* 22, 37–47.

Lynch, P. (1994), 'The 1994 European elections in Scotland: Campaigns and strategies', *Scottish Affairs* 9, 24–44.

Lynch, P. (1996), 'The Scottish Constitutional Convention, 1992–5', *Scottish Affairs* 15, 1–16.

Macdonald, C. M. M. (2011), 'The radical thread – Liberalism and the rise of Labour in Scotland, 1886–1924', *Mémoire(s), identité(s), marginalité(s) dans le monde occidental contemporain* 7 (online).

McEwen, N. (2005), 'Adapting to multi-level politics: The political parties and the general election in Scotland', *Scottish Affairs* 53, 119–35.

McInnes, A. (2019), 'Deindustrialisation and Gordon Brown's approach to devolution in Scotland', *Scottish Labour History* 54, 125–53.

McLean, R. (2001), 'Gallant crusader or cautious persuader? Donald Dewar's role in securing Scotland's parliament', *Scottish Affairs* 34, 1–10.

McLeish, H. (1999), 'The negotiation diaries: Diary of Scottish Labour Party negotiator: Henry McLeish MSP', *Scottish Affairs* 28, 56–61.

McVicar, M., G. Jordan & G. Boyne (1994), 'Ships in the night: Scottish political parties and local government reform', *Scottish Affairs* 9, 80–96.

Macwhirter, I. (1993), 'The road to nowhere: Scotland in Westminster, parliamentary session 1992/3', *Scottish Affairs* 4, 111–21.

Macwhirter, I. (1994), 'The year at Westminster: Parliamentary session 1993–1994', *Scottish Affairs* 8, 109–24.

Marwick, A. (1964), 'James Maxton: His place in Scottish Labour history', *Scottish Historical Review* XLIII:135, 25–43.

Marwick, W. H. (1973), 'James Barr: Modern Covenanter', *Scottish Journal of Science* 1:3, 183–98.

Mooney, G. & L. Poole (2004), '"A land of milk and honey"? Social policy in Scotland after devolution', *Critical Social Policy* 24:4, 458–83.

Nairn, T. (1968), 'The three dreams of Scottish Nationalism', *New Left Review* I/49.

Philippou, P. S. (2018), '"The fruits of long years of propaganda and unremitting effort": Labour's "breakthrough" in Scotland in 1922', *Scottish Labour History* 53, 142–84.

Phillips, J., V. Wright & J. Tomlinson (2019), 'Deindustrialization, the Linwood car plant and Scotland's political divergence from England in the 1960s and 1970s', *Twentieth-Century British History* 30:3, 399–423.

Riddell, N. (1997), 'The Catholic Church and the Labour Party, 1918–1931', *Twentieth Century British History* 8:2, 165–93.

Roddin, E. (2004), 'Has the Labour Party or the Liberal Democrats proved more successful in the Partnership for Scotland Coalition, 1999–2003? An initial assessment', *Scottish Affairs* 48, 24–49.

Rosie, M. & E. Hepburn (2015), '"The Essence of the Union ...": Unionism, Nationalism and identity on these disconnected islands', *Scottish Affairs* 24:2, 141–62.

Ross, W. (1978), 'Approaching the archangelic?', in H. M. Drucker & M. G. Clarke (eds), *The Scottish Government Yearbook 1978*, Edinburgh: Paul Harris, 1–20.

Shaw, E. (2003), 'Paper presented to the Annual Conference of the Elections, Public Opinion and Party Group of the Political Studies Association', Cardiff: University of Cardiff (online).

Sherwood, M. (2007), 'Krishna Menon, Parliamentary Labour Party candidate for Dundee, 1939–1940', *Scottish Labour History* 42, 29–48.

Simpkins, F. (2013), 'The 2011 Scottish Labour campaign: Changing tactics?', *Numéros* 5 (online).

Smyth, J. J. (2003), 'Resisting Labour: Unionists, liberals, and moderates in Glasgow between the wars', *Historical Journal* 46:2, 375–401.

Swan, C. Brown (2022), '"We're socialists not nationalists": British Labour and the national question(s)', *Nations and Nationalism* 29:2, 467–81.

Torrance, D. (2011), 'A tale of two elections', *Scottish Affairs* 76, 10–32.

Torrance, D. (2012), 'Better Together or Yes Scotland? Year one in the battle of Britain', *Scottish Affairs* 80, 69–87.

Torrance, D. (2013), 'Referendum debate: Year two', *Scottish Affairs* 84, 17–40.

Torrance, D. (2017), 'Scotland's progressive dilemma', *Political Quarterly* 88:1, 52–9.

Walker, G. & J. Greer (2019), 'Religion, Labour, and national questions: The general election of 1924 in Belfast and Lanarkshire', *Labour History Review* 84:3, 217–39.

UNPUBLISHED THESES

Brown, G. (1981), 'The Labour Party and Political Change in Scotland, 1918–1929: The Politics of Five Elections', Edinburgh: University of Edinburgh, PhD thesis.

Keating, M. (1975), 'The Role of the Scottish MP', Glasgow: Glasgow College of Technology, PhD thesis.
McFadyen, A. (2011), 'Agents and Institutions: Donald Dewar and the Politics of Devolution', Edinburgh: University of Edinburgh, PhD thesis.
Purves, A. (1978), 'Scottish Labour and British Entry: Labour Movement Attitudes to the European Community at Scottish and UK levels, 1960–1977', Edinburgh: University of Edinburgh, MPhil thesis.
Wood, I. S. (1981), 'Labour Politics in Glasgow', Edinburgh: Napier College.

BROADCASTS

The Dewar Years (2001), Glasgow: Scottish Television.
Rhodri Morgan – The Last Interview (2017), ITV Wales.

Index

Abse, Leo, 85, 107
Acheson, Dean, 277
Adams, Allan, 136
Adams, Irene, 184, 202, 228n
Adamson, Jennie, 45
Adamson, William, 16, 23, 36, 37, 39, 41, 45, 48n, 58, 63
Aitchison, Craigie, 42
Alexander, Douglas, 184, 196, 203, 221–2, 239, 242–3, 247, 248, 257, 266
Alexander, Wendy, 4, 155, 159, 196, 210, 216, 217, 219, 220, 221, 225–6, 266, 275
Allen, Clifford, 32
Allison, Jimmy, 79, 85, 94, 109, 133, 135, 140–1, 145, 153, 155, 159–60
Allison, Peter, 93
Anderson, William, 19
Anson, J. T., 60
Ascherson, Neal, 103
Ashdown, Paddy, 188, 206, 209, 221
Attlee, Clement, 46, 47–8, 62, 64, 67, 240

Baillie, Jackie, 257
Baird, Andrew, 217

Baldwin, Oliver, 45
Baldwin, Stanley, 37, 38, 45
Balls, Ed, 242
Barbour, Mary, 19, 28
Barnes, George, 14, 16, 17, 24, 26–7
Barr, Revd James, 33, 37–8, 39, 50n, 60
Baur, Chris, 141
Baxter, William, 85
Bealey, Frank, 2, 12, 80, 269
Begg, Anne, 184
Begg, David, 196
Benn, Tony, 94, 135, 165
Benn, William Wedgwood, 40
Bennie, Lynn, 4, 168
Better Together, 241, 245
Bevan, Nye, 40, 240
Bevin, Ernest, 61
Black, Mhairi, 248
Blair, Tony, 164, 182, 183–4, 185–90, 191, 192, 193–4, 197–8, 201, 202, 204, 209, 211, 213, 215, 216, 218, 220, 221, 222, 223, 224, 268, 269
Bleiman, David, 3, 36, 80
Bochel, J. M., 111, 114, 134, 137, 148, 158, 162

Bolton, George, 143
Boyack, Jim, 207
Boyack, Sarah, 206–7, 239
Bradbury, Jonathan, 219
Brand, Jack, 168
Breitenbach, Esther, 27–8
Brennan, Tommy, 274
Brexit, 250–1
Brown, Bob, 103, 126n
Brown, Ernest, 40, 58
Brown, Gordon, 40, 88, 93, 100–1, 107, 117, 118, 136, 140, 142, 143, 160, 183, 184, 186, 187, 194, 198, 201, 203, 204, 206, 207, 211–12, 215, 216, 222, 223, 224, 225, 226, 242, 244, 248, 250, 254, 255, 266, 267–8, 269, 272, 273, 276
Brown, Hugh, 96, 132
Brown, James, 27, 36, 46
Brown, Kenneth D., 3
Brown, Ron, 136, 150–1, 152, 162
Brown Swan, Coree, 244
Bryan, Pauline, 242
Buchan, Janey, 100, 166
Buchan, Norman, 91, 102, 115, 116, 127n, 135, 142, 273–4
Buchanan, George, 35, 36
Buchanan-Smith, Alick, 116
Budge, Ian, 83
Burnham, Andy, 256
Burns, John, 10, 97

Cable, Vincent, 101
Cairns, David, 215
Callaghan, James, 105, 106, 107, 114, 115, 118–19, 127n, 134, 274
Calman Commission, 226, 227
Cameron, David, 225, 245, 247
Cameron, Hollie, 255

Campaign for a Scottish Assembly (CSA), 139, 147, 155–6, 207
Campaign for Socialism, 183, 186, 213, 261n
Campbell, Alastair, 187, 188, 189, 191, 197, 204, 211–12, 229n
Campbell, Menzies, 213, 224
Campbell, Sam, 146
Campbell, Stuart, 253
Canavan, Dennis, 133, 139, 142, 149, 151–2, 184, 192, 199, 205
Cantley, Catherine, 108
Carmichael, James, 62–3
Carrigan, Dan, 217
Carson, George, 12, 14
The Case for Optimism, 154
Castle, Barbara, 97
Catholic Socialist Society, 16
Catto, Lord, 68
Chalmers, Philip, 203, 208
Champion, H. H., 10, 12
Chasing the Tartan Tiger, 220
Chisholm, Malcolm, 162–3, 195, 199, 217, 229n
Chisholm Robertson, R., 10, 12
Christie, Campbell, 143, 156, 274
Church of Scotland, 17, 28, 36, 67, 91–2, 99, 119, 157, 221
Churchill, Winston, 66
Claim of Right, 156–7
Clark, G. B., 11
Clark, Katy, 74n
Clarke, Charles, 216
Clarke, Tom, 133, 164, 166, 167, 168, 182, 247
Clyde Workers Committee, 24, 28
Clynes, J. R., 30
Co-operative Party, 26, 45–6, 49n, 86, 116, 125n, 144, 147, 241

Common Market, 99–100, 105
Common Wealth Party, 60
Communist Party of Great
 Britain, 30, 38, 39, 45, 119,
 143, 210
Connarty, Mike, 199
Conroy, Harry, 129n, 140
Cook, Robin, 101, 115, 116,
 118, 132, 142, 148, 151,
 152, 153, 161, 164, 187,
 203
Corbyn, Jeremy, 242, 249, 251,
 252, 253, 254
Craig, Carol, 211
Craig, Gordon, 140
Crawfurd, Helen, 19
Crick, Bernard, 161
Crick, Michael, 167
Crosland, Tony, 71, 92, 97, 124n
Crossman, Richard, 84, 89, 123n
Crowther-Hunt, Lord, 95, 97
Cullen, Alice, 70
Cunningham, George, 115, 133,
 189
Cunningham, Roseanna, 184
Cunninghame-Graham, R. B., 9,
 11
Curran, Margaret, 189
Curtice, John, 222, 257

Dalgety, Susan, 196
Daly, Lawrence, 140
Dalyell, Tam, 81, 84, 87, 96,
 97, 107, 114–15, 118, 134,
 138, 177n, 197, 220, 243,
 269
Dangerfield, George, 264
Darling, Alistair, 58, 160, 195,
 211, 214, 242, 245
Darling, Sir William, 58
Davidson, David, 96
Davidson, Ian, 199, 212
Davidson, Julie, 137

Davidson, Lorraine, 4, 202
Davidson, Ruth, 249–50
Day, Cammy, 255
Deacon, Susan, 148, 149–50,
 156, 160, 199, 206, 217
Dell, Edmund, 127n
Dempster, Jim, 262n
Denver, David, 111, 114, 134,
 136, 137, 140, 148, 158,
 162, 206, 208
Dewar, Donald, 4, 5, 71, 79, 83,
 88–9, 90–1, 92, 93, 95, 96,
 107, 112, 119, 120, 124n,
 132, 133, 136, 143–4, 145,
 147–9, 150, 151, 156, 157,
 159, 160–1, 163, 164, 165,
 170, 171n, 182, 185, 187,
 195, 196, 197–8, 199, 201,
 204, 205, 206, 207, 209–11,
 212–13, 214, 217, 234n,
 243, 266, 270, 274
Diana, Princess of Wales, 197
Dixon, Lord, 196
Doig, Peter, 115
Dollan, Agnes, 10, 19, 28, 69
Dollan, Patrick, 10, 28, 29, 30,
 34, 37, 38–9, 43, 44–5,
 46–7, 63, 66
Donnachie, Ian, 42
Donnelly, Mike, 191, 217
Donoughue, Bernard, 97, 99,
 100, 102, 109
Don't Butcher Scotland's Future,
 89
Dorey, Peter, 35
Douglas, Dick, 89, 150, 151, 152,
 162
Douglas-Mann, Bruce, 115, 133
Drakeford, Mark, 262n
Drucker, H. M., 2, 4, 83–4, 88,
 94, 101, 120, 134, 139, 264
Drummond, Archie, 135
Dudley Edwards, Owen, 241

Dugdale, Kezia, 246, 249, 250, 251, 252, 253, 261n
Dyer, Michael, 37

Eadie, Alex, 89, 95
Eden, Sir Anthony, 71
Elder, Murray, 152–3, 155, 157, 159, 160, 161, 163, 164, 196, 199
elections
 1892, 11
 1895, 12–13
 1900, 14
 1906, 14–15
 1910, 16
 1918, 26–7
 1922, 29–31, 37, 272
 1923, 33, 62
 1924, 36–7, 40
 1929, 40
 1931, 42
 1935, 45
 1945, 61–2
 1950, 67, 68
 1951, 68
 1955, 69, 78
 1959, 78
 1964, 82
 1966, 83
 1970, 91–2
 February 1974, 94–5
 October 1974, 98–9
 1979, 119–20, 131
 1983, 140–1, 269
 1987, 147–8, 269
 1992, 162–3, 193
 1997, 193–5
 1999, 205–6
 2001, 215
 2003, 218–19
 2005, 220–1
 2007, 222–3
 2010, 226
 2011, 226–8, 238
 2015, 247–8, 264
 2016, 249–50
 2017, 251–2
 2019, 253–4
 2024, 256–7
 2026, 258
Elger, William, 43
Elliott, Walter, 58
Evans, Gwynfor, 87
Ewing, Harry, 95, 99, 101, 112, 188
Ewing, Winnie, 87, 91, 274

Falconer, Lord, 251
Farage, Nigel, 258
Ferguson, Aitken, 30
Ferguson, Patricia, 206
Findlay, Neil, 234n, 242, 243, 245, 246, 247, 248, 249, 253, 254, 255, 258–9n, 261n, 276
Finlay, Richard, 33, 219
Finnie, Ross, 206
Foot, Michael, 106, 112, 134, 135, 138, 142, 143
Forgan, Robert, 42
Forsyth, Michael, 159, 162, 188
Forward, 17, 24, 46, 48, 57, 66, 67, 70, 87, 217, 275
Fotheringham, Peter, 2
Foulkes, George, 98, 107, 134, 138, 139, 141–2, 161, 173n, 271
Fraser, Douglas, 199, 213
Fraser, Sir Hugh, 111
Fraser, Tom, 70, 72, 78, 80, 81, 87
Freeman, Jeane, 199
Fulton, Tom, 96
The Future of Socialism, 71
Fyfe, Maria, 71, 79, 103, 151, 228n, 243

Index

Gaitskell, Hugh, 71, 72, 79
Galbraith, Russell, 7
Galbraith, Sam, 149, 171n, 195, 199, 207
Gallacher, William, 45
Galloway, George, 135, 136, 150, 152, 163, 165, 212, 271
Garro-Jones, George, 57
Geddes, Alec, 30
Geekie, Jack, 139, 146, 154, 268
General Strike, 38, 40
Gillespie, Bob, 153–4
Gilmore, Sheila, 103
Glen, Marilyn, 186
Godman, Norman, 142
Gordon, Eleanor, 27–8
Gordon, James, 170
Gormill, Frank, 96
Graham, David, 23
Graham, Duncan, 27, 36
Graham, Tommy, 196, 231n
Graham, William, 27
Grant, Alexander, 36
Gray, Charles, 159, 162, 163
Gray, Iain, 226–7, 266
Greenwood, Arthur, 61
Grieve, Christopher, 272
Griffiths, Jim, 78
Griffiths, Nigel, 250

Hamilton, William, 76n, 85, 115, 122n, 136
Hardie, Agnes, 15, 27, 47, 50n
Hardie, George, 15, 39, 47
Hardie, Keir, 3–4, 8–12, 15, 17, 20n, 24, 87, 91, 185, 186, 240, 244, 268, 273, 274
Hardie, Nan, 46
Harman, Harriet, 250
Harris, Tom, 210, 243, 250, 268–9
Hart, Judith, 69, 85, 133, 134, 242

Harvey, Malcolm, 220
Harvie, Christopher, 8, 59, 61, 62
Hassan, Gerry, 3, 4–5, 7n, 92, 185, 193, 200, 203, 208, 216, 217, 224, 225, 264, 265, 266, 275, 276
Hattersley, Roy, 143, 160
Hayward, Ron, 109
Hazell, Robert, 217
Heald, David, 107–8, 108–9
Healey, Denis, 135, 143, 147
Heath, Edward, 92
Heffer, Eric, 105, 115
Henderson, Ailsa, 254
Henderson, Arthur, 15, 18, 24, 25, 32, 38, 39
Herbison, Margaret (Peggy), 65, 68, 70, 72, 79, 85, 91–2, 124n
Highland Land League, 26
Highland Panel, 83
Highlands and Islands Development Board, 83
Hogg, Norman, 163, 274
Hood, Jimmy, 165, 210
Hopkin, Jonathan, 219
Hughes, Robert, 115, 116, 132, 142, 165
Hughes, Emrys, 9, 46, 48, 67, 71, 76n, 85–6, 87, 123n
Hughes, Hector, 80
Hutcheon, Paul, 258
Hutchison, I. G. C., 14, 15, 17, 29, 31, 39, 68, 71, 94
Hutton, Sadie, 96

Independent Labour Party, 11–13, 14, 17–18, 25–6, 29, 30, 31–2, 33, 34, 35, 36, 37, 39, 40, 42–3, 45, 58, 63, 65, 67, 217, 265, 272, 275
Ingram, Adam, 157
International Marxist Group, 214

Irvine, Derry, 170, 188, 195, 211

Jack, James, 93
Jackson, Nat, 61
Jamieson, Cathy, 186, 213, 217
Jenkins, Roy, 97, 133, 150
John Wheatley Centre, 161
Johnston, Douglas, 65
Johnston, Thomas (Tom), 4, 17, 24, 26, 30, 33–4, 36, 38, 40–1, 43–4, 51n, 52n, 57–9, 61, 62, 63, 76n, 105, 226, 273, 275
Jones, Peter, 160, 187–8, 189–90, 191, 211, 223, 229n
Joyce, Eric, 240–1

Kahn, Sadiq, 256
Kane, Pat, 163
Kane, Tommy, 242
Kaufman, Gerald, 140, 156–7
Keating, Michael, 3, 36, 44, 71, 80, 84, 93, 146, 158, 200, 218, 219, 220, 269, 271, 276
Kellas, James, 2, 10, 13, 16, 24, 85, 86
Kelly, James, 254
Kenefick, William, 24
Kenny, Meryl, 238
Kerevan, George, 103
Kerley, Richard, 217
Kerr, Andy, 226, 238
Kilbrandon, Lord, 90
Kinnock, Neil, 140, 143, 144, 145, 146, 147, 150, 151, 153, 157, 162, 164, 185
Kirkwood, David, 24, 30, 33, 37, 67
Kitson, Alex, 96, 97, 117, 139
Knox, William, 2, 29, 41, 44, 47, 62, 67, 264, 272

Labour and the Nation, 38
Labour Co-ordinating Committee (LCC), 135, 136, 152, 169
Labour Party
and nationalism/devolution, 9, 12, 26, 33–6, 37–8, 39–40, 47–8, 59, 61, 64–5, 68, 71–3, 77n, 80, 87–91, 93–4, 95–8, 101–3, 104–7, 109–10, 112, 114–20, 137–40, 142–3, 150, 152–3, 155–7, 162–3, 185–91, 196–8, 202–3, 207, 209, 213–14, 220, 225, 227, 239, 243–4, 250, 251, 255, 257, 267–71, 273, 276–7
and religion, 10, 12, 16, 17, 28–9, 30, 35, 37–8, 54n, 67, 83–4, 85, 91–2, 99, 113, 146, 164, 165, 166–7, 181–2, 196, 200, 246, 258–9n, 264–5, 266
in local government, 18, 28, 38, 40, 41, 44–5, 47, 51n, 62, 63, 67, 69, 87, 91, 92–3, 95, 104, 108, 110–11, 112, 113–14, 131–2, 134, 136, 145–6, 158–9, 166–7, 169–70, 192, 240, 255
relations between party in Scotland and rest of Great Britain, 18, 20, 24–5, 109, 116, 141, 145, 155, 160, 165, 168, 169, 179–80n, 200–1, 214–15, 249, 266–7
and mythology, 31, 165, 191, 248, 271–5
and Europe, 131, 146, 158, 176n, 181, 214, 250–1, 254
and women, 11, 13, 19, 27, 33, 35, 40, 50n, 57, 66, 70, 72, 78, 85, 117, 137, 166, 184–5, 200

Labour Party of Scotland, 92, 93
Labour Representation Committee, 14, 15
Laird, Mary, 19
Lally, Pat, 161
Lambie, David, 172n
Lamont, Johann, 239, 240, 242, 245–6, 257
Langdon, Julia, 113
Lansbury, George, 46
Laski, Harold, 60, 61, 74n
Laws, David, 245
Lazarowicz, Mark, 135, 199
Lee, Jennie, 40, 78, 85
Leishman, Brian, 257
Leonard, Richard, 249, 250, 252–3, 254
Let Scotland Prosper, 73
Let Use Face the Future, 61
Levitt, Ian, 28
Levy, Roger, 139, 146, 154, 268
Liddell, Helen, 98, 109, 111, 112, 113, 114, 115, 117, 119, 133, 135, 137, 140, 141, 145, 152, 155, 172n, 176n, 181–2, 195, 215, 235n
Lindsay, Isobel, 183
Lloyd George, David, 24
Lockhart, Mary, 241
London Scots Self-Government Committee, 48, 59
Lowe, David, 9, 10

Mabon, Dickson, 102, 106, 123n, 127n, 133
McAllion, John, 103, 151, 163, 182, 188, 192, 229n
MacAllister, Iain, 208
McAveety, Frank, 211, 240
McCabe, Tom, 226, 238
McCail, Coll, 257
MacCallum, R. B., 61, 62
McCluskey, Lord, 113
McConnell, Allan, 219
McConnell, Brigid, 216
McConnell, Jack, 147, 158–9, 163, 166, 167, 168, 169, 176n, 182, 183, 186, 187, 191, 196, 200, 202, 206, 209, 212, 213, 216–23, 270
MacCormick, John, 64, 65
McCrandle, James, 102
MacDiarmid, Hugh, 272
McDonagh, Margaret, 207
Macdonald, Alexander, 8
Macdonald, Catriona M. M., 205
MacDonald, James Ramsay, 9, 12, 14, 15, 16–17, 19, 20n, 23, 29, 30, 32, 33, 34–5, 36, 37, 38, 39, 40, 42, 45, 273
MacDonald, Margo, 94, 114
McDougall, Blair, 256, 257
MacDougall, Ian, 2, 17
McElhone, Frank, 91, 99
McFadden, Pat, 191
McFall, John, 163
McGahey, Mick, 88, 234n
McGee, Alan, 193
McGovern, John, 41, 54n, 63, 65, 71, 74n
McGowan, Alasdair, 188
MacGregor, Sir Ian, 145
McGuire, Anne, 161, 167, 184
Machin, George, 93
McIntosh, Alastair, 217
McIntyre, Dr Robert, 60, 94
MacKay, A. B., 59–60
MacKay, John, 157
Mackay, Fiona, 238
McKechin, Ann, 215
Mackechnie, Jim, 145
McKee, Gordon, 256
McKelvey, Willie, 149
McKenna, Rosemary, 192, 199
McKibbin, Ross, 3, 20, 25, 266

Mackinlay, Alan, 41, 44, 47, 272
McKinney, Paul, 201–2
Mackintosh, John P., 72, 83, 88, 89, 98, 100, 106, 107, 111–12, 114, 116
McLachlan, Davie, 253
McLaren, John, 222
McLean, Allan, 96–7
Maclean, John, 27, 52n, 274
McLean, Iain, 3, 9, 30, 31, 38, 87–8, 272
Maclean, Neil, 27, 36, 37, 73n
McLean, Robert, 3, 12, 68–9, 152, 166, 207
McLeish, Henry, 4, 111, 136, 164–5, 168, 199, 205, 210, 213–16, 224, 241, 271
Maclennan, Robert, 83, 102, 133
MacLeod, Revd George, 67
McCluskey, Len, 248
MacMahon, Peter, 213
McMaster, Gordon, 196, 202, 231n
Macmillan, Harold, 78
McMillan, Alistair, 9, 87–8
McMillan, James, 86
McNair, Alison, 195
McNeil, Duncan, 206
McNeil, Hector, 45, 68, 70
McNeil, Ian, 253
McNeill, Pauline, 206
MacNeill Weir, Lauchlin, 48
McNicol, Iain, 242
McShane, Harry, 17
McSweeney, Morgan, 254, 256
McTaggart, Bob, 132, 157
McVey, Jean, 96
Macwhirter, Iain, 163, 215, 216
Magnusson, Magnus, 81
Maguire, Patrick, 254
Major, John, 165, 193
Mann, Jean, 45, 70, 71, 72, 78
Marjoribanks, Edward, 10, 11

Marr, Andrew, 94
Marshall, David, 134, 173n
Marshall, William, 70–1, 72, 79, 86, 90
Martin, David, 157, 178n, 250
Martin, Iain, 202
Martin, Michael, 226
Marx, Karl, 271–2
Marwick, William H., 2–3, 14, 47, 65, 86
Mason, Stephen, 8
Mathers, George, 39, 67–8
Maxton, Annie, 65
Maxton, James, 4, 17–18, 25, 26, 30, 32, 33–4, 35, 37, 38–9, 41, 42, 43, 52n, 62, 67, 74n, 265–6, 273
Maxton, John, 120, 132, 142, 144, 173n
Maxwell, Jamie, 241
Maxwell, Robert, 176n, 181
Maxwell, Stephen, 102, 113–14
May, Theresa, 251
Menon, Krishna, 56–7
Middlemas, Keith, 3
Middleton, James, 35, 46
Midwinter, Arthur, 118, 272
Miliband, Ed, 239, 240, 245, 246
Militant Tendency, 136, 145
Millan, Bruce, 95, 98, 100, 106, 140, 143, 153, 158, 273
Millar, David, 161
Miller, William, 88, 107, 191
Milne, E. J., 72
Milne, Jimmy, 143
Mitchell, James, 3, 4, 154, 169, 256, 267, 270
Mitchell, Rosslyn, 37, 38
Mitchison, Naomi, 59, 67
Moffat, Anne, 226
Monklands District Council, 166–7, 181–2
Mooney, Gerry, 219

Moran, Michael, 69
Morel, E. D., 23
Morgan, Kenneth, 68
Morgan, Rhodri, 216, 251
Morrison, Herbert, 4, 61, 63, 64–5
Mosley, Oswald, 42
Mowbray, Richard, 133
Muirhead, Roland, 26, 39
Mulvey, John, 151
Murphy, Jim, 192, 239, 246, 247, 248, 264
Murray, Ian, 247, 248, 251, 253, 257, 262n

Nairn, Tom, 90, 101, 103
National Party of Scotland, 39
Naughtie, Jim, 141, 152
Neil, Alex, 98, 103, 113, 151, 157, 190
Network, 192
New Scotland, New Britain, 203
Noble, Michael, 83

O'Brien, Cardinal Keith, 221
Orr, Sir John Boyd, 60
Osborne, George, 241
Osborne, Sandra, 184
Our Changing Democracy, 102–3, 104

Palestine Liberation Organisation, 136, 160, 172n
Paton, John, 29–30, 31–2, 34, 35, 268
Pearson, Graeme, 246
Peattie, Cathy, 186
Pethick-Laurence, Frederick, 57
Philippou, P. S., 29, 31
Picken, Mary, 199
Pike, Joe, 238, 246, 247
Plan for Scotland, 47–8
Pogrund, Gabriel, 254

Poll Tax, 148, 150–1, 152–3, 154, 158, 159
Pollock, John, 90, 95
Poole, Lynne, 219
Price, Ian, 245
Purcell, Steven, 209

Quinn, Lesley, 200, 215

Radice, Giles, 197–8
Rafferty, John, 208
Ramsay, Meta, 248
Ratcliffe, Alexander, 44
Rawnsley, Andrew, 203
Readman, Alison, 61, 62
The Real Rulers of Scotland, 48
Red Clydeside, 30–1, 78, 151, 165, 248, 254, 272, 273
Red Paper Collective, 242
The Red Paper on Scotland, 101, 242
Reid, Fred, 10
Reid, Jimmy, 107, 119, 140, 274
Reid, Joani, 256
Reid, John, 140, 184, 210, 213–14, 215, 222
Reid, Kevin, 210
Reith, Lord, 59
Rennie, Willie, 221
Rentoul, John, 194
Rifkind, Malcolm, 132, 148
Ritchie, Murray, 201, 204–5
Roberton, Esther, 199
Robertson, George, 96, 103, 107, 112, 114, 134, 163, 168, 169, 182–3, 185, 187–8, 189, 190, 192–3, 195, 197, 202, 211
Robertson, John, 80, 95
Robertson, John Home, 114, 151, 172n, 173n
Roddin, Euan, 218
Rose, F. H., 27

Rosie, Michael, 28
Ross, Donald, 134
Ross, Ernie, 136, 139
Ross, Fiona, 198
Ross, Ricky, 163
Ross, William, 4, 74n, 79, 81,
    82–3, 84–5, 87–88, 89, 91,
    92, 95, 96, 97, 99–100, 102,
    104, 105–6, 107, 110, 119,
    127n, 198, 273, 275
Rougvie, David, 159
Rowley, Alex, 207–8
Roy, Brian, 247
Russell, Davy, 258
Russell, Peter, 154–5, 176n

Salmond, Alex, 149, 169, 197,
    202, 203, 204, 221, 222,
    223–4, 227–8, 234n, 242,
    243, 256, 270, 274
Sarwar, Anas, 239, 241, 243,
    252, 255, 256, 257, 258, 266
Sarwar, Mohammed, 169, 194–5,
    239
Scargill, Arthur, 144
Scotland: The Real Divide, 142
Scotland United, 163, 165
Scottish Advisory Council, 18,
    19–20, 23, 24, 25
Scottish Conservative and
    Unionist Party, 87, 88, 108,
    148, 150, 157, 264
Scottish Constitutional
    Convention, 155–7, 158,
    160, 161, 165, 184–5,
    187–8, 196, 197, 206
Scottish Council on Industry, 58
Scottish Council of the Labour
    Party, 25, 27, 28, 33, 37, 38,
    39, 43, 46, 47, 48, 56, 57,
    59–60, 61–2, 66, 69, 70, 72,
    73, 78, 79, 81–2, 88, 90, 92,
    94, 95, 100, 101, 104, 105,
    108, 109–10, 115, 116, 117,
    119, 134–5, 137–8, 142–3,
    147, 150, 151, 154, 160,
    162, 165, 166–7, 267
Scottish Covenant Association,
    64, 65, 68, 81, 274
Scottish Development Agency,
    100, 102–3, 126n, 161, 273
Scottish Home Rule Association,
    26, 35–6, 37, 39, 52n
Scottish Labour Action (SLA),
    152–3, 155, 156, 162, 165,
    166, 188, 191, 201, 206,
    207, 216, 270
Scottish Labour and Devolution,
    95
Scottish Labour College, 43, 54n
Scottish Labour Party (Jim
    Sillars'), 103–4, 110–11, 113,
    116, 120, 169
Scottish Labour Party (Keir
    Hardie's), 9–12, 169, 273
Scottish Labour Party, 168–9,
    183, 184, 187, 200–1, 213,
    225, 239, 246, 248, 249,
    250, 264, 276
Scottish Labour Women's
    Caucus, 166, 184–5, 189
Scottish Liberal Association,
    14–15
Scottish Liberal Democrats, 185,
    209, 218
Scottish Militant, 158, 162, 186
Scottish National Party, 34, 39,
    59, 60, 79, 80, 87, 93, 94–5,
    97, 98, 99, 102, 103, 110,
    111–12, 113, 115, 119, 131,
    139, 140, 147, 151, 154,
    155, 157, 162, 165, 181,
    190, 193, 202, 204, 220,
    222, 223, 227, 238, 242,
    243, 245, 248, 252, 268,
    269, 274

Index

Scottish Peace Congress, 56
Scottish Policy Forum, 200, 218
Scottish Protestant League, 44
Scottish Socialist Party, 43–4, 46, 47, 219
Scottish Socialist Party (1980s), 158
Scottish Socialist Party (1990s), 186, 223
Scottish Trades Union Congress (STUC), 13, 20, 28, 33, 36, 43, 58, 72, 79, 82, 88, 93, 109, 116, 135, 143, 144, 147, 149, 158, 188, 193, 199, 219, 241, 269
Scottish Unionists, 65, 69, 272
Scottish United Trades Councils' Independent Labour Party, 10
Scottish Workers' Representation Committee, 13–14, 15
Selby, Harry, 94
Sewel, John, 196, 199
Shanks, Michael, 256
Sharpe, Michael, 254
Shaw, Ben, 18, 25, 29, 43, 50n
Shaw, Clarice McNab, 27, 50n, 61, 74n
Shaw, Eric, 3, 199, 224, 225, 264, 265, 266, 276
Shaw, Geoff, 96, 106, 112
Shaw Maxwell, James, 11
Sheppard, Tommy, 169, 185, 190–1, 199, 201
Sheridan, Tommy, 158, 162, 186, 205, 212, 219
Shinwell, Manny, 43, 45, 51n, 60, 65
Signposts for Scotland, 82, 276
Sillars, Jim, 79–80, 89, 91, 93–4, 95, 97, 101, 103–4, 111, 113, 116, 120, 128n, 154, 157, 162, 217

Sinclair, Sir Archibald, 58
Skene, Danus, 103
Sloan, Alexander, 46, 60
Small, Willie, 112
Smart, Ian, 152, 153, 162, 188–9
Smillie, Robert, 13, 14, 15, 19, 87
Smith, Drew, 254
Smith, John, 5, 70–1, 92, 106, 115, 137, 138, 139, 144, 151, 160, 164, 166, 167–8, 169, 170, 181, 188, 198, 199, 213, 248, 274
Smith, Matt, 195–6
Smout, T. C., 32
Smyth, J. J., 45
Snowden, Philip, 42
Social Democratic Federation, 33
Social Democratic Party (SDP), 133, 134
Soutar, Brian, 210
Spiers, Bill, 135, 188, 189
Squire, Rachel, 228n
Stark, Davie, 189
Starmer, Sir Keir, 254, 256, 257, 258
Steel, David, 85, 112, 113, 141
Stephen, Revd Campbell, 38, 63
Stevens, Jim, 192, 197
Stewart, Allan, 167
Stewart, Andrew, 48
Stewart, Dick, 111, 146
Stewart, Donald, 91
Stihler, Catherine, 221
Stott, Gordon, 72, 77n, 82, 121n
Strachey, John, 71, 76n
Strang, Gavin, 138, 195
Strathclyde Regional Council, 91, 104, 106, 110, 111, 112, 113, 134, 141, 146, 159, 168, 184
Straw, Jack, 212, 248–9

Stronger Together: The 21st Century Case for Scotland and Britain, 222
Sturgeon, Nicola, 179n, 221, 246, 251, 255
Swinney, John, 218–19

Talbot, Peter, 96
Taylor, Brian, 194
Taylor, John, 57, 60, 66, 70
Taylor, Matthew, 209
Taylor, Teddy, 120
Taylor, William, 75n
Thatcher, Margaret, 120, 132, 142, 143, 147, 268–9, 274
Thomson, Bob, 158, 189, 201
Thomson, George, 72, 85, 93, 123n
Trench, Alan, 213
Turner, Ben, 16–17
Tweedsmuir, Lady, 69, 83
Tynan, Bill, 200

Ullrich, Kay, 181–2
Union of Democratic Control, 23
Upper Clyde Shipbuilders, 93, 100, 126n
Urquhart, Bunty, 72, 133, 171n
Urwin, Derek, 83

Walker, Imogen, 256
Wallace, Jim, 185, 206, 212
Walton Newbold, J. T., 30
Wardle, R. T., 65
Watson, Dave, 241
Watson, Mike, 131, 137, 157, 169, 194, 209, 210
Welsh, Ian, 212
Westwood, Joseph, 44, 63–4

Wheatley, John, 15–16, 18–19, 27, 32, 35, 37, 38, 41, 81, 275
Wheatley, John (nephew), 62–3, 67, 91
Wheatley, Kathleen, 81
Whitefield, Karen, 124
Whitton, David, 201, 208, 213
Whitty, Larry, 166
Williams, A. L., 72
Williamson, Neil, 108, 114
Willis, E. G., 72
Wilkie, Alexander, 14, 16
Wilkinson, Ellen, 41, 61
Wilson, Brian, 97, 118, 119, 130n, 138, 191, 211, 214, 234n, 243, 269, 270, 275
Wilson, Gordon, 93, 139, 157
Wilson, Harold, 82, 85, 87–8, 95, 96, 99, 100, 102, 105, 119
Wilson, Peter, 134
Wilson, R. F., 40
Wilson of Langside, Lord, 116, 119–20
Winning, Cardinal, 210
Wiseman, David, 133
Wishart, Ruth, 103
Wolfe, Billy, 81
Wood, Alex, 158
Woodburn, Arthur, 39, 42, 43, 44, 45, 46, 48, 56, 57, 64, 65–6, 67, 72, 87, 91
Wray, Jimmy, 145

Young, Alf, 113, 115
Young, Douglas, 60, 61, 86
Young, Hugo, 110
Younger, George, 132, 145
Yousaf, Humza, 262n

EU representative:
Easy Access System Europe
Mustamäe tee 50, 10621 Tallinn, Estonia
Gpsr.requests@easproject.com

www.ingramcontent.com/pod-product-compliance
Lightning Source LLC
Chambersburg PA
CBHW050203240426
4367ICB00013B/2227